The Illustrated Guide to Yachting Volume 1

THE JACK OF 1606 A.D.

St. Andrew of Scotland.

St. George of England.   St. Patrick of Ireland.

THE UNION JACK.

The Illustrated Guide to Yachting Volume 1

A Classic Guide to Yachts & Sailing
from the Turn of the 19th & 20th Centuries

Sir Edward Sullivan, Lord Brassey,
C. E. Seth-Smith, G. L. Watson,
R. T. Pritchett, Sir George Leach,
the Earl of Pembroke and Montgomery,
E. F. Knight and Rev. G. L. Blake

The Illustrated Guide to Yachting
Volume 1
A Classic Guide to Yachts & Sailing from the Turn of the 19th & 20th Centuries
by Sir Edward Sullivan, Lord Brassey, C. E. Seth-Smith, G. L. Watson,
R. T. Pritchett, Sir George Leach, the Earl Of Pembroke and Montgomery,
E. F. Knight and Rev. G. L. Blake

First published under the title
The Badminton Library of Sports and Pastimes
Yachting Volume 1

Leonaur is an imprint of Oakpast Ltd

Copyright in this form © 2013 Oakpast Ltd

ISBN: 978-1-78282-116-8 (hardcover)
ISBN: 978-1-78282-117-5 (softcover)

http://www.leonaur.com

Publisher's Notes

The views expressed in this book are not necessarily those of the publisher.

Contents

Dedication to H.R.H. the Prince of Wales	7
Preface	9
Introduction	11
Ocean Cruising	24
Corinthian Deep-Sea Cruising	44
The Evolution of the Modern Racing Yacht	51
Sliding Keels and Centreboards	109
Recollections of Schooner Racing	116
The Racing Rules and the Rules of Rating	152
Yacht's Sailing Boats	187
Small Yacht Racing on the Solent	216
Fitting Out a Fifty-Tonner to Go Foreign	287
Baltic Cruising	298
Five-Tonners and Five-Raters in the North	309
Yacht Insurance	382

Dedication to H.R.H. the Prince of Wales

Badminton: May 1885.
Having received permission to dedicate these volumes, the Badminton Library of Sports and Pastimes, to His Royal Highness the Prince of Wales, I do so feeling that I am dedicating them to one of the best and keenest sportsmen of our time. I can say, from personal observation, that there is no man who can extricate himself from a bustling and pushing crowd of horsemen, when a fox breaks covert, more dexterously and quickly than His Royal Highness; and that when hounds run hard over a big country, no man can take a line of his own and live with them better.

Also, when the wind has been blowing hard, often have I seen His Royal Highness knocking over driven grouse and partridges and high-rocketing pheasants in first-rate workmanlike style. He is held to be a good yachtsman, and as Commodore of the Royal Yacht Squadron is looked up to by those who love that pleasant and exhilarating pastime. His encouragement of racing is well known, and his attendance at the University, Public School, and other important mtches testifies to his being, like most English gentlemen, fond of all manly sports. I consider it a great privilege to be allowed to dedicate these volumes to so eminent a sportsman as His Royal Highness the Prince of Wales, and I do so with sincere feelings of respect and esteem and loyal devotion.

Beaufort.

Badminton.

Preface

A few lines only are necessary to explain the object with which these volumes are put forth. There is no modern encyclopaedia to which the inexperienced man, who seeks guidance in the practice of the various British sports and pastimes, can turn for information. Some books there are on hunting, some on racing, some on lawn tennis, some on fishing, and so on; but one library, or succession of volumes, which treats of the sports and pastimes indulged in by Englishmen—and women—is wanting. The Badminton Library is offered to supply the want. Of the imperfections which must be found in the execution of such a design we are conscious. Experts often differ. But this we may say, that those who are seeking for knowledge on any of the subjects dealt with will find the results of many years' experience written by men who are in every case adepts at the sport or pastime of which they write. It is to point the way to success to those who are ignorant of the sciences they aspire to master, and who have no friend to help or coach them, that these volumes are written.

To those who have worked hard to place simply and clearly before the reader that which he will find within, the best thanks of the editor are due. That it has been no slight labour to supervise all that has been written, he must acknowledge; but it has been a labour of love, and very much lightened by the courtesy of the publisher, by the unflinching, indefatigable assistance of the sub-editor, and by the intelligent and able arrangement of each subject by the various writers, who are so thoroughly masters of the subjects of which they treat. The reward we all hope to reap is that our work may prove useful to this and future generations.

The (original) Editor.

VICTORIA CUP. 1893.

Chapter 1

Introduction

By Sir Edward Sullivan, Bart.

It is related that Chrysippus, a cynic, killed himself in order that he might sooner enjoy the delights of Paradise. Philosophers do queer things sometimes. Many who are not philosophers kill themselves in order to avoid the miseries of this world; but, as far as I know, this is the only case on record of a man killing himself from impatience to enjoy the pleasures of the next.

Ideas of Paradise are exceedingly various. To the ancients Paradise meant a *dolce far niente* in the Elysian Fields; to the North American Indians it means happy hunting grounds and plenty of fat buffalo. The Scythians believed in a Paradise of immortal drunkenness and drinking blood out of the skulls of their enemies, and the Paradise that to-day influences the belief of one-fourth of the human race is contained in Chapter X. of the Koran. To Madame de Chevreuse it meant chatting with her friends in the next world. To one friend of mine it was galloping for ever over a grass country without gates. To another it meant driving four horses, with Tim Carter seated at his side. To some, I believe, Paradise means yachting, and for my own part, I think a 200-ton schooner, a ten-knot breeze, and a summer sea hard to beat.

Whether yachting approaches one's conception of Paradise or not, I think there are very few of us who, if they do not suffer from that hopeless affection the *mal de mer*, do not more or less enjoy a life on the ocean wave; it is so fresh and life-giving and so various. 'A home on the stormy deep' we won't say so much about. I have seen two or three storms at sea, but I have never found them pleasant; very much the contrary. There is grandeur, if you like, but there is also terror and horror.

As black as night she turned to white,
And cast against the cloud
A snowy sheet as if each surge
Upturned a sailor's shroud.

This is poetry; but it is true. You look to windward, and you look to leeward; you look ahead, and you look astern, and you feel that, if you are not already engulfed, you probably may be in the next minute.

Dr. Johnson said the pleasure of going to sea was getting ashore again; certainly the pleasure of a storm is getting into smooth water again.

The ideas of pleasure as connected with yachting vary as much as the ideas of Paradise; to one it means steaming at full speed from one port to another; but this becomes monotonous. A friend of mine used to write a letter at Cowes, address it to himself at Guernsey, and then steam, hard all, to Guernsey to get his letter. When he got it he would write to himself at Plymouth, then steam away, hard all again, to get that, and so on; even in steaming you must have an object of some kind, you know.

To another dowagering up and down the Solent, lunching on board, and then hurrying back to dine and sleep ashore are pleasure; to another, sailing with the wind, or against the wind, or drifting when there is no wind, is the ideal of yachting. Certainly that is mine. I have tried both. I have had a steamer and I have had sailing vessels, and if I lived to the age of the Hyperboreans and owned several gold mines I should never keep a steamer for pleasure. In sailing, the interest never flags; the rigging, the sails, the anchors, the cables, the boats, the decks, all have their separate interest; every puff of wind, every catspaw, is a source of entertainment, and when the breeze comes, and, with everything drawing below and aloft, you tear along ten or twelve knots an hour, the sensation of pleasure is complete—if you are not sick.

I can never allow that steaming, under any conditions, can give the same pleasure as sailing—nor a hundredth part of it. If you are in a hurry, steam by all means—steam, steam, steam, pile on the coal, blacken sea and sky with your filthy smoke, and get into your port; but that is the pleasure of locomotion, not of yachting. Even as regards locomotion, there are occasions when a fine sailing vessel will go by a steamer as if she were standing still.

Years ago I sailed from Plymouth to Lisbon in four days, and from Lisbon to Cowes in four days, and passed all the steamers on the way!

Atque haec olim meminisse juvabit. These are the happy moments, like forty minutes across a grass country, that fond memory brings back to us, and which Time's effacing fingers will never touch. Can steam at its best afford such delight as this? No; of course not. But, although this is my opinion of the relative pleasure of sailing and steaming, it is not by any means the general one; the race of steam *versus* canvas has been run, and alas! steam has won easily, hands down. I say alas! for I think that, from every point of view, yachting has suffered from the general employment of steam.

One of the objects of the Royal Yacht Squadron, when it was originally founded, was to encourage seamanship, and, as steam was supposed to destroy seamanship, steamers were not admitted into the Club; and the Royal Yacht Squadron was right. Steam does destroy seamanship; a steamship hand is certainly not half a sailor. Now more than half the tonnage of the Club is in steamers. I think it is a pity, and they are such steamers too! 800 tons, 1,000 tons, 1,500 tons. I do not see where they are to stop; but, I believe that in this, as in most things, we have run into excess. I cannot believe that the largest steam yacht afloat, with all the luxury and cost that upholsterers and cabinet-makers can devise, will ever give a man who is fond of the sea and seafaring matters a tithe of the gratification that a 100-ton sailing vessel will afford; one is a floating hotel, the other is a floating cottage. I prefer the cottage.

The worry of maintaining discipline in a crew of forty or fifty men, amongst whom there is sure to be one or two black sheep, the smoke, the smell of oil, the vibration, the noise, even the monotony, destroy pleasure. Personally, the game seems to me not worth the candle.

Thirty or forty years ago, yachting men with their sixty or hundred tonners went on year after year, fitting out, and cruising about the coast, as part of their yearly life. When their vessel was wearing out, they would sell her, and buy or build another; they seldom parted with her for any other reason. Now a man builds a floating palace or hotel at a fabulous cost; but as a general rule in about two years he wants to sell her and to retire from yachting life.

A sailing vessel and a steamer are different articles; you get attached to a sailing vessel as you do to anything animate, to your horse, or your dog; but I defy anyone to get attached to a smoky, oily steamer. There is an individuality about the sailing vessel; none about the steamer.

When the seven wise men of Greece delivered the oracular dictum that there were only two beautiful things in the world, women and roses, and only two good things, women and wine, they spoke according to their limited experience—they had never seen the new type of racing yacht under sail. Of course the perfection of animate beauty is represented by women, but certainly inanimate nature can show nothing more beautiful than *Britannia, Navahoe, Valkyrie, Satanita,* their sails well filled, the sun shining on them, streaking along twelve or thirteen knots an hour, apparently without an effort, scarcely raising a ripple. And then a yacht is so exceedingly feminine in her ways. One day everything goes right with her—she will not only do all she is asked to do, but a great deal more than her greatest admirers ever thought she could do: the next day everything goes wrong with her—she will not do anything she is asked, and indeed will not do what her admirers know she can do without an effort.

Some women—I speak it with all respect—bear being 'squeezed' and 'pinched,' they almost seem to like it, at any rate they don't cry out; whereas others will cry out immediately and vigorously. So will yachts.

The more you squeeze one vessel, the more you pinch her, the more she seems to enjoy it. Squeeze another, pinch her into the wind, and she lies down and calls out at once. The difference between vessels in this respect is quite funny, and essentially feminine.

Curiously enough, extremes meet; that is to say, if the pendulum of taste or fashion goes very much over to one side, it is sure to go over just as far on the other. Sailing yachts of 100, 200, 300 tons have gone out of fashion, and leviathan steamers of 800, 1,000, 1,500 tons have taken their place; but at the same time that a taste for immense steamers has driven moderate-sized sailing vessels out of the field, a taste for small boats, 5-raters, 3-raters, ½-raters—I don't quite understand their rating—has sprung up, and promises almost to supplant the big steamers themselves.

I believe the increasing popularity of these swallows of the seas—for turning, wheeling, skimming, doubling, as they do, I can compare them to nothing else—is a very good omen for yachting; they are expensive for their size and tonnage, certainly, but, after all, their cost may be counted in hundreds instead of tens of thousands. They have brought scientific boat sailing and racing within the reach of hundreds who cannot afford big racing yachts; and, moreover, the ladies join in these exciting contests, and of course very often win. In endurance, and courage, and nerve, and quickness, they are quite the equals of the other sex; and if they are occasionally a little too pertinacious, a little too eager to win, and don't always 'go about' exactly when the rules of the road require, what does it signify? Who grudges them their little victory?

A flight of these sea swallows skimming over the course at Calshot Castle, on a fine day with a good working breeze, is one of the prettiest sights in the world.

Independently of the health-giving and invigorating influences both to mind and body of a yachting life, it has advantages that in my opinion raise it above any other sport, if sport it is to be called. There is neither cruelty nor professionalism in yachting, except when certain foolish snobs in sheer wantonness shoot the too-confiding gulls that hover round the sterns of their yachts. There is no professional element in yachting, I repeat, not even in yacht racing, at least not enough to speak of, and it is an enormous advantage in its favour that it brings one into contact with what I believe is without doubt the best of our working population; for are not the toilers of the sea workers in the very fullest sense of the word?

Yacht sailors, as a rule, are sober, honest, obliging, good-tempered, original. During the many years I have yachted, I have had crews from north, east, west, and south, and I have almost without exception found them the same. A man must be hard to please indeed, if, after a three or four months' cruise, he does not part from his crew with regret, and with a sincere wish that they may meet again.

Amongst yachting skippers, I have come across some of the most honourable, trustworthy, honest men I have met in any class of life, men who know their duty, and are always willing and anxious to do it.

The chief peculiarity of all the seafaring class that I have been brought into contact with is their entire freedom from vulgarity. They are obliging to the utmost of their power, but never cringing or vulgar. The winter half of their lives is spent in fishing-boats, or coasters, or sea voyages where they have to face dangers and hardships that must be experienced to be realised. As a rule, they are religious; and their preparations for the Sabbath, their washings and soapings and brushings, show with what pleasure they welcome its recurrence. Yacht minstrelsy, with its accordion, its songs of twenty verses, its never-ending choruses, its pathos, is a thing of itself. Some day perhaps some Albert Chevalier will make it fashionable. Such as they are, I know no class of Englishmen superior, if any be equal, to the sailors who man our yachts. Of course there are sharks, or at any rate dog-fish, in all waters;

but where the good so immensely outnumber the bad, that man must be a fool indeed who gets into wrong hands.

To say there is no vulgarity in yachting is not true; there is; but it is not amongst the men or among the skippers. And, after all, the vulgarity one sometimes sees amongst yacht-owners does not go for much; it amuses them and hurts nobody. If the amateur sailor wishes to be thought more of a sailor than the sailor born, he soon finds out his mistake, and when he gets into a good club subsides into his proper position.

To those who are fond of the sea and of yachting, the yacht is the most 'homey' of residences; everything is cosy, and comfortable, and within reach; and the sensation of carrying your house and all its comforts about with you is unique.

The internal economy of a yacht constitutes one of its greatest charms. Your cook, with only a little stove for which a shore cook would scarcely find any use, will send you up an excellent dinner cooked to perfection for any number of guests; and the steward! who can describe the work of a yacht's steward? I doubt whether Briareus with his hundred hands could do more than a steward does with two. At seven in the morning he is ashore for the milk, and the breakfast, and the letters, and the flowers; he valets half a dozen people, prepares half a dozen baths, brushes heaven knows how many clothes, gets the breakfast, makes the beds, cleans the plate, tidies the cabin, provides luncheon, five-o'clock tea, dinner, is always cheerful, obliging, painstaking, and more than repaid if occasionally he gets a *petit mot* of compliment or congratulation. When he ever sleeps, or eats, I never can tell; and, far from grumbling at his work, he often resents the assistance of any shore-going servant.

The introduction of steam launches has added very much to the pleasures of yachting, and to my mind has greatly lessened the advantages, if any, that steamers possess over sailing vessels. Every vessel of 100 tons and over can now carry a steam launch, big or small, at the davits, or on deck. You *sail* from port to port, or loch to loch, in your sailing vessel, and when you have found snug anchorage, you 'out kettle' and puff away for as long as you like, enjoying the pleasure of exploring the rivers and creeks and neighbouring objects of interest. Everywhere this is delightful, at Plymouth, at Dartmouth, at Falmouth, the Scilly Isles, at St. Malo, and perhaps especially in Scotland.

To my mind, the West Coast of Scotland is, *par excellence*, the happy cruising grounds of yachtsmen. I know of none like it—the number and variety of the lochs, the wild grandeur of some, the soft beauty of others, the mountains, the rocks, the islands, the solitude, the forests, the trees.

> Oh! the Oak and the Ash, and the bonny Ivy tree,
> They flourish best at home in the North Countrie.

The heather, especially the white, the ferns, the mosses, the wild flowers, the innumerable birds and fish, the occasional seals and whales, the wildness of the surroundings, all combine to give it a charm that is indescribable. I have seen on the coast of Skye a whale, thirty or forty feet long, jump clean out of the water three or four times, like a salmon. Anchored close under a cliff in Loch Hourn, and happening to look up, I met the wondering eyes of a hind craning over the edge of the cliffs, and staring right down on the yacht. Go the world over, you will nowhere find so much varied beauty, above or below, on land or sea, as on the West Coast of Scotland.

Nobody can explore or appreciate the beauty of the Scotch lochs without a 'kettle.' It spoils one's pleasure to keep a boat's crew pulling for eight or ten hours in a hot sun, and therefore, if you have no steam launch, many expeditions that promise much interest and pleasure are abandoned; but with your kettle and a man, or a man and a boy, you don't care how long you are out or how far you go. This to my mind is the most enjoyable combination of sails and steam—a comfortable sailing vessel, schooner or ketch for choice, to carry you from port to port, and a steam launch for exploration when you get there.

The accommodation of a sailing vessel is, on a rough calculation, double the accommodation of a steamer of the same tonnage. The Earl of Wilton, Commodore of the Royal Yacht Squadron, had a schooner of 200 tons, and after sailing in her many years he decided, as so many others have done, to give up sailing and take to steam. To obtain exactly the same accommodation that he had on board his 200-ton schooner, he had to build a steamer, the *Palatine*, of 400 tons. Of course in an iron steamer of 400 tons the height between decks is very much greater than in a wooden schooner of 200 tons. Also the cabins are larger, but there are no more of them.

I think many people have erroneous ideas of the cost of yachting. Yacht *racing*, especially in the modern cutters of 150 or 170 tons, is very expensive. The wear and tear of spars and gear is incredible. I believe that in the yachting season of 1893 H.R.H. the Prince of Wales's vessel the *Britannia* sprang or carried away three masts; and some of his competitors were not more lucky. Then racing wages are very heavy: 10*s*. per man when you lose, and 20*s*. when you win, with unlimited beef, and beer, &c., mount up when you have a great many hands, and the new type of racer, with booms 90 feet long, requires an unlimited number; when you look at these boats racing, they seem actually swarming with men. In addition to 10*s*. or 20*s*. to each man, the skipper gets 5 *per cent.* or 10 *per cent.* of the value of the prize, or its equivalent.

So that a modern racing yacht with a crew of 30 men may, if successful, easily knock a hole in 1,000*l*. for racing wages alone, to say nothing of cost of spars, and sails, and gear, &c. Of course, in comparison with keeping a pack of hounds, or a deer forest, or a good grouse moor, or to pheasant preserving on a very large scale, the expense of yacht racing even at its worst is modest; but still in these days 1,000*l*. or 1,500*l*. is an item.

But yachting for pleasure, yacht cruising in fact, is *not* an expensive amusement. The wages of a 100- to a 200-ton cutter or schooner will vary from 50*l*. to 100*l*. a month at the outside, and the wear and tear, if the vessel and gear are in good order, is very moderate; and undoubtedly the living on board a yacht is infinitely cheaper than living ashore.

Thirty to forty pounds, or as much as fifty pounds, a week may easily go in hotel bills if there is a largish party. Half the sum will keep a 100- or 150-ton yacht going, wages, wear and tear, food, &c., included, if you are afloat for three or four months. Certainly for a party of four or five yachting is cheaper than travelling on the Continent with a courier and going to first-class hotels. Travelling on the Continent under the best conditions often becomes a bore; the carriages are stuffy and dusty, the trains are late, the officials are uncivil or at least indifferent, the hotels are full, the kitchen is bad, and you come to the conclusion that you would be better at home. Now, on board a yacht you are never stuffy or dusty, the accommodation is always good, everyone about you is always civil, anxious for your comfort, the kitchen is never bad, and you cannot come to the conclusion that you would be better at home, for you *are* at home—the most cosy and comfortable of homes!

The yachting season of 1893 will always be a memorable one. The victory of H.I.M. the German Emperor's *Meteor* for the Queen's Cup at Cowes; the victorious career of H.R.H. the Prince of Wales's *Britannia* and the *Valkyrie*; the series of international contests between the *Britannia* and *Navahoe*, with the unexpected victory of the latter over the cross-Channel course; and, finally, the gallant attempt of Lord Dunraven to bring back the cup from America, make a total of yachting incidents, and indeed surprises, that will last for a very long time. The victory of the *Meteor* in the Queen's Cup was a surprise: it was more than a surprise when the *Navahoe* beat *Britannia* to Cherbourg and back in a gale of wind. I don't know that it was a matter of surprise that the Americans kept the Cup; I think, indeed, it was almost a foregone conclusion. In yachting, as in everything else, possession is nine points of the law, and a vessel sailing in her own waters, with pilots accustomed to the local currents and atmospheric movements, will always have an advantage. Whether the *Vigilant* is a better boat than the *Valkyrie*, whether she was better sailed, whether her centreboard had anything to do with her victory, I cannot say. But there is the result: that the *Vigilant* won by seven minutes, which, at the rate they were sailing, means about a mile.

It would appear that the Americans are still slightly ahead of us in designing yachts for speed, but they are not nearly as far ahead of us as they were forty years ago. I remember the first time the *America* sailed at Cowes in 1851. I could not believe my eyes. It was blowing a stiff breeze, and whilst all the other schooners were laying over ten or twelve degrees, she was sailing perfectly upright, and going five knots to their four. It was a revelation—how does she do it? was in everybody's mouth. Now we are much more on an equality. The *Navahoe*, a beautiful vessel, one of the best, comes to England and is worsted: the *Valkyrie*, a beautiful vessel, also one of the best, goes over to America and is worsted.

The moral I think is 'race at home in your own waters.' I do not believe much in international contests of any kind, gravely doubting whether they do much to promote international amity.

It is a familiar sight to see H.R.H. the Prince of Wales taking part in yacht racing, but 1893 was the first occasion, in an English yacht race at any rate, that the *Kaiser* donned his flannels and joined personally in the contest. I suppose there is no monarch who is so dosed with ceremony and etiquette as the Emperor of Germany. What a relief, therefore, it must be to him to put aside the cares of monarchy for a whole week, and sit for hours in two or three inches of water, hauling away at the mainsheet as if his life depended on it, happy as the traditional king, if, when he has gone about, he finds he has gained six feet on his rival!

But beyond all this—the heartiness, the equality, the good feeling, the absorbing interest that attends yacht racing and yacht cruising—there are some very interesting questions that suggest themselves in connection with the great increase of speed lately developed by the new type of racing yachts.

There is no doubt whatever that whereas the Pleasure Fleet of England is progressing and improving every year, and is a subject of congratulation to everyone concerned with it—designers, builders, and sailors—the Business Fleet, the Royal Navy, is the very reverse: not only has it not improved, but it appears to have been going steadily the wrong road; and instead of being a joy to designers and sailors, it is confusion to the former, and something very like dismay to the latter.

In James I.'s time the fleet was not held in very high estimation. It was said of it that 'first it went to Gravesend, then to Land's End, and then to No End,' and really that appears to be its condition now. Whilst yachts are developing all the perfections of the sailing ship, our ironclads seem to be developing most of the imperfections of the steamship.

Whilst our yachts can do anything but speak, our ironclads can do anything but float. Of course this is an exaggeration; but exaggeration is excusable at times, at least if we are to be guided by the debates in Parliament. At any rate, it is no exaggeration to say they are very disappointing. If they go slow, they won't steer. If they go fast, they won't stop. If they collide in quite a friendly way, they go down. One sinks in twelve minutes, and the other with difficulty keeps afloat. In half a gale of wind, if the crew remain on deck, they are nearly drowned; if they go below, they are nearly asphyxiated.

They have neither stability nor buoyancy. But this does not apply to English ironclads alone. French, German, Italian, American, are all the same. Some of these monsters are fitted with machinery as delicate and complicated as a watch that strikes the hours, and minutes, and seconds, tells the months, weeks, and days, the phases of the moon, &c. &c. Some of them have no fewer than thirty to thirty-five different engines on board. If the vessel containing all this wonderful and elaborate machinery never left the Thames or Portsmouth Harbour, all well and good, very likely the machinery would continue to work; but to send such a complex arrangement across the Atlantic or the Bay in winter seems to me contrary to common sense.

The biggest ironclad afloat, a monster of 13,000 tons, in mid ocean is, after all, only as '*a flea on the mountain*'; it is nothing; it is tossed about, and rolled about, and struck by the seas and washed by them, just as if it were a pilot boat of 60 tons. It is certain that the concussion of the sea will throw many of these delicate bits of machinery out of gear: in the *Resolution* in a moderate gale the engine that supplied air below decks broke down; the blow that sank the unfortunate *Victoria* threw the steering apparatus out of gear, so that if she had not gone down she would not have steered; more recently still the water in the hydraulic steering apparatus in a ship off Sheerness froze, so that she could not put to sea. If such accidents can happen in time of peace, when vessels are only manoeuvring, or going from port to port, what would happen if two 13,000-ton ships rammed each other at full speed? Is it not almost certain that the whole thirty-five engines would stop work?

We have, I suppose, nearly reached the maximum of speed attainable by steam; have we nearly reached the maximum attainable by sails? By no means. When Anacharsis the younger was asked which was the best ship, he said the ship that had arrived safe in port; but even the ancients were not always infallible. The *Resolution* did not prove she was the best ship by coming into port; on the contrary, she would have proved herself a much better ship if she had been able to continue her voyage. What we want in a man-of-war, as far as I understand the common-sense view of the question, is buoyancy, speed, handiness, and the power of keeping the seas for long periods.

Racing cutters of 150 to 170 tons are now built to sail at a speed that two years ago was not dreamt of. Where a short time since the best of them used to take minutes to go about, they now go about in as many seconds. The racing vessels of the present day, (as at time of first publication), will reach thirteen or fourteen knots an hour, and sail ten knots on a wind; with hardly any wind at all they creep along eight knots. They do not appear to be able to go less than eight knots; double their size, and their speed would be immensely increased.

Now if thirteen and fourteen knots can be got out of a vessel of 170 tons, and seventeen knots out of one double her size, what speed might you fairly expect to get out of a racing vessel of 10,000 tons? Rather a startling suggestion certainly; but, if carefully examined, not without reason.

We have nothing to guide us as to the probable speed of a racing vessel of that size. Time allowance becomes lost in the immensity of the question.

I see no reason why a vessel of 10,000 tons, built entirely for speed, should not, on several points of sailing, go as fast as any torpedo boat, certainly much faster than any ironclad. Her speed, reaching in a strong breeze, would be terrific; and if *Britannia, Navahoe, Valkyrie, Vigilant*, and vessels of that class can sail ten knots on a wind, why should not she sail fifteen? She would have to be fore and aft rigged, with an immense spread of canvas, very high masts, and very long booms; single sticks would be nowhere; but iron sticks and iron booms can be built up of any length and any strength, and with wire rigging I see no limit to size. Such a vessel amply provided with torpedoes of all descriptions, and all the modern diabolisms for destroying life, would be so dangerous a customer that no ironclad would attack her with impunity.

Of course there would occasionally be conditions under which she would be at a disadvantage with ironclads; but, on the other hand, there are many conditions under which ironclads, even the best of them, would be under enormous disadvantages with her. She could circumnavigate the globe without stopping. I believe her passages would be phenomenal, life on board would be bright and healthy, she would be seaworthy, able to keep the seas in all weathers, easily handled, no complicated machinery to fail you at the moment when you were most dependent on it; and then what a beauty she would be! Why, a fleet of such vessels would be a sight for gods and men. We have sailing vessels of 3,000 and 4,000 tons, four-masted, square-rigged; they are built for carrying, not for speed, but even they make passages that to the merchant seaman of a hundred years ago would appear incredible.

I probably shall not live to see the clumsy, unwieldy, complicated, unseaworthy machines called ironclads cast aside, wondered at by succeeding generations, as we now wonder at the models of antediluvian monsters at the Crystal Palace; but that such will be their fate I have no doubt whatever. For our battleships we have gone back to the times of knights in armour, when men were so loaded with iron that where they fell there they remained, on their backs or their stomachs, till their squires came to put them on their legs again. I am certain that neither the public, nor the naval authorities of the world, realise what an ironclad in time of war means—positively they will never be safe out of near reach of a coaling station. Suppose—and this is tolerably certain to happen—that when they reach a coaling station they find no coal, or very possibly find it in the hands of the enemy. What are they to do? Without coal to steam back again, or to reach another station, they will be as helpless as any derelict on the ocean: a balloon without gas, a locomotive without steam, a 100-ton gun without powder, would not be so useless as an ironclad without coal.

But what has all this to do with yachting? it may be asked. Well, it is the logical and practical result of the recent development of speed in sailing vessels. It positively becomes the question whether racing sails and racing hulls may not, in speed even, give results almost as satisfactory as steam, and in many other matters results far more favourable.

Of course the model of the racing yacht would have to be altered for the vessel of 10,000 tons. Vessels must get their stability from beam and from the scientific adjustment of weights, not merely from depth of keel—the Channel would not be deep enough for a vessel that drew twenty fathoms; but this change of design need not affect their speed or their stability very much.

In the introduction to the Badminton Library volumes on Yachting, a great deal might be expected about the national importance of the pastime as a nursery for sailors, a school for daring, and all that sort of thing. But I think all this 'jumps to the eyes'; those who run may read it. I have preferred to treat the question of yachting more as one of personal pleasure and amusement than of national policy; and besides, I am sure that I may safely leave the more serious aspects of the sport to the writers whose names are attached to the volumes.

For myself, after yachting for nearly a quarter of a century, I can safely say that it has afforded me more unmixed pleasure than any other sport or amusement I have ever tried. Everything about it has been a source of delight to me—the vessels, the skippers, the crews, the cruises. I do not think I have ever felt dull or bored on a yacht, and even now, in the evening of life, I would willingly contract to spend my remaining summers on board a 200-ton schooner.

CHAPTER 2

Ocean Cruising
By Lord Brassey, K.C.B.

I fear that I can scarcely hope to contribute to the present volume of the admirable Badminton Series anything that is very new or original. Although my voyages have extended over a long period, and have carried me into nearly every navigable sea, I have for the most part followed well-known tracks. The seamanship, as practised in the *Sunbeam*, has been in conformity with established rule; the navigation has been that of the master-ordinary.

It would be hardly fair to fill the pages of a general treatise with autobiography. As an introduction, however, to the remarks which follow, my career as a yachtsman may be summarised in the most condensed form.

Voyages

Twelve voyages to the Mediterranean; the furthest points reached being Constantinople, 1874 and 1878; Cyprus, 1878; Egypt, 1882.

Three circumnavigations of Great Britain.

One circumnavigation of Great Britain and the Shetland Islands, in 1881.

Two circumnavigations of Ireland.

Cruises with the fleets during manoeuvres, in 1885, 1888, and 1889.

Voyages to Norway, in 1856, 1874, and 1885. In the latter year Mr. Gladstone and his family were honoured and charming guests.

Voyages to Holland, in 1858 and 1863.

Round the World, 1876-77.

India, Straits Settlements, Borneo, Macassar, Australia, Cape of Good Hope, 1886-87.

England to Calcutta, 1893.

Two voyages to the West Indies, 1883 and 1892, the latter including visits to the Chesapeake and Washington.

Canada and the United States, 1872.

The Baltic, 1860.

In 1889 the *Sunbeam* was lent to Lord Tennyson, for a short cruise in the Channel. The owner deeply regrets that he was prevented by Parliamentary duties from taking charge of his vessel with a passenger so illustrious on board.

The distances covered in the course of the various cruises enumerated may be approximately given:—

DISTANCES SAILED: COMPILED FROM LOG BOOKS

Year	Knots	Year	Knots	Year	Knots	Year	Knots
1854	150	1864	1,000	1874	12,747	1884	3,087
1855	250	1865	2,626	1875	4,370	1885	6,344
1856	2,000	1866	4,400	1876		1886	
1857	1,500	1867	3,000	1877	37,000	1887	36,466
1858	2,500	1868	1,000	1878	9,038	1888	1,175
1859	2,300	1869	1,900	1879	5,627	1889	8,785
1860	1,000	1870	1,400	1880	5,415	1890	8,287
1861	800	1871	5,234	1881	5,435	1891	1,133
1862	3,200	1872	9,152	1882	3,345	1892	11,992
1863	900	1873	2,079	1883	13,545	1893	8,500

Total, 1854–1893, 228,682 knots.

I turn from the voyages to the yachts in which they were performed, observing that no later possession filled its owner with more pride than was felt in the smart little 8-tonner which heads the list.

Date	Name of yacht	Rig	Tonnage	
1854–58	Spray of the Ocean	Cutter	8	—
1853	Cymba (winner of Queen's Cup in the Mersey, 1857)	,,	50	Fife of Fairlie's favourite
1859–60	Albatross		118	—
1863–71	Meteor	Auxiliary schooner	164	—
1871–72	Muriel	Cutter	60	Dan Hatcher's favourite
1872	Eothen	S.S.	340	—
1874–93	Sunbeam	Auxiliary schooner	532	—
1882–83	Norman	Cutter	40	Dan Hatcher
1891	Lorna	,,	90	Camper and Nicholson (1881)
1892–93	Zarita	Yawl	115	Fife of Fairlie (1875)

'Sunbeam,' R.Y.S. (Lord Brassey).

The variety of craft in the foregoing list naturally affords opportunity for comparison. I shall be glad if such practical lessons as I have learned can be of service to my brother yachtsmen. And, first, as to the class of vessel suitable for ocean cruising. As might be expected, our home-keeping craft are generally too small for long voyages. Rajah Brooke did some memorable work in the *Royalist* schooner, 45 tons; but a vessel of 400 tons is not too large to keep the sea and to make a fair passage in all weathers, while giving space enough for privacy and comfort to the owner, his friends, and the crew. Such vessels as the truly noble *St. George*, 871 tons, the *Valhalla*, 1,400 tons, and Mr. Vanderbilt's *Valiant*, of 2,350 tons (Mr. St. Clare Byrne's latest production), cannot be discussed as examples of a type which can be repeated in ordinary practice. Yachtsmen have been deterred from going to sufficient tonnage by considerations of expense. When providing a floating home of possibly many years, first cost is a less serious question than the annual outlay in maintaining and working.

A cruise on the eastern seaboard of North America, where the business of coasting has been brought to the highest perfection, would materially alter the prevailing view as to the complements necessary for handling a schooner of the tonnage recommended. The coasting trade of the United States is carried on in large schooners, rigged with three to five masts. All the sails are fore and aft. In tacking, a couple of hands attend the headsheets, and these, with a man at the wheel, are sufficient to do the work of a watch, even in narrow channels, working short boards.

The anchor is weighed and the large sails are hoisted by steam-power. The crews of the American fore-and-aft schooners scarcely exceed the proportion of one man to every hundred tons of cargo carried. For a three-masted schooner of 400 tons, a crew of twelve working hands would be ample, even where the requirements of a yacht have to be provided for. In point of safety, comfort, speed in blowing weather, and general ability to keep the sea and make passages, the 400-ton schooner would offer most desirable advantages over schooner yachts of half the tonnage, although manned with the same number of hands.

It is not within the scope of my present remarks to treat of naval architecture. The volumes will contain contributions from such able men as Messrs. G. L. Watson, who designed the *Britannia* and *Valkyrie*, and Lewis Herreshoff, whose *Navahoe* and *Vigilant* have recently attracted so much attention. I may, however, say that my personal experience leads me to admire the American models, in which broad beam and good sheer are always found. In 1886, I had the opportunity of seeing the International Race for the America Cup, when the English cutter *Galatea* (Lieut. Henn, R.N.), with a sail-area of 7,146 feet, and 81 tons of ballast, sailed against the American sloop *Puritan*, with 9,000 square feet of sail-area and 48 tons of ballast. On this occasion, the advantages of great beam, combined with a shallow middle body and a deep keel, were conspicuously illustrated. The Americans, while satisfied with their type, do not consider their sloops as seaworthy as our cutters. The development which seems desirable in our English building was indicated in a letter addressed to the *Times* from Chicago in September 1886:—

> Avoiding exaggerations on both sides, we may build up on the solid keel of an English cutter a hull not widely differing in form from that of the typical American sloop. It can be done, and pride and prejudice should not be suffered to bar the way of improvement. The yachtsmen of a past generation, led by Mr. Weld of Lulworth, the owner of the famous *Alarm*, were not slow to learn a lesson from the contests with the *America* in 1851. We may improve our cutters, as we formerly improved our schooners, by adaptations and modifications, which need not be servile imitations of the fine sloops our champion vessels have encountered on the other side of the Atlantic.

After the lapse of seven years, we find ourselves, in 1893, at the termination of a very remarkable year's yachting. The new construction has included H.R.H. the Prince of Wales's yacht, the '*Britannia*,' with 23 feet beam, Lord Dunraven's *Valkyrie*, Mr. Clarke's *Satanita*, and the Clyde champion *Calluna*, all conspicuous for development of beam, combined with the deep, fine keel which is our English substitute for the American centreboard. These vessels have proved doughty antagonists of the *Navahoe*, brought over by that spirited yacht-owner, Mr. Caryll, to challenge all comers in British waters.

Thus far as to sailing yachts. Though the fashion of the hour has set strongly towards steam-propelled vessels, the beautiful white canvas, and the easy motion when under sail, will long retain their fascination for all pleasure voyaging. It is pleasant to be free from the thud of engines, the smell of oil, and the horrors of the inevitable coaling. Owners who have no love for sailing, and to whom a yacht is essentially a means of conveyance from port to port and a floating home, do well to go for steam. The most efficient and cheapest steam yacht is one in which the masts are reduced to two signal-poles, on which jib-headed trysails may be set to prevent rolling. As to tonnage, the remarks already offered on the advantages of large size apply to steamers even more than to sailing yachts.

When space must be given to machinery, boilers, and bunkers, the tonnage must be ample to give the required accommodation. The cost of building and manning, and the horse-power of the engines, do not increase in proportion to the increase of size. The building of steamers for the work of tramps has now been brought down to 7*l*. per ton. I would strongly urge yacht-owners contemplating ocean cruising to build vessels of not less than 600 tons. Let the fittings be as simple and inexpensive as possible, but let the tonnage be large enough to secure a powerful sea-boat, with coal endurance equal to 3,000 knots, at ten knots, capable of keeping up a fair speed against a stiff head wind, and habitable and secure in all weathers.

Deck-houses are a great amenity at sea, but the conventional yacht skipper loves a roomy deck, white as snow, truly a marvel of scrubbing. Considerations of habitability at sea are totally disregarded by one who feels no need for an airy place of retirement for reading and writing. The owner, seeking to make life afloat pass pleasantly, will consider deck cabins indispensable.

There remains a third and very important type for ocean cruising, that of the sailing yacht with auxiliary steam-power. The *Firefly*, owned by Sir Henry Oglander, the pioneer in this class, suggested to the present writer a debased imitation in the *Meteor*, 164 tons. About the same date somewhat similar vessels were brought out, amongst others by Lord Dufferin, whose earliest experiences under sail had been given to the world in *Letters from High Latitudes*. All will remember the never-varying announcement by a not too cheering steward, on calling his owner, in response to the inquiry, 'How is the wind?' 'Dead ahead, my lord, dead ahead!'

The *Sunbeam* was launched in 1874; following in her wake, the *Chazalie*, 1875, *Czarina*, 1877, and the *Lancashire Witch*, 1878, appeared in rapid succession. The *Lancashire Witch'* was bought by the Admiralty for a surveying vessel, as being especially adapted to the requirements of that particular service. The *St. George*, 831 tons, launched 1890, is an enlargement and improvement on her predecessors already named. She does credit to her owner, Mr. Wythes; the designer, Mr. Storey; and the builders, Messrs. Ramage. The *Sunbeam*, as the first of this class,

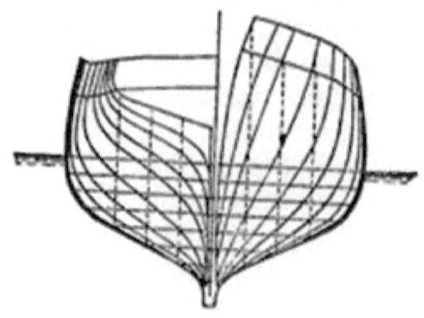

'SUNBEAM'—MIDSHIP SECTION.

has been a great success. She was designed by Mr. St. Clare Byrne, M.I.N.A., as a composite three-masted topsail-yard screw schooner, constructed at Birkenhead, and launched in 1874. The following table gives the leading details:—

Material of hull	Iron frame, teak skin
Length of hull	159 feet, overall 170 feet
Beam	27 ft. 6 in.
Depth of hold	13 ft. 9 in.
Displacement in tons	576 tons
Draught	13 ft. 6 ins.
Registered tonnage	227 tons
Engines, compound	By Laird of Birkenhead
Horse-power	70 nominal, or 350 indicated
Stowage of coals in bunkers	70 tons
Sail area	9,200 square yards
Weight of port anchor	12 cwt. 2 qr.
Weight of starboard anchor	12 cwt. 1 qr. 6 lbs.
Size of cable on board	1 1/16 inch }
Size of new cable on shore	1 2/16 inch} bower cables
Stowage of water	
Fore tanks	6 ½ tons}
After tanks	4 tons }
Reserve tanks	5½ tons} total 16 tons
Lead ballast	75 tons
Speed in fine weather	9 knots
Avge consumption coal daily	6 tons

Dimensions of Spars

	Length	Diam.
FORE	ft.	in.
Foremast, from deck to masthead	69½	—
Below deck	14½	—
Total	84	19½
Top and topgallant-mast	45	12
Fore-yard	50½	12
Topsail-yard	42¾	9
Topgallant-yard	33	7
Fore-gaff	29¼	7
Fore-boom	33¾	9
MAIN		
Mainmast from deck to masthead	74	—
Below deck	14½	—
Total	88½	19
Main-topmast	42¾	9¼
Main-gaff	29¾	7¾
Main-boom	35¼	8¼
MIZEN		
Mizenmast from deck to masthead	78½	—
Below deck	7½	—
Total	86	18½
Mizen-topmast	43½	9½
Mizen-gaff	33	9
Mizen-boom	52¾	13½

Jibboom, length 49 ft. 9 in., diameter 9¼ inches
Bowsprit ,, 21 ft. 9 in. ,, 17½ inches (outside knighthead)

It may be interesting to give some general account of the *Sunbeam's* performances at sea.

In making the voyage round the world in 1876-77 the total distances covered were 15,000 knots under sail and 12,800 knots under steam. The best run under steam alone was 230 knots. The most successful continuous performance was on the passage from Penang to Galle, when 1,451 knots were steamed in a week, with a daily consumption of 4-¼ tons of coal. The best runs under sail, from noon to noon, were 298 and 299 knots respectively. The first was on the passage from Honolulu to Yokohama, sailing along the 16th parallel of north latitude, and between 163° and 168° 15' east. The second was in the Formosa Channel. The highest speed ever attained under sail was 15 knots, in a squall in the North Pacific. On 28 days the distance under sail alone has exceeded, and often considerably exceeded, 200 knots. The best consecutive runs under sail only were:—

1. Week ending August 13, South Atlantic, in the south-east trades,

wind abeam, force 5, 1,456 knots.

2. Week ending November 19, South Pacific, south-east trades, wind aft, force 5, 1,360 knots.

3. Four days, January 15 to 18, North Pacific, north-east trades, wind on the quarter, force 5 to 9, 1,027 knots. The average speed in this case was 10.7 knots an hour.

The following were the average speeds of the longer passages:—

	Days at sea	Total distance	Distance under steam	Daily average
		miles	miles	miles
1. Cape Verdes to Rio .	18	3,336	689	185
2. Valparaiso to Yokohama .	72	12,333	2,108	171
3. Simonosaki to Aden .	37	6,931	4,577	187

On a later voyage to Australia, the total distance covered was 36,709 knots, 25,808 under sail and 10,901 under steam. The runs under sail included thirty-nine days over 200 knots, fifteen days over 240, seven days over 260, and three days over 270. The best day was 282 knots. Between Port Darwin and the Cape the distance covered was 1,047 knots under steam, and 5,622 knots under sail. The average speed under steam and sail was exactly eight knots. In the fortnight, October 13 to 27, 1887, 3,073 knots, giving an average speed of nine knots an hour, were covered under sail alone, with winds of moderate strength. Balloon canvas was freely used.

On returning from the voyage just referred to, the boilers of the *Sunbeam* (which are still at work, after nineteen years' service) required such extensive repairs that it was recommended to remove them and to replace with new. Hesitating to take this step, we went through two seasons under sail alone, the propeller being temporarily removed and the aperture closed. In 1889 a voyage was accomplished to the Mediterranean under these conditions. Making the passage from Portsmouth to Naples, in the month of February, we covered a total distance of 2,303 miles from port to port in ten days and four hours. The same good luck with the winds followed us in subsequent passages to Messina, Zante, Patras, and Brindisi, during which we steadily maintained the high average of ten knots. On the return voyage down the Mediterranean, the results were very different. As this novel experiment in running an auxiliary steam yacht under sail alone may be of interest, a few further details may be added.

The average rate of speed for the distance sailed through the water was approximately 6.4 knots. The total number of days at sea was 44. On 23 days the winds were contrary. On 21 days favourable winds were experienced. With much contrary wind and frequent calms the distances made good on the shortest route from port to port averaged 123 miles per day.

For the total distance of 3,020 miles from Portsmouth to Brindisi, touching at Naples, Messina, Taormina, Zante, and Patras, with fresh and favourable breezes, the distances made good on the shortest route averaged 201 miles per day.

On the passage down the Mediterranean, from Brindisi to Gibraltar, calling at Palermo and Cagliari, against persistent head winds, and with 60 hours of calm, the distance made good from port to port was reduced to 67 miles a day.

Homewards, from Gibraltar, against a fresh Portuguese trade, the distance made good rose to an average of 122 miles through the water per day, the average rate of sailing being 6-¼ knots. From a position 230 miles nearly due west of Cape St. Vincent to Spithead, the *Sunbeam* covered the distance of 990 miles in six days, being for the most part close-hauled.

	Total distances port to port	Distances sailed	Time under way		Fair winds		Calms
	miles	miles	days	hrs.	days	hrs.	hours
Portsmouth to Naples	2,200	2,303	10	4	9	0	11
Naples to Brindisi (calling at Messina, Taormina, Zante, and Patras)	820	841	5	0	4	0	16
Brindisi to Palermo	400	638	5	6	0	7	13
Palermo to Cagliari	224	353	3	19	—	—	11
Cagliari to Gibraltar	730	1,188	10	5	2	2	37
Gibraltar to Portsmouth	1,175	1,457	9	16	6	0	8
Total	5,549	6,780	44	2	21	9	96

In the course of the voyage numerous gales of wind were experienced, *viz*.: on February 12, a severe mistral, on the passage from Minorca towards Naples; March 28, heavy gale from westward off Stromboli; April 9 and 10, gale from S.W. at the mouth of the Adriatic; April 17, gale from S., off south coast of Sardinia; April 29 and 30, gale from W., off Almeria.

On the days of light winds and calms, balloon topmast staysails, a jib-topsail, and an extra large lower studsail, were found most valuable in maintaining the rate of sailing.

In ordinary cruising I find that, as a general rule, one-third of the distance is covered under steam, and that upon the average we make passages at the rate of 1,000 miles a week. The consumption of coal is very moderate. For a voyage round the world, of 36,000 miles, the coal consumed was only 325 tons.

If I were dealing with the question of rig, with the long experience gained on the *Sunbeam*, I should decidedly adopt the barque rig. In confirmation of this opinion, it may be interesting to note that when H.M. brig *Beagle* was under the command of Captain FitzRoy, R.N., for a lengthened service in the Straits of Magellan and the coasts of South America, the mizenmast was stuck through the skylight of the captain's cabin, an arrangement which, while of service to the ship, was not unnaturally a source of discomfort to the captain. In making passages in the Trades, with light winds on the quarter and the usual swell, fore-and-aft sails are constantly lifting, while sails set on yards keep asleep. They draw better, and there is no chafe. I have found great advantage from the use of large studding-sails, made of light duck. This material was highly esteemed when it was first brought out. In modern practice a combination of silk and hemp furnishes a greatly superior material for the huge spinnakers, of 4,000 square feet, carried by the *Navahoe* and *Valkyrie*. The new balloon sails can no longer be called canvas. They may more accurately be described as muslin.

I will not attempt a recital of nautical adventures in the present chapter; but a few experiences may be briefly described. The worst passage I ever made was in the *Eothen*, s.s., 340 tons, in 1872, from Queenstown to Quebec, touching at St. John's, Newfoundland. On August 14 we put to sea deeply laden, with bunkers full, and 15 tons of coal in bags on deck. In this condition we had 2 ft. 9 in. of freeboard. On the second day out we encountered a summer gale. Shortly after it came on, we shipped a sea, which broke over the bow and filled us up to the rail. At the same time the engineer put his head above the engine-room hatch, and announced that, the bearings having become heated, he must stop the engines.

For a short time we were in danger of falling off into the trough of the sea. It was a great relief when the engines once more slowly turned ahead. In the mid-Atlantic, we encountered a cyclone, passing through the calm but ominous centre into a violent gale from the north-west,

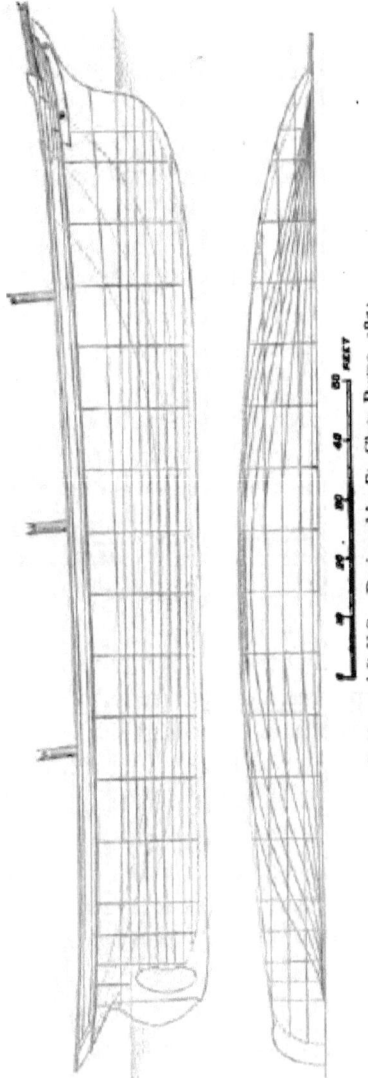

'Sunbeam,' R.Y.S. Designed by St. Clare Byrne, 1874.

which lasted twenty-four hours. We were battened down and suffered considerable discomfort. Fortunately, no heavy sea broke on board as we lay to under double-reefed main storm-trysail, the engines slowly turning ahead. Two days later we encountered another sharp gale, in which the barometer fell to 29.14°. Happily it soon passed over. After this third gale we had a change of wind to the eastward, and, pushing on, with all sail set, we reached St. John's in thirteen days from Queenstown, with four inches of water in the tanks, two tons of coal in the bunkers, the decks leaking in every seam, cabins in utter disarray, and a perfect wreck aloft and on deck. After leaving St. John's, where we had confidently hoped that the worst was over, we encountered a hurricane off Cape Race, which exceeded in violence anything that had been experienced in these waters for many years. We lay to for three days, and when the storm abated put into the French island St. Pierre, almost exhausted. It was an unspeakable relief when we entered the St. Lawrence.

The lesson to be drawn from my voyage in the *Eothen* is obvious. It is a great mistake to attempt to cross the stormiest ocean in the world in a steam yacht of such small size. For ocean steaming much more tonnage and power are necessary.

The heaviest gale ever experienced by the *Sunbeam* was off Flamborough Head, in 1881. I embarked at Middlesbrough on the evening of October 13, intending to sail for Portsmouth at daybreak on the following morning; but, finding the wind from the south and the barometer depressed, our departure was deferred. At 9 a.m. the barometer had fallen to 28.87°, but as the wind had changed to W.N.W., and was off shore from a favourable quarter, I determined to proceed to sea. We were towed down the Tees, and as we descended the river I conferred with the pilot as to what we might anticipate from the remarkable depression in the barometer. He was of opinion that a severe gale was at hand, that it would blow from the north-west, and that there was no reason for remaining in port. The tug was accordingly cast off at the mouth of the Tees, and we made sail.

Foreseeing a storm, topmasts were housed, boats were secured on deck, and we kept under close-reefed canvas, setting the main and mizen jib-headed trysails, double-reefed foresail and forestay-sail, and reefed standing jib. As the day advanced no change took place in the weather. The wind blew strongly, but not with the force of a gale, and the sea was comparatively smooth. Meanwhile the barometer continued to descend rapidly, and at 2 p.m. had fallen to 28.45°. As nothing had yet occurred to account for this depression, my sailing-master remarked that it must have been caused by the heavy showers of rain which had fallen in the course of the morning. I knew from former experiences that it was not the rain, but the coming storm, that was indicated by the barometer. It had needed some resolution to quit the mouth of the Tees in the morning, and at mid-day, when we were off Whitby, a still greater effort was required to resist the temptation to make for a harbour. No further incidents occurred until 3 p.m., when we were nearing Flamborough Head. Here we were at last overtaken by the long impending storm. Looking back to the north-west, over the starboard quarter, we saw that the sea had suddenly been lashed into a mass of white foam. The hurricane was rushing forward with a velocity and a force which must have seemed terrible to the fleet of coasting vessels around us.

Before the gale struck the *Sunbeam* our canvas had been reduced to main and mizen trysails and reefed standing-jib; but even with the small spread of sail, and luffed up close to the wind, our powerful little vessel careened over to the fury of the blast until the lee-rail completely disappeared under water—an incident which had never previously occurred during all the extensive voyages we had undertaken. Such was the force of the wind that a sailing vessel near us lost all her sails, and our large gig was stove in from the tremendous pressure of the gunwale against the davits. We took in the jib and the mizen-trysail, and, with our canvas reduced to a jib-headed main-trysail, were soon relieved of water on deck. For an hour and a half we lay-to on the starboard tack, standing in for the land below Burlington Bay. We were battened down, and felt ourselves secure from all risks except collision.

The fury of the wind so filled the air with spoon-drift that we could not see a ship's length ahead, and in such crowded waters a collision was a far from impossible contingency. At 6 p.m. we thought it prudent to wear, so as to gain an offing during the night, and gradually drew out of the line of traffic along the coast. At 9 p.m. the extreme violence of the hurricane had abated, and we could see, through occasional openings in the mist, the masthead lights of several steamers standing, like ourselves, off the land for the night. At midnight the barometer was rising rapidly, and the wind gradually settled down into a clear hard gale, accompanied by a heavy sea, running down the coast from the north.

At 6 a.m. we carefully examined the dead reckoning, and, having fixed on an approximate position, we determined to bear away, steering to pass in mid-channel between the Outer Dowsing and the Dudgeon, through a passage about ten miles in width. We were under easy sail; but, under the main-trysail, double-reefed foresail, staysail, fore-topsail, and reefed jib, we scudded at the rate of eleven knots. A constant look-out had been kept from aloft, and at 10 a.m., having nearly run the distance down from our assumed position when we bore away to the north end of the Outer Dowsing, I established myself in the crosstrees until we should succeed in making something.

After a short interval we saw broken water nearly ahead on the port bow. We at once hauled to the wind, steering to the south-west, and set the mizen-trysail. The lead showed a depth of three fathoms, and we were therefore assured that we had been standing too near to the Outer Dowsing. The indications afforded by the lead were confirmed by sights, somewhat roughly taken, and by the circumstance of our having shortly before passed through a fleet of trawlers evidently making for the Spurn. In less than an hour after we had hauled to the wind we found ourselves in the track of several steamers. At 3 p.m. we made the land near Cromer, and at 5.30 we brought up in the Yarmouth Roads, thankful to have gained a secure shelter from the gale.

In connection with this experience, it may be remarked that, as a general rule, our pleasure fleet is over-masted. We are advised in these matters by sailmakers, who look to the Solent and its sheltered water as the normal condition with which yachtsmen have to deal. When we venture forth from that smooth and too-much frequented arm of the sea into open waters, our vessels have to pass a far more severe ordeal, and they do not always come out of it to our satisfaction. Many are compelled to stay in harbour when a passage might have been made in a snugly rigged yacht.

One of the longest gales experienced in the *Sunbeam* was on the passage from Nassau to Bermuda, in November 1883. The gale struck us south of Cape Hatteras, on November 25, in latitude 31.54° N. The north-east wind gradually subsided, and we pushed on, under steam, for Bermuda at 7 knots. The head sea increased, but no change took place in the force or direction of the wind from 8 p.m. on the 25th till 4 a.m. on the 27th. Meanwhile, the barometer had gradually fallen to 29.82°, giving warning for a heavy gale, which commenced at north-by-east, and ended on November 30, at 4 p.m., with the wind at north-west. We lay-to on the 27th, under treble-reefed foresail and double-reefed mainsail, shipping no water, but driving to the south-east at the rate of at least one knot an hour. On the 28th we decided to try the *Sunbeam* under treble-reefed foresail and mainsail, double-reefed fore-staysail and reefed mizen-trysail. With this increased spread of canvas we were able to make two knots an hour on the direct course to Bermuda, and to keep sufficient steerage way to luff up to an ugly sea.

The behaviour of the vessel elicited the unqualified approval of our most experienced hands. Bad weather quickly brings out the qualities of seamen. Our four best men relieved each other at the wheel, and it was due in no small degree to their skill that, in a gale lasting three days, no heavy sea broke on board. I need not say that all deck openings were secured, especially at night, by means of planks and canvas. Our situation might perhaps excite sympathy, but we had no cause to complain. Meals could not be served in the usual manner, but by placing every movable thing on the floor of the cabins and on the lee side, and by fixing ourselves against supports, or in a recumbent position, we were secured against any further effects of the force of gravity, and did our best to enjoy the novelty of the situation. On the 30th the wind veered to the north-west, and the weather rapidly improved. The sea turned gradually with the wind, but for many hours we met a heavy swell from the north-east.

An acquaintance with the law of storms had proved invaluable on this occasion. There is no situation in which knowledge is more truly power, none in which, under a due sense of the providential care of Heaven, it gives a nobler confidence to man, than at sea, amid the raging of a hurricane. Mr. Emerson has truly said:

> They can conquer who believe they can. The sailor loses fear as fast as he acquires command of sails, and spars, and steam. To the sailor's experience, every new circumstance suggests what he must do. The terrific chances which make the hours and minutes long to the mere passenger, he whiles away by incessant application of expedients and repairs. To him a leak, a hurricane, a waterspout, is so much work, and no more. Courage is equality to the problem, in affairs, in science, in trade, in council, or in action. Courage consists in the conviction that the agents with which you contend are not superior in strength, or resources, or spirit, to you.

As a specimen of a dirty night at sea, I give another extract from the log-book. During our voyage round the world in 1876-77, after leaving Honolulu for Japan, as we approached Osima, on January 26, we were struck by a tremendous squall of wind and rain. We at once took in the flying square-sail, stowed the topgallant-sail and topsail, reefed the foresail and mizen, and set mainsail. At 6 p.m., the wind still blowing a moderate gale, the mizen was double-reefed. We pursued our way through a confused sea, but without shipping any water. All seemed to be going well, when, at 8 p.m., shortly after I had taken the wheel, a sudden squall heeled us over to the starboard side, where the gig was hung from the davits outboard.

At the same time a long mountainous wave, rolling up from the leeward, struck the keel of the gig and lifted it up, unshipping the fore davit, and causing the boat to fall into the boiling sea, which threatened at every instant to dash it to pieces. We at once brought to. A brave fellow jumped into the boat and secured a tackle to the bows, and the gig was hoisted on board and secured on deck intact. It was a very seaman-like achievement. A heavy gale continued during the night, and at 2 a.m., on the 27th, we met with another accident. The boatswain, a man of great skill and experience, was at the wheel, when a steep wave suddenly engulfed the jibboom, and the *Sunbeam*, gallantly springing up, as if to leap over instead of cleaving through the wave, carried away the spar at the cap. This brought down the topgallant-mast. The jibboom was a splendid Oregon spar, 54 feet long, projecting 28 feet beyond the bowsprit. It was rigged with wire rope, and the martingale was sawn through with the greatest difficulty.

The record of personal experiences must not be further prolonged. To the writer yachting has been to some extent part of a public life, mainly devoted to the maritime interests of the country. To conduct the navigation and pilotage of his vessel seemed fitting and even necessary, if the voyages undertaken were to be regarded in any sense as professional. There is something pleasant in any work which affords the opportunity for encountering and overcoming difficulties. It is satisfactory to make a headland or a light with precision after a long run across the ocean, diversified perhaps by a heavy gale. To be able to thread the channels of the West Coast of Scotland, the Straits of Magellan, the Eastern Archipelago, the labyrinths of the Malawalle Channel of North-East Borneo, or the Great Barrier Reef of Australia, without a pilot is an accomplishment in which an amateur may perhaps take legitimate pleasure.

To the yachtsman who truly loves the sea, it will never be satisfactory to remain ignorant of navigation. Practice of the art is not a relaxation. It demands constant attention, and is an interruption to regular reading. It may imply a considerable amount of night-work. On the other hand, the owner who is a navigator can take his proper place as the commander of his own ship. All that goes on around him when at sea becomes more interesting. He is better able to appreciate the professional skill of others. The confidence which grows with experience cannot be expected in the beginning. The writer first took charge of navigation in 1866, on a voyage up the Baltic. It was a chequered experiment. In the Great Belt we ran ashore twice in one day. In making Stockholm we had to appeal to a Swedish frigate, which most kindly clewed up her sails, and answered our anxious enquiries by writing the course on a black-board. On the return voyage to England we struck the coast some sixty miles north of our reckoning. Such a history does not repeat itself now.

It is not in books or at the library table that the art of the seaman can be acquired. Quickness of eye, nerve, promptitude of judgment, are the indispensable gifts, which must be gained by long and varied experience at sea. The seamanship required in a gale of wind on the open ocean, the seamanship displayed in sailing matches in oversparred yachts, sailed mainly in smooth waters, and the seamanship called for in pilotage waters not previously visited, and especially at night, are different branches of a wide profession. There is a skill of a very high order in docking an Atlantic liner at Liverpool. There is a skill of a different but equally high order in knocking huge ironclads about in fleet-exercising at sea. There is a skill in bringing the Channel steamers alongside the pier at Dover. The skill of every description of nautical specialist will never be combined in one individual. There is some risk that the more careful the navigator, the less dashing the same man may be as a seaman.

I must not conclude without some reference to the most attractive cruising grounds. To begin near home, the Seine, the Meuse, the coast of Holland, the Baltic, the coast of Norway, the grand West Coast of Scotland, the East Coast of England (a cruising ground too much neglected by yachtsmen), and the Channel are all favourite haunts of mine. Going further afield, in my own case nothing was more satisfactory than a voyage along the East Coast of North America, in which every river was ascended to the head of the navigation for sea-going vessels. Certain parts of the Mediterranean offer a perfect cruising ground for the winter months. Most suitable waters for yachting are those bounded by the Straits of Gibraltar on the west and the Balearic

Islands on the north-east.

Here the mistral of the Gulf of Lyons is not felt. The Spanish coast offers many places of shelter and many points of interest. In westerly winds keep to the eastward of Cape de Gata; in north-easterly winds to the westward. There is another charming cruising ground between Corsica and the Italian coast, as far north as Spezia, and south down to Civita Vecchia. Sicily is admirable for yachting. A weather shore can be always made upon its beautiful coasts. In the spring or autumn the Archipelago and eastern side of the Adriatic can be confidently recommended. In the winter months the West Indies are a most perfect cruising ground. It will be well to make Barbados the landfall, then run to Trinidad, proceeding thence to Grenada, and following on from island to island down to Jamaica. The return voyage should be by Havana, and thence to a port in the United States, and by an ocean liner home, or by the Bahamas, Bermuda and the Azores to England. The Pacific, Japan and Eastern Archipelago will well repay those who can give the time required for such distant voyages.

Lastly, let no yachtsman speak contemptuously of the Solent. It is no exaggeration to say that if the splendid natural breakwater of the Isle of Wight were removed, half the tonnage of yachts under the British flag would disappear. The Solent offers a sufficient space of sheltered water for all but the very largest yachts to manoeuvre in conveniently. Breezes are seldom wanting, and the shores of the Wight are most pleasing. In this miniature ocean many have formed tastes for the sea which have led to more ambitious voyages. The estuary of the Clyde merits equally high praise, but the puffs off Bute are less gentle than those off the Wight, and the racing partakes of a hard-weather character, with streaks of calm.

In the preceding observations it has been assumed that I have been addressing readers who love the sea in all those varying phases which have given inspiration to some of the finest creations of poetic genius. The Greeks were lovers of the sea. We have been reminded of their admirable descriptions by Mr. Froude, in a brilliant passage:—

The days pass, and our ship flies past upon her way.

γλαυκὸν ὑπὲρ οἶδμα κυανόχροά τε κυμάτων
ῥόθια πολιὰ θαλάσσας.

How perfect the description! How exactly in those eight words Euripides draws the picture of the ocean; the long grey heaving swell, the darker steel-grey on the shadowed slope of the waves, and the foam on their breaking crests. Our thoughts flow back as we gaze to the times long ago, when the earth belonged to other races, as it now belongs to us. The ocean is the same as it was. Their eyes saw it as we see it.

Time writes no wrinkle on that azure brow.

Nor is the ocean alone the same. Human nature is still vexed with the same problems, mocked with the same hopes, wandering after the same illusions. The sea affected the Greeks as it affects us, and was equally dear to them. It was a Greek who said: '*The sea washes off all the ills of men*,' the '*stainless one*,' as Æschylus called it, the eternally pure.

The Romans had in Virgil a poet of the sea, who could attune his lyre to perfect harmony, alike with freshening or subsiding breeze:—

Vela dabant læti et spumas salis ære ruebant.
******
ferunt ipsa æquora classem,
Æquatæ spirant auræ, datur hora quieti.

The sea has been the favoured theme of our English poets. There has been none in any language who has excelled our own Byron:—

Oft had he ridden on that wingèd wave,
And loved its roughness for the speed it gave.

For me, the sea was a dream in my earliest years. I have spent upon its waters some of the brightest, and, alas! some of the saddest of my days; and now, in the autumn of my life, the unforgotten past, and the aims and work of the present, are more than ever bound up with the sea.

Our hearts, our hopes, are all with thee;
Our hearts, our hopes, our prayers, our tears,
Our faith, triumphant o'er our fears,
Are all with thee—are all with thee.

CHAPTER 3

Corinthian Deep-Sea Cruising
By C. E. Seth-Smith, C.B.[1]
(Late commanding London Brigade Royal Naval Volunteers)

The record of Corinthian sailing would not be complete without some account of deep-sea voyages in yachts manned by amateur seamen. The cruises of Corinthian yachtsmen are naturally chiefly confined to the estuaries of rivers and the seas immediately adjacent, and, as a rule, are within sight of the coast. Considerations of time and expense are generally sufficient to impose these limits. That the dangers of the sea and the difficulty of navigation are no impediments is amply proved by the records of more extended voyages in craft of all sizes, made public from time to time. There are, however, certain other difficulties which, as a rule, stand in the way of Corinthian seamen extending their experience of the sea still further. For an ocean voyage of any extent a craft of some size is necessary, and it must be manned by a crew of considerable number.

Amateur yachtsmen are scattered, and find it difficult to take their cruises together in any large numbers. The yacht-owner, who wished to man his yacht for an ocean voyage solely or mainly with Corinthian seamen, would not find it easy to obtain a sufficient number to make up his complement. A movement was made some twenty years ago to develop and utilise for the national defence the seafaring instincts and tastes latent in many of our young countrymen, and until it was abandoned in 1892[2] provided a body of men, Corinthian yachtsmen

---

1. I am deeply indebted to Mr. D.W. Marsden, late honorary secretary of the London Corps Royal Naval Artillery Volunteers, for his assistance in the compilation of these notes.
2. The late corps of Royal Naval Artillery Volunteers of London, Liverpool, Bristol and Glasgow.

and others possessing seafaring capacities, and formed an exceptional reservoir on which yacht-owners could draw who desired to give opportunities of more extended seafaring to the amateur seaman. The more extended voyages of the schooner *Hornet* were undertaken to give a pleasurable holiday to the members of the corps and to increase their efficiency as Naval Volunteers. The *Hornet* was a powerful yacht of 101 tons register and about 140 tons Thames measurement, she was 85 feet on the water-line and nearly 20 feet beam, and drew about 10 feet of water in sea-going trim. She was built at Cowes, and was rigged as a topsail-yard schooner, carrying in addition to her ordinary fore and aft sails a square foresail, a fore-topsail and topgallant-sail, and fore-topmast and lower studding-sails.

All her gear was fitted as far as possible in man-of-war fashion, and both on deck and below she was arranged as one of the small old-fashioned vessels of Her Majesty's service. A wardroom and four separate sleeping cabins for her officers were arranged aft, and a very large forecastle gave ample lower deck accommodation for some thirty-five or forty petty officers and men.

The majority of the *Hornet's* voyages were restricted by the limited holidays of her amateur crew, but she was occasionally manned by crews not tied in such a degree by business engagements, and during the summers of 1879, 1880 and 1881 sailed round the coast of Ireland, visited the Cattegat Sound and Danish Islands, Christiania and some other Norwegian ports, the coasts of Spain and Portugal, and Gibraltar, and made a short trip down the coast of Morocco. The latter terminated in an exciting passage home from Lisbon in stormy weather, during which the Corinthians were for upwards of three weeks out of sight of land on a strictly limited scale of provisions, hove to in a gale of wind for some days, and driven into the vicinity of the Azores. Since the present chapter is concerned solely with Corinthian yachting on the ocean, nothing need be said about the many short cruises round and about the English and French coasts and up and down the Channel, during which the *Hornet's* ever-varying crew were gaining some practical knowledge of seamanship and testing their individual fitness for their voluntary duties.

About the end of June 1879 the *Hornet* sailed from the Thames, manned by thirty-five amateurs, Mr. Edward Dodd, who was rated as boatswain, and the galley staff being the only professional seamen on board. Mr. Samuel Brooks (recently thrice mayor of Redhill) acted as chief petty officer, chief quartermaster and occasional watch-keeper, and Mr. R. T. Pritchett was borne on the books and drew rations as the 'staff officer,' the guide, philosopher and friend of the whole ship's company. The weather of the summer of 1879 is notorious, and the *Hornet's* first ocean cruise was a trying one for her Corinthian crew, who experienced to the full the miseries of a month at sea in bad weather. From the day she left Dartmouth in June to her arrival in the Solent in July her log-book records no single fine day. The afternoon of Friday, July 17 (the ship having left Queenstown July 16) is the only day on which 'light airs and sunshine' are entered even for a few hours.

Nevertheless the crew expressed themselves as thoroughly delighted with the experiences of their month's cruise. Some account of this trip appeared in the *Graphic* of October 18, 1879, with illustrations by the staff officer, of which the principal represented 'stowing the foresail off the Longships at midnight in a gale, June 30, 1879.' On this occasion the *Hornet* was compelled by a heavy gale from the south-west to force a passage round the Land's End, and make for the Bristol Channel, running up to the Mumbles. As the author remarks, such weather on a dark night was a severe trial for the practical seamanship of gentlemen sailors, but they proved themselves equal to it, and were afterwards complimented on their efficiency by the Admiral, Sir William Dowell, on arrival at Queenstown.

The following year—1880—a much longer and most enjoyable cruise of six weeks was undertaken on which the Captain, Mr. C. E. Seth-Smith, was assisted by Messrs. A. B. Woodd and E. Graham as lieutenants. The crew numbered twenty-five all told; Mr. Dodd again acted as boatswain, and Mr. Brooks as chief petty officer. The *Hornet* reached Copenhagen on July 10, and after cruising among the lovely Danish islands for some days, her officers and crew were hospitably entertained by the Royal Danish Yacht Club, then holding their annual regatta at Svendborg. From Denmark she passed to Christiania, and on July 25 the ship's company landed in Norway and enjoyed a cariole trip of two days across the country to the Falls of Hönefos. After cruising for two or three days along the southern coasts and up the Fjords the *Hornet* left Norway and returned to England, arriving at Greenhithe on August 4 after a well-managed and most successful expedition. She was the largest vessel, manned entirely by amateur sailors, that had appeared in those seas.

The account from which the above particulars are taken appeared in the *Illustrated London News* for February 12, 1881, and was accompanied by illustrations from photographs by Mr. Henry Denison Pender, son of Mr. (now Sir John) Pender, M.P., who was a member of the crew and an enthusiastic Royal Naval Artillery Volunteer, and whose lamented death soon after was the occasion of much grief to his many friends.

The following year—1881—a cruise of even more extended scope was undertaken. The *Hornet* left Dover on May 20, and proceeded down Channel to Dartmouth under the command of Mr. C. E. Seth-Smith, assisted by Mr. A. B. Woodd, Mr. Dodd again acting as boatswain and Mr. Brooks at his old post. At Dartmouth all hands signed articles. On Tuesday, May 24, the steam launch and boiler having been got on board, the *Hornet* left England for the South at 9 a.m. and lost sight of the English coast at 11.15 a.m., Prawl Point being her point of departure. The weather on her passage out was on the whole favourable, and on Tuesday, May 31, the Burlings, fifty miles west of Lisbon, was sighted, the ship's run from noon of the 30th to noon of the 31st having been 218 knots. On June 3, after a period of light winds and calm, the ship being about 120 miles west of Gibraltar, it came on to blow from the eastward, and the square fore-topsail was got in for the first time since leaving Dartmouth.

On June 4, the wind increasing to a whole gale from the east with heavy sea, they stood in shore to south of Cape Spartel and lay to 'up and down' in Spartel Bay all night. Next day, the weather moderating, the *Hornet* stood over to the Spanish coast and sighted Gibraltar Rock at 6.15 p.m., for which she stood steadily in; but at midnight, being becalmed, she was towed in by the gig, and at 2.30 a.m. the anchor was dropped in six fathoms off the Ragged Staff in Gibraltar Bay, after a passage from Dartmouth of thirteen days. The interval between June 6 and 11 was spent at Gibraltar in necessary cleaning and repairs, in exploring the Rock and its neighbourhood, and in giving and receiving hospitalities; and at noon on June 11 a start was made for Tangier, where the *Hornet* arrived at 5 a.m.

There she remained until the afternoon of June 12, when, the sights of the old Moorish town having been seen and various Oriental purchases made, the anchor was weighed for Cadiz. At 4 a.m. next day Cadiz was sighted, a pilot taken on board, and at 9.30 a.m. the anchor was let go in Cadiz Bay. At Cadiz a halt was made until June 17, employed by the ship's company in excursions to Seville and Jerez, and in seeing at Cadiz the procession of *Corpus Christi* and a bull-fight, distinguished on this occasion by the bull-ring taking fire. At 11.30 on the 17th a start was made for Lisbon. From Cadiz to Cape St. Vincent was a beat to windward, until on the 20th they were becalmed off the Cape. A breeze springing up in the afternoon, Cape Epischol was sighted, and at 9 a.m. on the 22nd a pilot was taken on board for Lisbon, and the *Hornet* sailed in with a light breeze by the south channel, and let go her anchor between Belem and Lisbon at 2 p.m.

The voyage home was destined to prove a much less agreeable experience. Anchor was weighed at 4 p.m. on June 24, wind blowing strong from the north-east, which continued next day with a heavy sea. Standing out to sea some fifty miles, the *Hornet* was put on the port tack and sighted the Burlings Light at 8.30 p.m., when she was again put about for sea room. On the 26th the ship was under three-reefed mainsail, reefed foresail, staysail, and jib, and on the 27th she was hove to under three-reefed mainsail and reefed foresail to a strong north-east gale. The 28th, still hove to, the gale blowing furiously, with tremendous seas, the mainsail and fore-staysail were taken in, and the ship put under fore-trysail alone.

On the 29th the gale appeared to be moderating, but at 8 a.m. it was found that the rudder-head had started, the steering-wheel and gear had to be unshipped, and the tiller shipped, tended constantly by two helmsmen. A jib-headed trysail was set on the mainsail to ease the steering gear. On the 30th the mainsail was again set, and, the stores having been overhauled, everyone was put on rations, which were further reduced next day. The weakness of the rudder-head rendered the most careful steering necessary, which, during the rest of the voyage, threw more work on the experienced hands. On July 3 she was again close hauled to a strong breeze from the north-east, which continued all day, the ship being under three-reefed mainsail and reefed foresail, and so continued through the whole of the 4th; but on the 5th the wind shifted to the north-west and moderated. All available sail was gradually made, and by noon of that day, the position having been verified by observation, under square foresail, topsail, and topmast stun'sails, topgallant-sail, and main topmast skysail, the course was set for home.

Next day the wind again shifted, and all hands were called in the morning watch to reduce sail. Their misfortunes had not ended, for on July 8 it was discovered that the fore-masthead was sprung, and the cap and crosstrees damaged. A lashing was, however, put round the heel of the fore-topmast, and the fore-masthead, and all the rigging and gear carefully overhauled and made good where possible. The rations, also, were still further reduced. However, on the 9th, having again got sights, the commander decided to bear up for the Channel, and at 10.30 sighted Ushant. A fair wind then sprang up, and the ship ran along gaily at an average of eight knots. On the 10th, and at 5.45 a.m., the English coast near Plymouth was sighted, the Start at 6.30, Portland at 2 p.m., and the Wight at 7. At 6 a.m. next day the anchor was dropped in Shanklin Bay, but permission to land being refused by the Customs authorities, sail was again set for Ryde, where the *Hornet* arrived at 7.30 p.m., thus terminating an eventful cruise. Although its unexpected prolongation had been rather trying for some of the ship's company, and their experience had been of a nature to try severely the physique and capacity of amateur sailors, they seem to have gone through it well.

Several other yachts, among which may be mentioned the *Titania*, belonging to the Marquis of Ailsa, the *Dawn*, to Mr. Klein, and *Diligent*, to Mr. C. E. Chadwick Healey and Mr. Sydney Hoare, have been manned by naval volunteers.

It now only remains to add a few considerations on the advantages and disadvantages of Corinthian crews for ocean-going yachts.

First, then, as to expense: the owner does not save anything by shipping an amateur crew. It is true he pays no wages to his Corinthian deck hands, but he must be prepared to incur a considerable outlay in alterations to the internal arrangements of the vessel, to buy new bedding and mess traps, and to provide a better class of ship's cooks and a more numerous galley staff. Good temper will not prevail, nor can discipline be easily maintained, unless Corinthian Jack is well fed. If, as is sometimes the case, the amateur crew arrange to cater for themselves, the owner and captain must occasionally add to the luxuries of the lower deck mess. Some expense is also unavoidable from the extra wear and tear arising from the want of skill of novices who have not yet learned to handle sails and gear with a view to their preservation.

The safety and comfort of one's ship's company, too, is a double source of anxiety when some or the whole are not seafaring by profession. For it must not be forgotten even in the finest weather that there is no such thing as 'playing at sailors' when at sea. The risk involved is not appreciably increased by manning the vessel with amateurs, if the officer in command will take certain precautions; and this view was endorsed by the insurance companies, who in no instance increased the premium on the *Hornet*. The owner must insist on shipping a due proportion of old hands in each crew, and take care to train them as helmsmen and leadsmen. He should relieve the 'wheel' and 'look-out' as often as practicable.

Above all, he should be careful to shorten sail in good time, and always at dusk, until he can depend upon his crew. Active and courageous as the amateur seaman invariably is, he has not the practice aloft of the professional, he cannot shorten sail so rapidly, nor does his knowledge of the lead of the ropes enable him to identify them so readily in the dark. The services of a good professional boatswain, with an enthusiastic love for his profession and a cheery sympathetic manner as an instructor, are absolutely essential for the proper working of a Corinthian ship. A minute and careful observation of the barometer, and constant verifying of position by reckoning and by observation, are the duties of the officer rather than the crew. Unless the yacht-owner be an enthusiastic navigator, delighting in his sextant and mathematical formulæ as well as a keen sailor-man, he had better not attempt this exacting if fascinating method of sailing his ship.

On the other hand, the Corinthian crew is a cheery one, well mannered and enthusiastic, grateful for any instruction which is given them, and happy in an exceptional and delightful holiday.

As a Corinthian crew is in general more numerous than one composed of professional sailors, when they have learnt their stations and become accustomed to the work, the vessel may be handled with that old-fashioned man-of-war smartness which is so attractive.

In conclusion, the national aquatic instinct, fostered as it is by the healthy sea-breezy tone prevailing in so much of our boyhood's literature, can only be cultivated by the majority of us as Corinthian seamen. Love for shipping and boats is not necessarily love for the sea and seafaring. Those who take to the sea as a profession are not always constant in their love. A voyage in a passenger ship, or even a trip as an honoured guest on board one of the floating batteries of Her Majesty's Navy, quite satisfies the still keen boyish aspiration. It is only as one of the crew of a large yacht on a deep-sea voyage that the amateur can personally experience that 'life at sea' which has so fascinated his imagination. Though I dare not advise all yacht-owners to man their ships with their friends, I should hail with pleasure an opportunity of sailing again with some of my old shipmates.

CHAPTER 4

The Evolution of the Modern Racing Yacht
By G. L. Watson

Seven years ago, (as at time of first publication), the task of describing the form of racing yachts would have been a much simpler one than it is today.. Then even the cruising vessels were more or less under the influence of the old tonnage rule, or of its later modification, and big and little were pretty much of a type;—a model of, say, a 'forty,' representing with sufficient accuracy a 'ninety,' or a 'five,' if we supposed the scale changed; and the individual yachts in each class, while presenting differences to the eye of the amateur, were not to be distinguished apart by the general yachting public, except perhaps by the racing flag.

Under the present length and sail-area rule, the variety of type is enormous. Broad, narrow, deep, and shallow; boats with centreboards and boats without; single boats and double boats; plain keel, fin keel, and bulb keel, have all their representatives, and each has had its successes. But few of these types could have been successful under the old tonnage rule, and few of them may be successful under rules yet to come. Any history, therefore, of the development of the form of racing yachts would fail did it not take account of, and run parallel to, the history of the tonnage rule of the time.

Throughout the modern story of yachting the tonnage question has been the all-absorbing one. Looking back, through the pages of those sporting papers and periodicals which forty years ago devoted a meagre portion of their space to yachting, one is struck by the same feature that shows prominently in the *'Field'* or *'Yachtsman'* of today. For one letter on any other subject, there are a dozen on the measure-

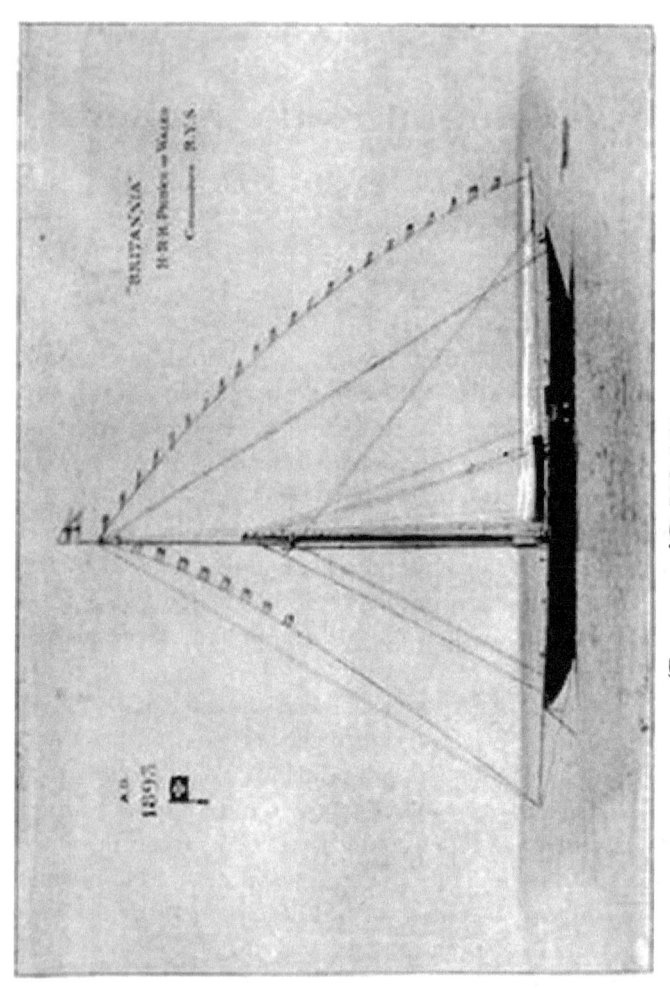

'Britannia' R.Y.S. 151-rater.
Designed by G. L. Watson, 1893.
Winner of R. Victoria Gold Cup, September 1893.

ment question, and the writers handled their pens in much the same energetic way then as now, in abuse of rival theorists; but, more merciful than the moderns, spared us their elaborate formulæ.

These controversies happily have served the useful purpose of preserving for the historian of today a good many facts which might otherwise have been lost; for our dear old friend *Hunt's Magazine*, in his flowery youth, is fonder of treating us to an *Ode to the Yachtsman's Bride*' or a relation of 'How Miss Delany married an Officer,' than to facts regarding measurement, or time allowances, and these are only to be picked up incidentally as it were from the correspondence of the quarrelsome gentlemen aforesaid. It is to be hoped that the yachting historian of the twentieth century may reap a like benefit from our controversialists of today, and that those mathematicians who now brandish their tonnage formulæ to the terror of all quietly disposed yachtsmen will find a reader in the searcher after facts of 1950.

Yachting, then, may be said to have begun with this century; for although, as is shown elsewhere in these volumes, yachts are mentioned long before that date, it was hardly until the century opened, or indeed until after the Crimean War, that yachting as a sport became fairly established in this country.

The yachts of those days were round-headed things, of about three beams in length, in most cases innocent of metal ballast, and kept on their feet by gravel or by iron ore. What little racing there might have been was confined to scratch matches between the owners, and time allowance for tonnage was not thought of, though doubtless the tonnage rule as then used for the merchant shipping of the country was recognised as a useful measure for the purchase and sale of these vessels. Racing became commoner; soon more than two yachts came together to try conclusions, and it was presently discovered by some astute yachtsman that a good big ship, other things being the same, was faster than a good little ship, and therefore, where their purses admitted of it, owners built yachts as large as could be handled. *Arrow*, 84 tons; *Lulworth*, 82 tons; *Alarm*, 193 tons; and *Louisa*, 180 tons, were the crack cutters on the Solent about forty-five years ago, and, as may be well understood, little boats had a very poor chance with these giants, except perhaps in light and fluky weather.

Mr. Holland-Ackers called attention to this fact, and proposed a table of time allowances between large and smaller yachts based on the length of the course and the difference of size between the vessels. The measure of this size was the tonnage, as ascertained by the then tonnage law of the land, which had been in force since 1794, or rather a slight modification of this rule, adapted to the peculiar form of yachts. In this, 'the old 94 rule,' as it was called, only length of keel and breadth were taken into account, the depth being assumed as half the breadth. Breadth was thus penalised twice over in the formula, and perhaps the most extraordinary fact in connection with this rule is, that it was in force for years before it seems to have occurred to our yacht-builders that a success was to be made by increasing those dimensions which were untaxed, or only moderately taxed, and reducing the beam which was taxed twice over.

This is all the more remarkable, as builders of the mercantile marine seem to have caught this point much earlier, and were building vessels with enormously increased depth and reduced beam, though it is true the slowness of these ships did not invite imitation, as the American clipper ships, built under a fairer tonnage law, were rapidly sailing them off the seas. Happily, in 1854 the law was changed for the present method of measurement by internal cubic capacity, and the genius of our shipbuilders, thus left unfettered, was equal to the task of regaining our supremacy on the ocean.

But among the yachts the old $L\text{-}B \times B \times (\frac{1}{2}B)/_{94}$ prevailed, and gradually builders discovered that, by increasing draft and amount of ballast, beam could be pared down, and a boat of nominally the same tonnage made longer and to carry more sail than her predecessor. Lead ballast was slowly introduced, despite all sorts of adverse prophecies from old salts that it would strain the ship and would cause her to plunge so heavily as to go under; and presently, when some unknown genius first put lead outside, and from a timid hundredweight or two this increased to tons, the veterans gave the new type up altogether as past praying for, and left them to their well-merited fate. I have been unable to get any definite information as to the first application of outside ballasts, but in 1834 Messrs. Steele built the *Wave* for Mr. John Cross Buchanan, and on this vessel a metal keel was fixed.

There may, however, have been earlier instances of this in the South. But Providence was on the side of the heavy lead keels, and each year yachts got longer, and deeper, and narrower, and had more and more lead outside, until there was none left inside at all, while they more and more nearly approached Euclid's definition of a line as having length but no breadth. *A propos* of these proportions, a good, and it may possibly be true, story is told of an enthusiastic cutter-man on the other side of the Atlantic, who, intensely prejudiced against the

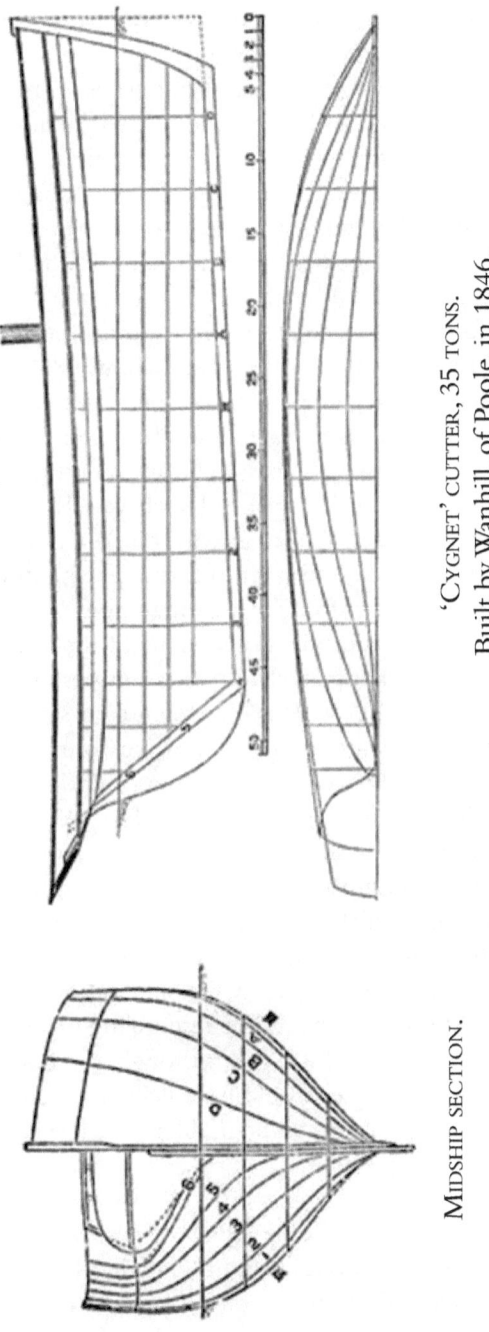

'Cygnet' cutter, 35 tons.
Built by Wanhill, of Poole, in 1846.

Midship section.

fine broad ships of America, asked a friend here to buy, and have sent across to him, a typical British 5-ton cutter, stipulating only that she should be fast, and at least as narrow as anything of her class. The little craft was safely brought across and put in the water in New York Bay, and after a trial sail the owner invited one or two friends to come off for a day's pleasuring in the new ship, with the object of showing the advantages of five feet of beam against ten. But, on coming alongside, the first to get out of the dinghy took hold of the runner, and taking a nice wide step, so as to get well into the centre of the boat, stepped clean into the water on the other side.

But long before the advantage of substituting untaxed depth for the heavily taxed beam was discovered, and about 1850 Mr. Wanhill, of Poole, introduced the raking sternpost, thus getting, on a given length of keel, a much longer water-line. But even this device was used in moderation, 50° to 60° being the utmost rake given, with the sternpost showing at the water-line, and such vessels as our modern cutaway fives, tens, twenties, or forties, with the keel a fourth of their over-all length, were as yet unthought of, though the direct inducement to build them was far stronger then than now.

I may cite an exception to this, however, in a vessel called the *Problem*, built at Kirkcaldy about 1850 or 1851, and described in *Hunt's Magazine* of August 1852. The *Problem* presented a similar profile to that of our fashionable fives or 2½ of three or four years back, the stem and sternpost sloping down and meeting in a point as in the *Lily*, 2½-rater; *Natica*, 5-rater; and *Varuna*, 40-rater. But the vessel was built without any idea of racing, she having three masts, square-rigged on each mast, and whatever advantages she may have possessed seem to have escaped the notice of the regular yacht-builders. A much likelier idea was struck by *Vanderdecken*, in a letter to *Bell's Life* in 1852, where he proposes a 'tonnage cheater,' in which he had got the sternpost pretty nearly amidships, with the profile resembling in an exact degree that of our most modern small craft. But though, if properly designed otherwise, the proposed vessel would have been a certain success, the jump was too big a one for our yacht-builders, and *Vanderdecken's* idea lay on the shelf for many years.

The evasion of length by this method, however, raised a terrible storm of discussion. *Bell's Life* and *Hunt's Magazine* were inundated with indignant letters on the subject, until, in 1854, the Royal London Yacht Club, followed by the Royal Thames, arranged to measure the length on deck, subtracting from this length the whole beam,

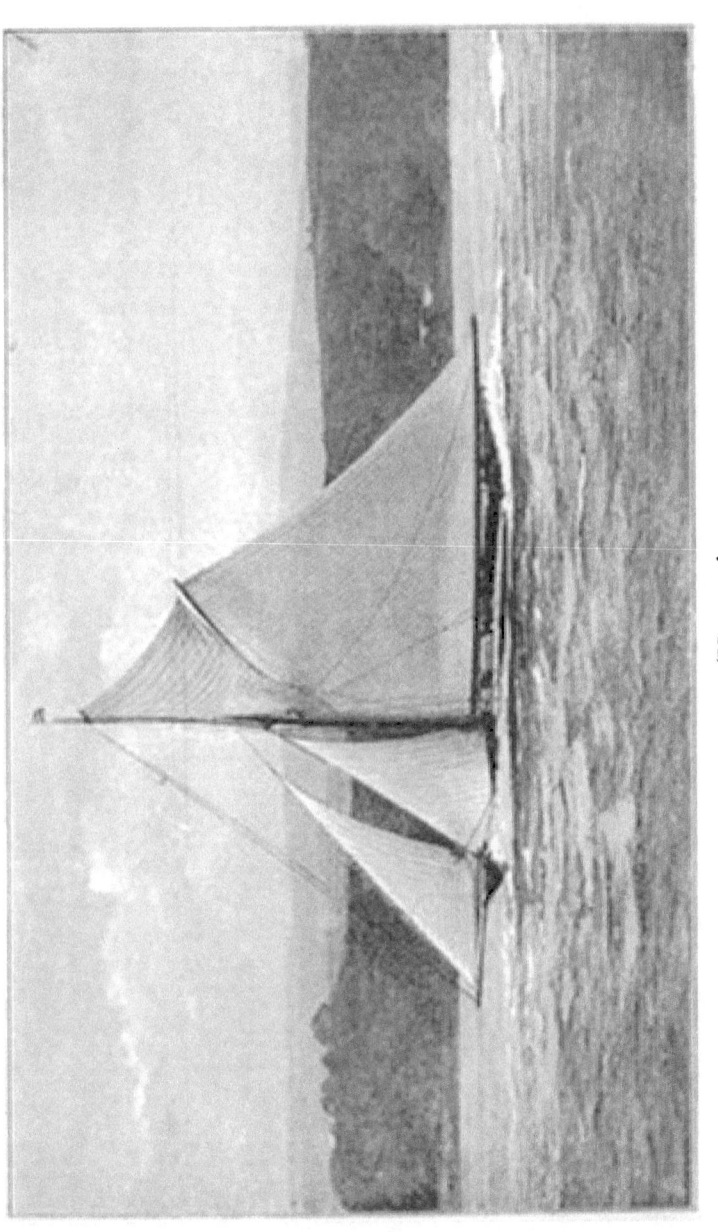

'Varuna'
40-rater (Capt. J. Towers-Clarke). Designed by G. L. Watson, 1892.

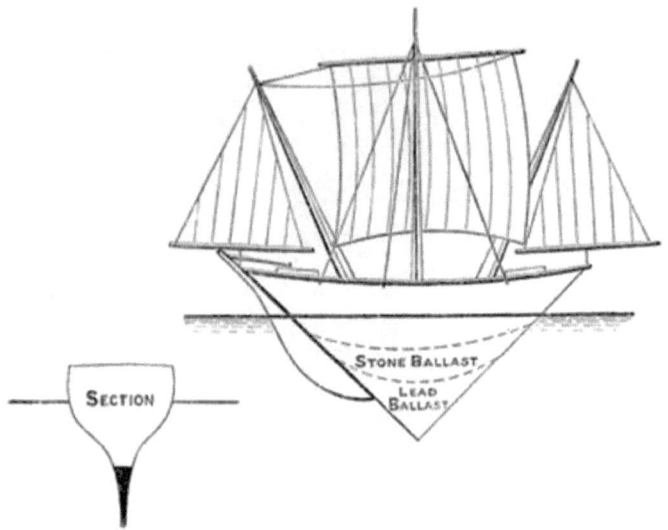

'Problem,' 1852.

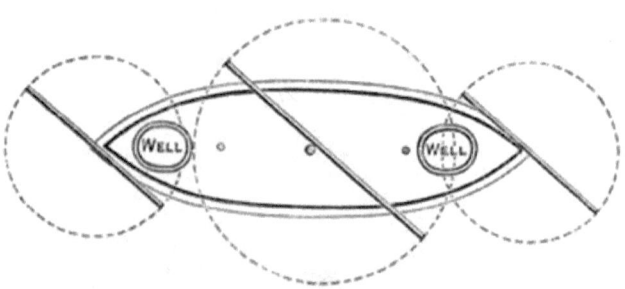

Deck plan of 'Problem'.

Profile of the 'Varuna,' 1892.

instead of three-fifths of the beam, so as not to dis-class those vessels with excessive rake already built. This rule, under the name of the 'Thames Rule,' became the recognised method of measuring yachts, and, indeed, still remains the standard measurement for rates for buying, selling, and hiring.

Slowly at first, but steadily, yachts became longer, narrower, and deeper; the crack yacht of one year being displaced the next by something with more length, less beam, and more ballast. Here and there, it is true, an occasional vessel of exceptional excellence held her own for a year or two with the newer ones; but what looked for a little like high water was but the mark of an exceptional wave which in its turn was covered, and the true flood seen to be a bit away yet.

To check the growing tendency towards length and depth at the expense of beam, the New Thames Yacht Club, at a meeting on March 12, 1874, adopted the following rule:—

The length shall be the distance from the fore part of the main stem to the after part of the main sternpost measured in a straight line along the deck.

The breadth shall be the distance between the outsides of the outside planks or wales, measured where that distance is largest.

The depth shall be the distance between the top of the covering board and the bottom of the keel at the middle point of the length.

The product of the length, the breadth, and the depth, divided by 200, shall be taken as the tonnage of the yacht.

But the influence of this rule was not far-reaching, and confined to the New Thames Club, and (in a slightly modified form) to the Queenstown Model Yacht Club; few yachts were built under it, and these were not conspicuously successful. Nor was the reason of this very far to seek. The tax on depth induced builders to cut down freeboard, and, so far as might be, draft, while to make up for this latter deficiency the amidships draft was carried well forward and aft, and only little rake given to the post, with the result that the few boats built under this rule carried an extremely awkward sail-plan, and were abnormally slow in stays.

The great general effect of the 94, or Thames Rule, has been described; but among its minor influences may be mentioned the inducement to have the utmost water-line length on a given deck or measurement length. One obvious manner of attaining this was by keeping the sternpost upright or nearly so; while the writer, in a little cutter called the *Peg Woffington*, built for himself in 1871, took a farther

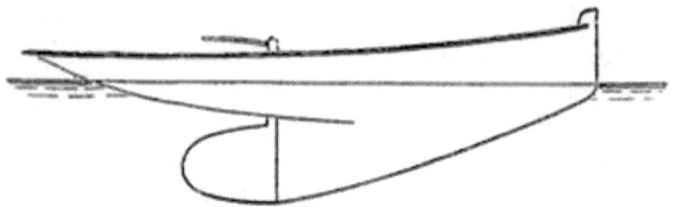

Vanderdecken's tonnage cheater.

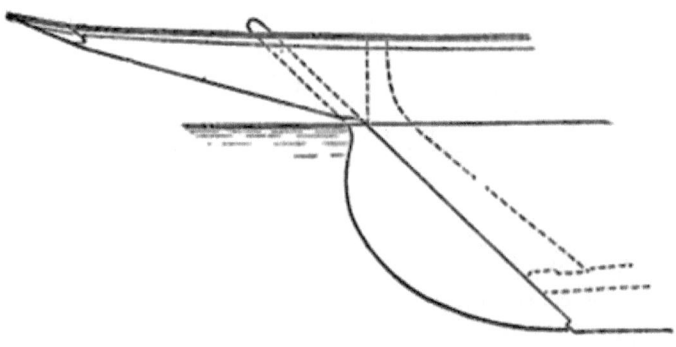

Dog-legged sternpost.

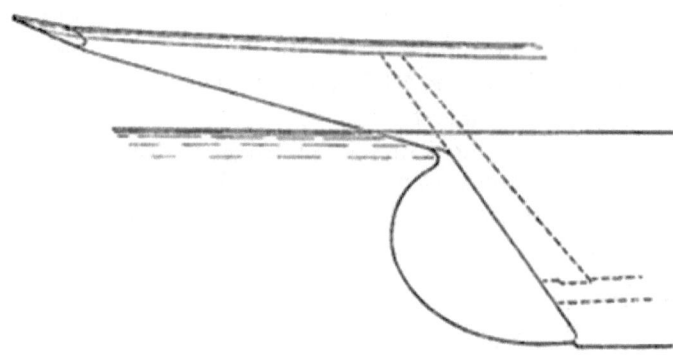

Immersed counter of 'Quiraing,' 1877.

advantage of the rule by putting a ram bow on her, thus getting the water-line even longer than the measurement on deck. An additional interest attaches to this yacht as being the earliest sailing yacht, so far as I have been able to ascertain, which had all her ballast outside.

In 1873 Mr. James Reid, of Port Glasgow, just then beginning to make his mark as a yacht designer, devised what was called the 'dog-legged' sternpost, fitting one in the 10-tonner *Merle*. This, as will be seen from the sketch, retained all the advantages of a raked sternpost, and yet gave as long a water-line length as the length on deck; but the device had but a short life, as in the spring of 1877 the Yacht Racing Association, which had been formed the previous year, decreed that the length should be measured to the fore side of the rudder stock.

This regulation, made so late in the building season, somewhat unjustly threw out three yachts built under the existing rule. Unfortunately, a policy of procrastination seems to have haunted the Yacht Racing Association since its inception, as in most instances where the building rules have been changed, these changes have been decided on so close to the coming season that builders have been unfairly pushed in the designing and getting ready new vessels.

I would venture to suggest to that body, and this in the interests of yacht-owners quite as much as of builders, that no rule affecting the construction of racing yachts should be considered after the end of October.

In the fall of 1877, in designing *Quiraing*, and with the same end in view, I got the water-line the same length as the length for measurement by immersing the counter as in the sketch.

In 1878 the Yacht Racing Association recognised the right of builders to have the same length on load-water-line as that for which they were taxed on deck, and that without forcing them into adopting abnormal shapes, and therefore determined that the length should be measured on the load-water-line. Though it was at once pointed out that this would lead to overhang, so strong was prejudice in favour of the old-fashioned straight stem, that no advantage was taken of this until the advent of the 10-ton *Buttercup* in 1880, and in her the outreach was extremely moderate. Indeed, it was impossible, with the deep, narrow style of yacht produced by the 94 rule, to use overhang to excess, this device only becoming objectionable when used in combination with a flat, shallow section. *Buttercup* made a most excellent record; and though this was from causes quite apart from her clipper stem, yet she marks a stage as being the first cutter to reintroduce this

'DORA'
10-rater, centreboard (R. G. Allan, Esq.) Designed by G. L. Watson, 1891.

adornment. *Buttercup* was the work of an amateur, Mr. Robert Hewitt, and the following particulars of her may be of interest:—

'BUTTERCUP,' LAUNCHED FROM YARD AT BARKING, SEPTEMBER 1880

L.W.L.	42 ft. 3 in.
Extreme beam	7 ft. 4 in.
Draught	8 feet
Least freeboard	2 ft. 9 in.
Displacement	22 tons
Lead	14 tons
Ship and gear	8 tons
Sail-area	2,580 feet

First match, May 9, 1881; sailed 20 starts in 1881, won 15 firsts, 2 seconds; designed, owned, and sailed by Robert Hewitt, Esq., R.T.Y.C, now commodore.

I may mention that the first design for the 90-ton *Vanduara* was drawn with a clipper or out-reaching stem; but I had not the heart to disfigure the boat (as I then considered I should be doing) by building her in this fashion. The rising generation of yachtsmen, however, is entirely reconciled to the clipper bow on a cutter-rigged yacht, and may eventually (though this seems improbable) look with complacency on such cutwaters as *Dora's* or *Britannia's*.

About this date—1875—builders were becoming more and more impressed with the value of a low centre of gravity got by outside lead, which, in combination with increased displacement, allowed of beam being reduced and length added almost indefinitely. Indeed, Mr. Dixon Kemp, probably the best authority on the subject in this country, declared somewhat later that there was no limit to this process of drawing out; and though I never could quite agree with him on that point, the beginning of the end was approaching, and yachts, more especially in the smaller classes, were getting most uncomfortably narrow.

The older men, however, were naturally timid about the introduction of external ballast, and it was left to 'the boys,' with the happy audacity and confidence of youth, to design 100-tonners with 70-ton keels, which, perhaps fortunately, did not get beyond the length of paper. But fives, tens, and twenties were built with nearly all their lead outside, and did not from that fact tear themselves asunder. Mr.

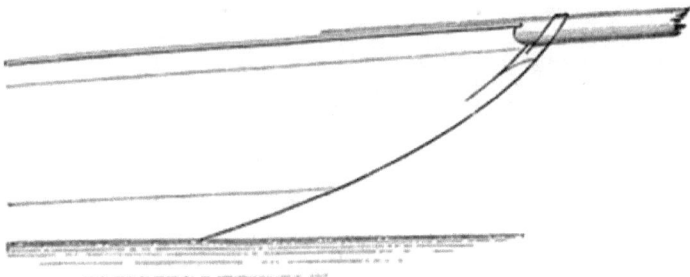

'Britannia,' 1893.

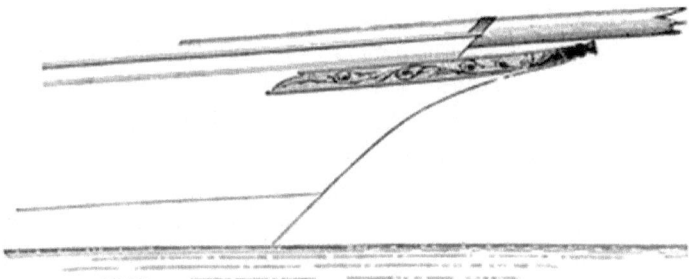

'Thistle,' 1887.

Sketch of cutwaters.

James Reid, of Port Glasgow, designer of the beautiful 10-tonner *Florence* and many other fast boats, closely followed by Mr. John Inglis, of Pointhouse, and later by the writer, put all or nearly all of the ballast outside, and the practice in a few years became general.

Length and displacement went merrily on, as will be seen from the following tables and diagrams:—

Elements of 5-Tonners (94 and 1730 Rules)

Description	Diamond	Vril	Trident	Olga	Doris	Oona
Length on load-line	25 ft. 3 in.	28 ft. 4 in.	32 ft.	33 ft.	33 ft. 8 in.	34 ft.
Breadth extreme	7 ft. 2¼ in.	6 ft. 7 in.	6 ft.	5 ft. 8¾ in.	5 ft. 7 in.	5 ft. 6 in.
Draught of water extreme	4 ft. 6 in.	5 ft. 2 in.	6 ft. 3 in.	6 ft. 4 in.	7 ft.	8 ft.
Displacement	4·92 tons	7·18 tons	8·9 tons	10·4 tons	12·55 tons	12·5 tons
Total area of lower sail	671 sq. ft.	830 sq. ft.	912 sq. ft.	985 sq. ft.	1,116 sq. ft.	—
Designer	W. Baden Fowell	G. L. Watson	W. E. Paton	W. E. Paton	G. L. Watson	W. E. Paton
Date when built	1873	1876	1879	1883	1885	1886

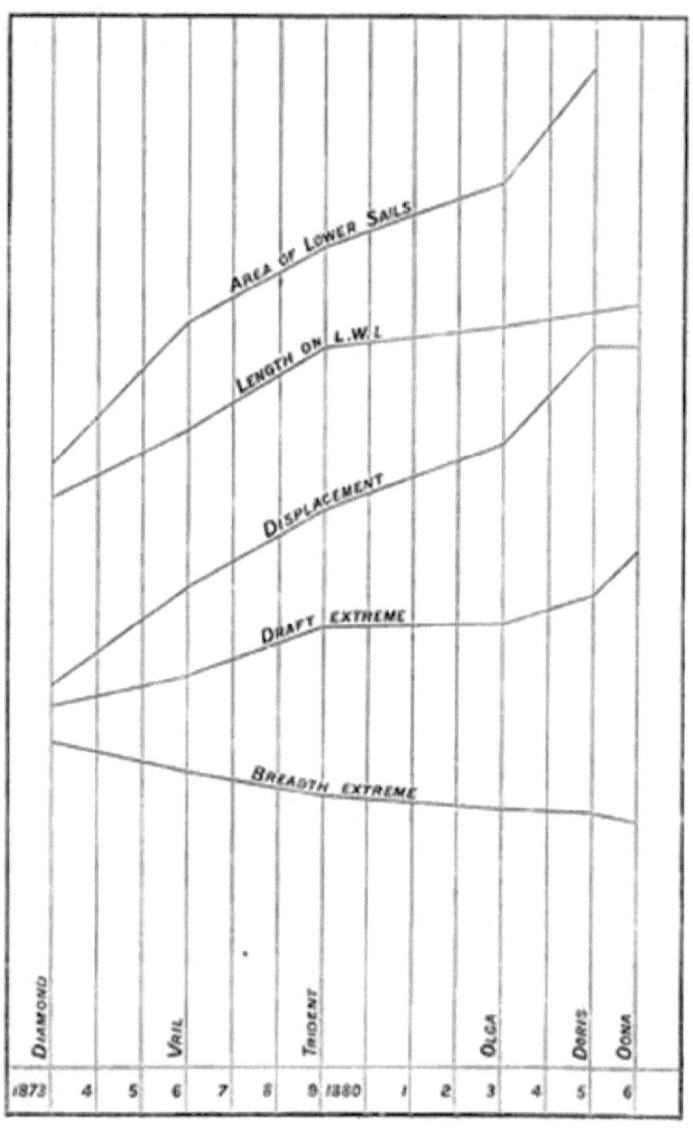

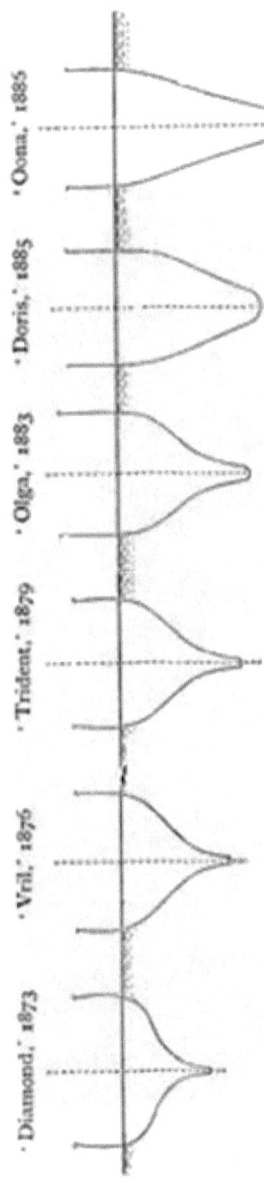

SECTIONS SHOWING DECREASE OF BREADTH AND INCREASE OF DEPTH IN 5-TONNERS—UNDER 94 AND 1730 RULES.

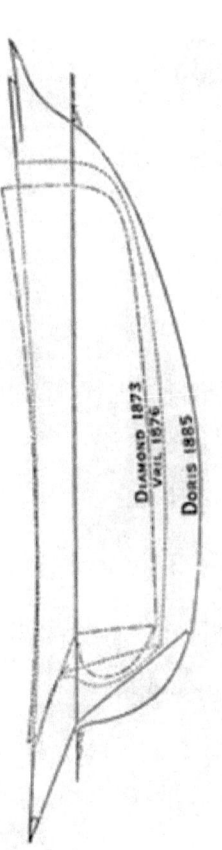

PROFILES OF 5-TONNERS.

In the autumn of 1881 it was thought a check might be put on this development by adopting a rule somewhat easier on beam than the existing 94 one, and in 1882 it was determined that the tonnage should be reckoned in accordance with the formula:—

(L+B)2 x B ·/· 1730

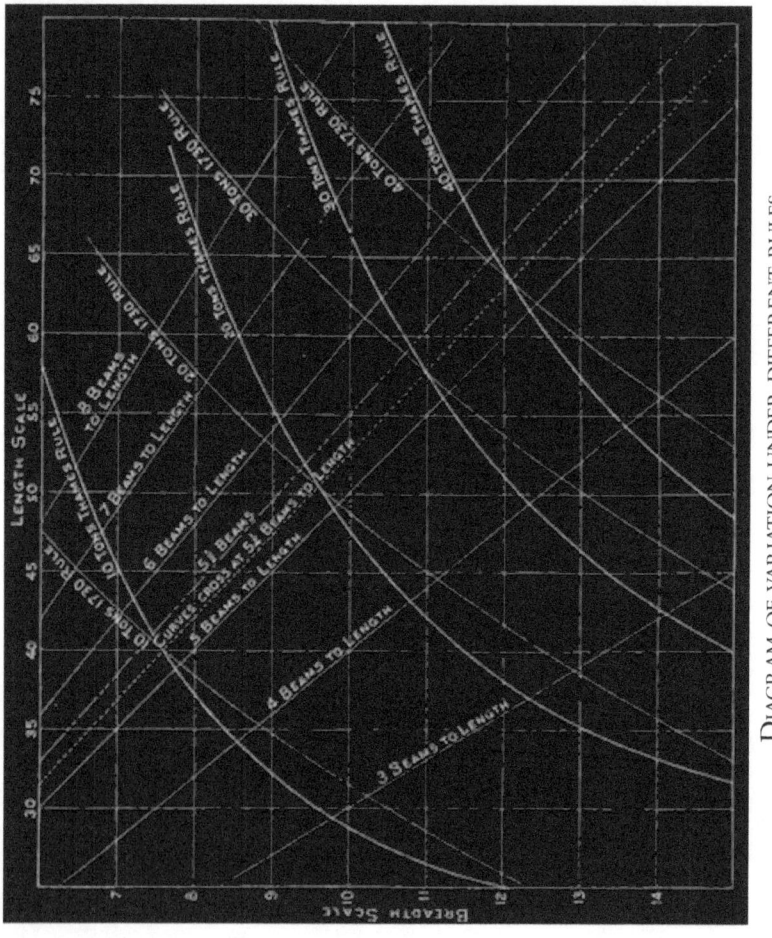

DIAGRAM OF VARIATION UNDER DIFFERENT RULES.

The incidence of this rule is clearly enough shown by the diagram, where the possible dimensions for a 10-, 20-, 30-, and 40-tonner are plotted under both rules; the two curves crossing at a point where the vessel is about 5-¼ beams in length. Below this point the new rule was easier on beam, and above it more severe; and it was thought that the extra beam admissible below the five-beam point would have induced builders to avail themselves of this quality; but beam, as we learn by the light of later years, was then altogether undervalued, and length was taken at any price, with the result that the adoption of extreme proportions was hastened rather than averted, till in 1886 a radical change in the rule was demanded, and in the autumn of that year a Committee of the Yacht Racing Association, after taking most exhaustive evidence from the various experts, decided on the adoption of a rule proposed by Mr. Dixon Kemp, based solely on length (which was measured on the load-water-line) and on sail-area.

In this rule, breadth, so sorely taxed by the 94 rule, was left absolutely unfettered; depth as heretofore being also untaxed, so that infinite scope was left for experiment in the way of beam. Simultaneously with this change, the use of the centreboard was permitted; and, as the pessimists declared, the road made clear for all manner of skimming dishes and consequent caprices.

I ventured to point out at the time the possible dangers of unlimited beam, and proposed that the rule should be (L+B) x sail-area/constant but this limitation was held to be unnecessary, as, indeed, it appeared to be for a year or two. With the exception of the *Thistle*, built immediately on the passing of the rule, and built probably more with a view to American racing than performance in home waters, builders were somewhat chary of availing themselves of the advantages of beam, and, in the larger classes at least, successive yachts, though getting broader, only 'slowly broadened down from precedent to precedent.' To Mr. Alfred Payne, of Southampton, is due the credit of showing what could be done with large beam and moderate displacement.

In 1889 he built the *Humming Bird*, 2½-rater, for Captain Hughes; this boat was 26 feet on water-line, 7.5 feet beam—that is, 3.46 beams in length—and was extremely successful against other and narrower boats, notably *Thief* and *Queen Mab*, of like rating and designed by the writer.

Elements of 40-Raters (Length and Sail Area Rule)

Description	Mohawk	Deerhound	Creole	Thalia	Varuna	Centreboard cutter—Queen Mab	Lais	Vendetta
Length on load line	61·23 ft.	58·85 ft.	59 ft. 6 in.	59·14 ft.	59 ft.	59 ft. 8 in.	59·92 ft.	59·96 ft.
Breadth extreme	14·5 ft.	13 ft. 5 in.	13 ft. 2¼ in.	13·9 ft.	14 ft. 7 in.	16 ft. 4 in.	17 ft.	17·05 ft.
Draught of water extreme	9·5 ft.	11 ft. 6½ in.	12 ft.	12 ft. 6 in.	13 ft. 4 in.	10 ft. 9 in.	—	—
Displacement	58·8 tons	58 tons	58 tons	57 tons	55 tons	54·8 tons	—	—
Designer	C. P. Clayton	G. L. Watson	G. L. Watson	W. Fife jun.	G. L. Watson	G. L. Watson	W. Fife jun.	A. E. Payne
Date when built	1888	1889	1890	1891	1892	1892	1893	1893

In 1890 *Iverna* was built, of practically the same length as, and of less beam than, *Thistle*, and no great advance was made until the present year (1893) in the adoption of beam in the larger classes; but the progress in this direction may be easily traced in the 'forty' and 'twenty' rating classes, where the growth of beam and decline in displacement are very well marked, as the table and diagram show.

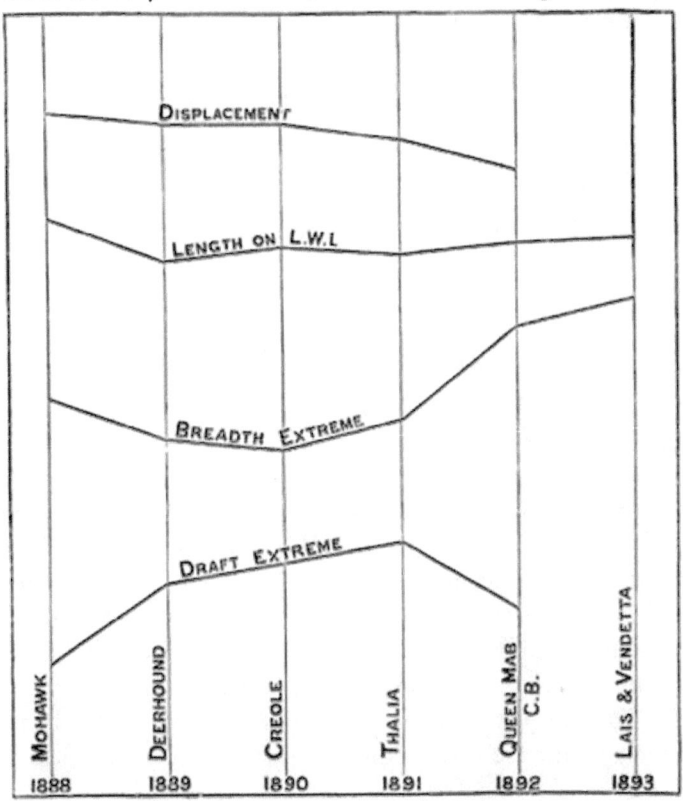

DIAGRAM SHOWING VARIATION OF DIMENSIONS, &C., WITH YEARS. 40-RATERS. L. AND S.A. RULE.

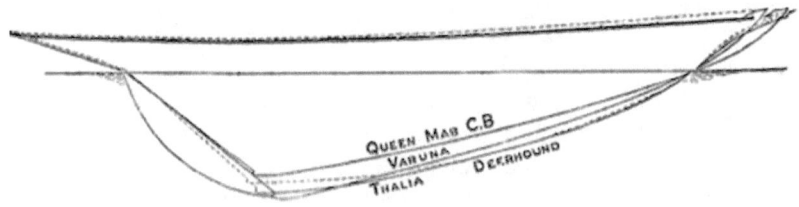

PROFILES OF 40-RATERS.

1893 will be remembered as having produced four notable boats on this side of the Atlantic, and five in America; and in all nine due prominence is certainly given to beam, if, indeed, more breadth has not been taken, in some of these at least, than can be advantageously used.

The dimensions of these boats, so far as they have been obtainable, will be of interest.

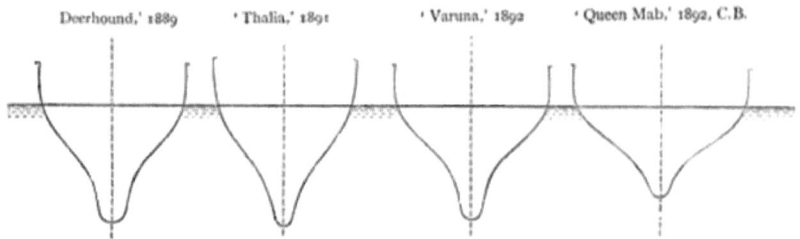

MIDSHIP SECTIONS OF 40-RATERS.

How far under the present rating rule beam may yet be increased with advantage to speed is still matter for debate and experiment. Personally I am inclined to think we have pretty nearly approached the limit. But of this much I am confident, that we have long ago exceeded the limit where beam improves a yacht as a comfortable sea-going craft, and that we should have a much more wholesome and useful vessel for all purposes, except possibly for international racing, with somewhat less beam and somewhat more displacement.

The diagram given *ante* may serve to give the reader an idea of the influence that the various tonnage or rating rules have had on the proportions and form of yachts.

British Yachts, 1893

Name	Length on L.W.L.	Breadth ext.	Y.R.A. sail area	Length over all	Draft	Y.R.A. rating
	feet	feet	square feet	feet	feet	
Satanita	97·7	24·7	9,923	131·0	16·5	161·58
Britannia	87·8	23·66	10,328	121·5	15·0	151·13
Valkyrie	86·8	22·33	10,271	117·25	16·3	148·58
Calluna	82·0	24·3	10,305	—	15·0	140·83

American Yachts, 1893

Name	Length on L.W.L.	Breadth ext	Y.R.A. sail area	Length over all	Draft	Y.R.A. rating
	feet	feet	square feet	feet	feet	
Navahoe, C.B.	86·93	23·0	10,815	128	13	156·7
Vigilant, C.B.	86·19	26·25	12,330	124	14·0	178
Colonia, K.	85·00	24·00	—	124	14·0	—
Jubilee, C.B. and Fin	84·00	22·5	—	123	16·0	—
Pilgrim, K.	85·00	23·0	—	122	22·0	—

But an entirely false impression has been conveyed should it be understood that the only advance made in yacht designing was due to more or less ingenious methods of evading the existing measurement rule; and it will be sufficient if the fact has been impressed, that a designer is as unlikely to make a successful vessel if he ignores the measurement under which the yacht is to race as by failing to recognise those laws of nature which govern the stability of bodies in water and their resistance in passing through it.

What has to be done by the yacht designer, besides getting the very utmost out of the tonnage rule, has never been more happily put than by Lord Dunraven in an article on International Yachting, from which I venture to quote:—

> How most successfully to drive a body through the water by the means of the motive power of the wind acting upon the sails, is the question that puzzles men and turns them greyheaded before Nature should have thinned or whitened their locks. The designer has not merely to discover the form of solid body which, at various rates of speed, will excite the smallest degree of resistance in passing through the water, for the body is not solid, it is hollow. It must have buoyancy, and suitable accommodation for all the living and dead freight on board. It must possess stability, real and acquired; that is, natural by means of breadth, and artificial by means of ballast, if the expressions are allowable.
>
> It does not proceed on a level keel or at any uniform angle, but at angles varying at every moment, and the contour of the body must be adapted to these various angles. Neither does the wind exert its force upon it from a fixed direction, nor propel it through water uniformly smooth or constantly rough. On the contrary, the propelling power strikes from various angles on

the surface of the sails; and the sea, as we all know—and some of us to our cost—has a reprehensible habit of becoming, on the shortest notice, agitated in the most disagreeable manner.

Every point of sailing suggests an appropriate and different form of hull. The shape that is well adapted for one kind of weather is ill adapted for another sort; vessels that move as by magic in light airs may be of little use in a whole sail breeze; one that is by no means a flier in smooth water may be very hard to beat in a sea-way. In short, a vessel must be light enough to be driven easily by a moderate breeze, stiff enough to stand up to her canvas in a hard wind, shallow enough to be docked with ease and to run with speed. She must have depth enough to hold her up to windward, breadth enough to give her stability; she should be long enough to reach well, and short enough to turn well to windward; low in the water so as not to hold too much wind, with plenty of freeboard to keep the sea off her decks. The satisfaction of any one requirement necessitates something antagonistic to some other requirement equally clamorous for satisfaction.

Your vessel, to be perfect, must be light, of small displacement, and with the centre of gravity brought very low; she must also have large displacement, and the ballast must not be too low, in order that she may be easy in a sea-way; she must be broad, narrow, long, short, deep, shallow, tender, stiff. She must be self-contradictory in every part. A sailing ship is a bundle of compromises, and the cleverest constructor is he who, out of a mass of hostile parts, succeeds in creating the most harmonious whole. It is not strange that designers pass sleepless nights, and that anything like finality and perfection of type is impossible to conceive. No wonder that yacht designing is a pursuit of absorbing interest.

It has been shown, then, how from the three beam yachts of fifty years ago, the proportions drew out, under the 94 rule, to five, five and a half, and in some instances six beams in length, the *Evolution* reaching even 7.8 beams; and even more rapidly, under the length and sail-area rule, fell back to something like three again. But the proportions are about all that remain in common to the clippers of 1845 and 1893 and it will be interesting now to trace how form, mode of construction and equipment have developed, as well as proportions.

Prior to 1820, what yachts there were afloat seem to have presented but little individuality of form, and showed, in common with the faster smugglers and fishing vessels of the day, a round barrel-like bottom, full round bow and fairly clean run, the buttock lines and after riband lines being generally fair and easy. These yachts were, one and all, built of timber, were ballasted with stones or gravel, the more advanced possibly with ore, while the sails and equipment were of a piece with the hull, the main rigging being of hemp, and no attempt being made after flatness in the sails.

The original *Arrow*, of 84 tons, built somewhere about 1823 by Mr. Joseph Weld, seems to have been a fairly representative craft of that time, and raced with considerable success, even against much larger vessels than herself.

This original *Arrow* was 61 ft. 9½ in. long by 18 ft. 5-¼ in. beam, with a depth of hold of 8 ft. 8 in.—that is, she had a proportion of length to breadth of 3.35—not very much differing in proportion from our present cutters of 1893: *Calluna*, the 40-raters *Lais* and *Vendetta*, being about 3.4 and 3.5 beams to length, and the American *Vigilant* about 3.32.

Arrow had the usual round barrel-like bottom, and, so far as can be learned, a round, short bow, the run being fair and easy, the small midship section lending itself pleasantly to this.

Racing with the *Arrow*, but without any very conspicuous success, was the cutter *Menai*, designed by that famous sportsman, Mr. T. Assheton-Smith, and memorable from being the first vessel in which hollow lines were adopted. But little notice seems to have been taken of this very radical alteration in form, and although Scott Russell in 1840 elaborated a system of construction, based on hollow lines, and the famous *Mosquito*, built in 1848, and *Tiara*, built by Simons of Renfrew in 1850, all showed this feature strongly, it was not till the 'America' schooner appeared in 1851 that the old round bow was utterly condemned, and everyone went more or less crazy on the long hollow bow.

Meanwhile the original old *Arrow* was being sailed with fair success against craft much larger than herself, until in 1827 she was laid aside by her owner in favour of the first *Lulworth*, of 130 tons, known for little else than that she was of the same name as the famous *Lulworth* of 80 tons, also built by Mr. Weld in 1857.

Meantime, Mr. Weld built the famous *Alarm* of 193 tons in 1834, and for a long time this enormous cutter was Queen of the Solent.

But the old *Arrow* was to begin a second career. Bought in 1846

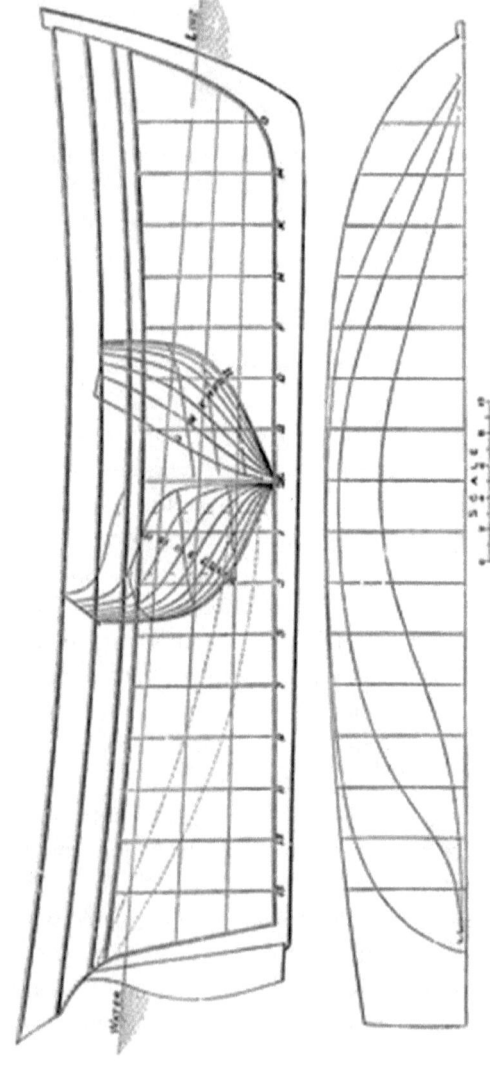

MIDSHIP SECTION.

'LEOPARD,' BUILT BY LINN RATSEY, COWES, ISLE OF WIGHT, 1807.
These lines are accurately reproduced from the original by his grandson, Michael E. Ratsey.

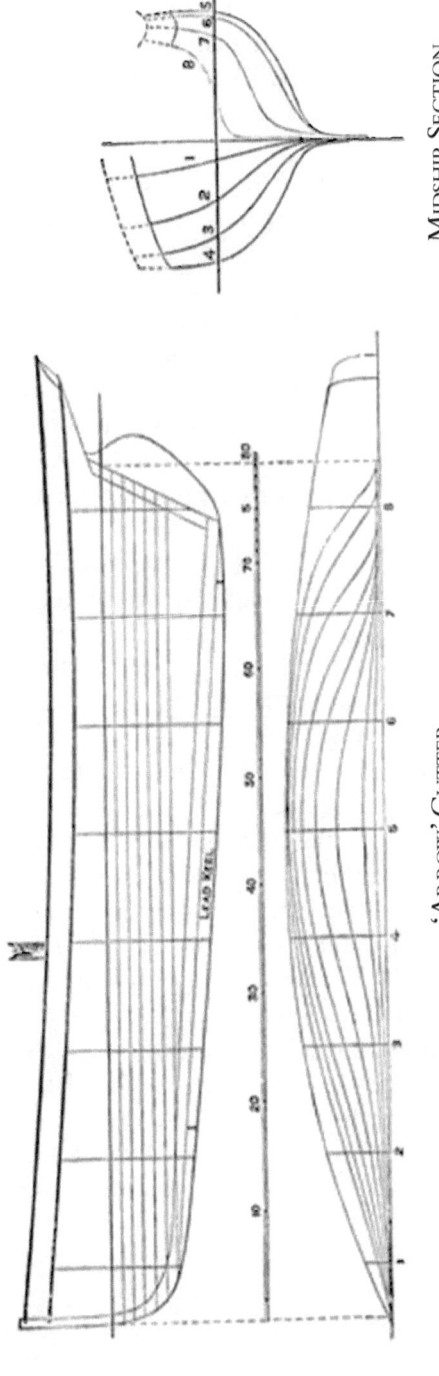

MIDSHIP SECTION

'ARROW' CUTTER

113 tons. Length on L.W.L., 79' 2"; beam extreme, 18' 9"; draught extreme, 11' 6". (The original 'Arrow,' 84 tons, was built by Mr Joseph Weld about 1823. In 1846 she was bought by Mr. Thomas Chamberlayne and rebuilt; but it was not until 1852 that her bow was lengthened and she appeared as shown above.)

from a dealer by Mr. Thomas Chamberlayne for a few pounds, that gentleman had her replanked and some alterations made in the bow and run, indeed not very much more than the amidship frame seems to have been preserved. Anyway the resuscitated vessel appeared again in 1847, recommencing a career which has certainly been an extraordinary one.

In 1848 *Mosquito* was built and fairly tackled the older ship, but the *Arrow* was not yet the boat she now is, or as represented in the plate, as it was not till 1852, and until after the advent of the *America*, that she appeared with her present long, hollow bow, having been pulled out some 17 feet in the winter of 1851, as indeed was pretty well everything else that aspired to be in the fashion. As is often the case, the pendulum swung too far the other way; bows were built on old boats, and new boats were designed with fore bodies, altogether out-Heroding Herod; and the *America's* graceful, well-proportioned and moderately hollow bow was caricatured in some instances to a ridiculous extent.

The *America* showed also a decided departure in form of midship section, the bottom being much straighter than in our British-built craft, and the bilge higher and quicker—altogether a fine form for stability. The run, though somewhat short, was very fair, the buttock lines especially (as will be seen by the plate given in the second volume) showing beautifully easy curves.

But the lesson hinted at by *Menai*, reiterated by *Mosquito* and *Tiara*, insisted upon by Scott Russell, but only brought home to us by the American schooner, was not the only one to be gleaned from that graceful vessel. Previous to her advent, our British-made sails were most baggy productions, kept decently flat only by drenching the luffs with water, a process called 'skeating.' This defect could not altogether be laid at the door of our sailmakers, as they did fairly well, considering the material they had to work with; but flax canvas at that date was still made by hand and was little firmer in texture, if indeed as firm, as the unbleached merchant canvas of the present day. The *America's* sails were of machine-spun cotton, and, farther, were laced to the booms as well as the gaffs and masts, the staysail also being laced to a boom. These flat sails certainly suited the easy form of the *America*; but here again the reaction was too strong, and it is undoubtedly the fact that for some years afterwards sails were got too flat, at least, for many of the full-bodied boats that they were put over, and the want of flow of the older-fashioned loose-footed sails was sadly missed when there came to be any work off the wind.

For some years then after 1851 (the year of *America's début* here), sails were probably flat enough for the forms they had to drive; and American sailmakers apparently arrived at this conclusion, as they first of all gave up lacing the head sails, and later cut those rounder and rounder, until now American head-sails are cut much fuller than our own, and their mainsails also somewhat fuller. But while the *America* was undoubtedly the great epoch-making vessel in yacht designing, the cutter *Mosquito* possessed quite as many original features, and had she only come from abroad instead of being a home production, would have made a far greater stir than the schooner.

The *Mosquito* was turned out by the Thames Iron Works Shipbuilding Company. She was designed by that great original genius, Tom Waterman, who had already produced many successful merchant steamers and sailing ships: notably the steamer *Himalaya*, built originally for the Peninsular and Oriental Company, but afterwards sold to Her Majesty's Government for a troopship, and still a gem of the ocean and mother of the troopers.

The *Mosquito*, besides presenting novelties in form, in the way of an easy and hollow bow, large displacement, well-raked post and deep heel, also upset all preconceived notions of what was yacht fashion, by being built of iron. Great was the discussion over this departure; but, among many prophets of evil, a writer in *Hunt's Magazine*, in 1854, discussing wood *versus* iron, predicts that 'the *Mosquito* is likely to be well and hearty when the present wooden craft have gone to that "bourne from which no traveller returns."'

This prediction has been exactly fulfilled, as *Mosquito*, after as long and brilliant a career as has fallen to any yacht, is now, or was a few years ago, doing good work as a pilot boat off Barrow-in-Furness.

In 1852, Mr. William Fife, of Fairlie, in Ayrshire, who, with his father before him, had for some years been turning out fast and weatherly boats, produced *Cymba*, a notable cutter. His father had made Scotch-built yachts, well known by his *Gleam*, built in 1832, though only fitted out for racing by Sir Robert Gore Booth in 1837; but *Cymba* was a marked improvement on this model, having a far longer and easier bow, larger displacement, considerable rake of post, and great drag aft.

The dimensions of *Cymba* are appended, and it will be seen that she was just under four beams in length.

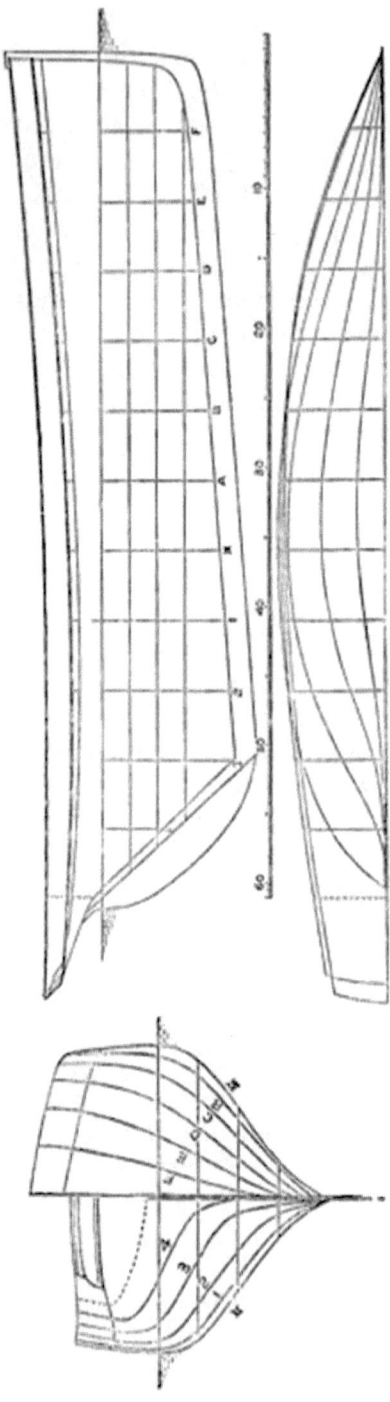

'Mosquito,' 50 tons, 1848.

Midship Section.

Cymba, built 1852, by Fife

Length of keel	52	feet
Length between perpendiculars	59	"
Breadth, extreme	15.3	"
Draft aft	10	"
Forward	5.6	"
Mast from stem	23	"
Length of mast	56	"
Boom	53	"
Bowsprit	32	"
Lead outside	3 tons	
Lead in all	23 to 24 tons	

Meanwhile in matters of equipment steady progress was being made. Wire rope was rapidly ousting hemp for all standing rigging. Sailmaking, in the hands of Messrs. Lapthorn and of Charles Ratsey, was rapidly becoming a science. Machine-spun and woven flax canvas was in universal use, even cotton canvas was fitfully tried, and from the first strongly upheld by Charles Ratsey, of Cowes; but prejudice was too strong as yet for this material, and flax held the day for many a year to come. It is gratifying that Mr. Ratsey should have lived to see his favourite material triumphant, and to have looked, as he might have done in 1893, at the finest fleet of racing yachts the world has seen, clothed, from the Prince of Wales's majestic *Britannia* to the tiny half-rater, entirely with cotton.

A considerable factor in modifying form was the gradual abolition of shifting ballast; this, though not yet actually illegal, was being more and more looked upon with disfavour, and as the use of outside lead increased, it was found that depth was a more than sufficient substitute for weather ballast, especially as beam was being squeezed down by the tonnage rule, and a long lever in this direction rendered impossible.

Timber was still the favourite material for building (*Mosquito, Torpid,* and one or two others being the sole exceptions to this rule); but about 1860 a new system of construction was tried in which an iron framework was combined with a wooden skin or planking. This system came rapidly into vogue on the Clyde, and was adopted by several firms there in the building of those beautiful creations, the China clipper ships. The annual race home with the season's teas was the subject of discussion in the great Clyde shipyards, and I can well remember the highest ambition of every spirited lad in the drawing office was to live to design a China clipper. The Suez Canal closed for ever this avenue to fame.

Among the most successful builders of these ships were Messrs. Robert Steele & Co., of Greenock, who had, so early as 1807, built yachts for the Excise and for various Scotch owners. Mr. William Steele of that firm being an able designer of yachts as well as of ships, it was natural that this method of construction should be adopted by him in the building of *Nyanza*, *Oimara*, *Garrion*, and the majestic *Selene*, today one of the handsomest schooners afloat; while many of that firm's large steam yachts, notably the *Wanderer*, 850 tons, the finest auxiliary yacht of her day, were built on this plan.

Dan Hatcher of Southampton carried out this system in building several vessels, commencing with a schooner, the *Bella Donna*, of 119 tons, in 1867; *Seabird*, 126 tons, 1868; *Lizzie*, of 20 tons, 1868; then, in one of his finest craft, *Muriel* which he built for Mr. Bridson in 1869; and in the famous *Norman* he also adopted this construction. But, owing to the steel frame being considerably more expensive than timber, the composite build has never become popular until within the last few years, when the naturally weak shape of the modern yacht, the fact of all the lead being outside, and her enormous stability, have so increased the racking strains on the structure, that a merely wooden frame cannot be got to hold together without making the weight of the hull altogether prohibitive; and the composite racing yacht, for everything except very small vessels, seems likely to push all the others from the field. As illustrating this method of construction, a midship section is given of *Lethe*, 163-ton yawl, and one of the finest of our cruising yachts. The photograph shows the lead keel, the heaviest ever cast, and also the method of securing the same to the bottom of the ship.

Since *Mosquito* astonished the yachting world in 1848, until today, (as at time of first publication), when *Navahoe* and other American racing yachts have been constructed of metal, iron and steel yachts have been more or less successful; but the difficulty of keeping a smooth and perfectly clean bottom is a considerable source of expense and worry, although the immense strength of the steel shell, and in a large yacht its lightness, will always be a set-off to the trouble of the uncoppered bottom.

In a lecture on 'Progress in Yachting and Yacht-building,' which I delivered early in 1881, in a fanciful specification of the yacht for the season 2000, I required that the plating below water should be of

'LETHE'
163 tons, showing lead keel and construction. Designed by G. L. Watson. Built by Fay & Co., 1889.

manganese bronze. Curiously enough, a few years later saw an attempt to combine the strength of steel and the smoothness, anti-fouling, and non-corrosive properties of copper, in the building of a torpedo-boat of this material; while this year the chosen defender of the America Cup has been plated with a similar bronze on a steel frame, the builders claiming, and not without reason, that the additional smoothness of bottom gives her an advantage of five to seven minutes on a forty-mile course. But such a practice seems hardly likely to become general for ordinary racing yachts built for men with a normal depth of pocket, and whilst, as in the old Mississippi steamboat days, it sometimes paid to burn hams, most of us have to try and get along with good coal.

I was going to build the topsides, frames, and beams of my ideal vessel of aluminium, and the other day a small yacht has been built, on the Continent, of this lightest of metals; but the present cost of this material, and, as yet, its unreliability, place it, for the present at least, outside the range of practical material for yacht-building. There seems more hope for some of the very beautiful and immensely strong alloys of aluminium, but they too are expensive, and also heavy. It may be some years before the complete realisation of my design is accomplished, and platinum is substituted for lead as ballast, though when syndicates of millionaires start yacht-building there seems very little limit to extravagance in construction.

In nickel-steel there is promise of a very perfect material. This is an alloy of the ordinary Siemens-Martin steel with nickel, and called by the makers Yolla metal. It can be made to comply with all the ordinary tests applied to ship steel, in the way of ductility under stress, and at the same time have a breaking strength of 40 tons to the square inch as against 27 for ordinary steel. This metal was used by Mr. Fife in 1893 for the frames and beams of the 20-rater *Dragon* (third), and although the few pounds of weight saved by no means accounted for the phenomenal success of this little ship, yet the gain was all in the right direction.

Wire standing rigging continued to improve in quality, and very rapidly pushed out the old hemp rigging. From being made at first of good charcoal iron wire, it is now manufactured of the very highest class of steel, of such perfect character that the breaking strength of each wire is equal to 130 tons per square inch.

Used at first for standing rigging only, flexible wire rope takes the place of Manilla or hemp for the runners, and runner tackles, topping

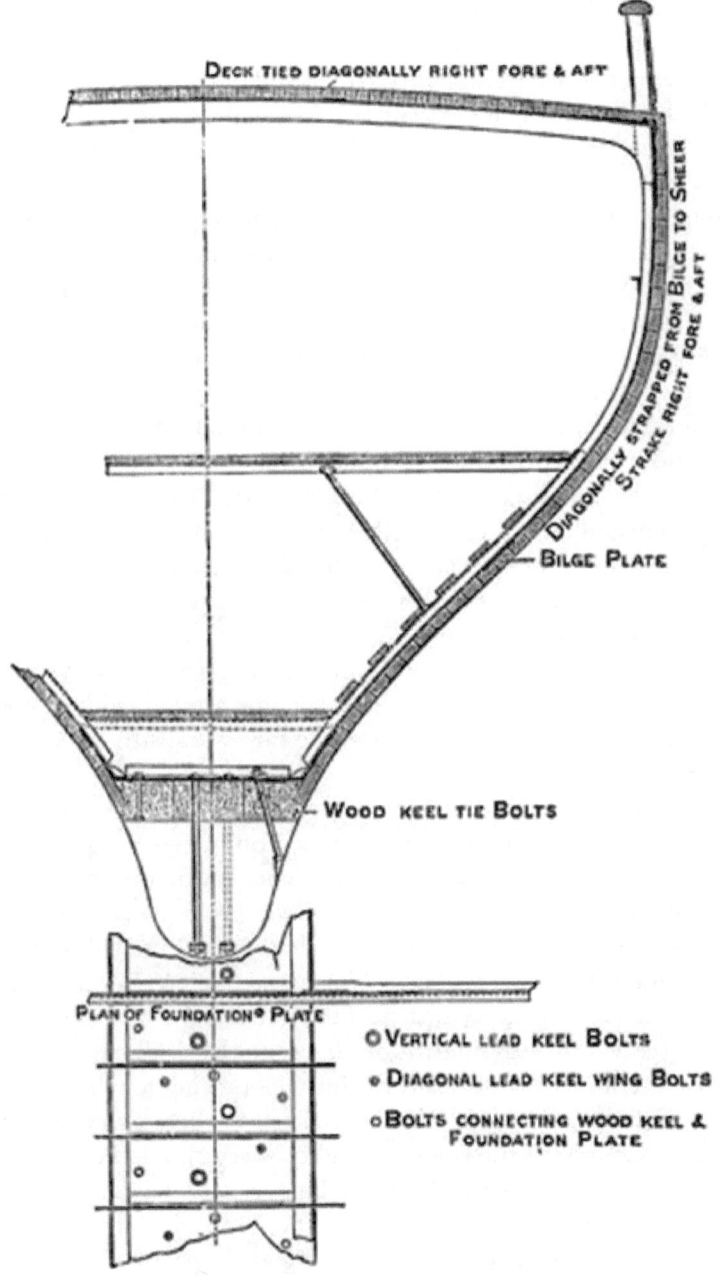

'LETHE,' 163 TONS. BUILT FOR S. C. WATSON, ESQ.—
MIDSHIP SECTION.

lifts, bobstay falls, outhauls, topsail and jib-topsail halliards, and latterly even for throat and peak halliards.

Other details were also perfected. Instead of the heavy and clumsy windlass, neat and light capstans are arranged of cast steel and gun metal, made so that the whole thing can be lifted away and stowed below while racing.

Right- and left-handed screws have superseded the old dead-eyes and lanyards, although these held their own desperately for many years. Introduced first in the 10-tonner *Verve*, in 1877, the chain-plates were torn up in an extra heavy squall; but this occurred from the great stability of the boat and the fastening having been insufficient; the rigging screws, however, were blamed for all the trouble, and were laid aside for ten years or thereabouts, until re-introduced in the 5-tonner *Doris*. Now no racing boat is without them.

Attention was also given to the lightening of deck fittings, sky-lights, companions, and the like, these in the racing vessels being kept lower and flatter, and the scantling reduced perhaps rather farther than advisable, as one certainly thinks on getting a stream of water down the neck from a leaky skylight.

Bulwarks have been reduced so as to save weight and windage, until in the smaller yachts they have become a mere ledge or foot-hold, whilst even in the largest class the rail is less than a foot from the deck.

Below, fittings have been lightened correspondingly. Cedar, yellow pine, and cretonnes or tapestries stretched on frames or light panels, take the place of the good solid oak and mahogany framing of the years gone by. Indeed, in some of the classes under 40-rating, cabin fittings have been dispensed with altogether; although this is not altogether a novelty, as the Marquis of Ailsa, in *Bloodhound* (built 1874), and *Sleuth-hound* (built 1881), had at first no fittings beyond a seat along each side. *Thistle* in 1887 was similarly arranged, nor had *Valkyrie* or *Vigilant* much more inside than a coat of paint when racing for the America Cup; but these last are of course special cases, where everything was sacrificed so that the uttermost second of speed should be taken out of the yachts. In cruising yachts the cabins are infinitely more elegant and comfortable now than formerly. The good old birdseye maple panelling with rosewood mouldings and gilded 'egg and dart' cornice has given place to tasteful cabinet-work designed in many cases by high-class artists. The main cabin of the *Lethe*, designed by Mr. T. L. Watson, F.R.I.B.A., is a good example of this, and the *Thistle*, now called *Meteor*, the property of the German emperor, has since been very beautifully fitted up from designs by the same gentleman, the photographs reproduced here giving but an indication of the elegance and richness of the interior.

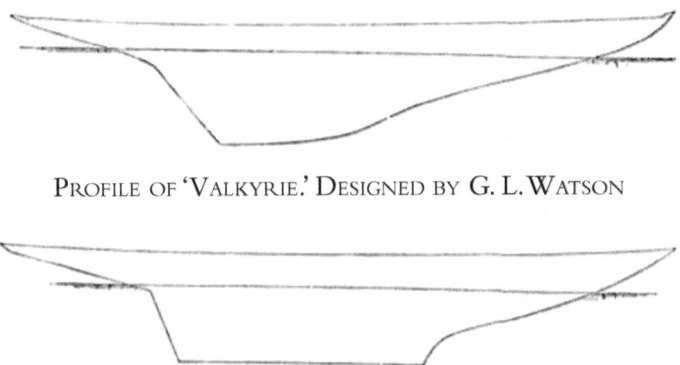

PROFILE OF 'VALKYRIE.' DESIGNED BY G. L. WATSON

PROFILE OF 'VIGILANT.' DESIGNED BY N. HERRESHOFF.

One of the happiest combinations of lightness of structure with taste and comfort is in the Prince of Wales's *Britannia*. The fittings throughout are of polished yellow pine and mahogany, with tapestries and cretonnes above the polished wood dado, the effect being extremely bright, cosy, and unostentatious.

To return to the story of the evolution of the modern racing yacht, no striking change in form was made for some little time after *America's* advent, beyond, of course, the steady lengthening and deepening of the model. Dan Hatcher, with the *Glance* in 1855, entered on the wonderful series of successes which culminated perhaps in *Norman*, 1872. These were all reasonably long boats with nice bows, fine after ends, and of big mid-area and displacement, but beautifully fair and easy all over, and showing a slight but not inordinate hollow forward. In 1866 Mr. Fife, of Fairlie, built the *Fiona*, and though Clyde builders had already turned out successful yachts, it was *Fiona* that put the fame of Scotch builders on a solid footing.

This beautiful vessel was a cutter of 80 tons, of great length in proportion to beam (73 ft. 6 in. × 15 ft. 9 in.) and of large displacement for those days (108 tons); but she had singularly long, fair and easy lines, and, sailed in a masterly manner by John Houston, of Largs, more than held her own with the Solent-built craft. However, beyond being exceptionally fair and easy, *Fiona* presented no striking novelty in form, nor did the big cutters *Kriemhilda*, *Vol-au-Vent*, or *Formosa*, built

Saloon of 'Thistle' (Now 'Meteor').

by M. Ratsey, of Cowes, in 1872, 1875, and 1878 respectively, and it is an outsider and amateur yacht-builder that we have to thank for the daring departure in form that was made in *Jullanar*

Prior to 1870 but little was known of the laws governing the resistance to bodies moving through water. It is true that eighty years before this, towards the close of last century, Colonel Beaufoy had made an elaborate series of experiments in towing bodies through water, beginning first in one of the tanks of his father's brewhouse. These were elaborated in the Greenland Dock near London, and included the determination of the resistance of all manner of shapes, except unhappily shipshape ones, the nearest approach to these being double wedges, and double wedges with a straight amidship piece inserted.

But while Colonel Beaufoy also made experiments for the determination of the value of surface friction on planes pulled through the water, no great importance seems to have been attached to these by shipbuilders in general, and the subject of surface friction was more or less lost sight of by them until again brought forward by Maquorn Rankine, first in a series of papers in the *Mechanic's Magazine*, and more elaborately in his *Shipbuilding, Theoretical and Practical*, published in 1866. In this Rankine, basing his deductions on Weisbach's experiments on the flow of water through pipes, concluded on mathematical principles that the entire resistance at moderate speeds of a fair and easy formed vessel was due to surface friction—*i.e.* the rubbing of the water against the sides and bottom of the ship. Rankine showed also that at higher speeds the forming of waves was a material and ever-increasing element in the resistance.

It is fully twenty years ago, (as at time of first publication), that the late Mr. William Froude began to give to the world the results of his experiments on the resistance of planes of different lengths, coated with various substances and towed at varying speeds through the water. These experiments were conducted under the most favourable conditions, and with the nicest regard for accuracy, and practically confirmed Maquorn Rankine's deductions, although it was found that Rankine had somewhat overestimated the value attachable to surface friction, and had also overestimated the increase in frictional resistance, due to increased speed. Still the great fact remained that practically the entire resistance to a fairly formed body, moving through water at moderate speeds, is due to friction and to friction alone.

Rankine's reasoning, early in the sixties, had been too subtle for those fathers of shipbuilding at that date engaged in the art. Able, hon-

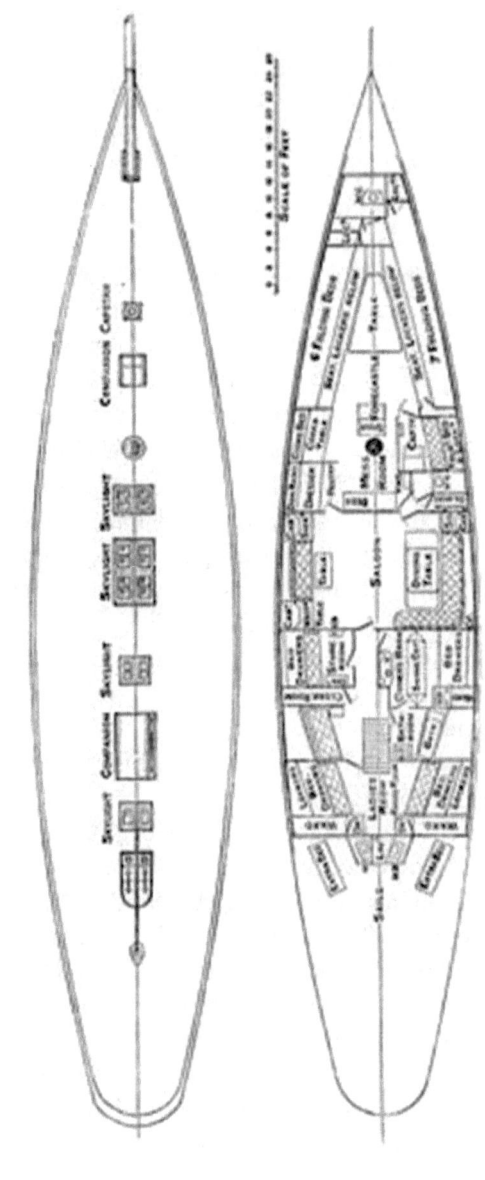

Cutter yacht 'Britannia'—General arrangement plan.

est, practical men, most of them could have handled an adze, or maul, with the best of their workmen, and were more at home fairing a sheering batten, or directing a launch, than in analysing speed curves, or investigating strength calculations.

But one or two of the younger and brighter minds in the profession, more especially those who had the advantage of Rankine's direct tuition, felt that the old beliefs as to resistance presented such anomalous and unreconcilable results that they could not be founded on any true law of nature. John Inglis, jun., then a mere boy, instituted in Pointhouse Shipyard Rankine's method of estimating the resistance of ships, and for many years was alone in this mode of investigation.

But with Froude's experiments all doubt on the matter vanished. It was no longer a question of 'condemned mathematics.' Froude had the happy knack of writing so that the proverbial schoolboy could understand him; and the schoolboy could see the value of resistance to motion through water weighed out as simply and accurately as a pound of currant bun. These experiments for the determination of the frictional resistance of water, published in 1874, were supplemented presently by experiments on models of actual ships, and also by towing a full-size ship, the *Greyhound*, her resistance at various speeds being recorded by means of a dynamometer on board the *Active*, the vessel towing her. The results of the experiments on model and ship were set out in a curve, when it was found, after the necessary corrections were made, that both curves were of precisely similar character.

A basis of comparison between model and ship was thus established, the measure of this being set forth in what is known as Froude's law of comparison, which may thus be stated. The equivalent speed of a ship and the model it represents will vary as the square root of their lengths. Thus, in the case of a ship 100 feet long represented by a model 4 feet long, the equivalent speed of the ship would be five times that of the model, and at these equivalent speeds would present similar phenomena connected with resistance as the model does. This fact enormously increased the knowledge of investigators, and it was belief in it that gave the writer absolute confidence in carrying out the design of the *Vanduara*, though he possessed experience in small boats only. Mr. Froude also split up the several elements of resistance to motion through the water into their component parts, assigning a value to each, and showing what was due to surface friction and eddy-making, and what to wave-making.

Scott Russell had already argued for a given length of fore and after body for any given speed, and this was recognised by yacht-builders to some extent by their gradually lengthening out their vessels; but the disadvantages as well as the advantages of length could only be thoroughly realised on investigating Froude's experiments. An example is given of such an experiment in the diagram, which shows the resistance curve of a model of the *Merkara*, built by Messrs. Denny Bros., at Dumbarton, where the several resistances are shown, each in its place. In this diagram the resistance due to surface friction is indicated by the dotted line, and the total resistance by the full line. Up to a speed of 250 feet per minute (for the model) the resistance is almost entirely due to skin friction, but after that the wave-making becomes more and more serious until at 370 feet per minute the wave-making takes more power than the surface friction.

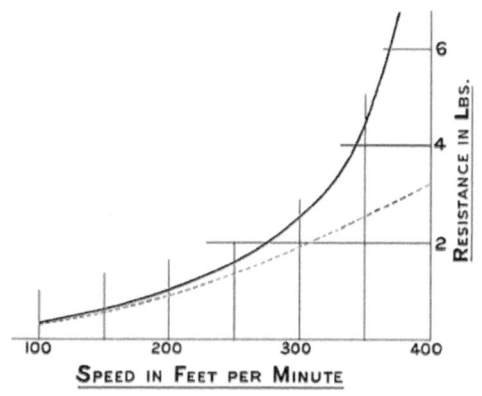

RESISTANCE CURVES
Model of S.S. 'Merkara.'

While surface friction thus plays a very large part in the resistance of all vessels, and more especially in that of ocean-going steamers and ships, which from their large dimensions seldom attain serious wave-making speeds, yet undue importance may be placed upon friction, and, in the smaller yachts, especially, surface may be inordinately cut away. A notable example of this was the *Thistle*, built in 1889 to compete for the America Cup; here the surface was so cut down that sufficient lateral plane was not left to hold her to windward, and although she sailed the water as fast as the American champion, the *Volunteer*, she drifted bodily to leeward.

A short history of Mr. Froude's discoveries in resistance was advisable before touching on *Jullanar*, as this wonderful vessel, whether the result of intuition or of early and immediate appreciation of Froude's investigations, was a remarkable example of the modern theories regarding naval architecture.

The same year that *Jullanar* was built, I designed my first racing yacht, the 5-ton *Clotilde*, but whilst I had the advantage, through my friend Mr. John Inglis, jun., of specially early access to Professor Froude's investigations, I cut her away in a somewhat timid fashion, though sufficient for her at that time to be compared to a 'cart-wheel,' with the accompanying prediction that she might 'run on land, but would never sail in salt water.'

Meanwhile, with splendid audacity, and with no timid reverence for precedent, Mr. Bentall built the *Jullanar*. An Essex plough and agricultural implement maker, Mr. E. H. Bentall had but little training in naval architecture, but from boyhood had been fond of yachting and of yacht modelling. He fancied he could do something in the way of improving the form of the existing racing yacht. After cutting several half-models, he got one that pleased him, and on a piece of his own property adjoining the Blackwater River in Essex, the famous yawl, afterwards to be known as *Jullanar*, was laid down.

Great length was taken in proportion to beam, as length means capacity for speed, and beam in those days was doubly taxed. Draft was untaxed, and was used boldly to obtain stability and weatherly qualities; but while such proportions would have been impossible with the ordinary form of forefoot and sternpost, as the boat would have been clogged up with wet surface, this was got over by cutting all deadwood clean away both forward and aft, in such daring fashion as was not attempted until *Thistle* was built, years afterward and I should not have essayed such a form of profile in her had not *Jullanar's* success given me a precedent. Add to these features the fact that every line in

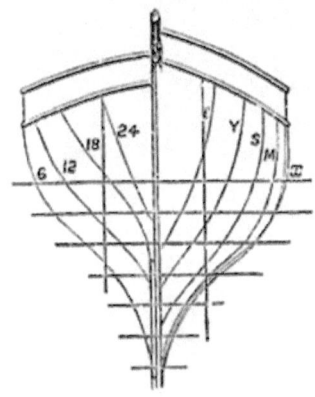

'JULLANAR'—
MIDSHIP SECTION.

'JULLANAR'
126 tons. Built by E. H. Bentall, Esq., 1875.

the vessel was easy and fair, and the only wonder is that the famous yawl was not even more phenomenally successful than she was.

Mr. Hunt, publisher of *Hunt's Yachting Magazine*, has kindly supplied the following measurements of the *Jullanar*, which were given to him by Mr. Bentall himself, when he would not let anyone else have them. Coming therefore from the fountain-head they are accurate, and should be preserved as a register of detail.

JULLANAR[1] 126 TONS, YAWL

	ft.	in.
Length over all	110	6
Depth of hold	12	0
Length on load-line	99	0
Beam extreme, one sixth of load-line	16	10
" on water-line	16	5
" on deck	16	8
Depth after under load-line	13	6
" at forefoot load-line	1	6
" at midship	13	6
Height of freeboard aft	6	3
Height of freeboard forward	7	9
" " midships	3	8
Height of freeboard bulwarks	2	0
Rake of sternpost, upright		
Distance the greatest transverse section is abaft centre of vessel at load-line	10	6
Distance of centre of gravity of displacement below water-line	3	4
Length of mainmast	75	0
" deck to hounds	53	0
" masthead	9	6
Diameter at deck	1	4
Length of main-topmast, fid to pin	38	6
" main-boom	56	6
Diameter centre of main-boom	1	0
Length of main-gaff	40	0
" bowsprit outboard	24	6
" gaff topsail-yards, No. 1	63	0
" " " No. 2	46	0
" " " No. 3	22	0

1. Vide *Arabian Nights*, the *Princess Jullanar of the Sea.*

Length of mizzen-mast		51	6
"	deck to hounds	36	0
"	mizzen-boom	26	0
"	mizzen-yard	35	0

To my mind the genius, daring, and originality of mind of Mr. Bentall were even more fully displayed in the design of the unsuccessful *Evolution* than of the successful *Jullanar*.

The *Evolution*, as her name implied, was the logical outcome of the then tonnage rule, and of the laws of resistance rediscovered, or at least popularised, by Froude. It seems self-evident now that with a belief in these laws only one type of boat could be the result; but Mr. Froude alone had the courage of his opinions, and built the extraordinary 10-tonner which, if it did nothing else, scared the authorities into changing the tonnage rule. *Evolution* was by far the longest of the 10-tonners, her dimensions being 51 ft. × 6 ft. 6 in.—indeed about the same water-line length as the twenties. To get moderate wet surface the ends were cut away; but as *Jullanar* already represented the utmost that could be done in that direction, while preserving a fair line of keel, this was cast aside in 'Evolution,' and the profile was that of a true 'fin' boat.

More than this, it was found after a trial sail or two that she was very deficient in stability when the lead slab forming the keel was recast in the form of a bulb on the bottom of the plate, the completed design simply forming one of our modern bulb fin keels, but of course, owing to the 94 rule, with vastly less beam. *Evolution* was not a success because of her insufficient stability, but with the meagre data in possession of the designer as to the stability of boats of this class, it would have been marvellous had the difficulty been overcome in a first trial. To those able to see the beauties in a design, it matters less whether the ultimate outcome has been successful or not, and while to 'the general' nothing succeeds like success, a few have a kindly sympathy and hearty admiration for those who have laboured, that *we* may enjoy the increase.

Many of the best and kindest thoughts and brightest ideas never reach fruition in this world, and so in the mechanical arts there is often more genius displayed in a failure than in a success, with this difference, that a mechanical idea seldom dies, but, 'blossoming in the dust' of one brain, is plucked and worn by another. *Evolution* lay dead for fifteen years. She has had a striking resurrection on both sides of the Atlantic.

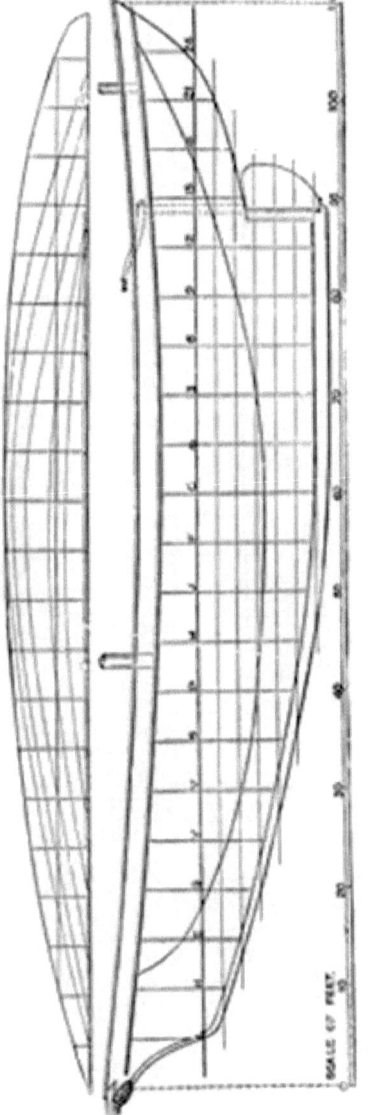

'Jullanar,' yawl, 126 tons, 1875. Designed by E. H. Bentall, Esq.

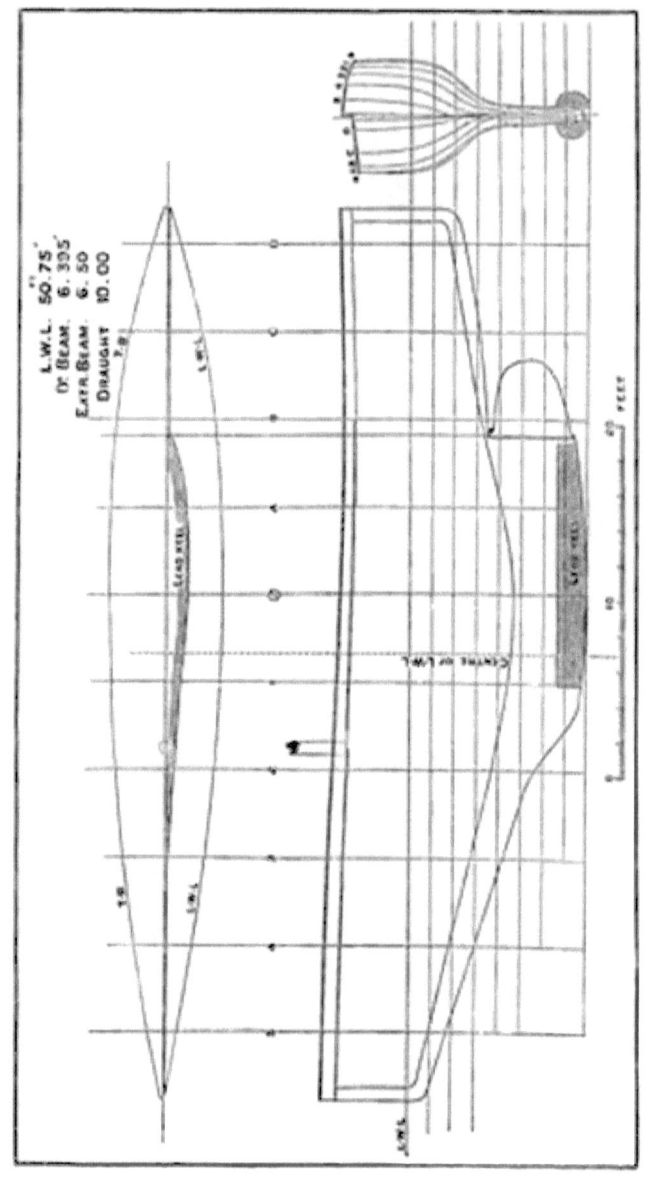

'Evolution,' October 12, 1880, 10 tons, Y.R.A.
Designed by E. H. Bentall, Esq.

In the autumn of 1886, as has been stated, the tonnage rule was changed to that of rating, the only taxed dimensions being length on water-line and sail-area. This change, though at once affecting dimensions, did not materially affect form, though even in the earlier boats designed under this rule more hollow was given to the sections, this being of course a necessity, as with the added beam abnormal displacement would otherwise have been the result. But displacement was not immediately cut down, and for a given length of load-water-line yachts had quite as much displacement as formerly; *Thistle*, 120-rating, and *Mohawk*, 40-rater, the only two large yachts built the first year for the new classification, both being wholesome big-bodied boats, with 130 and 58 tons displacement respectively.

Overhang naturally increased somewhat, as it was apparent that this could be more usefully adopted with a shallow-bodied boat than with a narrow one, it being evident that the natural way of forming the stem and counter was to follow the general buttock lines of the fore and after body. This overhang on the fairly deep boats built up till 1890, so far from being objectionable, was a distinct advantage, as it gave a fine, easy, and at the same time lifting, bow in a sea, eased the bow riband lines when the boat lay down and was hard driven reaching, and carried the side fairly out aft in the long counter.

But beam was now steadily increasing, as untaxed dimensions are apt to do, while extreme draught also increased, and these two giving ample stability, displacement was more and more cut down. Length still had to be got somehow, but length ran up wet surface, and in the 'classes' for every foot of length a considerable amount of sail-area had to be given, making, as it were, a direct and indirect tax thereon. With an ordinary form of profile, the longer yachts would have been clogged up with wet surface; so profiles first imitated *Jullanar* and then *Evolution*, while displacement was cut down to a minimum, to give an easily driven form, and stability got in another way, by lengthening the righting lever of the ballast, by giving immense draft of water, and in the smaller classes concentrating this ballast in the form of a bulb, as in the altered *Evolution*. With the shallow body, overhang has of course increased, the flat section carrying out naturally into overhangs forward and aft, which almost double the water-line length of the boat on deck.

That such a type of boat sails fast for a given sail-area and water-line length is beyond dispute, but this exhausts almost all that can be said in its favour. For ½-raters, 1-raters, and 2½-raters, the type is per-

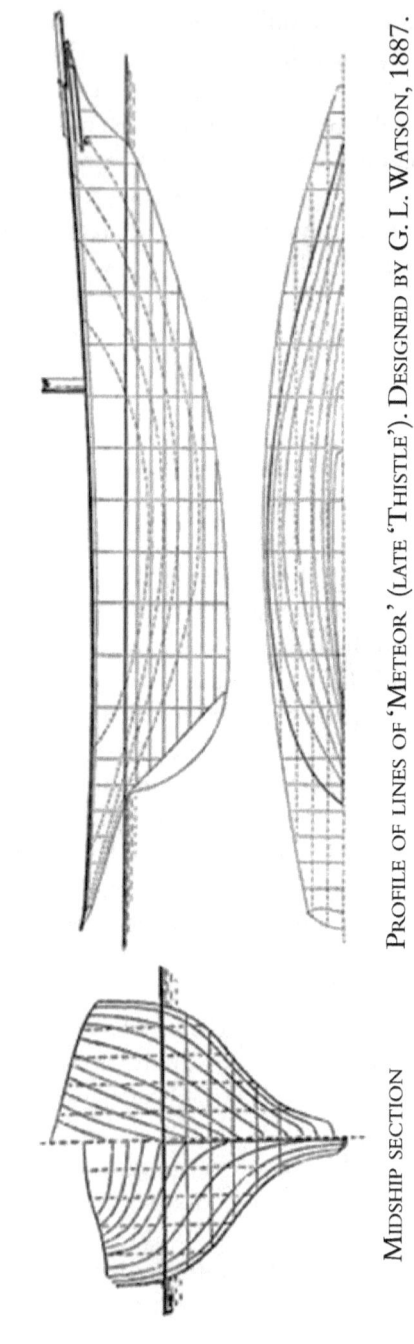

Profile of lines of 'Meteor' (late 'Thistle'). Designed by G. L. Watson, 1887.

Midship section

haps suitable enough, as these are only used as day boats, and extended cruising was never contemplated in them. But from 5-up to 40-rating the type is nothing like so good as that of the boats built prior to 1890. Expensive to build, expensive to handle, without head-room, or indeed room of any kind inside, they would thrash themselves to pieces in any sea but for the admirable manner in which they have been put together. A season, or at most two, sees the end of their success as racers; then they must be broken up, or sold for a mere song, as they are quite useless for cruising. So strongly was this felt by the various yacht-builders and designers, that in the autumn of 1891 they, in response to the invitation of the Yacht Racing Association, addressed a joint circular to that body, and, with I think exceptional abnegation of what looked to be their more immediate interests, pointed out the undesirability of the present type of yacht, in the following letter:—

Langham Hotel, London: October 6, 1892.
We (C. P. Clayton, William Fife, jun., Charles Nicholson, Arthur E. Payne, H. W. Ridsdale, Joseph Soper, and G. L. Watson) have met for the consideration of the questions put before us in the circular of the Council of the Yacht Racing Association, dated September 27, 1892.

We have considered that, besides the saving in time to the Council and to ourselves, it would be more satisfactory for many reasons to have such a preliminary meeting for interchange of ideas on the important issues raised in this circular, and we trust that this course of action will be approved of by the Council. We may state that we are practically unanimous in the opinions hereinafter expressed, the only exception being on the one point of taxing overhang, Mr. Ridsdale feeling that he could not go with the majority in this.

We would, then, most respectfully submit to your Council that as designers of racing yachts we have no desire whatever to interfere with the present rating rule. It has the merit of being the existing rule, and is a perfectly fair one for racing yachts together by, as indeed is any rule whatsoever, so far as designers are concerned, provided its conditions are clearly stated beforehand. But as naval architects, and, if we may be permitted to say so, as trustees for the yachting public, we think it our duty to point out any deteriorating tendency in a rule. We cannot help fearing that the present length and sail-area rule has such a tendency, and is leading, if it has not already led, to an unwholesome type of boat.

We take it that the general yachting public require in a yacht: That she shall be safe in all conditions of wind and weather; that she shall combine the maximum of room on deck and below with the minimum of prime cost; and that she shall be driven as fast as may be with the least expenditure of labour—*i.e.* that she shall have a moderate and workable sail-area. Therefore, as but few men can afford to build for racing, and for racing only, and as the racer of today is the cruiser of a few years hence, any rating rule should by its limitations encourage such a wholesome type of vessel.

On the above assumptions we have based our advice, and it is for your Council, as representing the general body of yachtsmen, to determine whether these assumptions are correct or not.

We are all agreed, then, that the present length and sail-area rule is a most admirable one for the classification and regulation of time allowance of racing yachts. But we are also of opinion that the tendency of this rule is such as to induce a vessel of so large dimensions, relative to displacement and internal capacity (*i.e.* the useful living room on board the ship), that it is advisable to so alter or modify this rule that a type of vessel having more body may be evolved.

We suggest that length and sail-area (as being the leading elements in speed) should be preserved in some form, but modified so as to make it the interest of builders to produce a bigger-bodied boat.

The direct method of doing this would be to introduce displacement or register tonnage in some way as a divisor in the formula, but we foresee so many difficulties in the practical working of this that we are not prepared to advise it.

By taxing breadth and draft or, alternatively, girth, and by reducing the tax on sail, we think this result may be arrived at indirectly. As to the precise value that each element should take in such a formula, we, at this stage, are not prepared to venture an opinion.

The above on the general principles of the rule.

But we also feel that the details of measurement, &c., require revision.

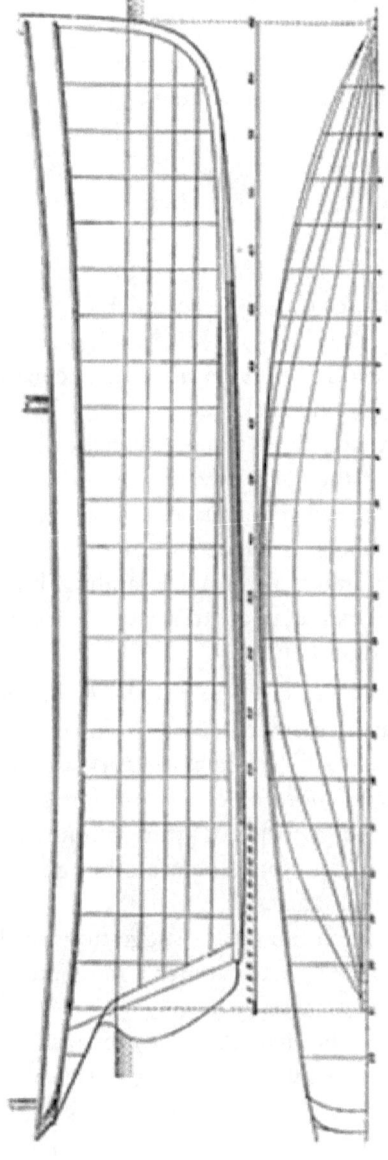

'Florinda,' yawl, 126 tons. Built by Camper and Nicholson, 1873.

On the hull.—The overhang, at least forward, should be taxed, as it may be carried to such an extent as to be a source of danger, but it need not be taxed excessively or to extinction.

The L.W.L. should be marked forward and aft.

Should girth or draft be used in the formula in centreboard vessels, some proportion of the drop of board should be added, and a limit should be placed on the weight of the board.

In the smaller classes, at least, the crews should be limited.

On the sails.—The perpendicular of fore triangle should be measured from top of deck to where the line of luff of sail would cut mast.

That the question of limiting the relative area of mainsail to total sail in the various classes be considered.

Mr. Alexander Richardson, of Liverpool, was unable to be present at this meeting, but this note has been submitted to him, and receives his endorsation:—

The Council of the Yacht Racing Association, however, took the view that what the yacht-owning public want in a racing yacht is speed, and speed at any price, and on the yacht-builders clearly understanding this they withdrew their objections as having been made under a misunderstanding, but asked to be tied down to some extent, in a letter dated November 8, and in the following words:—

> Our opinions, as expressed in that letter of October 6, practically remain unaltered; but so far as we are able to interpret the wishes of yacht-owners, as stated in the public prints, and more especially as expressed by your chairman and the majority of your committee, we now take it that speed, and speed before other good qualities, is what is to be aimed at.
>
> We consequently withdraw any suggestions made in that letter, as having been made under a misapprehension as to your requirements.
>
> But while it may be determined to retain a length and sail-area rule, either in its present or in some slightly altered form, we would most respectfully suggest that, at least in the classes above 5-rating (if, indeed, a lower line should not be drawn), the tendency toward abnormal and un-shipshape form should be curbed in some way. The main direction in which we would propose such

'KRIEMHILDA,' 106 TONS. BUILT BY RATSEY, 1872.

limitation in form would be in the outline of longitudinal section, and we would suggest that this should be bounded by a fair line, concave, or at least not convex, toward the water-line. That the sternpost should show, say, a quarter of an inch above the water-line aft, and the rudder be hung thereon. That overhang forward and aft should be restricted, as also the extreme forward position of mast; but as we deem it undesirable to absolutely prohibit any form, we would simply propose to tax such variations from this normal one so heavily as to make their adoption unprofitable.

The Yacht Racing Association, however, thought it undesirable to limit form in any way, and beyond the adoption of the proposed method of measuring the fore triangle, and marking the L.W.L., the rule remained unaltered.

1893 therefore saw new boats in the classes, fast, it is true, in fresh breezes, but undesirable from anything but a racing point of view. In the unclassed vessels above 40-rating things were not quite so bad, as with a practically unlimited sail-area a fair amount of body was required to carry it. Besides, men who did not mind spending two or three thousand on a 'machine' hesitated before putting down ten or twelve. In America, however, where money is spent like water when the national honour is at stake, 85-foot machines were built on the off chance of their being successes; but it is gratifying alike to American and British yachtsmen that the cup should have been defended by such a wholesome type of vessel as *Vigilant* undoubtedly is.

In a short chapter showing the evolution of the modern racing yacht, many links in the chain of descent must be left unnoticed. I have had to leave almost undescribed Dan Hatcher's wonderful fleet, beginning in *Glance* and *Muriel*, and culminating, perhaps, in *Norman*; Nicholson's famous schooners and yawls (*Florinda* was a standing miracle for years); Michael Ratsey's equally fine ships; Richardson's grand cutters and Clayton's clever 'length classers'; the work accomplished, and still being accomplished, by the famous William Fifes, besides many others whose labours are more fully recorded in other parts of these volumes. But I think no one of all that band who have loved and worked for the sport of yacht racing cares for the type of ship which has been evolved by their own ingenuity and the present Y.R.A. rule, and I am convinced that they would thankfully welcome

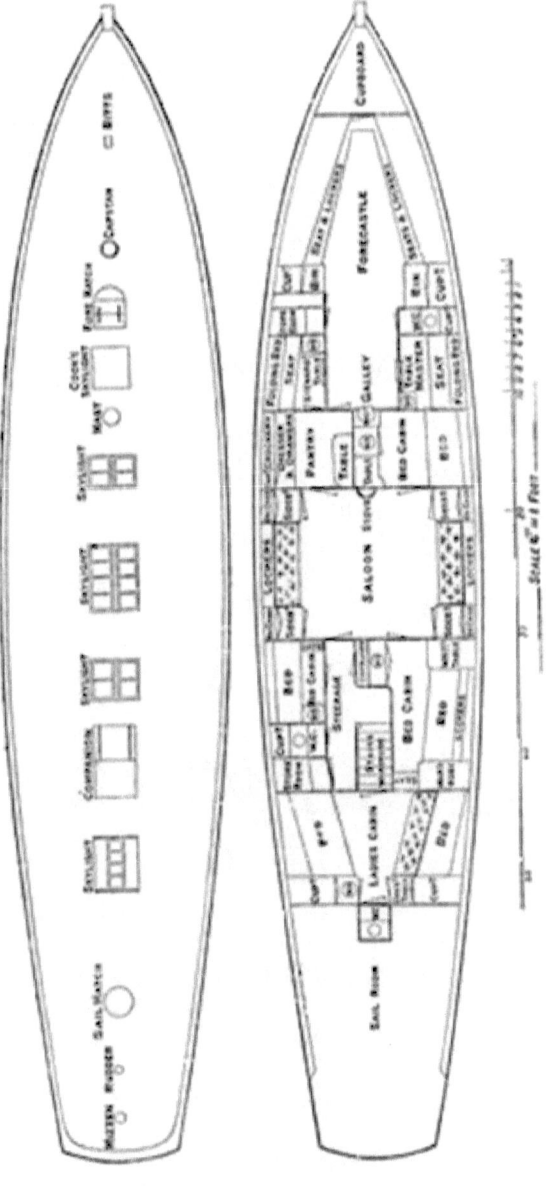

'FLORINDA,' YAWL.

any legislation which should protect the yachting public against the present extravagant, costly, and by no means seaworthy type of boat.

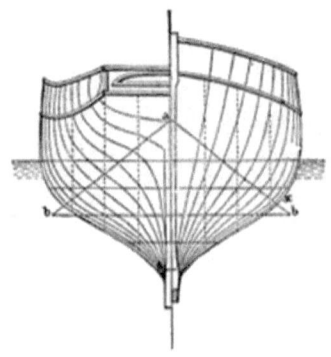

'Florinda'—
MIDSHIP SECTION.

H.M. brig 'Lady Nelson,'[2]
60 tons (1797), to Australia.
Three keels, 1798, 1800-1-2.

---

2. The first ship to discover that Tasmania was an island.

CHAPTER 5

Sliding Keels and Centreboards
By R. T. Pritchett[1]

Centreboards have been so prominently before the yachting world of late that, endeavouring carefully to avoid the argumentative phases of the question, it may be well to notice certain points of their history which may be generally unknown. Centreboards are essentially American in general adoption. Their origin was the natural outcome of the shallow coasts and sand-banks of New York Bay and the New Jersey coast, where wild fowl flock, and the fowler finds happy hunting grounds. Sportsmen originally sank boxes in the marshes; in the course of time these developed in length, and became 'scows' or floating blinds; then the corners forward were rounded off, to facilitate their being hauled up on a beach or bank. This mobility led to their passing into deeper water, the scows were developing into boats, and then came the practical germ of centreboards.

To give stability to the box, a hand board was dropped through a well slot, as the simplest way of achieving the object, until they reached land or some other marsh. The board was not hinged or pivoted in any way, and when no longer required was pulled up and laid on the floor of the craft, ready for any emergency. These boards were first known as 'dagger boards,' and as they were likely to touch the sand unexpectedly, they were rounded off at the bottom, curving aft, so that notice was given, and before the hull touched the ground the boat could be put about into deeper water. This was the early form of American centreboard. On this side of the Atlantic, it is to be noted, our forefathers were not so prejudiced against their introduction as many are inclined to assume. In 1774 A.D. Lord Percy had a boat built in Boston, New

---
1. The original editor desires to express his acknowledgments to Mr. Pritchett for much energetic service kindly rendered during the preparation of these volumes.

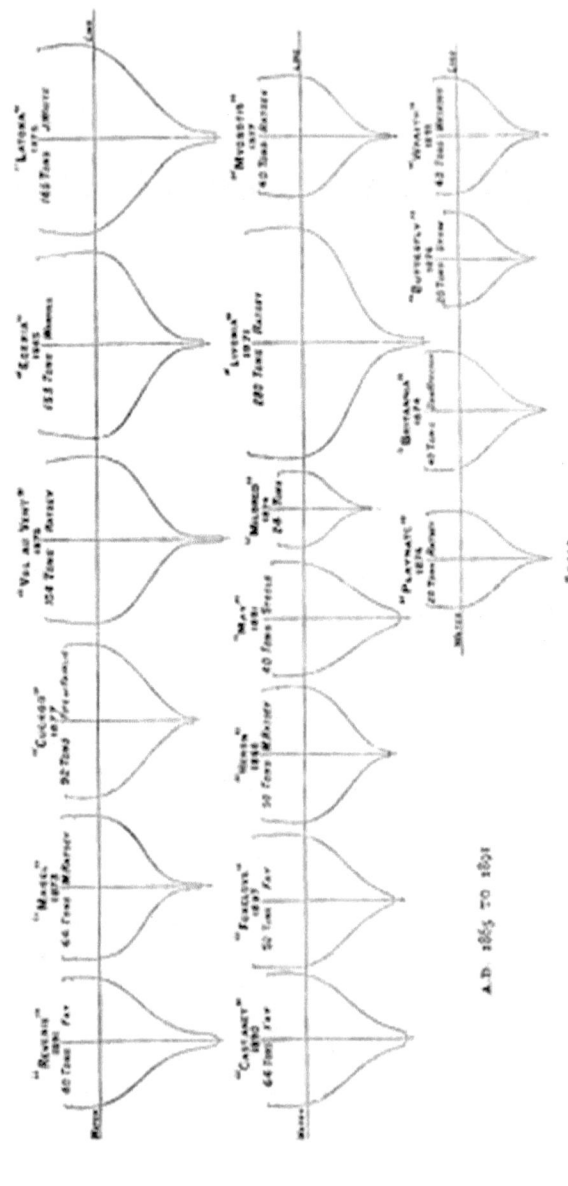

Midship Sections, Dates, and Tonnage of Schooners, Yawls, and Cutters
Drawn to scale by J. M. Soper, M.I.N.A.

England, with one long centreboard, and sent over here in order that he might try the new system in this country. In 1789 a boat was built at Deptford with three centreboards or sliding keels.

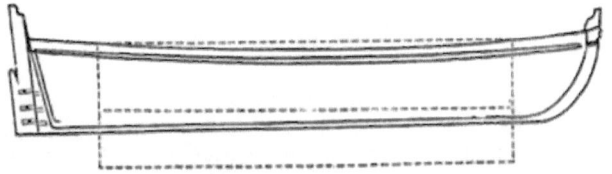

BUILT IN BOSTON FOR LORD PERCY, 1774,
WITH ONE CENTREBOARD.

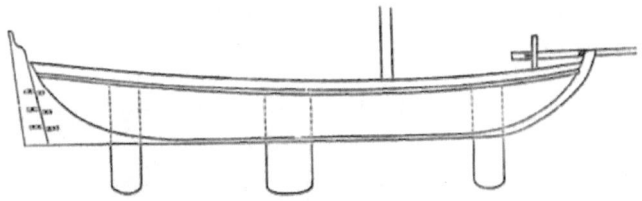

BUILT AT DEPTFORD, 1789, WITH THREE SLIDING KEELS.

The Admiralty in 1790 A.D. had a revenue cutter called the *Trial*, built with three sliding keels. The report was most satisfactory, and a note on their application describes—

Use of fore keel in tacking and laying to.

Use of keels on a wind, raised or depressed according as necessary to assist helm or gain the wind.

Use of after keel, in wearing or scudding in a gale of wind.

Keels hove up going over shoals or before the wind.

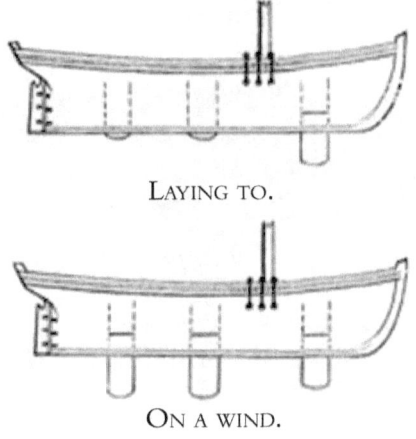

LAYING TO.

ON A WIND.

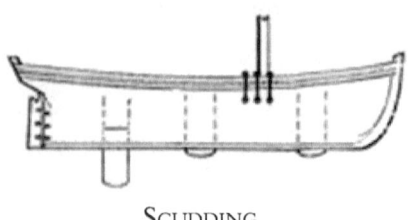

SCUDDING.

The Admiralty soon after this proceeded to make a bold experiment, and built a 60-ton brig, the *Lady Nelson*, with three sliding keels, designed to perform a voyage of discovery to New South Wales. She was built in 1797, and began her expedition of 1800-1-2 under the command of Lieutenant James Grant, R.N., when she first sailed round Tasmania, at the same time as the *Flinders's* voyage to Australia. A full account was published in 1803. The whole report was favourable to the keels, and H.M. sloop *Cynthia* was built. Private individuals also made experiments, and some cargo boats at Teignmouth were fitted with them for river-work. About this time a very prominent personage in the yachting world was the Commodore of the Cumberland Sailing Society in the Thames. Commodore Taylor had a yacht built with five sliding keels, the illustration here given being his from a photograph of the model now in possession of Mr. Richard Taylor, his grandson. The original lines of this vessel have been presented to the Royal Thames Yacht Club, together with the pennants and ensigns flown by the Commodore during his period of office, and are now carefully preserved in the Club House in Albemarle Street; the cups are still retained in the family, by Messrs. Robert and Richard Taylor. Early in the present century the sliding keels were pivoted (1809) here in England, by Captain Shuldham, R.N.

CUMBERLAND FLEET: COMMODORE TAYLOR'S 'CUMBERLAND,' WITH SLIDING KEELS.

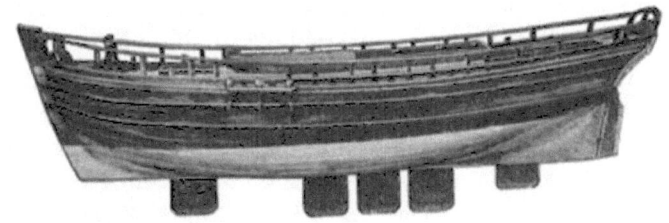

SHOWING THE FIVE KEELS DOWN, AS ON THE WIND.

In America centreboards became general, in fact almost universal, from scows to catboats, catboats to sloops, sloops to schooners and coasters. As regards their application to English modern racers, Mr. Jameson, who is always to the fore either in adopting improvements or sailing races, built *Irex* in 1873 with a centreboard; but after careful trials to thoroughly test its capabilities, it was discarded, the slot filled up, and *Irex* became the crack of the season without it.

Dora, 10-tonner, by Mr. G. L. Watson, was a success with a centreboard. In 1892 *Queen Mab*, 40-rater, designed also by Watson, had a centreboard, and at first sailed with it in the Thames; but after Dover it was not used. Still *Queen Mab* became the *Queen of the 40-raters* for the year 1892.

Recent yacht-building in America offers some interesting data. Mr. Edward Burgess, a very successful designer, planned a keel boat, *Gossoon*, which was a great success in 1890, and many was the close tussle between her and Fife of Fairlie's *Minerva*, built in 1888. After the death of Edward Burgess, 'Nat' Herreshoff produced a keel boat, the *Gloriana*, with new ideas of form and bow, and she acquitted herself well (1891). In 1892 he followed on with the *Wasp*, keel boat, and in 1893 two cup defenders were designed and built by Messrs. Herreshoffs of Rhode Island, the *Vigilant*, centreboard, and *Colonia*, keel boat. The *Vigilant* was victorious in the best races, and afterwards won the race for the America Cup; nevertheless *Colonia*, the keel boat, was the designer's favourite.

The battle of centreboard *v.* keel will doubtless be continued. Among the cup defenders, General Paine, one of the most scientific and earnest yachtsmen in America, decided to throw aside all conventionality, and to have advanced science carried out in a real racing machine 'up to date.' Full details are not obtainable, but they are understood to be: Canoe hull, canoe bow, hull drawing 5 feet. Fin keel of 12 feet with bulb, through both of which drops centreboard; a small centreboard forward like Commodore Stevens's *Black Maria* sloop, and the rudder slung on a small fin. It is a matter of general regret that the gear of the boat gave way during the trials. The aluminium blocks were not strong enough, and the jaws of the gaff were carried away. General Paine may, however, be expected to try again.

The general feeling on this side among the very best authorities on the subject is certainly that a keel racing cutter can be designed and built to compete with any centreboard vessel, and the victory of 'Vigilant' in the late races has not yet convinced that excellent sportsman and practical yachtsman the owner of *Valkyrie* that nothing but a centreboard can win the America Cup. One thing must be remembered: it is neither centreboard nor keel *per se* that makes a perfect racer; it is the happy combination and balance of quantities that get the much-coveted 'gun' at the finish.

It is curious that in the very early days of sliding keels a patent for a design should have been taken out, not by a practical sailor or naval architect, but by a London coach-builder. In 1785, Lionel Luken, who followed that trade, wrote a pamphlet upon the 'invention, principle, and construction of insubmergible boats'; such boats were to be protected by bands of cork round the gunwales, to be made buoyant by using air compartments, especially at bow and stern, and 'to be ballasted with or by an iron keel.' Apparently after much trouble Luken found an opportunity of testing his idea, and the first iron-keel boat at Bamborough Head saved lives from shipwreck.

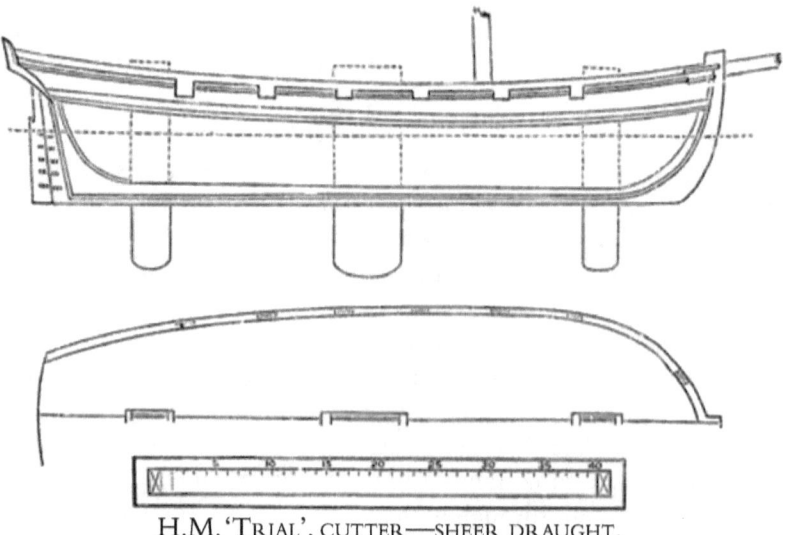

H.M. 'Trial', cutter—sheer draught.
Designed by Captain Schanks, 1791.

'Kestrel,' 202 tons (Earl of Yarborough, Commodore R.Y.S.), 1839.

CHAPTER 6

Recollections of Schooner Racing
By Lt.-Col. Sir George Leach, K.C.B., Vice-President Y.R.A.

Schooner racing has unfortunately for the present become a thing of the past; but the prominent position it at one time occupied makes it desirable to refer to the subject in any publication relating to yacht racing, for the purpose of reviving recollections of the times when races between the 'two-stickers,' or in which they took part, were considered a leading feature of the regattas of all the principal yacht clubs.

The decadence of schooner racing was primarily due to the more extensive use of steam; wealthy men preferred steam yachts, in which they had better accommodation and could move with certainty from port to port, to sailing yachts, in which the accommodation was less spacious and the powers of locomotion were dependent on the winds and tides. But to the true lover of the world of waters the pleasures of steaming do not bear comparison with the pleasures of sailing.

Another reason for schooners going out of fashion was no doubt due to the improvement of the speed of the cutters and yawls. Formerly schooners could compete with success in races open to all rigs, for though their powers of turning to windward were inferior to those of the single-stickers, their reaching powers, with the wind free, were generally superior, so that in mixed races they had always a fair chance of carrying off the prize. No schooner has yet been produced which could compete successfully with the cutters of the present day, even with the benefit of the large allowance of two-fifths of her tonnage made under the rules of the Yacht Racing Association for difference of rig. The last schooner of note which appeared under racing colours—the *Amphitrite*—brought out in tiptop condition by her owner, with an able skipper in command, though she had some success, was not on a par with the best of the racing cutters of her day. Again, the building of large yachts for racing purposes has declined for some years past, owing to the great increase in the expense both of building and maintaining them, and because yachting men found that as much, if not more, pleasure was to be obtained in racing small vessels, in the handling of which they could take a large share, than in larger vessels which, as a rule, were sailed wholly by their skippers.

Under all these circumstances, it is not surprising that schooner racing should, for the present, have passed away; though it is by no means impossible that it may hereafter be revived, especially if further experience shall show that the very large cutters which have been brought out this year, with sail-areas of over 10,000 square feet—about a quarter of an acre—are too large for the sometimes turbulent winds and waters round our coasts.

In the early times of schooner racing the yachts were, as a rule, vessels of comparatively large tonnage, with raking masts, standing bowsprits, and jibbooms; and the old salts had then a conviction on their minds that sails with a good belly in them were the right thing. In 1851 the American schooner yacht *America* appeared in our waters. As compared with our yachts she was remarkable for two things. She had a much longer and finer bow than was usually given by our designers, 'a cod's head and mackerel's tail' being the principle which in those days appears to have been accepted; and, secondly, her sails were made to stand much flatter than ours, so much so that it was remarked that when by the wind close-hauled her sails were barely visible if seen edge on.

One peculiarity in the *America's* sails was that the foot of the mainsail, instead of being fixed to the boom only at the tack and clue, its two ends, was laced to the boom along its whole length, which tended to make the sail stand flatter. This improvement was quickly adopted by our schooners, but it was many a day before it was taken to by the cutters, the impression being that cutters would not sail with laced mainsails, and that a certain amount of curve in the foot was necessary 'to let the wind out.' Now, however, cutters as well as schooners have laced mainsails, with appreciable improvement in their weatherly qualities.

The Royal Yacht Squadron arranged a race without time allowances round the Isle of Wight for a 100*l*. cup, the *America* being one of the competitors, which included both cutters and schooners. The *America* quickly showed her superiority over our schooners, being more weatherly and going more smoothly through the water, and she won the cup, but would not have done so if the conditions of the race had been enforced, as she did not go round the Nab Light, thus gaining a considerable advantage; but she was treated generously and not disqualified. She would also probably have been beaten by the cutters *Alarm*, *Arrow*, and *Volante* if the two first had not been put out of the race by the *Arrow* running aground in Sandown Bay, the *Alarm* going to her assistance, and the *Volante* by the carrying away of her bowsprit in a collision with the *Freak*. All these cutters were well known to be much faster than the *Aurora*, which came in only eight minutes after the *America*.

The cup thus won by the *America* was presented by her owners to the New York Yacht Club as a perpetual Challenge Cup to be sailed for by yachts of all nations, and is known as the 'America Cup.' It has since been competed for by several English yachts, the *Cambria* and *Livonia* schooners, the *Genesta*, *Galatea*, and *Thistle* cutters, and lastly—up to the time of writing—by the cutter *Valkyrie*, owned by Lord Dunraven. The conditions under which the cup is held, however, appear to unduly favour the holders, and do not commend themselves to yachtsmen on this side of the Atlantic.

We were not slow to learn and take advantage of the lessons taught us by the *America*. In the following year the *Alarm* cutter, 193 tons, owned by the veteran yachtsman Mr. Joseph Weld, of Lulworth Castle, was lengthened, given a longer bow, and converted into a schooner of 248 tons; and for some years, with Jack Nicholls at the helm, was the fastest schooner in the fleet.

In 1855 the *Wildfire*, of 59 tons, owned by Sir Percy Shelley, was brought out as a schooner with a running bowsprit and head-sails like those of a cutter, in substitution for the usual standing bowsprit and jibboom of a schooner. She was the first racing schooner so rigged. The alteration of the head-sails greatly improved her weatherly qualities, and she was raced with success by Captain John Herbert against both cutters and schooners.

No further material improvement was made in the schooner rig until 1860, when Camper and Nicholson, of Gosport, built the *Aline*, 216 tons, for Mr. Charles Thellusson. Up to this time it had been usual to give the masts of schooners a considerable rake aft with the idea that it made their sails more lifting, but the *Aline* came out with masts nearly upright like the masts of a cutter and quickly dispelled the illusion. She also, like the *Wildfire*, had a running bowsprit. In the hands of her able and experienced owner the *Aline* proved a great success, and, with variations in model, was the type on which all the best schooners which followed her were based. Although several other schooners were built to beat her, notably the *Evadne*, 206 tons, by the same builders, for Mr. John Richardson in 1862, she remained up to 1865 the most successful schooner afloat.

In that year two new schooners, which were destined afterwards to make their mark in the yacht-racing world and to wrest some of the laurels from the *Aline*, made their *début* in the Royal Yacht Squadron race for Her Majesty's Cup at Cowes: the *Egeria*, 153 tons, built by Wanhill, of Poole, for Mr. John Mulholland (now Lord Dunleath), and the *Pantomime*, 151 tons, built by Michael Ratsey of Cowes for Lieut.- Colonel Markham. The *Witchcraft* 240 tons, built by White of Cowes for Mr. Thomas Broadwood, also came out this year, and with the *Alarm*, which had passed into the hands of Mr. George Duppa, again commissioned, and a fleet of racing schooners made up of such vessels as *Aline*, 216 tons; *Evadne*, 184; *Titania*, 184; *Albertine*, 153; *Galatea*, 143; *Viking*, 140; *Gloriana*, 133; *Circe*, 123; *Fleur-de-Lys*, 90; *Iolanthe*, 75; *Intrigue*, 72; 'Madcap,' 70; *Fiery Cross*, 51, and *Reverie*, 43, it probably would not be wrong to date the approach to the zenith of schooner racing from this period.

The races this year were chiefly of the mixed order, that is to say, races which included yachts of all rigs, schooners, cutters and yawls. The principal schooner race of the season was that for the Queen's Cup at Cowes, for which the entries were the *Aline*, 216 tons; *Aquiline*, 55; *Albertine*, 156; *Egeria*, 153; *Galatea*, 143; *Pantomime*, 151; *Titania*, 184; and *Viking*, 142. There was a strong north-westerly wind, which gave them a reach to the eastward, and a close haul with some turning to windward when going west, over the usual Queen's Cup course, round the Nab Lightship and a mark-boat off Lymington. The *Egeria* proved a very smart vessel on all points of sailing, coming in neck and neck with the *Aline*, and winning the Cup in her maiden race. Two days afterwards, she again beat all the schooners in a race round the Isle of Wight.

In the following year the racing season opened early, with a memorable contest from the Nore to Dover, under the auspices of the Royal Thames Yacht Club. There was a large entry—six schooners, nine cutters, the *New Moon*, lugger, 209, and the *Xantha*, yawl, 135—seventeen in all. The schooners were *Evadne*, 206; *Blue Bell*, 170; *Egeria*, 153; *Gloriana*, 140; *Iolanthe*, 83; and *Fleur-de-Lys*, 82. The *Blue Bell* was a new

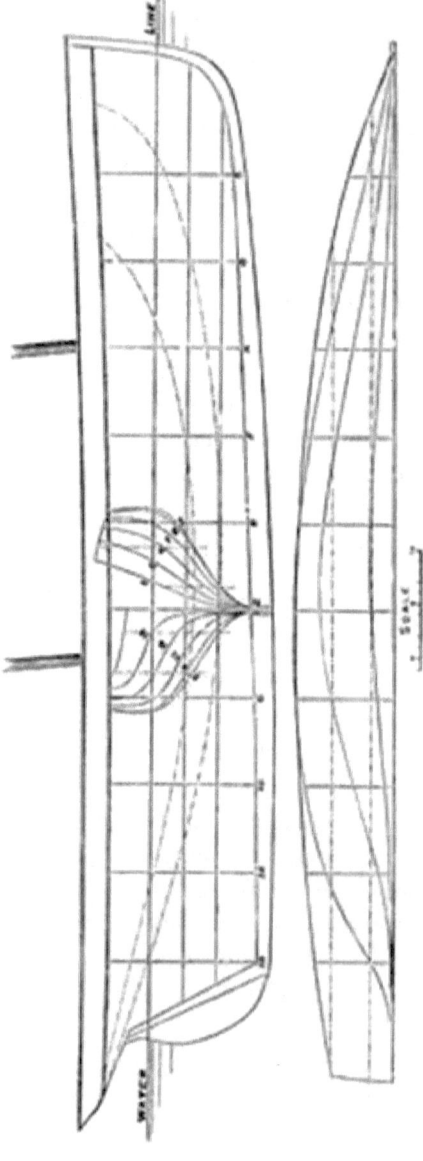

'Pantomime,' 1865 (formerly Colonel Markham's schooner). Designed and built by M. E. Ratsey, Cowes, Isle of Wight. Length for tonnage, 92 ft. 3 in.; breadth for tonnage 19 ft. 3 in.; tonnage T.M. 144.

vessel built by Camper and Nicholson for Mr. Edwards. Among the cutters was the *Lulworth*, 80, formerly owned by Mr. Weld, but then recently purchased by Mr. George Duppa. The other cutters ranged from 65 tons to 40, and included many of the cracks of the day. A hard E.S.E. wind was blowing, which, with a lee-going tide, kicked up such a sea as is not often seen in the Thames channels. Those who sailed in the race will remember it.

The *Xantha* snugly canvassed though with a jib-headed topsail aloft, went away from all the other vessels in the beat to windward, but the *Sphinx* and *Christabel*, though much smaller, sailed remarkably well against the heavy head sea. The *Lulworth*, from which much had been expected, proved too tender for so strong a wind, and when off the Prince's Lightship was put out of the race by starting her chain-plates, with considerable risk of her mast going over the side. The race between the schooners was a good one, but the new vessel, *Blue Bell*, did not come up to expectation. The *Egeria* was soon in front of all but *Gloriana,* and eventually passed her just before they reached the North Sandhead Lightship.

When it was rounded sheets were eased off, the troubles ended, and it was an easy reach along the edge of the Goodwin Sands, in which the power and weight of the schooners quickly began to appear by their overhauling the smaller cutters, the *Egeria* being carried by the send of a heavy sea past the leading cutter, the *Christabel*, not more than a few hundred yards from the winning line. *Xantha* finished 20 min. before any other vessel, *Egeria* being second, thus establishing her reputation as one of the fastest of the schooners. Only seven out of the seventeen were timed, several having either come to grief or given up. Fortunately the tide was sufficiently high to let the yachts into dock. *Egeria* got pooped by a heavy sea when running in under small canvas, luckily without any unpleasant consequences beyond a ducking for all in the after part of the ship.

Blue Bell raced again in the schooner match of the Royal Thames Yacht Club, and was beaten by the *Gloriana* and *Circe*. But in the R.Y.S. race round the Isle of Wight she was successful against both *Egeria* and *Pantomime*. A little later, however, she raced against, and was beaten by, the *Aline* at Ryde.

It was not until 1868 that anything noteworthy occurred in schooner racing. In that year the *Cambria*, 188 tons, was added to the schooner fleet. She was built by Michael Ratsey of Cowes for Mr. James Ashbury, and was destined to obtain some celebrity, not only

'EGERIA'
153 tons. J. Mulholland, Esq. (Lord Dunleath), 1865.

in our own waters, but also from winning the race across the Atlantic with the *Dauntless*, American schooner, belonging to Mr. Gordon Bennett, and from being the first to challenge and compete, though unsuccessfully, for the 'America Cup.' She made her first appearance in the matches of the Royal Thames, New Thames, and Royal London Yacht Clubs, but was beaten by both *Egeria* and *Gloriana*. The contests between the *Cambria* and the *Egeria* during the time the former was owned by Mr. Ashbury were frequent, and keenly contested. They met in most of the principal races, with varying results, but on striking a balance the *Egeria* appears to have been the victor. Mr. Charles Thellusson sold the celebrated *Aline* to Sir Richard Sutton, and brought out the *Guinevere*, 308 tons, which was built for him by Camper and Nicholson of Gosport.

There was good racing in the Solent among the schooners, in which *Guinevere*, *Aline*, *Cambria*, *Egeria*, and *Pantomime* took part. *Cambria* proved herself to be a fast and powerful vessel, especially in strong winds, and sailed about level with the *Aline*. *Egeria* also sailed well, but there was little opportunity of estimating the qualities of *Guinevere*, as she was only entered for one race. Two of the races were across the Channel, one from Ryde to Cherbourg, the other back to Ryde. The latter was not completed until long after dark, and the night will be remembered as one of the dirtiest in which a race was ever sailed; a hard, squally wind, intense darkness, and blinding rain made the sailing anything but agreeable. *Cambria* won, beating the *Aline* by 7 min., but it was not until after their arrival that they were aware they had been in the darkness such close competitors.

A challenge was given this year by Mr. Baldwin, of New York, on behalf of the American schooner *Sappho*, 310 tons, which was promptly taken up by the schooners *Aline*, 215 tons, and *Cambria*, 188 tons, and the cutters *Oimara*, 165 tons, and *Condor*, 129 tons, and a race was arranged round the Isle of Wight under the direction of the Royal Yacht Squadron. It took place in August, after the Cowes week. The yachts were started to the eastward at 10 a.m. before a light northwesterly breeze. In the run and reach to the Bembridge Ledge Buoy all the English vessels were ahead of the *Sappho* except the *Oimara*. Just after rounding the buoy *Sappho* carried away her martingale, and a little further on the *Oimara* carried away her big topsail-yard. It was now a beat to St. Catherine's against tide, and *Oimara* soon passed *Sappho*.

At 1 hr. 15 mins., when *Sappho* was going about under Ventnor cliffs, she carried away her jibboom, which destroyed any winning chance she might otherwise have had. After rounding St. Catherine's the yachts were all able to lay their course for the Needles, which were rounded in the following order:—*Oimara, Condor, Cambria, Aline,* and *Sappho.* In the run back to Cowes against an ebb tide the two schooners got ahead of the cutters, the order of arrival being *Cambria,* 6 hrs. 17 mins. 50 secs.; then the '*Aline, Oimara,* and *Condor,* the last being 7 mins. behind the leader. The *Sappho* did not get in until nearly an hour and a half after the leader. The breaking of the *Sappho*'s jibboom was unfortunate, but before the accident it was made tolerably clear that in a light wind the English vessels had the heels of her, both with the wind free and sailing close hauled.

In 1869 Count E. Batthyany brought out the *Flying Cloud,* 75 tons, which in his hands proved to be one of the fastest of the smaller class of schooners. The old *Alarm* was also again in commission, and with such a fleet of schooners as *Guinevere,* 308; *Alarm,* 243; *Witchcraft,* 221; *Aline,* 216; *Pleiad,* 205; *Cambria,* 188; *Egeria,* 156; *Pantomime,* 151; *Siesta,* 127; *Gloriana,* 133; *Flying Cloud,* 75; *Amy,* 72; and others, the racing could not fail to be keen and interesting.

One race deserves special notice, because an American schooner, the *Dauntless,* 336 tons, the property of Mr. Gordon Bennett, was one of the competitors. The Emperor Napoleon, desirous of encouraging aquatic sports, gave two prizes to be sailed for by yachts of all nations from Cherbourg round the Nab Lightship and back, a distance of 130 miles. A third prize, open to French yachts only, was also given. The entries were: *Dauntless,* 336, Mr. Gordon Bennett; *Guinevere,* 308, Mr. Charles Thellusson; *Shark,* 204, the Duke of Rutland; *Egeria,* 156, Mr. J. Mulholland; *Mystère,* 118, Count de Sesmaisons; *Diane,* 98, Mons. Bescoit Champy. Bar accidents, the race for the first two prizes lay between the *Dauntless, Guinevere,* and *Egeria.* The yachts were started at 2 p.m. on August 16. The weather was fine and bright, with a northerly 7-knot breeze, which enabled them to lay their course close hauled for the Nab. Every stitch of canvas that would draw was set, the *Dauntless* putting up a jib-topsail of a size which made those carried by the other yachts pale into insignificance.

The jib-topsail having been long known as the 'topmast breaker,' it was felt that if there came a puff the *Dauntless* would have a good chance of losing hers, and this soon afterwards happened, topmast, jib-topsail, and gaff-topsail all going over the side. The wreck, however, was very smartly cleared away, and a jury-foretopmast rigged with a small gaff-topsail upon it. A large balloon jib was also set, as well as a larger main-topmast staysail. The *Dauntless* had edged a good bit up to windward, and she was right in doing so, for when the Isle of Wight was sighted about 7 o'clock it was broad on the weather bows of *Guinevere* and *Egeria*. The position of the yachts at this time was, *Guinevere* leading by about 1½ mile, *Egeria* second, with *Dauntless* on her weather quarter and a little astern; the others from two to three miles behind. The *Egeria*, having to luff, did not go so fast through the water, and the *Dauntless*, closing up upon her, the two yachts rapidly approached each other, and then occurred one of the most interesting incidents of the race. The *Dauntless* tried to pass the *Egeria* to windward, but the latter luffed to prevent her doing so, and it became a neck-and-neck race between them.

In a short time it was evident that *Egeria* was sailing a little closer to the wind, and slowly drawing ahead of her powerful rival; and in the course of an hour she was well clear, and had the *Dauntless* under her lee, dropping astern fast. The sea was smooth, which was no doubt much in favour of the smaller vessel. The *Guinevere*, sailing splendidly, considerably increased her lead during this little by-play, and was rapidly nearing the Nab Lightship, which she ultimately rounded without a tack, thus gaining a considerable advantage, especially as she carried the last of the ebb tide until she was clear of the island. The *Egeria* and *Dauntless* were not so fortunate; the wind fell lighter and headed them, so that they had to make several tacks before they could round, and all but the *Guinevere* met the flood tide against them after rounding the Nab. The times taken by a French steamer were as follows: *Guinevere*, 10 hrs. 17 mins.; *Egeria*, 11 hrs. 12 mins.; *Dauntless*, 11 hrs. 22 mins.; *Diane*, 11 hrs. 57 mins.; *Mystère*, 12 hrs. 40 mins.

After rounding, sheets were eased well off to the port side, but about 2 a.m. the wind came out from the north-east, and a gybe had to be made, and square-sails and square-topsails were set. When morning broke *Guinevere* was out of sight of the other yachts; *Dauntless* and *Egeria* nearly abeam, the former about a mile and a half further to the eastward, 'Diane' and *Mystère* a long way astern. *Dauntless* and *Egeria* had apparently run very evenly all through the night, and continued to do so to the end. The times of arrival at Cherbourg were: *Guinevere*, 7 hrs. 1 min.; *Egeria*, 9 hrs. 43 mins.; *Dauntless*, 9 hrs. 53 mins.; *Diane*, 10 hrs. 42 mins.; *Mystère*, 10 hrs. 52 mins. *Guinevere* won the Emperor's Cup, a beautiful work of art; the *Egeria* the second prize and gold medal; and the *Diane* the prize for French yachts.

Those who had seen the *Dauntless* in dock at Cowes were impressed with the idea that, from her small body, she would run and reach fast, but that she would not go to windward with our schooners. It was a surprise, therefore, that in the run back from the Nab she did not outpace the *Egeria*, a vessel of so much smaller tonnage. The loss of the fore-topmast of the *Dauntless* was to be regretted, but probably it did not affect the issue of the race, and as these two were never much more than a mile apart, and there was an average 7-knot breeze, the race was a fair test of their respective merits in smooth water.

The successes of the *Egeria* led to her being classed as a sort of standard or test vessel, and, taken all round, she was probably the fastest schooner we had, although in strong winds she was often overpowered by her larger rivals. Year after year vessels were built to beat her, but, kept up as she was in the best racing condition and well sailed by her skipper, John Woods, she proved, even to the end of her racing days, no easy nut to crack.

A memorable race from the Nore to Dover at the beginning of the season of 1870 showed how good she was even in heavy weather. It was the Channel Match of the Royal Thames Yacht Club, a mixed race with fifteen entries, embracing some of the best vessels of the day, and including the schooners *Cambria*, 188 tons; *Pleiad*, 187 tons; *Gwendolin*, 171; *Egeria*, 152; *Gloriana*, 133; and *Flying* Cloud, 75. The *Gwendolin* was a new and very handsome vessel, built by Camper and Nicholson for Major Ewing, her characteristic being considerably greater depth than any of her predecessors. The Nore to Dover course is one in which strong winds and heavy short seas may occasionally be looked for; and those who are in the habit of crossing the Channel know what a sea in it can be like. On this occasion there was a strong westerly to south-westerly wind, so that it was running and reaching to the North Sandhead Light, and from there a dead beat along the outside edge of the Goodwin Sands against a very heavy head sea.

All were diving their bowsprits deeply into the seas, and taking in green water over their bows. The *Pleiad* split the foot of her staysail and lowered it to reef; while this was being done she was struck by a sea, and two men were carried overboard. By great good luck one of them was washed on board again near the counter and saved, but the other poor fellow was never seen afterwards, although the *Pleiad* remained about the spot for upwards of an hour. It was supposed that he was struck by one of the staysail sheet blocks and went to the bottom at once. The *Cambria* was overdone with canvas, but was unable to reef, owing to something having gone wrong with her peak-halliard blocks. The *Egeria*, which had wisely started with a reefed mainsail, also reefed her foresail and staysail, and went faster for it, riding over the waves in a style which astonished some old salts who were sailing in her. *Cambria* passed *Egeria* in Dover Bay, but could not save her time. Seven only out of the fifteen starters crossed the winning line, in the following order: *Cambria, Oimara, Egeria, Julia, Rose of Devon, Gwendolin,* and *Fiona.*

Egeria won the first prize, taking her time from the *Cambria,* and *Julia* the second prize, taking her time from *Oimara*.'

The sea was exceptionally heavy off the South Foreland, and the casualties were numerous, seven bowsprits having been either broken short off or sprung, including those of *Oimara, Egeria, Rose of Devon,* and *Fiona. Egeria,* when staying to go off round the mark-boat, was met by a very big comber which reared her nearly on end, and it was doubtful for some seconds whether she would pay off or miss stays with some risk of being carried against the pier-head. All agreed that the day had been one of the heaviest in their experience.

Two of the American schooners, the *Dauntless* and *Sappho*, were in our waters during the early part of the season, and in order to do honour to them, and to give them an opportunity of testing their speed against some of the fastest of our English schooners, as well as to encourage friendly competition between English and American yachts, H.R.H. the Prince of Wales liberally offered a cup to be sailed for by English and American schooners of 100 tons and upwards, on terms and conditions to be arranged by the Royal Yacht Squadron. The Sailing Committee of the Squadron decided that it should be a Challenge Cup, not to become the property of any yacht-owner unless won by him three times, though not necessarily with the same vessel.

The course was to be from Cowes round the Shambles Lightship off Portland, and thence round the south side of the Isle of Wight and the Nab Lightship, back to Cowes, about 120 miles. The first race was fixed for June 22, but as it did not suit the convenience of the owners of either the *Sappho* or *Dauntless* to remain for it, the race was postponed until the Cowes week, and was sailed on August 5. *Guinevere,* 295 tons; *Shark,* 201; *Pleiad,* 185; *Gwendolin,* 182; and *Egeria,* 152, were entered. They were started at 4 o'clock in the afternoon in a nice topsail breeze with the wind W.S.W., which made the race a dead beat all the way to the Shambles. There was some pretty turning to windward down to the Needles; but, as the chronicler of the day remarked, the race soon resolved itself into contests between *Guinevere* and *Egeria,* and between *Pleiad* and *Gwendolin; Shark*, which had not adopted the running bowsprit, being left far astern. *Guinevere* passed the Needles first, with *Egeria* close in her wake, *Gwendolin* and *Pleiad* being about 10 min. behind in the order named.

Outside the Needles there was a jump of a sea, and the two leaders drew still further away from their competitors. The night was fine, with a clear sky, and so far the breeze held true and strong. The Shambles Lightship was rounded by the *Guinevere* at 11.20, with *Egeria* close up to her, then *Pleiad, Gwendolin,* and *Shark*. After this it was a run of forty miles to St. Catherine's Point, and as the tide had just turned to the eastward a speedy passage home was anticipated. But oh, the glorious uncertainties of yachting! The wind fell, and *Guinevere* did not pass St. Catherine's until 6 o'clock the next morning, about three-quarters of a mile ahead of *Egeria*, and from four to five miles ahead of *Pleiad* and *Gwendolin*. Off St. Catherine's they met the ebb tide, and as the wind was light and dead aft the progress to the Nab was slow.

With varying luck in wooing the gentle breezes, these two rounded the Nab Lightship together about half-past 10 o'clock; *Pleiad* and *Gwendolin*, bringing up a much stronger breeze, were rapidly overhauling them. After rounding, it became a close haul, and *Guinevere* and *Egeria* still had the wind very light while the others were rejoicing in a breeze, and at the Noman the *Pleiad* was not more than a mile astern. This state of things, trying to the patience of the leaders, exhilarating and enjoyable to the others, continued until they were off Ryde, when, welcome sight! a breeze from the southward was seen curling the surface of the water.

All hands were immediately at work trimming the sails for the new wind, which carried the yachts past Osborne and through Cowes Roads at a spanking pace; the stately *Guinevere* leading, the beautiful *Egeria* closely following her, and the fine schooners *Pleiad* and *Gwendolin* coming in soon after them. The official timing was *Guinevere*, 1 hr. 17 mins. 1 sec.; *Egeria*, 1 hr. 20 mins. 20 secs.; *Pleiad*, 1 hr. 26 mins. 34 secs.; *Gwendolin*, 1 hr. 35 mins. 24 secs. *Egeria* was thus by time the first winner of the Prince of Wales Challenge Cup. It was a curious coincidence in so long a race that *Guinevere* and *Egeria* rounded all the principal points—Needles, Shambles, Nab, and winning flagboat—almost together. The schooners continued well to hold their own against the cutters and yawls in the regattas of the season.

The records of this year would be incomplete without some account of the races of the *Cambria* with the American schooner yachts.

After much correspondence a series of three races were arranged to take place in May between the *Cambria* and the *Sappho*, then owned by Mr. Douglas, without time allowance. The first race was to be a beat of sixty miles to windward, and it was sailed on May 10. The yachts were towed out to the Nab, and as the wind, a light breeze, was then south-east, they were instructed to sail sixty miles to windward on that course, which would bring them to a point in mid-channel about twenty-eight miles south of Beachy Head. They were started at 8.30, and when round the Owers worked eastward, not very far off the Sussex shore, *Sappho* quickly showing herself to be the faster vessel. Off Brighton she was about two miles ahead of her opponent, and when they tacked to the southward off Newhaven, she had considerably increased her lead. As they stood off, the wind freshened and went round to the west of south, and with eased sheets they were able to fetch the terminal point where the steamer ought to have been; but, by an unfortunate mistake, it was not in position. The *Sappho* covered the point about 6.30 p.m., full five miles ahead of the *Cambria*, and won the race, having, it was computed, sailed about 89 miles in the ten hours.

The second race was on May 14. It was agreed by the umpires and referee, with the consent of the owners, that the course, on this occasion, should be to a fixed point, provided one could be obtained not more than two points off the direction from which the wind was blowing, so as to give a beat to windward. The morning broke with a strong W.S.W. wind, and every prospect of its increasing to a gale, as it had done the previous day. The yachts had two reefs in their mainsails, and other sails snugged down to correspond. Here was *Cambria's* chance, a strong wind and heavy sea; but unfortunately when the signal to start was made she refused to go, on the ground that the fixed point decided on Cherbourg breakwater—was more than two points off the direction of the wind. The umpires and referee were, however, of opinion that Cherbourg breakwater, when fixed upon, complied with the conditions, and, moreover, that it would have been impossible in such weather to bring up a steamer out at sea, so after notice to Mr. Ashbury the *Sappho* was allowed to sail over the course, and the second race was given in her favour.

The third race was sailed over a triangular course, from the Nab round a steamer about eight miles off St. Catherine's, thence eastwardly to another steamer and home to the Nab, about sixty miles in all. It was a beat along the island shore to the first mark, and in the short turnings with a light wind the *Cambria* got rather the better of her rival, but the *Sappho* by good handling managed to round the steamer a few minutes ahead of her. They then had the wind free, but it died away almost entirely; the *Sappho*, however, managed to scrape round the second steamer, and completed the race about 9 o'clock in the evening, thus winning all the three races. The *Cambria*, a long way astern, signalled to the steamer to come and tow her in. The *Sappho* had been altered in various ways since she sailed the match round the island in 1868, and was obviously a very much improved vessel, the *Cambria* being no match for her except in short turnings to windward.

On July 4 the *Cambria* and the *Dauntless* started for a race across the Atlantic to New York. The *Cambria* took the northern passage, going as far north as latitude 55°; the *Dauntless* a more southerly and a straighter course. The *Cambria* passed the Sandy Hook Lightship a few hours before the *Dauntless*, and won the race, an account of which, with a chart of the courses sailed, will be found in the *Field* of August 13 and 27, 1870. The *Dauntless* unfortunately lost two men, who were swept off the jibboom when endeavouring to take in the flying jib, and this delayed her for some hours. Such a race was obviously but a poor test of the relative speed of the two yachts, as throughout they were sailing under different conditions, and it was curious under these circumstances that they should have reached their destination so nearly together.

The race for the America Cup, in which the *Cambria* took part, was sailed on Monday, August 8, in New York harbour. She had seventeen competitors, all the best schooners of the New York Yacht Club, of sizes varying from 262 down to 83 tons, N.Y.Y.C. measurement; the *Cambria* being rated at 227 tons. The course was through the Narrows, round Sandy Hook Lightship, and return. The race was not a satisfactory one, as in the narrow waters she was much hampered by other vessels, with one of which she came into collision, carrying away a fore-port shroud and fore-topmast backstay, and springing the port arm of her fore-crosstrees. Later on she also carried away her fore-topmast, losing all chance of even a good place. The race was won by the *Magic*, a small schooner of 93 tons, the *Cambria* being eighth, and the Cup therefore remained in the possession of the New York Yacht Club. Even if nothing had gone wrong with the *Cambria*, pitted as she was against seventeen other vessels, her chance of winning the Cup would necessarily have been small.

MR. ASHBURY'S 'CAMBRIA,' 188 TONS, BEATING
'DAUNTLESS,' 321 TONS, 1870 RACE.

In 1871 Mr. Ashbury, who was determined to have another try for the America Cup, brought out the *Livonia* schooner, of 265 tons. She was built for him by Michael Ratsey of Cowes, with the express object of challenging for the Cup. She made her first appearance in the three Thames River matches, one of which she won, but was beaten in the other two by the *Egeria*, and does not seem to have won again during the season. She, however, sailed a very close and interesting match with the *Aline* for the Prince of Wales Cup, the *Egeria*, the holder of the cup not competing, owing to a misunderstanding. The race was started under way at 1 p.m. on Friday, August 4. The wind was strong from the north-west, with an ebb tide, and smooth water inside the Needles. Each had whole lower sails set, but no topsails. *Livonia* was a little to windward of the *Aline*, and if the wind held it would be a beat all the way to the Shambles Lightship.

Soon after the start both set jib-headed main-topsails, but *Livonia*, obviously the more tender of the two, was rather overdone with canvas, and in the squalls had plenty of water in her lee scuppers. They passed out through the Needles passage together, *Livonia* leading by about a cable's length. Outside there was more wind, with a good deal of sea, which did not seem to suit the *Livonia*, for the *Aline* slowly but steadily gained, and tried to pass her to windward, but this was denied. After a quarter of an hour's jockeying the *Aline* suddenly eased her sheets a trifle, put her helm up, and shot through the other's lee. Off Darleston they took in topsails and housed topmasts. They had a roughish time of it in St. Alban's race, *Aline* going the more easily through the seas.

The Shambles Light was weathered by *Aline* at 6.18, and by *Livonia* a minute afterwards. 'Gybe oh! Up topsails and square-sails,' was then the order of the day, and with the young flood tide in their favour they made quick tracks homewards. About seven o'clock the *Aline* carried away her square-sail-yard, which might have seriously damaged her chance of winning, but fortunately for her the wind about the same time became so much more northerly that *Livonia* had to take in her square-sail also. Off Darleston the wind backed to the old quarter N.W. by W., and *Livonia* at once got up her square-sail again and gradually lessened the distance, previously about half a mile, between herself and the *Aline*. They rounded St. Catherine's at ten o'clock, the *Aline* being then about half a mile astern. When round, they came again upon even terms, as *Livonia* had to luff and to lower her square-sail.

The wind continued strong, and in the reach to the Nab they tore along at great speed. Nearing the Nab both prepared for the beat back to Cowes, and took in fore-topsails and main-topmast staysails; *Aline* also took in her main topsail. *Livonia* passed the Nab at 11 o'clock, 4 mins. ahead of the *Aline*, when sheets were hauled taut in all round for the beat to windward. *Aline* was rather the quicker in stays, and, as she kept gaining little, by little she was close up to *Livonia* by the time they had reached the Stourbridge Shoal. *Aline* continued to work the Island shore by short boards, but *Livonia* made one or two longer tacks over to the north shore, and when they again neared each other off Osborne, *Aline* just cleared her rival to windward, immediately went round, and planted herself on her opponent's weather-bow.

This was fatal to *Livonia's* chance, even of the honour of coming in first, for *Aline* had her pinned and never let her go in the few more tacks which were made before they crossed the winning line, *Aline* at 1.45 a.m., and *Livonia* a minute and a half later. It was a remarkably closely contested and fast-sailed race, the wind being strong, and the tide favourable both ways. The time occupied was 12-¾ hrs., and the length of course was 120 miles; but as it was a beat all the way to the Shambles, and again from the Nab to Cowes, the distance actually sailed was considerably greater, and the average speed over the bottom could not have been less than 11 knots an hour, which was exceptionally fast. The performance of *Livonia*, however, was disappointing, as it was considered that, being so much the larger vessel, and built expressly for speed, she ought in such a wind and sea to have easily given the *Aline* a fair and square beating all round.

Her defeat by the *Aline* led to the insertion of the following amusing couplet in *Punch:*—

Oh! Livonia, I wouldn't own yer
Now I've seen the grand Aline.

Though a more beamy vessel than the *Aline*, she had comparatively small displacement, and did not carry her canvas so well. The result of the race did not augur favourably for her success in America, and there was little chance of her winning the America Cup unless she could be given more canvas, with an increased weight of ballast placed lower down to enable her to carry it.

Soon after the race for the Prince of Wales Cup, the *Livonia* went to New York to compete for the cup, and had a very boisterous passage across the Atlantic, but proved a first-rate sea-boat, and arrived safely without material damage. Subsequently to the race by the *Cambria* in 1870 against seventeen American schooners, the New York Yacht Club, owing to representations made by the surviving donor of the cup, had decided that, in accordance with the intention of the deed of gift, only one vessel should in future matches compete against the challenger; but they reserved the power to select the defender of the cup on the morning of the race, according to the state of the weather, a light-weather vessel for a light day, a more powerful vessel if the wind was strong. This was so manifestly giving an undue advantage to the holders of the cup that it was surprising such good sportsmen as the Americans should not have seen the one-sidedness of the reservation.

After some not very satisfactory correspondence with the New York Yacht Club, it was ultimately arranged that there should be five matches, the club naming four yachts from which to select the defender of the cup in each match; namely, the *Sappho* and *Dauntless*, keel boats, and the *Palmer* and *Columbia*, centreboard schooners.

The first match was sailed on Monday, October 16, over what was known as the New York Yacht Club course, from the head of the Narrows round the S.W. Spit Buoy and Sandy Hook Lightship, and return, about 36 miles. The wind being very light from the N.W., the club

'DAUNTLESS,' N.Y.Y.C, 268 TONS, 1871

selected the *Columbia*, a light-weather centreboarder, as *Livonia's* opponent. The tide had just begun to ebb when the yachts were started at 10.40. There were not so many steamers or other vessels out as on the occasion when the '*Cambria* raced. It was a run nearly all the way to the Lightship, and in the light airs the *Columbia*, drawing little water with her centreboard up, slipped away from the *Livonia* and rounded the Lightship about 15 mins. ahead of her. There they came on a wind, and it was a beat as far as the Spit Buoy, about 8½ miles. *Columbia* both weathered and fore-reached *Livonia*, and at the Spit Buoy led by 29 mins. After rounding the buoy the wind became abeam and freshened for a short time, but died away again in the Narrows. The *Columbia* completed and won the race about 5 o'clock, beating '*Livonia*' by 25 mins.

The second race was on the following Wednesday, Oct. 18, and the *Columbia* was again selected to defend the cup. There was a good breeze from the W.N.W., and the course was intended to be 20 miles to leeward from Sandy Hook Lightship, and return; but the Committee, contemplating a change of wind, decided to send the steamer, which was to mark the turning point, 20 miles E.N.E. instead of E.S.E., with the result that there was no beating to windward either going or returning. There was also a misunderstanding as to the way in which the turning mark was to be rounded. The point was not referred to in the sailing instructions, but as the usual practice in American waters was to leave the turning marks on the starboard hand, and this had been done in rounding Sandy Hook Lightship in the previous race, no doubt was felt on board the *Livonia* that the same course was to be followed.

The owner of the *Columbia*, however, more wary, put the question to the committee, and was informed in reply that he might round as he pleased; but this instruction was not given to the *Livonia*, and in consequence *Livonia* gybed, and *Columbia* stayed round the steamer, the latter gaining thereby a considerable advantage. In the broad reach out the *Livonia* gained a little and rounded the steamer nearly 2 mins. ahead of *Columbia*, but from the fact that the former rounded to leeward, and the latter to windward, *Columbia* quickly became the leading vessel. After rounding they were nearly close hauled, and in consequence felt the wind more, and all flying kites were taken in.

On the way home they were struck by a squall, *Columbia* had to lower her foresail, and *Livonia* was a good deal pressed; but it soon passed over, and they were able to hold their reach without a tack back to the starting line, *Columbia* arriving at 3 hrs. 7 mins., 3 mins. ahead of *Livonia*. Mr. Ashbury protested against the race being given in favour of *Columbia* on the ground that she had rounded the steamer on the wrong side, but the committee disallowed the protest.

The third race was sailed on Friday, October 20, over the New York Yacht Club course. The wind was fresh from W.S.W., blowing pretty straight up the Narrows. The committee had some difficulty in selecting their representative vessel. The *Dauntless* had been named, but Mr. Gordon Bennett declined to sail owing to some mishap which had befallen her. The *Palmer* and *Sappho* were also disabled, and the *Columbia* had started the hounds of her foremast; the Committee were therefore considering whether the *Livonia* should be allowed a sail over alone, when Mr. Osgood, rather than that such should be the case, said he would again start the *Columbia*, but it was not until half-past one that the vessels were ready and given the signal to go. At this time the wind was strong, and they were able to lay their course close hauled through the Narrows. The *Livonia* rounded the S.W. Spit buoy 6 mins. before the *Columbia*, and then stood away with freed sheets for the Lightship, which was tacked round at 3 hrs. 20 mins. 30 secs., about the same distance separating the two vessels. Coming back, something went wrong with *Columbia's* steering-wheel, the clew of her main-topmast staysail, foresheet, and her fore-gaff topsail split, and shortly after she lowered her mainsail and gave up, the *Livonia* finishing the race alone at 5 hrs. 18 mins., her first win.

The fourth match was against the *Sappho*, 20 miles to windward from Sandy Hook Lightship, and return. The wind was fresh from S.S.E. The yachts were started at twelve o'clock, and *Sappho* beat the *Livonia* as easily as she had done the *Cambria* in our waters in 1870, rounding the turning point 27 mins. ahead of her, and rather increasing her lead in the run home, eventually winning by over half an hour.

The fifth and last match was again against the *Sappho*, over the inside course. There was a good topsail breeze from the S.W. which gave them a reach through the Narrows to the S.W. Spit Buoy, and a run from there to the Lightship. *Livonia* got the start of the big vessel, and at one time was about half a mile ahead, but the *Sappho* was not long in overhauling her, and rounded the Lightship 12 mins. ahead. In the beat back to the Spit Buoy, and in the reach from there home, the *Sappho* continued to gain, and ended the race 26 mins. ahead of *Livonia*. The result of the matches was, therefore, that the America

Cup remained in the possession of the New York Yacht Club. This was the last occasion on which an English schooner competed for the cup, though there have since been several contests for it by English cutters.

There was another good race for the Prince of Wales's Cup the next year, 1872, in which the following yachts took part: the *Livonia*, 265 tons; *Aline*, 215; *Gwendolin*, 179; and *Egeria*, 152, schooners, and the *Dauntless*, yawl, 162 tons. They were started at 2 o'clock, with a good topsail breeze from the W.S.W., and an ebb tide. The *Gwendolin* had been altered and fined at both ends, and was much improved this year. She and *Egeria* were first off, and they made a close race of it out to the Needles. There was a pretty little bit of sailing between them off Newtown; both were standing in to the island shore, *Gwendolin* to windward, *Egeria* a little ahead. The latter hailed for water, and was so much more nimble in coming round, that she managed to get on *Gwendolin's* weather before she had gathered way, and gave her such a complete blanketing as left her almost in irons. This left *Egeria* the lead, and she was first to pass through the Needles, with the others not far astern.

All but *Aline* and *Dauntless* held on towards Swanage; these two stood off from the land on the other tack, but lost a good deal by doing so, as the wind chopped round to the southward, enabling all to lay their course easily for the Shambles. *Gwendolin* passed *Egeria* off Darleston Head, and *Livonia* did the same in the lumpy water off St. Alban's. As they neared the Shambles the wind went further round to S.S.E., and sheets were eased well off. *Gwendolin* luffed round the Lightship at 6 hrs. 33 mins., closely followed by *Livonia* at 6 hrs. 34 mins., *Egeria* 6 hrs. 39 mins., *Aline* 6 hrs. 42 mins., and *Dauntless* 6 hrs. 47 mins. It then became a close haul for St. Catherine's, but as the breeze kept steadily increasing in strength and the ebb tide was pretty well done, the yachts travelled fast through the water. The *Aline* collared the *Egeria* before they reached the Needles, but all were surprised at the speed of the smaller ship in such a breeze and sea.

The night closed in very dark, and the wind continued to freshen, backing round again when the yachts were crossing Scratchell's Bay to the west of south, which admitted of the sheets being eased considerably. Off St. Catherine's they were caught in a heavy squall, and *Egeria* lost her main-topmast, and of course supposed that her chances of the race were gone; but she kept on, and as after rounding the point the wind became more aft, the wreckage was got in and secured. *Livonia* in the run to the Nab had got a good lead of *Gwendolin* and *Aline*, but when within about two miles of the Nab she also came to grief like the *Egeria*, her main-topmast going, and in its fall damaging the gaff. She hauled round the Nab at 11 hrs. 20 mins., and it was then a reach to Cowes with a beam wind so strong that she made very rapid progress, notwithstanding her crippled state. The night was so dark that the yachts could not see each other, but *Gwendolin* was supposed to have passed *Livonia* off Ryde.

The times of arrival were: *Gwendolin*, 12 hrs. 38 mins. 30 secs.; *Livonia*, 12 hrs. 40 mins.; *Aline*, 12 hrs. 42 mins.; *Egeria*, 12 hrs. 50 mins.; and *Dauntless*, 1 hr. 20 mins. In the morning it was reported that *Gwendolin* had run down the mark-boat, and was thereby disqualified, and that as *Egeria* had saved her time from *Livonia* and *Aline*, she was again the winner of the cup. Major Ewing, however, represented that, as the lesser of two evils, he had run down the mark-boat in order to avoid a gig which was bringing ladies and others out from the Squadron Ball to the American yacht *Sappho*. The squadron considered that under the circumstances the *Gwendolin* ought not to be disqualified, and Major Ewing accordingly became the third holder of the cup.

The race was sailed in even a shorter time than that of the previous year; but this was to be expected, as the conditions were quite as favourable as to tide and strength of wind, with less turning to windward, so that the yachts had not to sail over so long a distance.

The *Egeria* won the Queen's Cup at Cowes, but in the races of the Royal Victoria Yacht Club the schooners found a strong opponent in the *Corisande*, yawl, 140 tons, built by Michael Ratsey of Cowes, for Mr. John Richardson, which beat them in the races both for the Commodore's and the Vice-Commodore's Cups. In those days it was the practice to class schooners and yawls together simply from the fact that both had two masts, and without reference to their relative sailing powers. In order to give the yawl as large a mainsail as possible, the mizen was placed at the extreme end of the counter, the yawl became in fact a cutter with a short boom, and like the cutter was superior to the schooner in going to windward and running, though not in reaching with the wind abeam.

In 1873 another yawl appeared which was also destined to prove a thorn in the side of the schooners, namely the *Florinda*, 140 tons, built by Camper and Nicholson for Mr. Lessop. She was a very successful vessel, and a worthy rival of the *Corisande*, and subsequently of Mr. Rowley's *Latona*, 160 tons, and other fast yawls. These yawls

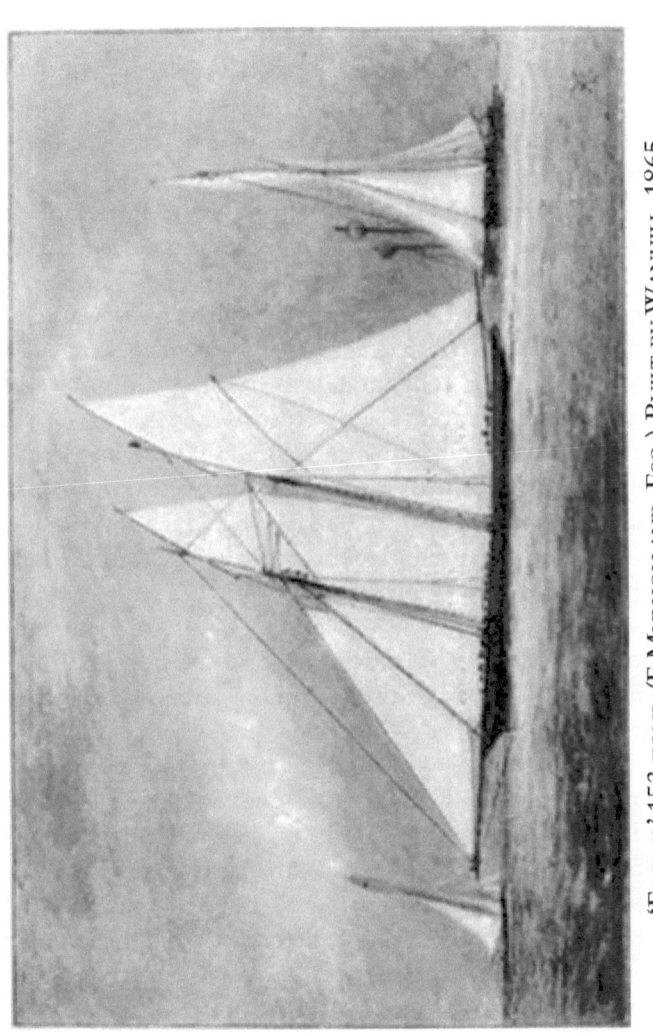

'EGERIA' 153 TONS. (F. MULHOLLAND, ESQ.) BUILT BY WANHILL, 1865.
'OIMARA' 163 TONS. 1867.

took many prizes from the schooners in the schooner and yawl races, as well as in the mixed matches. The *Kriemhilda* cutter, 105 tons, built by Michael Ratsey and brought out by Count Batthyany in the latter part of last season, also made her mark this year, beating the old *Arrow*. She was the first material advance both in size and speed in the cutter class, and with the improved yawls made it hot work for the schooners in the mixed races.

In the schooner racing the contests were very keen, but the most successful vessels were the *Egeria*, 152, and *Pantomime*, 140. The latter had passed into the hands of Mr. F. Starkey, and with Captain John Herbert at the helm was hard to beat.

The race this year round the Shambles for the Prince of Wales's Challenge Cup was practically a match between the *Morna*, 257, and *Egeria*, 152 tons. The *Shark*, 201, was also entered, but had no chance. The *Morna* was built in the early part of the year by Camper and Nicholson for Mr. W. Houldsworth, and was intended, as the Americans say, to 'lick creation,' but though a very fine vessel she did not turn out a success as a racer. They were started at 8 a.m. on August 9, the weather being all that could be desired for pleasant sailing, fine and bright with a nice topsail breeze from the westward. *Egeria* kept ahead of the *Morna* in the beat to the Needles, which she passed at 11 o'clock, with *Morna* about a quarter of a mile astern. Outside the wind was fresher from the S.W., with a gentle swell.

Here was a chance for the big vessel, but she did not improve her position, and when they cross-tacked off Darleston Head she was some two miles to the bad, with *Shark* about a mile astern of her. As they progressed the wind fell lighter, and when within a short distance of the Shambles they were enveloped in a fog. Beating to windward in a fog was not an easy or a pleasant task; however, all managed without much difficulty to pick up the Lightship, which was rounded by *Egeria* about 3.45, when she received the welcome news that she was the first vessel; *Morna* rounded about a quarter of an hour, and *Shark* half an hour, after. Shortly afterwards the fog lifted a little and the competitors were able to make out their respective positions, but it soon returned and they were again lost to sight.

The wind being aft and very light, little progress was made, and at 10 o'clock, when about six miles from St. Catherine's, the tide again turned to the westward. It now became very doubtful whether the progress over the ground was ahead or astern, so the hand-lead was dropped to the bottom, and quickly showed that it was time to anchor, and kedges were accordingly let go. The full moon, bright and clear, had, as the sailors expressed it, squandered the fog; the night was beautifully fine and the sea smooth as glass. All quietly turned in to await events, leaving a trusty watch on deck.

At 4 o'clock a.m. the tide began to flow and kedges were hauled in, but there was scarcely a breath of air, and drift, drift was all that could be done. However, about 8 o'clock a light breeze came out from the N.E., which *Egeria*, being most to the eastward, was the first to feel, and so considerably increased her lead. The Nab was rounded by the *Egeria* at a little past 9 a.m. and by the *Morna* at 9.50, *Shark* a long way astern. From the Nab to Cowes the wind continued very light and variable, with the sun scorchingly hot, but with a strong tide in their favour they reached and were timed at Cowes: *Egeria*, 12 hrs. 3 mins. 30 secs., and *Morna*, 1 hr., the former becoming for the second time the holder of the cup.

In 1874 three new schooners of heavy metal appeared upon the scene—the *Cetonia*, 203 tons, built by Michael Ratsey for Mr. William Turner; the *Corinne*, 162, by the same builder, for Mr. Nicholas Wood; and the *Seabelle*, 142, built by John Harvey at Wivenhoe for Mr. Harry Taylor. They were all fast vessels, and with such a splendid fleet of schooners as *Morna*, 257 tons; *Modwena*, 223; *Aline*, 215; *Cetonia*, 203; *Gwendolin*, 182; *Corinne*, 162; *Egeria*, 152; *Pantomime*, 142; and *Seabelle*, 142, besides others, schooner racing continued at its zenith. *Guinevere* was not raced this year. It would be difficult to say with certainty which was the fastest vessel without a much more critical examination and record of their respective merits than it is the object of this chapter to give; but, on the whole, probably the *Cetonia* would have been considered to have carried off the palm.

Challenge cups are not popular with English yachtsmen, and some satisfaction was felt when the *Egeria* won the Prince of Wales's Challenge Cup for the third time, thus making it the absolute property of her owner, Mr. J. Mulholland, M.P. The race had an interest of its own, from the fact that for the first time an American yacht, the *Enchantress*, 329 tons, the property of Mr. Lubat, competed for it. Mr. Fish, the well-known American yacht-builder, had been brought over to superintend the preparation of the yacht for the contest. The entries were *Enchantress*, *Egeria*, and *Shark*. The Cowes week this year was characterised by blustering winds and rain. The *Egeria* had sailed for the Town Cup on the Wednesday, and as the weather was bad, and she had got everything soaked, the race was postponed by consent from Thursday until Friday, the 7th, to give her a chance of drying her sails.

The morning broke with a strong S.W. wind, and as *Egeria's* skipper knew well what he was to expect in the Channel, he reefed mainsail and bowsprit, and housed topmasts. Although the *Enchantress* had to allow the *Egeria* a lot of time, being more than double her tonnage, it was felt on board the latter that, if the *Enchantress* got round the Shambles first, she would in all probability reach clean away and save her time: therefore that *Egeria's* chance was to beat her adversary in the turn to windward, and so if possible increase the time she would have to receive from the Shambles home. The race was to be started at 6 a.m., and *Egeria* was early under way, prepared, with such a wind, which kept increasing every minute, for a hard fight. To the great satisfaction of those on board *Egeria*, the *Enchantress* was observed soon after coming down with a cloud of canvas over her. 'Hurrah!' was the word; 'something must go before long!'

Egeria gained five minutes at the start, and as in coming round after the first board on the Calshot shore her opponent got in irons, she gained full another five minutes. They had not made many tacks before the man who was looking out on *Egeria's* lee side cried, 'There goes *Enchantress's* jibboom!' which made *Egeria's* crew feel that, although the weather was getting more stormy and dull, their prospects had considerably brightened.

Without her jibboom *Enchantress* was no match for *Egeria* in the beat to windward, and when the latter was well outside the Needles, and had passed the Shingles Buoy, *Enchantress* had hardly reached Hurst Castle.

Just before she got opposite Yarmouth, *Egeria's* second jib was blown clean out of the bolt-rope. This will give some idea of the strength of the wind, which made the sea outside exceedingly heavy. *Egeria* was standing in for Christchurch Bay with the view of smoothing the water, when she observed that the *Enchantress* was put before the wind, and turned back for Cowes, having carried away her forestay.

Her competitor being placed *hors de combat*, *Egeria* was immediately put under snug canvas, and sailed easily until she rounded the Shambles Lightship at 4 o'clock. The run and reach home to Cowes round the Island were comparatively easy sailing, and she showed her blue light passing the Squadron Castle at 11 hrs. 50 mins., thus winning the cup for the third time.

'SEABELLE'
153 tons. (M. F. Taylor, Esq.) Built by Harvey, 1874.

A race was sailed at the beginning of the season of 1875 between the two schooners *Egeria* and *Seabelle*, in a stronger wind than had probably ever been experienced in a race on the Thames. It blew a gale from the S.W.; the ground tackle which had been put down in the Lower Hope for the yachts to start from would not hold them. *Egeria* dropped her anchor, and *Seabelle* got under canvas; the others all drifted, got up head-sails and sailed away, and the steamer carrying the Committee of the Royal London Yacht Club, which gave the prize, did not make its appearance. What was to be done? *Seabelle* sailed close by the *Egeria*, and asked Mr. Mulholland if he would start under way.

The reply was, 'Yes, but stay round the Mouse instead of gybing.' *Egeria* had previously got both her topmasts on deck, and all hands were at once at work getting up the sails, two reefs in the mainsail, reefed foresail, reefed staysail, and small jib. *Seabelle* was also under reduced canvas, and had her fore-topmast on deck, main-topmast being only housed.

The start was a very even and fair one. Soon afterwards the Club steamer was observed in the distance, but she had little chance of catching the racers before they reached the Mouse. They tore away before the wind without attempting to set any additional sail, and as they stayed round the Mouse got in sheets for the beat back, *Egeria* with a lead of about 2 mins. *Seabelle* was a trifle the quicker in rounding, but she could not prevent *Egeria* getting on her weather, and it was a case of tack and tack for at least twenty tacks, *Seabelle* doing all she knew by feints and otherwise to shake off her rival, and *Egeria* doing her best to get sufficiently ahead to properly smother *Seabelle*, which she eventually succeeded in doing, and then reached away from her, increasing her lead little by little every tack.

Presently the wind southerned, and they were able to start sheets for a long reach to the Lower Hope, through which they had another beat, but were able to lay their course up Gravesend Reach, crossing the winning line, *Egeria* at 5 hrs. 31 mins. 20 secs., and *Seabelle* at 5 hrs. 37 mins. 52 secs. *Egeria*,' having to allow *Seabelle* about five minutes, saved her time by a minute and a half, and won the 100*l*. prize, a very beautifully designed silver salver. The *Egeria* had been altered and given more stability in the early part of the year, without which she might not have won in so strong a wind against so good and powerful a vessel as the *Seabelle*.

In 1876 the *Phantom*, 176 tons, was built for Mr. Arthur Wilkinson, from designs by Mr. Weymouth. She was a handsome, roomy vessel, and was entered for a few races in 1876 and 1877, but as a racer was not a success.

Mr. C. Thellusson also brought out the *Boadicea*, 378 tons, this year. She was built by Camper and Nicholson, but was intended for a cruiser rather than a racer, though she raced occasionally. One of the races in which she sailed was the memorable one from Torquay round the Eddystone and return, when the weather was so tempestuous and the seas so steep and heavy, that even *Boadicea* and *Latona* were compelled to run for shelter under the Start headland, and it was some hours before they were able to continue the race. *Boadicea* beat the *Latona* by two hours.

Their competitors, unable to face the weather, were disabled, or retired very soon after they got round the Start and fairly into the Channel.

The following year—1877—the *Miranda*, 139 tons, was built by Harvey, of Wivenhoe, for Mr. G. E. Lampson, and with Lemon Cranfield in charge proved one of the fastest and most weatherly of the schooner fleet.

Her specialities were that she had large displacement, with a fine run aft, a considerable weight of ballast in proportion to her tonnage, and the mainmast placed far forward, so as to increase the size of her mainsail, and make her as near an approach to a cutter as practicable. She was raced for several seasons, and frequently competed both in the schooner and mixed races, with varying results.

In 1879 the schooner *Fiona*, 150 tons, was built for Mr. E. Boutcher, the owner of the famous cutter of the same name; and the following year the *Waterwitch*, 160 tons, was commissioned by Mr. E. Baring, afterwards Lord Revelstoke. Both were by the same builders, Camper and Nicholson.

They did not race for long, but sufficiently to show that they were powerful and fast vessels, though they did not make any great reputation in the racing world.

Schooner racing began to decline in the early eighties, and indeed the building and racing of all large yachts rapidly fell off, for the reason given in the early part of this chapter. But a race took place in 1887 which is worthy of record.

In commemoration of Her Majesty's Jubilee, the Royal Yacht Squadron gave large prizes to be raced for by schooners, cutters, and yawls. The match was open to all yachts above 30 tons, English and foreign, but no foreign yachts entered. The prizes were 500*l*. for the

RACING FLAGS

SCHOONERS

 Aline
 Cetonia
 Egeria
 Amphitrite

CUTTERS

 Iverna
 Meteor
 Valkyrie
 Mad Marion
 Esperance
 Samœna
 Vanduara
 Dolphin

YAWLS

 Lorna
 Lethe
 Columbine
 Latona

40's

 Queen Mab
 Corsair
 Varuna
 Thalia
 Reverie
 Creole
 Castanet
 White Slave

20's

 Mohawk
 Sleuthhound
 Dragon
 Siola

10's

 Ghost
 Ptarmigan
 Iris
 Yseult

RACING FLAGS

first vessel within her time allowance, 200*l*. for the second vessel of a different rig within her time, and 100*l*. for the winning vessel of the third rig.

The course was from Cowes round the Nab Lightship, Cherbourg Breakwater, and the Eddystone Lighthouse, returning to Cowes round the south side of the Isle of Wight and the Nab Light, a distance of about 330 miles.

The entries were:—

	Rating	Owner
	Schooners	
Enchantress	281	General Owen Williams
Aline	149	H.R.H. the Prince of Wales
Cetonia	157	Sir Edward Guinness
Egeria	118	Mr. John Mulholland
	Cutters	
Irex	93	Mr. John Jameson
Lorna	90	Mr. S. Hope Morley
Genesta	88	Sir Richard Sutton
Moina	85	Captain Bainbridge, R.N.
Sleuthhound	54	Lord Francis Cecil
Arethusa	54	Mr. Stuart Lane
	Yawls	
Atlantis	—	Mr. L. M. Ames
Dauntless (ketch)	108	Mr. F. L. Popham
Anemone	58	Mr. E. Liddell
Viking	—	Earl of Caledon

The ratings are those of the yachts under the new length and sail-area rule of measurement, which is altogether different to the old tonnage rule.

The time allowances settled by the Royal Yacht Squadron were as follows:—

	h.	m.	s.
Irex	0	0	0
Lorna	0	4	57
Genesta	0	6	15
Enchantress	0	59	22
Sleuthhound	1	31	8
Cetonia	2	28	21
Aline	2	36	36

Moina	2	43	32
Egeria	3	13	50
Arethusa	4	15	10
Dauntless	5	29	21
Viking	5	43	6
Anemone	6	30	30

The yachts were started at 10 o'clock on the morning of August 8 before a light W.S.W. breeze, making it a run to the Nab, which the cutters rounded about 2 hrs. after the start, some 10 mins. ahead of the schooners. The day being beautifully fine and the sea smooth, the sail across the Channel close hauled on the starboard tack was very enjoyable. The east end of Cherbourg Breakwater was rounded by the *Irex* at 7.30, just at dinner-time, with *Genesta* and *Lorna* only a few minutes astern.

Then followed *Egeria* at 7.50 with *Cetonia* in close attendance, and *Moina* and *Aline* respectively 16 and 35 mins. behind. The *Irex*, as soon as she passed the west end of the breakwater, stood away close hauled for the English coast, and the other cutters followed her lead; but *Egeria* and *Cetonia* tacked to the westward along the French coast with the view of getting an easier tide when working to the westward, and it was not until about 11 p.m. that they started off to cross the Channel. The yachts had a nice breeze all night, and in the morning *Irex* struck the English coast somewhere to the west of Portland. *Egeria* found herself about 1½ mile to windward and nearly abeam of *Cetonia*, both heading a good deal further to the westward.

Unfortunately *Egeria* had to bear down upon *Cetonia* to request Sir Edward Guinness to allow his steamer *Ceto*, which was accompanying the race, to take one of the former's passengers, who had broken his arm by a fall, back to Cowes, which he very kindly did. This delayed *Egeria* fully an hour, and more than lost her the advantage she had gained, but she picked it up again during the day. The weather throughout was fine and bright, but the wind very paltry. The yachts were widely scattered, and as there was a good deal of haze it was difficult to make each other out. *Irex* did not get round the Eddystone until about 10 p.m., *Egeria* and *Cetonia* about 11.30, and the other two schooners some time afterwards.

The next day the wind continued light, but the *Irex* being lucky with the wind, managed to save the tide round all the headlands, and reached Cowes at 3 hrs. 51 mins., nearly 8 hrs. before any other vessel.

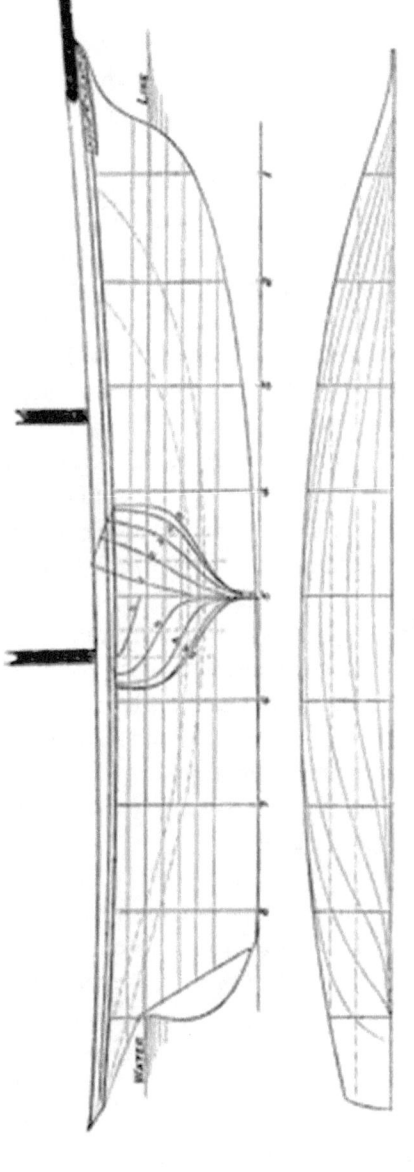

'CETONIA,' 203 TONS (NOW BELONGING TO LORD IVEAGH; 1892). Designed and built (1873) by M. E. Ratsey, Cowes, Isle of Wight.

Egeria and *Cetonia'* made an exceedingly close race of it the whole day, never being as much as a gunshot apart. The wind had headed them when off the Isle of Wight, and several tacks had to be made after they passed Dunnose. The *Egeria*, when making her last board off on the port tack to round the Nab, found she could not quite weather *Cetonia*, and had to bear away under her stern. *Cetonia* was also obliged to tack, and when they again crossed was in the same predicament, which put *Egeria* round the Nab a minute or two before her. The *Aline*, which had not been seen by the others for some time, had stood more out to sea, got a better wind, and, to the surprise of the others, rounded the Nab only a short distance astern of them.

The run to Cowes was an exciting one, as they were all very evenly matched, but *Egeria* managed to keep the pride of place and crossed the winning line at 1.15 a.m., 1 min. ahead of the *Cetonia* and 6 mins. ahead of the *Aline*. The '*Enchantress*' arrived about 2 hrs. later. It was a curious sight to see the three schooners come in so close together after so long a race, and the fact of *Egeria* and *Cetonia* rounding the three principal points, Cherbourg Breakwater, the Eddystone, and the Nab, almost together was also remarkable. *Egeria* of course thought she had won the schooner prize, but to the surprise of her owner he was told that the *Dauntless* ketch had been classed with the schooners, and that, as she arrived at 2 hrs. 56 mins. within her time, she had been awarded the prize for the schooner rig. It was pointed out to the Sailing Committee that no intimation had been given that the *Dauntless* was to sail as a schooner, that the race was sailed under the rules of the Yacht Racing Association, and that a recent decision had been given by the council of that Association, that ketches were to be classed as yawls; but the Sailing Committee adhered to their decision, and declined to refer the question to the Association.

The 'last of the schooners' was the *Amphitrite*, 161 tons, by Camper and Nicholson, brought out in 1889 by Colonel Macgregor, but by that time schooner racing had practically ceased, and she only sailed in mixed races. Her performances in these, however, were so good that competent judges believed that, had schooner racing been in vogue, she would have been one of the fastest of the class.

It may probably be considered that on the whole the *Egeria* was the most successful of the schooners. She made her *début* in 1865 in the race for the Queen's Cup at Cowes, beating the *Aline*, the crack of the day, and her last race was sailed in 1889. She has had a longer career than any other schooner, won seven Queen's Cups at Cowes, and about 70 other cups and prizes, each of which has an interesting story of its own.

The writer sailed in many of the races described, and of these the accounts are chiefly from personal recollection; but he must not conclude without recognising the admirable descriptions of the races published in the *Field*, which has done so much to encourage and improve yacht racing.

Chapter 7

The Racing Rules and the Rules of Rating
By 'Thalassa'

Part 1. The Racing Rules

We race yachts in home waters under the rules of the Yacht Racing Association.

For a long time yacht racing was conducted without any central authority or court of appeal, and the difficulties which arose in consequence enabled a few racing owners to start the Association ('For the promotion of the interests of yacht racing,'—General Rule 1) in the year 1875; since which it has gradually and surely increased its authority until, at the present time, it is acknowledged by clubs and owners alike as the ruler of the sport, owing much to the energy and ability of Mr. Dixon Kemp, the secretary of the Association, and to the solid work done by many of the older councillors, among whom should be specially mentioned the Marquis of Exeter, Sir George Lampson, Bart., Sir William Forwood, Sir George Leach, K.C.B., Major Frank Willan, Colonel Fitzroy Clayton, Major Percy Hewitt, Mr. E. R. Tatchell, Mr. F. Cox, Mr. A. Manning, and, last but not least, Captain J. W. Hughes, who, with Prince Batthyany Strattmann, took a most active part in starting the Association.

The qualification for the Association embraces 'the owners of racing yachts, and such other gentlemen interested in yacht racing as the council may elect'; . . . . 'also the representatives appointed by recognised yacht clubs' (General Rule 2). It is astonishing to find, by an examination of the list of members, how few racing owners belong to the Association and how many old cruisers and steam-whistlers show their active interest in the sport of yacht racing by paying two guineas a year to support the court of appeal. We touch our caps to them for doing so—but pray them to allow the men actually engaged in the sport to settle the details as far as possible. Indeed, it would appear desirable that the Council should be mainly composed of racing owners, and that each class of racing yacht should be represented, say, by two councillors. Thus—two for racing cruisers of the *Columbine* type, two for the large class of racers, two for each Y.R.A. class, and two for each of the *Minima* classes (1 and ½-raters), or 18 in all. The other six members of the Council might with advantage be selected from the appointed representatives of the yacht clubs (General Rule 3).

At present the Council is practically a self-elected body, General Rule 4 stating that 'vacancies occurring between the annual meetings *shall* be filled by the Council.' Evidently the word 'shall' should be replaced by *may*.

Four councillors retire annually by rotation (General Rule 4), but are eligible for re-election, and changes seldom occur from this cause, except through compulsory retirement due to non-attendance for an entire year. Quite right; when you have a good man keep him if you can; but the self-election clause is wrong in principle, and quite unnecessary in a council beginning each year with 24 members.

General Rule 5 describes the procedure for electing councillors.

General Rules 6 and 7 refer to the Annual General and Special General Meetings, and No. 8 to the annual subscription—which is two guineas.

General Rule 9 should form part of the measurement rules. It refers to the payment of measurement fees, and their non-payment is mingled in a most curious manner with the non-payment of subscriptions to the Y.R.A., on which latter point there is a penalty in Rule 8. So far as measurement fees are concerned all owners should be on the same footing. The general rules are of course only binding on the members of the Association.

General Rule 10, concerning the meetings of the Council, is vague, and might well have another rule, to be spoken of presently, incorporated with it.

General Rule 11 describes the duties of the Council which are tantamount to the objects of the Association, and might with advantage be mentioned in Rule 1. The measurement of yachts for racing and the issue of certificates of rating should be added to the rule, as now being duties which are governed by the Council.

THE START.

General Rule 12 describes the procedure necessary for effecting any alterations in the rules (general or racing), a two-thirds majority of the Council, and, subsequently, of a general meeting, or of a general vote, being necessary for any *amendment or addition* to the rules. A member may, however, persevere in a proposal, although the Council report unfavourably upon it; in which case it is brought before a general meeting, or a general vote, and then requires a favourable majority of three-quarters to pass it into law.

This rule is perhaps too stringent in its conservative tendencies, a two-thirds majority being ample under any circumstances. When such a majority is obtained in face of the Council's opposition the case must be very strong. Nothing of the kind has ever occurred; but in 1891 certain alterations, recommended by the Council, failed to obtain the requisite two-thirds majority at the Annual General Meeting.

The Rules for the Guidance of the Council:

have never been passed by a General Meeting, although some of them (like No. 7) are important. All of them should be incorporated with the General Rules. These unauthorised Rules are:—

No. 1, that the Council may be assembled by the president, or by a vice-president, or by a requisition of three councillors addressed to the secretary.

No. 2, that five shall be a quorum.

No. 3 refers to the chairman; and

No. 4 to the minute book of the proceedings.

No. 5, that a quorum of three may be assembled at any time and notice, to settle questions on the measurement of yachts.

No. 6 regulates the procedure on General Rule 4, last paragraph, the election of councillors.

No. 7 regulates the procedure on General Rule 2, first paragraph, the election of members of the Association.

The Racing Rules

There are thirty-two 'sailing rules' under which yacht racing in British waters is conducted. Many of these rules have nothing to do with 'sailing,' but refer to the measurements for rating, entries, sailing committees' work ashore, and cognate matters; the rules and paragraphs of rules connected with any one subject being dotted about in the most bewildering manner, and the whole forming a general hotch-potch, no great credit to the yachting Fathers.

The rules, being numerous and complex, must always be difficult to follow; but this difficulty is increased tenfold by unmethodical arrangement, and by the absence of any code whereby the law-making decisions of the Council can be discovered and kept in view by racing owners, by 'sailing' committees, and by the Council itself.

The rules have been examined and explained with much ability by Mr. Dixon Kemp, in his book on *Yacht and Boat Sailing*, chapter viii. being devoted to the subject. Every racing owner should possess this book: it is, therefore, unnecessary to repeat the treatment of the rules therein contained. Nor is a criticism of the rules necessary, as this has been done by the present writer in a series of articles published in that excellent paper *The Yachtsman*, on April 28, and May 5, 12, 19, and 26, 1892; which back numbers can be obtained for a few pence by applying to the publisher, 143 Strand, London. Moreover, a summary of the rules was given in the *Almanac* for the Solent Racing, published by King & Co., Southampton, in 1893, and will probably be repeated in succeeding years.

An attempt will therefore be made in these pages to treat the Racing Rules in a different manner, by an examination and description of the duties of each important actor in connection with a yacht race.

Duties of a Designer

The principal object and duty of a designer is to build yachts capable of winning prizes fairly. He must, therefore, study every peculiarity and custom of the sport, the average climate during the racing season, and, above all, he must study the rule of rating and measurement (Rule 3), to be examined at the end of this chapter. Other rules must not escape his attention; for instance, the designer of Mr. Carrol's yacht, when building in America for races in British waters, would note that by Rule 9 shifting keels may only be moved by manual power, and, consequently, that if any hydraulic appliance be used, anything in the nature of an accumulator would be contrary to the spirit of the rule, and would be matter for protest. The same remark applies to working and hoisting the sails (Rule 13).

A designer must note that, by Rule 15, yachts over 10-rating must be fitted below deck as yachts, including two wooden transverse bulkheads. Also that, by Rule 16, yachts of 30 to 90-rating must carry on deck a boat not less than 10 feet by 3½ feet, and yachts of 90-rating, or more, a boat not less than 12 feet by 3½ feet.

Designers must also consider Rule 33, which defines 'cruising trim'—especially Clause 2, which prohibits the placing of 'sails or other gear' 'in the main cabin' of yachts which race in this trim; and Clauses 3 and 4, concerning the anchors and chains, and boats.

Private Match

A yacht race can only be said to occur when the competitors have carefully prepared for it, and when it is under the direction of some competent nautical authority. In arranging a private match, it is therefore important to appoint both a race officer and a referee, the latter having the power to decide any dispute or to refer the same to the Y.R.A., should he think fit to do so.

Club and Open Matches

Private matches are less frequent than of yore, and modern racing is generally for prizes given by yacht clubs or by town regattas.

Duties of a Yacht Club

The object of a yacht club is usually defined somewhat as follows:—

R.S.Y.C.—The encouragement of yacht sailing in the Southampton Water and Solent.

R.P.C.Y.C.—To encourage amateur yacht racing in the Solent.

C.Y.C.—To encourage the racing of yachts in the small classes Y.R.A.

B.S.C.—To promote the interests of amateur boat-sailing.

The executives of such clubs should keep these objects in view by choosing flag officers who are keen sportsmen and patrons of yachting; by appointing sailing committees well versed in details; by raising funds for the prizes; and, generally, by constantly endeavouring to further the yachting interests of the club members.

Unfortunately the development of a yacht club only too frequently produces a dual government, the house being governed by a committee mainly consisting of *habitués* who are not yachtsmen, and the yachting by a sailing committee.

Duties of a Sailing Committee

The first duty of a sailing committee is to perfect itself. Each member should study, and be well acquainted with, the racing rules. The chairman should be a good business man, and well versed in the intricacies and dodges of yacht racing. If one of the flag officers fulfil these conditions, so much the better. The chairman should be elected by the committee, not by the club.

The committee should discover the amount of cash available for racing, the average cost of a regatta, and consequently the balance which can be devoted to prizes.

Other clubs whose regattas are held at the same period of the season should be addressed, and dates arranged to suit both clubs and owners.

The committee is then in a position to settle its programme, which should be done as early in the year as possible, in order that owners may prepare their yachts' programmes for the season. A summary of the club programme should then be published or advertised; and this should be strictly adhered to, if possible.

A clause is frequently inserted stating that the committee reserves the right to alter the programme; but it should be remembered that no change in the conditions of a race can be made after an entry has been received, because, by Rule 8, Y.R.A., the yacht is then 'entitled to a prize of not less than half the value of the first prize offered for competition,' if she 'sail over the course' under the conditions.

The advertisement may conveniently take the following form:

The . . . . . . .Yacht Club will hold a Regatta on the . . . . day of . . . . 189 . . at . . . .
Race 1.—Fee . . . . Prizes £ . . . , £ . . . , £ . . . , for yachts exceeding . . . ., and not exceeding . . . . . . .R.
Race 2.—Fee. . . . . . . .Prizes £ . . . , £ . . . , for yachts exceeding . . . . . , and not exceeding. . . . . R.
And so on.
Open to yachts owned by members of recognised yacht clubs.
Entries close at noon on the. . . . . of. . . . . 189. . .
For full programme apply to the Club Secretary.

This summary is sufficient. It is better to insert a short notice twice than a long notice once.

The full programme should be drawn up with much care, and everything mentioned, thus avoiding numerous inquiries and much correspondence.

The programme should state the matters already mentioned in the summary, and, in addition, the time of start for each race; the method of starting; the course of each race; the starting line; the finishing line (Rule 17); time limit (if any) for finishing race or shortening course; the exact length of each course in sea miles and decimals, for time allowance (if any); and the regulations special to the club or town regatta (Rule 4. Also Rec. 6 of Appendix).

Some good sportsmen on the Solent hope soon to see a code of regulations universally adopted for the Solent classes, in which event it will only be necessary to state on the programme or the race card that the Y.R.A. rules and the Solent class regulations will be observed.

The regulations might deal with the following matters:—

The sailing-over rule; the conditions on which second or third prizes (if any) will be awarded; the payment of entrance fees; the certificate of rating (Rule 3); the declaration at entry (Rule 5); the declaration at end of race (Rule 10); the deposit (if any) on a protest (Rule 30); the owner; the helmsman; rig allowances (if any). (Rec. 1 of Appendix.)

The race card can only be drawn up at the last moment, after the entries have closed. It is similar to the programme, but contains the names of the yachts which have entered, their colours, their recall numerals, and sometimes the names of their owners (Rule 12). It also generally contains the names of the flag officers, and the names of the race officers for the day.

Duties of the Secretary

As the date of a regatta approaches, entries will be received, and the secretary should acquaint the sailing committee of any irregularity (Rule 5). He should also discover if the sailing committee wishes to 'refuse any entry.' An entry by telegram should finish thus: *Written entry follows*; and this should be made in strict accordance with Rule 5, Y.R.A. The entry (when filled in) and the declaration amount to nearly 150 words, which cost an owner 12*s.* 6*d.* if sent entirely by telegram. It was never intended that an entry by telegram should relieve an owner from making the declaration.

The secretary must see that the race cards are printed promptly as soon as the entries are closed, and one should be sent to each yacht in accordance with Rule 12, Y.R.A., which states that 'written or printed instructions as to the conditions of the race, the course to be sailed, marks, &c., shall be supplied at the time of entry, or as soon after as possible, to every yacht entered for a race.'

The secretary must see that recall numerals, 'white on a black ground, and the figures not less than 2 ft. 6 in. in height,' are placed conveniently for use by the race officers (Rule 12); also that the white peter, the blue peter (Rule 4), the commercial code flags B, C, D, F, and so on (Rule 17), and the means and trained labour for hoisting them promptly are similarly provided.

He must also have a care that the gun, or guns, and the ammunition are in good order and position, and properly manned, in order that Rules 4 and 17 may be complied with.

He must see that the two inner marks for the alignment of the starting line are correctly fixed, and that the outer mark is moored as nearly as practicable in the same alignment.

He must take measures for having the mark-boats (if any) correctly moored, in good time.

He should see that the race officers are provided with a chronograph, a book of the Y.R.A. rules, a race card, a chart showing the courses, a coloured diagram showing the racing colours of each competing yacht, and a description of each yacht giving any peculiarity by which she may be identified, such as the colour of the hull, the rig, the shape of the bow or stern, &c.

He should provide lanterns for use at the winning line in the event of a finish after sunset.

After the racing he should endeavour to obtain the declarations from the owners (or their representatives) on board the winning yachts (Rule 10).

During these stirring times a secretary must not rely on receiving any assistance; on the contrary, everyone expects help from him; and should anything go wrong his broad shoulders must carry the blame.

Yet there are some men who do all this and much more a dozen times in a season, and toil year by year 'for the good of the club,' and 'the fun of the thing,' as honorary secretaries.

The Duties of Race Officers

It is customary, and a good plan, for the sailing committee to appoint two race officers for each day of a regatta (Rule 1). If the services of a flag officer, or of an active member of the sailing committee, can be obtained, well and good; but anyone, whether a member of the club or not, may be appointed.

A race officer should be at his post *at least* half an hour before the first race begins (Rule 1). This gives him only fifteen minutes to see that things are 'shipshape' before flag B is hoisted (Rule 17). During this time he must decide whether the regatta or any race must be postponed on account of bad weather, in which case letter N is hoisted over the flag denoting the race or races so postponed (Rule 2). He should discover from the secretary that the marks are all correctly moored, the flags and guns ready, and everything in order. It is a great convenience to sailing masters to have a *time gun* fired half an hour before the start for the first race; but this should not be done unless it be mentioned on the race card.

The race officer should time this gun to the fraction of a second, and start all the races in strict accordance therewith. The officer should also make himself acquainted with the racing colours (Rule 11), and, if possible, with any peculiarities in the appearance of the yachts which are about to compete, in order that they may be easily identified at the start. As the time for hoisting flag B (race 1) approaches, the officer should warn the man at the signal halliards, who will hoist the flag, *furled*, at the peak, and the instant the officer gives the time signal the flag should be 'broken out' by a sharp jerk on the halliard.

As the time for *first gun* approaches, the blue peter is hoisted similarly by another halliard, and is 'broken out' the instant the officer gives the time signal; the gun is fired simultaneously, and should it miss fire the blue peter is the signal. The 'preparative flag' is also lowered.

The yachts in the race are under the rules at first gun (Rule 17). The only apparent exception being that a *paid* hand may join or leave a yacht before the 'signal to start' (Rule 14), but not afterwards. N.B.—Corinthians may join or leave a yacht at any time during a race. The race officer should recall any yacht at the start which breaks any racing rule, such as being towed or propelled by any means other than her sails, after first gun (Rule 25).

The 'member of a recognised yacht club' (Rule 10) must be on board at *first* gun, and so with all the other racing rules.

One of the race officers must very carefully watch the alignment as the starting time (*precisely* five minutes after first gun) approaches, and the other officer should watch the chronograph and shout the word 'fire' at the fraction of a second. 'Should the gun miss fire the simultaneous lowering of the blue peter is the signal to start' (Rule 17). The officer attending to the starting line should carefully note whether 'any part of the hull, spars, or other equipment' (Rule 17) of any of the yachts 'be on or across the line *before* the signal to start is made.' If so, the recall numerals of such boats should be at once displayed, and kept displayed until they return and recross the line or give up the race (Rule 12). The second race is started in the same way, the preparative flag C being hoisted when the starting gun for the first race is fired.

Sometimes there is an interval of time between these actions; but there is no difficulty in starting races every fifteen minutes in strict accordance with the rules, if the officers know their duties and the signalmen are well trained.

The work of starting shows the necessity of appointing *two* race officers; and, subsequently, during the racing it enables at least one officer to be always on duty. The officers should watch the racing as much as possible, and should they see or learn that any yacht has broken any rule, they should disqualify her whether she be protested against or not (Rule 30).

'Should it be necessary during a race to shorten the course' (Rule 4), the officers will order 'the signal flag denoting the race' (or races) to be 'hoisted under the white peter; or, in case of fog or darkness, two guns' to be 'fired,' to show that the race is to finish with the round about to be completed, 'or at such mark as the sailing committee or officer of the day may appoint.' In practice, the sailing committee never interferes with the race officers.

Of course the time allowance, if any, is adjusted to the altered distance (Rule 4).

If there be more than one round in a course, each yacht should be timed at the end of each round; but there is no rule to this effect. The time at the end of a round or race is taken when any part of a yacht's hull or equipment *first* cuts the line. When the competing yachts pass the race officer, he should also notice whether any of them 'show an ensign conspicuously in the main rigging' (Rule 30), this being the preparative signal of a protest; and consequently, the race officers must be prepared to receive such protest 'within two hours of the arrival of the protesting yacht,' but they cannot decide it. This rests with the sailing committee.

Race officers must also be prepared to receive from a yacht, or yachts, a claim for a resailed race under the 'man overboard' rule (Rule 29), which states that competing yachts 'shall use their utmost endeavours to render assistance in case of a man falling overboard from a competing yacht; and if it should appear that any yacht was thereby prevented from winning the race, the committee shall have power to order it to be resailed between any yacht or yachts so prevented, and the actual winner.'

By the wording of the rule the race officers can only report the matter to the committee, and cannot settle it themselves. Nevertheless, they have the power to 'award the prizes' (Rule 1) in the absence of any such claim, or protest; but this is seldom done in practice, because owners rarely send their declaration (in accordance with Rule 10) to the secretary of the club until it is demanded. *See* Duties of Owners.

Practically, therefore, race officers can only declare the probable winners; and in some clubs, where the same yachts race frequently, this is done at the termination of the racing, by hoisting the colours of the apparent winners under the signal flags denoting their races.

Duties of Owners

The principal duty of a racing owner is to see that everything in connection with the racing of his yacht is done in a perfectly fair and honourable manner. An owner who breaks or infringes any racing rule flagrantly 'may be disqualified by the Council, for such time as the Council may think fit, from sailing his yacht in any race held under the rules of the Y.R.A.' (Rule 33).

When a yacht is officially measured, the owner should be on board, or have an experienced racing friend on board to represent him. He should note the position of the inside ballast, ship's stores, unbent sails, and other gear, entering same in his note-book. He should see that the crew is properly placed, *viz.* 'amidships' (Council's instructions to official measurer, March 1, 1883), as, by a resolution passed December 6, 1892, a yacht (Rule 3, December 1892) must now be marked by the owner, such marks being clear above the water surface in smooth water in 'racing trim,' which evidently means with crew and all weights (live or dead) carried in a race on board.

The taxable length will in future be officially measured to the 'outer edges' of said marks, a length somewhat greater than the yacht's L.W.L.

An owner should take the greatest care to see for himself that his yacht's taxable length is never increased, and that any alteration to her ballast trim, sanctioned by a recent addition to Rule 15, is never made after 9 p.m. of the day previous to a race.

As regards the sail-area, an owner should hand the sailmaker's certificate to the official measurer and give him every assistance in measuring the yacht's spars, &c.; and, subsequently, should any alteration be made to the sails or spars affecting the yacht's rating, the owner should at once inform the secretary Y.R.A. in writing, and return the certificate if required (Rule 3). In short, an owner is held responsible for the rating of his yacht being absolutely correct.

His next duty is to enter her properly for any race he may wish to compete in. 'Entries shall be made . . . . . *at least* forty-eight hours previous to noon of the race day'—twenty-four hours being added for a Sunday. Clubs have asserted the right to close entries at a longer interval. Owners must therefore note these times for closing the entries, and act accordingly (Rule 5).

Post entries are not provided for in the Y.R.A. rules, and must therefore be considered irregular, whether sanctioned by the other competitors or not.

The long declaration given in the rule is a nuisance, and should be cut out, as there is no reason for mentioning one rule more than another on this declaration. So long, however, as the Y.R.A thinks it necessary, it must be enforced, and owners should help the clubs to do so by carrying it out. As before stated, an entry by telegram (*sent off* before the hour of closing entries) should be followed at once by this written declaration.

An owner should know that if a race be postponed or resailed all the yachts *entered* may start; but the entry is closed to other yachts (Rule 5).

An owner must belong to some 'recognised yacht club' or his entry is void. A hired yacht cannot be entered for any race under Y.R.A. rules (Rule 6).

An owner cannot enter two yachts to compete for one prize, but he can enter one yacht for two simultaneous races (Rule 7).

An owner who has entered his yacht for a prize may sail over the course for half the value of the prize should no other competitor start (Rule 8), and should the race officer not postpone the race for bad weather (Rule 2).

The owner (or a member of a recognised yacht club, to represent him) must be on board during a race, and after the race he should sign a declaration that the yacht has been sailed in strict conformity with the Y.R.A. rules and with the conditions on the programme (Rule 10), and forward same to the race officer at once, or to the secretary if later.

An owner (or his representative) should see that his yacht is supplied in good time with the written or printed instructions for a race (Rule 12).

Should an owner (or his representative) decide to protest against a competitor, or otherwise (removal of a mark, for instance), the protest-flag should be displayed at the proper time, and the protest in writing lodged without delay. Certain time-limits are given in Rule 30.

An owner having flown a protest flag should continue the protest, as it is often unfair to other competitors to withdraw it. Moreover, it may be fairly argued that an owner who observes an infringement

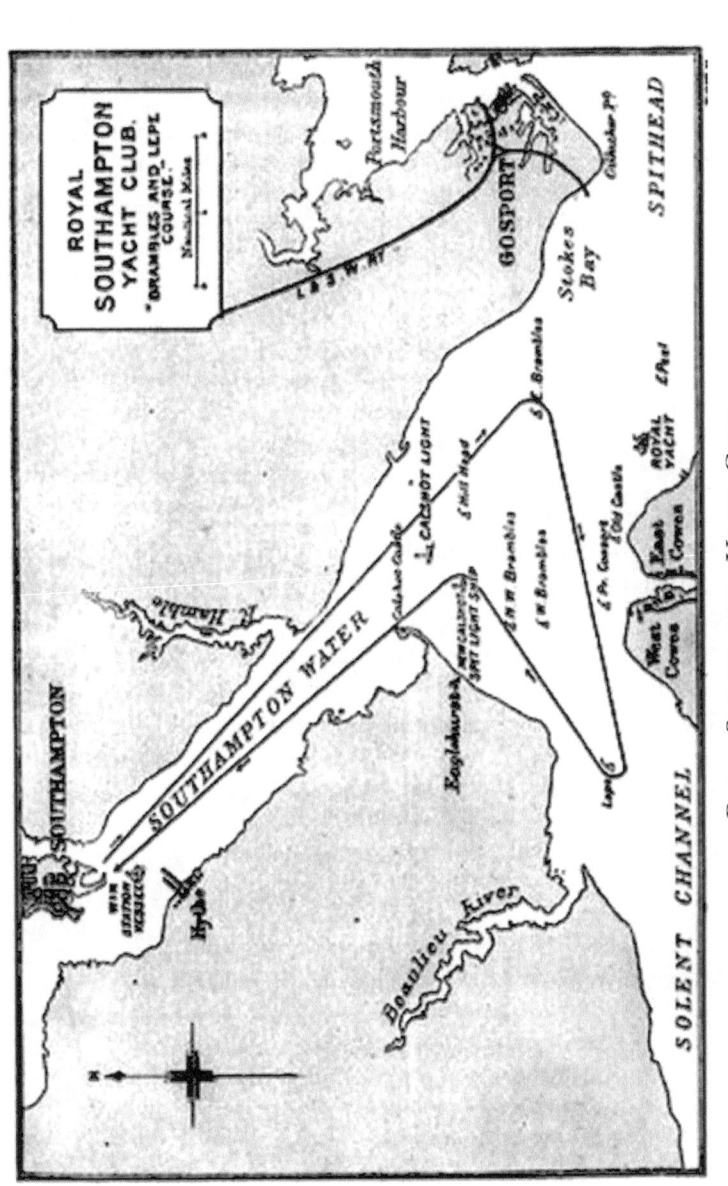

Royal Southampton Yacht Club.
"Brambles and Lepe Course."

of the rules by a competitor, and does not protest as ordered in Rule 30, himself breaks the rules by such omission, and subjects himself to disqualification by the sailing committee. If there were more protests there would soon be far less necessity for them.

Duties of a Sailing Master

A skipper is responsible to the owner, his employer, for the correctness of the yacht's rating, as shown on her certificate; he must also see that she is properly prepared for each race, and properly raced; thus:—

He should not start unless the owner or a qualified representative is on board (Rule 10).

He should have the yacht's colours carried properly (Rule 11).

He should carefully study the written or printed instructions and follow them in every detail (Rule 12).

At the start he should look out for his recall numeral (Rule 12).

He should prevent any paid hand joining or leaving the yacht after the signal to start (Rule 14).

He should be careful to comply with the ballast rule, and see that the dead-weight is not altered after 9 p.m. of the day previous to a race (Rule 15).

He should see that boats and life-buoys are carried in accordance with Rule 16.

He should be specially careful not to infringe any sailing rule between the guns at the start (Rule 17).

If late at the start, he should know that the yacht is not disqualified (Council Y.R.A., 1881).

A good skipper will know Rules 18 to 29 by heart. By Rule 18:—

(a) *A yacht going free keeps clear of a yacht close hauled.*
(b) *A yacht close hauled port keeps clear of a yacht close hauled starboard.*
(c) *When going free on opposite tacks the yacht with wind on port keeps clear.*
(d) *When going free on same tack the windward yacht keeps clear.*
(e) *A yacht with wind aft keeps clear of all others.*

By (b) a yacht on port tack can be disqualified: first, if she strike or be struck by a yacht on starboard tack; secondly, if the latter luff, tack, or bear away to avoid being struck.

When yachts which overlap are rounding a mark or passing an

obstruction, the outside yacht must give room to and keep clear of the inside yachts (Rules 19 and 20).

When yachts approach an obstruction close-hauled, and the leeward yacht cannot tack and clear the windward yacht, the helmsman of the former should 'hail for water' when required, and the two yachts must then tack together (Rule 22).

An overtaking yacht must keep clear of an overtaken yacht, which may luff, but must not bear away out of her course to obstruct the passage on her leeward side (Rule 21).

'A yacht running ashore or foul of a vessel or other obstruction may use her own anchors, boats, warps, &c., to get off,' but must take them on board again, and must receive no assistance except from the crew of a vessel fouled (Rule 23).

A yacht which touches a mark or competitor, or which wrongfully causes another yacht to do so, forfeits all claim to the prize (Rule 24).

A yacht must be propelled by her sails alone after first gun (except as stated in Rule 23). She may anchor, but not slip. She must not make fast to buoys, &c. She must not send an anchor out in a boat (except as stated in Rule 23). Any sounding must be done with lead and line alone (Rules 25, 26, and 27).

Yachts racing at night must carry lights by Board of Trade rules (Rule 28).

When accidents occur, competing yachts must help to save life (Rule 29).

A skipper should also remember that, 'should a flagrant breach of the racing rules be proved' against him, 'he may be disqualified by the Council,' for any stated period, 'from sailing in any race held under the Y.R.A. rules' (Rule 32).

Duties of the Official Measurer

An official measurer should be prepared to measure a yacht promptly at short notice. Consequently no person should accept the post whose time is much engaged in other business or pursuits.

The measurement of a racing-yacht's *sails* is left very much in the hands of the sailmakers. The only check usually applied is the measurement of the spars on which the sails are set. The secretary of the Y.R.A. is then able to check the accuracy of the sailmaker's measurements as recorded on a 'sailmaker's certificate,' which is guarded afterwards by the secretary, Y.R.A.

For instance, to check a cutter's mainsail, the boom and gaff are measured.

It would occupy too much space to describe the whole of the sail measurements, which are detailed on six or seven pages of the Y.R.A. book of rules—under Rule 3. Let it suffice to say that the actual area of each sail abaft a mast is found, and that the head-sail tax is obtained by the measurement of the fore-triangle; which will be done in 1894 as follows:—

> The perpendicular will be taken from the deck at the foreside of the mast to where the line of the luff of the foremost head-sail when extended cuts such perpendicular, and the base will be taken from foreside of mast to where the line of luff of foremost head-sail cuts the bowsprit, other spar, or hull (General Meeting, Y.R.A., December 6, 1892).

The instructions to the measurer issued by direction of the Council on May 8, 1889, are, briefly, as follows:—

He must not measure a yacht in which he is interested as owner, designer, builder, or otherwise.

The taxable length must be obtained at slack water by measuring the L.O.A. on deck, and deducting the O.H. at stem and stern, found by hanging a lead-line from the bow and taffrail and measuring its distances from the outer edges of the owner's marks on the stem and stern. He must ascertain that the yacht is in correct racing trim, and the crew amidships (mid over-all length) when measuring these overhangs.

Sails, spinnaker gear, tackles, &c., may be put amidships at this time.

He should note and record the position of any movable ballast.

Each measurement should be taken twice, and recorded twice in the book, and a third time if there be material disagreement. The mean should be adopted. (*This is wrong mathematically. The 'mean adopted' should be that of the observations which agree, the one with a 'material disagreement' being cancelled.*)

By a new rule passed on December 6, 1892, 'owners are required to mark the rating length of their yachts at the bow and stern, which marks shall at all times be clear above the surface of the water when the yacht is lying in smooth water in her usual racing trim,' *i.e.* with crew amidships. See previous instructions.

The following matters connected with measurements are contained in Rule 3, and should be remembered:—

Notches cut away from the fair-line of the stem or stern post are not allowed for when the rating length is measured.

The segmental area bounded by the bent yard of a lug or other sail, and its chord, is included in the sail-area.

If the length of the spinnaker boom when shipped in its place square to the keel, and measured from its outer end to the fore-and-aft line of the mast, be greater than the base of the yacht's fore-triangle, it is substituted therefore in calculating the taxed area of head-sails.

The perpendicular for same triangle has already been referred to.

A measurer should send his measurements to the secretary, Y.R.A., by the first post in order that the owner may receive his yacht's certificate of rating as soon as possible.

At present the regulations on measurements are divided, some being placed in Rule 3, and some in the printed instructions to measurers. It would be far better to combine them into one appendix, which measurers, builders, designers, and owners alike could then refer to, and note precisely how matters should be arranged. Rule 3 should simply describe the rule for rating racing yachts and the Y.R.A. certificate of rating.

The remarks on the Y.R.A. rules end here, but the writer has been requested to include in this chapter a short examination of the various Rating Rules of different nationalities.

Part 2. The Rating Rules

Extract from Letter to the Field in 1892.—

With shame I confess that the problems and calculations, the combinations of straight and crooked lines, with large and small numerals and Latin and Greek letters, the mathematical contortions and algebraic hieroglyphics ... are meaningless to my uncultured eyes. They are fascinating; I admire their beauty, and can well understand that inventing rules for rating must be a most charming pursuit for intellectual yachtsmen....

Dunraven.

An attempt will be made to treat the subject as simply as possible, so that anyone who knows a little arithmetic may follow it.

The following 'hieroglyphics' will be used:—

B. ......Beam
D. ......Draught
F. ......Freeboard
G. ......Girth
L. ......Length
L.O.A. Length over all
L.O.M. Length between official marks
L.W.L. Length on W.L.
M. ......Area of immersed mid-section
M.S. ...Mid section
R. ......Rating, whether Y.R.A., or corrected length, or other
S. ......Sail area
T. ......Tonnage
U.Y.F. Union des Yachts Français
W. ......Weight of yacht complete in English tons dead weight same as her displacement
W.L. ....Water level
Y.R.A. Yacht Racing Association

If the subject of rating were treated historically, it would be necessary to begin with the old tonnage rules; but we live in the present, and the more important of the existing rules will therefore be examined first. The old tonnage rules will more conveniently be described at the end of the chapter, with existing tonnage rules.

England and America have used rating rules for some years, and France determined to do the same in October 1892.

The efficiency of a sailing yacht can be calculated very similarly to that of a steam yacht, the sails being the motor in one, the engines in the other. But we know that the efficiency of a steamer should vary directly as her indicated horse-power, and inversely as her displacement. The same idea should apply to sailing yachts. It is, in fact, almost impossible to rate a sailing yacht satisfactorily without taking into account both her sail-area and her displacement—or something very closely allied with the latter.

A length and sail-area rule proposed by Mr. Dixon Kemp in 1880 was adopted in 1883 for second-class racing, and in 1886 this alternative rule was adopted as the sole rule. It is—

English $R = L \times S \div 6,000$ (I.)

This important step was taken after a careful and exhaustive inquiry conducted by a special committee appointed by the Council, Y.R.A., and presided over by Sir William Forwood. The committee took the evidence of our most noted yacht architects, and finally reported in favour of Rule (I.), and of the present classification (except 2½ rating, which was afterwards added by the Council). The report met with general approval; the Y.R.A. put its seal upon it, and gave it a tenure of seven years; subject, however, to General Rule 12, by which any change at any time can be made by the requisite majorities.

The tonnage time scale in use before 1886 was altered to agree with the new rating, which cannot be said to represent anything but what it really is—*viz.* the product of a yacht's taxable length and her sail-area.

The classification and the divisor do not alter the rule one iota. They are purely arbitrary, as was very clearly stated in an excellent letter by Mr. G. B. Thompson, published in the *Field* of December 17, 1892. He said very truly that the 5-rating class is in reality the 30,000 class, and the 10-rating class is the 60,000 class. If the divisor 6,000 be altered alone, the result is precisely the same as altering the rating itself in like ratio, and in the same direction. Thus (R. × divisor) and (L. × S.) must each equal 120,000 in the 20-R. class, and must each equal 240,000 in the 40-R. class, and so on. In short, the Y.R.A. rule may be regarded thuswise:—In each class L. × S. = a constant, for boats at the top of the class.

By a recent decision in general meeting, Y.R.A., December 6, 1892, L. will in future be measured between the outer edges of the official marks, which must be affixed by the owner and always show clear above W.L. when a yacht lies in smooth water in racing trim.

L., therefore, is no longer L.W.L., but L.O.M. (length by owner's marks), rather longer than L.W.L.

By Rule 3, Y.R.A., in calculating a yacht's R., a fraction of or exceeding 0.01 counts as 1.0 in classes exceeding 10 R.; but in classes exceeding 1.0 R. and not exceeding 10 R., a fraction less than 0.1 counts as 0.1; and in classes not exceeding 1.0 R. fractions from 0.01 to 0.99 inclusive count for their value.

Example: 'Dacia's' certificate, June 1892, recorded S. = 887.6 and L. = 33.83 and R. = 5.00. But her S. × L. ÷ 6,000 = 5.005 and 0.005 is 'a fraction smaller than 0.1'; consequently, by the wording of Rule 3, her R. = 5.01, and she was over-rating; but the secretary, Y.R.A., when questioned, stated that the 'Y.R.A. only recognises two places of decimals,' and words to this effect were added to Rule 3 at the general meeting February 22, 1893.

The Time Allowance

The time scale for differences of R. under Rule 1. was based on the conception that a racing yacht's 'capability for speed varies as the fifth root of the rating,' the argument leading to this being that—

speed varies as $\sqrt{L}$ (1)
and that sail varies as $L\sqrt{B}$ (2)
and by the rating rule, R varies as $S \times L$
it therefore follows from (2) that R varies as $L^2\sqrt{B}$
and, assuming that B varies as L   (3)
it follows that R varies as $L^2\sqrt{L}$ or $L^{5/2}$
   therefore ... L varies as $R^{2/5}$
Hence, by (1), speed varies as $\sqrt{R^{2/5}}$ or $^{[5]}\sqrt{R}$.—Q.E.D.

The Y.R.A. time scale therefore rests not only on the two assumptions (1) and (2) mentioned in the book, but on the further assumption (3), which we know to be incorrect.

However, the 5th root of R. gives a time scale which is found to act fairly well in practice, and this being so, the theory of the time curve is a matter of minor importance.

At first (1886 and 1887) the adoption of the unrestricted rule met with some opposition, especially in the small classes, where a few of the most experienced yachtsmen advocated restrictions in L.W.L. or L.O.A., and in mainsail area. But the majority determined, and rightly, to give the rule free scope; and the results on the whole have been highly satisfactory, fine seaworthy vessels, driven by a small sail-area at great speed, having been produced in the large classes. The evolution in the small classes has been more rapid, and in 1892 some rather undesirable types were prize-winners, and yachtsmen who wished to protect themselves against similar vessels in the large classes induced the Y.R.A. to appoint a special committee to consider whether the unrestricted and unaltered rule should be continued beyond the seven-years period, terminating in 1893.

This committee, under the presidency of Sir George Lampson, obtained the opinions of our leading designers, as was done in 1886, and the designers themselves met in conference twice, and jointly addressed two letters to the Rule Committee in which they finally recommended the adoption of the Seawanhaka rule for rating racing yachts and a classification of corrected lengths suitable for our existing racing fleet; also other details, the most important being a proposal to tax overhang above the W.L. and cut away keels below it.

The Rule Committee adopted the recommendation as to change of rating rule, but proposed a modification whereby the British rating and time scale could be retained.

When this report was brought before the Council it was upset, some of the committee themselves voting against their own report.

But the action of the Council has since been justified by the production of several splendid specimens of yacht architecture to race under the Y.R.A. rule of rating.

The elements of the fastest types which have developed in small yachts under the rule can be studied in the tables given in the chapter on Racing in the Solent Classes.

One of our ablest designers has consistently advocated the introduction of a tax on beam into the formula. He did so in 1886, and again in 1892, when he proposed to tax draught also.

Unfortunately the mathematics of the rule make it difficult, if not impossible, to do so, because the blow on L. is lessened when it is shared by other quantities.

Thus by Mr. Watson's modification of the rating rule, proposed in October 1892, *viz*.

$$\text{English } R = (2L + 2B + D) \times S \div \{\text{constant, say } 17{,}000\} \qquad \text{(II.)}$$

Doreen is of smaller rating, although both longer and more beamy than *Decima*. They are of the same rating for racing by the Y.R.A. rule. Mr. Watson's formula would therefore encourage even greater length of hull than the Y.R.A. rule. No such difficulty is encountered by the introduction of such taxes into the Seawanhaka rule, where the plus sign replaces the multiplying sign used by us. This rule was adopted by the American Yacht Club of its name in 1882, the form being

$$\text{American } R = (L + \sqrt{S}) \div 2 \qquad \text{(III.)}$$

The New York Yacht Club has raced for a number of years under a similar rule for time allowance,[1] *viz*.

$$\text{American } R = (2L + \sqrt{S}) \div 3 \qquad \text{(IV.)}$$

and just as the Y.R.A. rule can take the form

$$L \times S = \text{constant in any class,}$$

so these rules can take the forms

$$L + \sqrt{S} = \text{constant, in any class} \qquad \text{III.}$$
$$2L + \sqrt{S} = \text{constant, in any class} \qquad \text{IV.}$$

It then becomes evident that any sacrifice of S. to obtain greater L. under Rule IV. is only half as effective as the same process under Rule

---

1. But not for classification, which latter has been simply the length of hull on water-line. Hence, yachts built for the same class have varied much in their sail-area; *Vigilant* and *Valkyrie* for instance.

III. Conversely, any sacrifice of L. to obtain more S. is twice as effective under Rule IV. as under Rule III.

Again, as comparisons between L. and S. must be brought to some common measure, the Y.R.A. form ... L. × S. = constant in any class, may be read L. × √S. × √S. = constant, and it then becomes clear that any sacrifice of S. to get L. is twice as effective as in Rule III., and four times as effective as in Rule IV.; and conversely, that any sacrifice of L. to get more S. is half as effective as in Rule III., and one-fourth as effective as in Rule IV.

The author of the Y.R.A. rule has pointed out that it can be converted into the American form of 'corrected length,' thus:—

$$\text{American R} = \sqrt[3]{L \times S} \qquad (V.)$$

See his second edition of 'Yacht Architecture.' The sail curve is precisely the same as that from the Y.R.A. rule.

An examination of this form of the Y.R.A. rule is interesting. By cubing V, and comparing it with I., it will be seen that six thousand times the English rating equals the cube of the American rating derived from formula V.

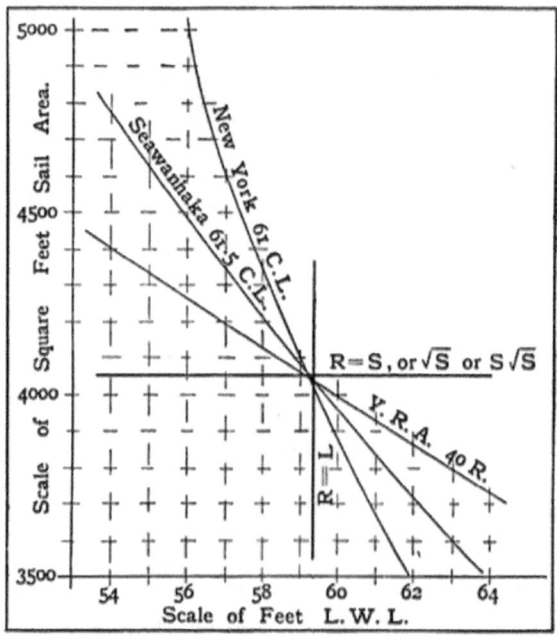

DIAGRAM OF SAIL CURVES, SHOWING THE RELATION OF SAIL TO L.W.L. IN THE Y.R.A., NEW YORK, AND SEAWANHAKA RULES. 40-RATING CLASS.

When English and American rules are examined diagraphically, the sail-curves take three positions that differ considerably in their steepness—the Y.R.A. rule giving a curve nearest to the horizontal which indicates R. = S. ÷ constant, proposed by Mr. Richardson in 1886 (or R. = $\sqrt{S}$ ÷ constant if expressed in American measure; or R. = S. $\sqrt{S}$ divided by a constant if expressed in English measure); and the New York rule taking a position nearest to the vertical denoting R. = L., under which the Solent Length Classes used to sail.

The Seawanhaka rule gives an intermediate curve—perhaps the 'happy medium.'

The curves have been plotted for yachts of 40-rating by our rule, and the following table gives the actual numbers:—

L.W.L.	40-raters, Y.R.A. Rule	Sail-area allowed to	
		61·5 Corrected L. Seawanhaka Rule	61 Corrected L. New York Rule
ft.	ft.	ft.	ft.
54	4,444	4,761	—
56	4,286	4,489	5,041
58	4,139	4,225	—
59	4,068	4,096	4,096
60	4,000	3,969	—
62	3,871	3,721	3,481
64	3,750	3,481	—

The Turning-point of Maximum Efficiency, or best Length

Each L. and S. rule for rating racing yachts must have a turning-point, or best length, in each class for winning prizes in a given climate. It depends far more upon the average wind-pressure during the racing season than on any assumed connection between L. and $\sqrt{S}$. It will vary on different days, and for different seasons, and for different localities. The average wind-force is stronger on the Solent than on the Clyde, and stronger at Rothesay than at Sandy Hook. But type is another matter. Type is governed by the racing rule, and differences of climate have very little effect upon it. The best proportional length also varies in different classes, the water being rougher and the wind harder, comparatively speaking, on small than on large yachts, thus causing the former to develop L. and sacrifice S. to the utmost. Under the tonnage rules it is true that the small yachts carried the larger comparative sail-plan, but this was due to other causes, such as their greater comparative draught and ballast.

The *best length* under L. and S. rules also varies with the rating rule, those rules having sail-curves nearest to the line R. = S. developing the greatest length, and those having sail-curves nearest to the line R. = L. developing the greatest sail.

Still another factor governs the *best length* in any class, *viz.* lightness of construction; and this depends on four other factors: cost, design, workmanship, and strength of materials.

We are therefore met by quite a crowd of considerations when endeavouring to determine *best length*; but in comparing the rating rules we can eliminate many of them by making a few assumptions and reasoning therefrom.

First, assume that a new boat is built with the lightest possible hull consistent with strength, and of the best possible design for the 40-R. class 1894, and that her L.=62 ft., therefore S=3,871. (See preceding table.)

Second, assume that a longer boat and a shorter boat equally well built and designed are tried and are beaten, and that 62 ft. is then acknowledged to be *best length* for 40-ratings in our climate.

Third, assume that the class is converted in 1895 into one rated at 61.5 American R., *Queen Mab* being thereby placed at the top of the class by the Seawanhaka rule without alteration. The 62-ft. yacht, however, must clip to 3,721, or 150 off her S. as a 40-rater.

But the shorter boat, say a *Queen Mab* 59 ft. L.W.L., which we assumed to fail when racing under our rule, could now *add* 30 ft. and sail against the crack 62-footer with an advantage of no less than 180 sq. ft. of canvas.

Evidently, the best length under our rule being 62, the best length under the American rule is something less; how much less being only determined by trial, and depending on the numerous factors before mentioned. Moreover, an arbitrary limit of L.W.L. is thus shown to be less necessary under the American rule than under ours; and with L. so greatly developed in our racers at the present time, it may be that we have already gone beyond the best length for the American rule, especially in the small classes. This was carefully pointed out by the present writer in two letters to 'Land and Water,' October 5 and 9, 1892. Mr. R. E. Froude also stated the case very clearly in the 'Field,' December 31, 1892; but it is very difficult to convince the defenders of the Y.R.A. rule that any other rule is superior.

Mr. Dixon Kemp, in his excellent work on 'Yacht Architecture,' says (p. 15, 2nd edition) in comparing rules I., III., IV.: 'Of these rules, that of the Y.R.A. admits of the employment of the greatest length for any given rating'; and the length referred to was evidently *best length* in a given climate.

The Seawanhaka rule is therefore superior to ours if excessive length be feared; and being a plus formula, it lends itself readily to the adoption of any desired tax on other linear dimensions.

For instance, Mr. Watson's proposal (II.) might be put into the plus form, thus:—

$$\text{American R} = (2L + 2B + D + \sqrt{S}) \div 3.8 \qquad \text{(VI.)}$$

This shows the value of a plus rule over a multiplying rule and the value is not lost when a plus rule is converted into an English rating rule by cubing the former and dividing by a constant. Thus, the recent Rule Committee proposed to convert the Seawanhaka rule into an English rating rule by cubing it and dividing by 6,000, the result being:

$$\text{English R} = (L + \sqrt{S})^3 \div \text{constant, say } 48{,}000 \qquad \text{(VII.)}$$

The variable within brackets in VI. can be cubed and divided by a constant in a similar manner. But the cubic forms of the 'plus' rules are clumsy, and seem difficult to those who cannot compute by logarithms. No real advantage is gained by adhering to the English rating and time scale and classification. In fact, the American time scale is simpler. If, therefore, a 'plus form' of rating be ever adopted, it would be much better to adopt 'corrected length' as the rating, together with the American time scale. The classification could, of course, be chosen in such a manner that our own racing yachts would be at the top of the classes without any important alterations.

Another rule was proposed in a leading article of the *Field* on October 15, 1892. It is:—

$$\text{English R} = L^2 \sqrt{S} \div \text{constant, say } 6{,}000 \qquad \text{(VIII.)}$$

(p. 177) It gives a sail-curve nearly parallel to the one produced by the New York rule, and may almost be regarded as that rule dressed in Y.R.A. uniform; but the advantages of a plus rule are lost, whereas in the conversion of the Seawanhaka rule proposed by the Y.R.A. Committee 1892 they are retained.

Similarly, the Y.R.A. rule—varying as $\sqrt[3]{L.S.}$ (see V.), or as $\sqrt[3]{L.} \times \sqrt{S.} \times \sqrt{S.}$—may be considered as equivalent to the plus formula $L + 2\sqrt{S.} \div$ constant, and the English and American rules may therefore be regarded to vary as follows:

	In linear measure
New York as	$2L + \sqrt{S}$
Seawanhaka as	$L + \sqrt{S}$
Y.R.A. as	$L + 2\sqrt{S}$

Mr. Herreshoff has recently proposed a rule of rating based on $L\sqrt{S}$, which is an area, but the cube root of tonnage is placed in the divisor; and this being linear, it converts the rating into linear measure, an area divided by a line being a line. The result being linear, it is translatable into American rating and time allowance.

Mr. Herreshoff's proposed rule is:—

$$\text{American } R = (L\sqrt{S} / \sqrt[3]{T}) \div \text{constant, say 15} \qquad (IX.)$$

A critique on this rule by the editor of the *Field*, December 17, 1892, suggests that the cube root of 100 T. should be taken, as there are 100 cubic feet in a registered ton. This is unnecessary. So long as S. is superficial, and T. cubic, the $\sqrt{S}$ and the $\sqrt[3]{T}$ will be linear; and a constant can be selected which will convert the quotient resulting from the rule into corrected feet or inches, or metres, as required for the linear rating adopted.

Mr. Herreshoff's rule when tested is not encouraging; 'Doreen's' length so corrected being 2½ *per cent.* smaller than *Decima's*. The rule evidently does not encourage that compactness of hull-dimension which Mr. Watson considers desirable. It also appears to put a premium on abnormal freeboard, so as to increase T. by means of a large body over the water-level.

This was pointed out by the editor of the *Field*, December 24, 1892, and an improved rule suggested in which displacement was used as a divisor in place of tonnage. W. the total weight of yacht in English tons dead weight is of course her displacement, and the rule proposed may be written:—

$$\text{English } R = L^2 S / \sqrt[3]{W} + 10{,}000 \qquad (X)$$

So far as L. and S. are concerned this rule would produce a similar sail-curve to the Y.R.A. rule (see diagram); but the divisor would encourage a large powerful hull, and the rule would therefore produce a shorter type with more sail than now exists in English racers. The practical difficulty of discovering W., either by measurement or by some system of weighing the yacht complete, has to be considered in connection with this rule.

The most important point to be noted about these rules (IX. and X.) is the fact that Mr. Herreshoff and Mr. Dixon Kemp proposed them—showing that two of the leading experts consider it necessary to encourage greater displacement by means of the rating rules. The question, therefore, arises whether the desired result cannot be effected in a less objectionable manner; and it appears to the writer that dividing the present Y.R.A. rule by some area proportional to that of the immersed mid-section would have the desired effect, and would avoid the difficulties already mentioned. The actual area of M.S. cannot be found without encroaching on the secrets of a yacht's design; but M. the area of immersed mid-section can be easily found if measured internally, and the Y.R.A. rule may take the form:—

$$\text{American R} = L S/M \div \text{constant (say 72)} \qquad (XI)$$

L.S. being cubic, and the variable divisor M. being superficial, the quotient is linear, and a constant divisor can be chosen which will convert the result into American rating, which is expressed in 'corrected' feet.

The general tendencies of the Y.R.A. rule would be modified by the introduction of M. as proposed in XI., a large immersed M.S. being encouraged, without the necessity of employing a deep narrow body, as may be seen on the following table, where *Bedouin* figures out very well owing to her large but not deep immersed M.S. The author claims with some confidence that this modified rule presents the best solution of the problem yet suggested. But there is really no problem requiring solution at present. So long as yachts like *Britannia* and *Satanita* are built for racing under the Y.R.A. existing rule of rating, grumblers will not command an audience. In the event, however, of yachts like *Pilgrim* or *Jubilee* winning in our waters a change of some sort will be required.

The measurement of M. can be easily done in a few minutes, with yacht afloat, as described on p. 87 of the *Field*, January 21, 1893.

The Seawanhaka rule (III.) can be treated similarly, the divisor 2 being thereby avoided. It becomes

$$\text{American R} = L + \sqrt{S} - \sqrt{72M} \qquad (XII.)$$

The action of these rules may be seen from the table on p. 180; column headed XI. giving the rating under the modified Y.R.A. rule, and column headed XII. giving the rating under the modified Seawanhaka rule. Each result is in 'corrected length.'

The dimensions in above were obtained from the drawings in Dixon Kemp's *Yacht Architecture*, 2nd ed., except *Decima's* and *Doreen's*, which were kindly given by their designers.

It will be found on trial that 72 M. is approximately equal to the mean value of S. and L^2 in successful yachts.

The New French Rule

On November 5, 1892, it was announced in the *Field* that the *Union des Yachts Français* had decided to adopt a hull- and sail-area rating, it being considered by the 'active element in French yacht racing' that 'the type .... produced by the French length and girth rule is inferior to the type produced by the British and American rules .... British yachts having defeated those of France, although handicapped by the French rule of rating.' The conclusion was scarcely a logical sequence from the premises. It should have been that French racing yachts were not the correct evolution of the French rule of rating. But we are now concerned with the new French rule (proposed by M. Godinet) in which sail is an important factor.

In its simplest form, it is:—

$$\text{English R} = (4L - G) \, G \, \sqrt{S} \div 520 \qquad \text{(XIII.)}$$

G. being the greatest girth from top of deck planking port, round keel to ditto starboard, plus extreme beam. Each of the three factors L. G. $\sqrt{S}$. being linear (metric measure) the result is given in cubic form, and is converted into English rating by the divisor selected, and the Y.R.A. time scale has been adopted by the *Union des Yachts Français*.

The editor of the *Field* considers that 'the rule is calculated to produce a poor kind of vessel for match sailing or anything else'; but it is hazardous to prophesy the evolution of any rule, more especially one which taxes L., B., D., bilge, and S. No doubt the tax on D. is doubtful policy, and it seems very unnecessary when we consider the small depth of water in many French harbours, which is the most efficient check on D. it is possible to conceive for large yachts, and in the small classes D. gives grip and power to windward, and seaworthiness.

A careful analysis of the rule by the writer leads him to believe that the conclusion arrived at by the editor of the *Field* is correct. It certainly appears that the rule has a sail-curve nearly as steep as the New York rule, which has been abandoned because it encouraged such large sail-plans. For this reason, therefore, if for no other, the new French rule seems to be inferior to the Y.R.A. and the Seawanhaka

Name of yacht	L	S	√S	M	XI.	XII.
Genesta	81·0	7,643	101·40	91·27	94·21	87·39
Volunteer	85·9	10,270	87·43	105·42	100·24	93·30
Chiquita	45·5	2,636	51·36	31·32	53·20	49·35
Ghost	46·5	2,577	50·77	34·60	48·10	47·38
Minerva	40·0	2,700	52·00	29·73	50·39	46·00
Dis	36·0	1,658	40·71	22·37	36·23	36·00
Decima	35·67	1,679	40·94	22·17	37·23	36·71
Doreen	38·05	1,572	39·62	21·67	38·34	38·23
Oread	28·2	1,063	32·60	13·33	31·25	29·82
Quinque	33·0	900	30·00	13·33	30·93	32·02
Valentine	29·8	996	31·56	14·47	28·50	29·08
Bedouin	30·0	1,000	31·62	14·96	28·00	28·92
Madcap	21·0	714	26·72	9·97	20·89	20·97
Lady Nan	23·0	653	25·55	8·63	24·16	23·63
Dolphin	25·7	581	24·10	8·27	25·07	25·41

rules. A good letter on the subject of girth, by one of our leading designers, was published in the *Yachtsman*, September 8, 1892.

On the whole, English yachtsmen would probably feel very disinclined to adopt the new French rule for British yacht-racing.

This concludes the examination of the more important national rules in which sail-area and some hull dimension or dimensions are combined in the formula for the rating, whether the result be cubic, linear, or otherwise.

We therefore now pass to the simple sail-area rule proposed by Mr. Richardson in 1886, *viz*.

$$R = S \div 100 \quad \text{(XIV.) A}$$

The rating so obtained being neither cubic nor linear, but superficial, difficulties as regards time scale arose, and neither Mr. Richardson nor the Council appeared to notice that the rule could easily be made linear by putting it in the form

$$\text{American } R = \sqrt{S} \quad \text{(XIV.) B}$$

when American rating and time scale could have been adopted. Also that it might have been rendered

$$\text{English } R = S \sqrt{S} \div \text{constant} \quad \text{(XIV.) C}$$

which is the cubic form, suitable for the Y.R.A. rating and time allowance.

The graphic result in the sail-diagram is the same in each case, viz. a horizontal line for any given class, the limit for each class being one of sail-area alone.

It was not adopted because the Council considered that the type evolved from it would be one of excessive length and small displacement; and our experience with the Y.R.A. rule, which approaches it more nearly than any other hull- and sail-area rule, has shown that this estimate was correct.

We will now examine a few of the rules which rate yachts entirely by hull-measurement. The simplest of the kind is the pure length rule, used for some years on the Solent for racing small yachts up to 30 ft. of L. *See* chapter on Solent Racing.

$$\text{American } R = L \qquad\qquad (XV.) \text{ A}$$

Some trouble was taken in 1884 to produce a special time scale for this formula. It was quite unnecessary, because the time scale for tonnage (see XVIII.) then in use could have been employed, (XV.) A being modified to

$$R = L^3 \div \text{constant} \qquad\qquad (XV.) \text{ B}$$

and by adjusting the constant this form of the length rule can be adapted to the time scale of *any* cubic rule. Thus, the divisor 5,000 adapts it to the Y.R.A. time scale for *rating*.

The type resulting from the length rule was, of course, a very fast and powerful boat for its L., carrying an enormous sail-spread—somewhat costly to build and race.

Our grandfathers raced their yachts under the old tonnage rule,

$$\text{Tonnage } R = L \times B \times H \div 96 \qquad\qquad (XVI.)$$

H. being depth of hull to deck beam, and L. being measured in various ways at different times. After 1854 it was taken on deck from stem-head to sternpost, and certain deductions made for rake. Eventually the Thames Rule,

$$(L - B) \times B \times \tfrac{1}{2}B \div 94 \text{ or } B^2(L - B) \div 188 \qquad\qquad (XVII.)$$

N.B.—G is only approximately correct. It is measured in the French way was evolved and adopted by the Y.R.A. in 1876. And in 1878 it was decided to measure L. on the water-line. In 1880 the Y.R.A. altered the rule to

The Rating Rules and Proposals

Date	No. in text	Name of rule or proposal		Rule or proposal		Examples	
		Cubic rules		Variable+constant		Decima	Doreen
1886 ?	I.	Y.R.A. rule (Dixon Kemp)		L S	÷ 6,000	9·98	9·96
1892	II.	Ditto modified (Watson)		(2 L + 2 B + D) S	÷ 17,000	10·06	9·89
1892	VIII.	New York modified (Dixon Kemp)		$L^2 \sqrt{S}$	+ 6,000	8·69	9·56
1892	X.	Y.R.A. modified (Dixon Kemp)		$\dfrac{L^2 S}{\sqrt[3]{W}}$	÷ 10,000	8·80	?
1892	VII.	Seawanhaka modified Y.R.A. Committee's rule		$(L + \sqrt{S})^3$	÷ 48,000	9·39	9·75
1892	XIII.	U.Y.F. rule (Godinet)		$G (4 L - G) \sqrt{S}$	÷ 520	8·57	9·02
1892 ?	XIX.	Old French rule		$G^2 (2 L - B)$	+ 176	12·58	13·53
1876 ?	XVI.	Old English tonnage rule		L B H	÷ 96	?	10·60
1876–80	XVII.	Thames tonnage rule		$B^2 (L - B)$	÷ 188	15·9	?
1880–86	XVIII.	Y.R.A. tonnage rule		$B (L + B)^2$	+ 1,730	13·8	17·9
	XIV. c	Richardson's rule, cubic form		$S \sqrt{S}$	÷ 6,000	9·97	15·7
	XV. B	Length rule, cubic form		L^3	÷ 5,000	9·08	11·01

183

The Rating Rules and Proposals—continued

Date	No. in text	Name of rule or proposal		Rule or proposal		Examples	
		Linear rules		Variable ÷ constant		Decima	Doreen
1882 ?	III.	Seawanhaka rule		$L + \sqrt{S}$	÷ 2	38·33	38·82
?	IV.	New York rule		$2L + \sqrt{S}$	÷ 3	37·45	38·57
?	V.	Y.R.A. Rule (Dixon Kemp)		$\sqrt{LS}$	÷ 1	39·12	39·11
1893	XI.	Y.R.A. modified (Thalassa)		$\dfrac{LS}{M}$	÷ 72	37·23	38·34
1893	XII.	Seawanhaka ditto (Thalassa)		$L + \sqrt{S} - \sqrt{72\,M}$	÷ 1	36·71	38·23
1893	IX.	Herreshoff's new rule		$\dfrac{L\sqrt{S}}{\sqrt{T}}$	÷ 15	38·69	37·01
1892	VI.	Watson's rule, linear form		$2L + 2B + D + \sqrt{S}$	÷ 3·8	37·60	38·58
? –86	XV. A	Length rule		L	÷ 1	35·65	38·05
1886	XIV. B	Richardson's rule, linear form		$\sqrt{S}$	÷ 1	41·00	39·60

The following Dimensions were used in the Examples

	L	L'	S	$\sqrt{S}$	B	D	G	M	W tons
Decima	35·67	1272	1679	41·0	11·0	8·5	·36	22·2	14·3
Doreen	38·05	1448	1572	39·6	11·2	8·5	·36	21·7	?

N.B.—G is only approximately correct. It is measured in the French way

$$\text{English } T = B(L + B)^2 \div 1730 \qquad \text{(XVIII.)}$$

The type evolved, as might have been anticipated, had a long, narrow, heavily ballasted, deep-bodied, wall-sided hull, possessing little beauty, small *initial* stability, and no great speed, considering the sail-area employed to drive it. There was little scope for improvement, and the energies of our best designers were directed to producing yachts which carried large sail-plans on narrow hulls, their L.W.L. often approaching and sometimes exceeding six beams. Nevertheless, this '1730 Rule,' as it is often called, governed first-class racing in British waters from 1880 to 1886.

Another hull-measurement rule is the one used for some time in France, and often called the 'Girth Rule.' In its simplest form, it was:—

$$\text{French } T = G^2(2L - B) \div 176 \qquad \text{(XIX.)}$$

G., the girth, is taken as in Rule XIII. The rule taxes draught heavily, and does not appear to have given satisfaction, or it would not have been changed last October to No. XIII.

Many other hull-measurement rules might be mentioned; in fact, a short time ago the yachting press was full of such proposals; but those who make them must be aware of the general feeling among sportsmen in England, France, and America, *viz.* that sail-area should be taxed in the formula for rating.

Any lengthy discussion on rules which do not conform with this opinion is, therefore, a waste of time and energy, and the hull rules just described have been noticed principally on account of their historical interest.

The rules are numbered consecutively in the order in which they have been examined; the tonnage rules last, although some of them are the most ancient. But it may be convenient for the student to have them grouped somewhat differently and this has been done in the tables shown, which also afford an opportunity to compare two yachts of similar hull-dimensions, but differing in regard to their length and sail-area, except that the product is equal. *Doreen* and *Decima* make an excellent pair for such a comparison, being each 10-rating by the Y.R.A. rule, and of nearly the same beam, draught, girth, and depth of hull, but differing in length and sail-area.

The tendencies of those rules which aim at encouraging larger body, like Mr. Herreshoff's, or larger immersed body, like X., XI., and XII., are shown in the tables shown, and the student is invited to work out some examples for himself to test their action, as the New York committee has reported in favour of some such modification of existing rules.

CHAPTER 8

Yacht's Sailing Boats
By The Earl of Pembroke and Montgomery

'Why in the world do not yachting people make more use of their sailing boats?' I have often thought, while gazing on a bright breezy morning at some great steam yacht, capable of carrying one or more fine sailing boats, and presently observing her owners and their guests, all arrayed in faultless yachting costume, departing for the shore in their steam launch to spend their time pottering about some dull and dirty little seaport town, when they might, some or all of them, be enjoying the most glorious sail, with who knows what possibilities in the way of fishing thrown in. Even landing and putting off to the ship become a pleasure when they are done under sail instead of steam or oars. I have had many an interesting and exhilarating day's sailing which has been made up entirely of trips between the yacht and the shore with passengers, luggage, provisions, telegrams, and what not.

Yet, though in these days large yachts may be numbered by the hundred, and many of them carry fine sailing boats, I can count on the fingers of one hand the vessels I happen to have met which both carry and habitually use a sailing boat for the purposes of cruising, landing, and fishing. It is really very curious; and I can only account for it by supposing that many people who go to sea in large yachts do not know how much amusement there is to be got out of such a boat, and the ease and nicety with which she can be handled. For when there is any wind at all a sailing cutter can land anywhere where it is safe to take a steam launch, and with a little practice it is as easy to take her alongside a ship's ladder as a six-oared gig.

And when a yacht is on a cruise, moving daily from port to port, a sailing cutter takes considerably less time to get ready than a steam launch. Anywhere on the coast she can generally be carried in the davits with her mast stepped and rigged, so that there is nothing to do but to lower the ballast into her and loose the sails, and she is ready to start. Of course there are places and days when the steam launch is of use and the sailing boat is not; but they are not so numerous as one might suppose. One year when, after a severe illness, I spent all the spring and early summer cruising in the Mediterranean, and the autumn on the coast of Scotland, I thought it advisable to take a steam launch as well as my sailing cutter. I found that at the end of this long cruise I had used her just three times. I have never carried one since. It is not advisable on vessels of less than 400 tons (yacht measurement) to carry two such heavy boats. They are not safe in the davits on an ocean voyage, and two of them carried inboard completely block the deck amidships; but a yacht of 500 tons or more can perfectly carry both, if a steam launch is considered necessary.

As for the fun to be got out of her, a good sailing boat simply doubles the pleasure of yachting. It combines the amusement of small yacht sailing with all the advantages and comforts of a large vessel to sail in from port to port. When the anchor goes down, and fires are banked or put out, your fun begins rather than ends. In less than half an hour you are off in your cutter, to sail, to fish, or to explore; perhaps, when you are tired of sailing, to land in some snug, inviting cove, and to feel the fascination of a ramble in strange and beautiful ground; to sit on the hillside and watch the sun go down in glory, and to make your way back to the ship as the rosy light dies out and the purple hills grow black.

And the next day, let us suppose, is a fine one. Sea and sky are of a rapturous blue, and a pleasant summer breeze is blowing in from the sea. The great yachting question of the morning, 'What shall we do today?' is scarcely debated at breakfast at all. It is pre-eminently a day for sailing. The cutter is got ready at once, and you beat out towards the open water. In all probability there are fish to be caught, for you noted a quantity of birds fishing off the mouth of the bay when you steamed in yesterday—but you really hardly care whether there are fish or not, it is so good simply to be alive and sailing the sea on such a day. The sun warms you through in your shirt sleeves, the steady breeze is balmy to feel, and though it is the coast of Scotland you are vaguely reminded of coral islands and trade winds.

As you work out to seaward it becomes evident that you are in a fishy sea, for the foolish confidential little guillemots and razorbills (he that shooteth such knoweth not how to live nor the nature and

WHALES.

object of things) are squeaking and croaking and ducking under water all round. And lo! close ahead appear two whales, not mere black fish (whatever they may be), but great fellows looking 40 feet long on a moderately calm computation, spouting and showing their black backs at intervals. You go as close to them as they will let you and watch with breathless fascination their oily movements so full of lazy strength and sensuous enjoyment; and you call them bottle-noses or finbacks or rorquals according to your individual taste and fancy; for the scientific classification of whales is in an extraordinarily imperfect state, and even the Encyclopaedia, that settler of disputes and averter of quarrels that no yacht should ever be without, will give you but little assistance.

But you must tear yourself away from the whales, for half a mile to windward there you sight a cloud of birds fishing furiously, the gannets swooping and soaring, and then suddenly shutting their wings and dropping in quick succession, *pop, pop, pop*, like bullets into the sea; and a dense mass of gulls flying and swimming, screaming and squattering, and flapping their wings on the surface of the water. How a gull ever gets a living is a wonder; he seems so dainty and hesitating and afraid to commit himself. A gannet will soar, plunge, dive under water, and swallow half a dozen little fish while a gull is apparently making up his mind whether it is worthwhile to risk wetting his feet.

As soon as your boat will fetch, you go about and stand straight for the birds, overhauling meanwhile the 'whiffing' or 'railing' lines that are towing astern, to make sure that there is nothing foul, and that there is no seaweed on your silvery spinners. You are all keen, but not too sanguine, for there is never a certainty of catching fish like this. Sometimes you may sail backwards and forwards till you are sick of it through a mob of feeding seabirds, trying every sort of bait and never getting a ghost of a bite. Either it is herring that they are after, or else it is that the unknown big fish who are hunting up the small fry to the birds from below will not take a bait. You are close now, and there is a noise not unlike that of the parrot-house in the Zoological Gardens. Mackerel is what you hope for; gurnard you will put up with; pollack will not be caught in any numbers so far from the shore. You shake your sails to reduce your pace, and then, filling them again, stand straight in amongst the screaming gulls, and as they reluctantly rise from the water and the little guillemots squatter away and dive, you get a rapid vision of fish shooting about near the top of the water and little tiny silver things rippling its surface and hopping feebly above.

A moment more and the lines tauten: 'Mackerel it is, by Jingo!' and as soon as the lines are out again and no one feels another bite, round goes the boat again, and back through the school. So you go on, sometimes catching them slowly and singly, sometimes two at once as fast as the lines can be got out, until you have several dozen in the bottom of the boat. All of a sudden the fish cease to bite and the birds fly away. They gather again into a new cluster half a mile off, and away you go for it as fast as you can sail, and begin catching fish once more. Once more the fish stop biting, and the birds move off, and you can see no more of them fishing except a very few a long way to windward. It seems a sin to go home on such a day, and it is too early to try for pollack with so bright a sun. But your chart shows you a fishing-bank close to, and you have got a few herrings for bait; so you make for this place, and get the exact spot by the relative bearings of points and islands, and drop your anchor in twenty fathoms.

Hardly are the lines down before it becomes evident that you are in the right place. Whiting, haddock, and gurnard come up with rapidity, varied by an occasional cod, skate, or bream. You have caught quite a lot before the dog-fish set in. Then it is all over. First comes one, then another, and then nothing else. In vain you despatch them with knives and throw their bleeding corpses back into the sea to terrify the rest. Dogfish have no nerves that you can work upon in this way. The sight and smell of their murdered relations and friends only whet their appetites and make them the more greedy. You give it up in despair, haul your anchor up, and get under sail once more.

It is now late in the afternoon. The day has changed for the worse—

weather changes quick in these latitudes—and looks rather wild and windy, with promise of more to come before long. But your port is to leeward, so you need not be anxious, and you make up your minds to fish for pollack round the headlands and the islands at the mouth of the bay; for just before sundown is the best time of all, especially if it is about half flood. You take a reef down in both sails to make the boat slower and easier to handle, for you do not want to have to devote all your attention to keeping her right side up when you are fishing for pollack close in to the rocks.

The tack is triced up so as to let the steerer see under it; a crutch is shipped on each side of the boat, and a couple of oars are cleared and made ready for instant use if required. One man stands up in the bows to look out for rocks, and also to attend to the peak halliards when called upon; two others handle the lines on which a red or a white india-rubber sand-eel has been substituted for the spinners; while the steerer takes tiller in one hand and mainsheet in the other, and concentrates all his faculties on regulating the pace of the boat, and going as near as he can to the rocks without incurring shipwreck or fouling the lines.

In this order you coast slowly along about twenty yards from the steep cliffs, running out occasionally to avoid reefs and shoal places, the steerer keeping the speed to something under three knots an hour by slacking the mainsheet and spilling the sail when the wind is abeam, and hauling it right in when it is aft, occasionally dropping the peak as well. Every now and then, generally off a point, you catch

THE SWOOP OF THE GANNET.

a fish, and when you do you go about to see if there are more in the same place. But fish seem scarce, and the sport is rather slow until you sail through a narrow channel between two islands. Then in a moment there is a heavy fish on each line, and no sooner are they hauled on board and the lines thrown out again than the same thing happens. You have struck fish at last in earnest.

While the hooks are being disengaged up goes the peak, and you stand back close-hauled through the narrow channel. Backwards and forwards you go, again and again, with varying luck. Now you haul in two at a time, now you give a groan of dismay as a monster gets off as you are in the act of swinging him in. Sometimes the boat will not go fast enough to make the fish bite, and there is agony of mind; sometimes it *will* go too fast. But on the whole the fishing is fast and furious, and you are all wild with excitement; and then—snap goes a snooding with a particularly big fish, and you must fish with one line till the other is refitted. The wind heads the boat off standing back through the channel this time; the centreboard hits a rock and bumps up into its case; there is no harm done, but alas! the remaining line gets foul of the rock before it can be shortened up, and snaps above the lead, and there is nothing for it but to stand off until the tackle is repaired; the steersman, who has to look on, grinding his teeth with impatience as the precious moments slip away.

But, though minutes seem hours, you are soon at work again, and by the time that darkness brings the sport to an end you have caught some four dozen fine pollack, the larger ones 9 lb. or 10 lb. apiece. And you sail home full of that sense of physical well-being and mental contentment that comes of a long day spent in pure air, healthy enjoyment, and freedom from care. And, somehow, it is not on days like these that one looks back with the keenest sense of having wasted time.

Or imagine a morning of quite another sort. The sky is gloomy; the sun is quite invisible; it is raining occasionally, and a strong searching wind is blowing. The seas are running up in magnificent white masses on the islands outside the mouth of the loch. It is too cold to sit on deck; indeed it seems cold everywhere on board. It is impossible to do anything with the yacht, for you want to go south, and it is evidently blowing a gale outside from the south-west. It is the sort of day on which, if you had no boat, and there was nothing to do on shore, you would sit shivering most of the time below, trying to read, thinking what a miserable business yachting is in bad weather, and feeling ill from defective circulation. But if you have a good boat such a day has positive charms.

You and your boating pal look in each other's eyes and say, almost in a breath, 'Let's beat out round the islands and see what the sea is like.' Indeed you almost persuade yourselves that it is a duty to do so with a view to the possibility of getting away tomorrow. So your boat is hauled alongside, and a little extra ballast is put in, and you and your mate get your oilskins, and, dropping into her, double reef your mainsail and foresail, and shove off. And by the time you have got your sheets trimmed, your halliards coiled away, and everything made snug, you are already as warm as any reasonable men can wish to be.

It is a long leg and a short one out of the harbour, and you get a heavy puff now and again from over the high land that brings your lee-rail level with the water, and makes you luff in a hurry. Three or four tacks bring you to the headlands of the bay, and as you stand out from under the weather-shore you begin to feel the real wind and sea. There is plenty of both, and you have to do all you know with tiller and sheet to negotiate the big seas that roll up on the weather-bow and to keep the lee-gunwale out of the water at the same time. It is just a little more than you can manage.

A couple of steep combers that you have to luff up to knock all the way out of the boat and make her stagger; the next sea throws her head off the wind, while at the same time a heavy puff forces her lee-side under water. You put the helm down, but she has had no time to gather much way, and is slow coming to; you are forced to let go the sheet, but she has taken a good drop on board before she comes up, and there are more big seas coming. 'It won't do,' you say to your mate; 'we must have another reef in.' So you drop your peak, and wear, and run back under the shelter of the point, and take your third reef down.

Then you stand out and try again; and it is wonderful what a difference the reduction of canvas has made. She stands well up, and rides beautifully over the big seas, hardly shipping a cupful of water as she rears up and lets them pass under her. It is an art, if a simple one, steering a boat to windward in a big sea. You have to put her almost straight at the worst seas, and yet you must never let her lose way, or she will fall off broadside to the sea, and perhaps be too 'sick' to come to again in time to prevent a vicious wave from breaking on board or capsizing her. And there are few things more exhilarating. Every big sea successfully surmounted is a triumph in itself, and the winning of ground to windward foot by foot against wind and sea feels like an arduous but steadily victorious struggle against a sturdy foe.

And now you find you can weather the island, and, choosing a 'smooth,' go about for the last time. If the seas breaking on it looked fine from the yacht nearly three miles off, they look awe-inspiring now close under your lee with their roar thundering in your ears. Now you are no longer riding head first over the seas, but running free at a slashing pace, sheet in hand, watching the sea narrowly over your shoulder, ready to luff instantly if some specially dangerous monster should make it necessary.

And when you are well clear of the rocks you bear up and run before it—most glorious and exulting sensation of all. The big seas come hissing and growling up in pursuit, and lift up her stern on high, and the boat seems positively to fly as she tears down their steep faces. You have to use all your strength at the tiller to keep her straight, and your mate keeps the peak halliards in hand and lowers the peak now and again to ease your task and avert a possible broach to. In less than half an hour you are back on board the yacht; a little wet, maybe, but tingling with exhilaration, and warmed through for the rest of the day.

These are but two typical sails out of many that might be sketched, for the variations of weather and sea and coast are nearly endless, and the yachtsman who is a persistent boat-sailer will find his memory stocked with glowing recollections of rapturous sails and fascinating explorations wherever his yacht has taken him—in breezy English waters, and on the wild west coasts of Scotland and Ireland; in Greece and Italy, and many a pleasant land in the Mediterranean Sea; perhaps even the Coral Islands of the South Pacific, and the wooded bays of far New Zealand.

Of course there is a reverse side to the picture—days when storms make sailing too dangerous to be quite pleasant, and more often, days when want of wind makes it almost intolerably tiresome. To row, or be rowed in, a heavy boat halfway across the Bay of Naples by night is certainly an experience in tediousness. Though even such an ordeal as that is not quite without its compensations. But I feel it is rash of me to say so.

Like so many things material and other in the world we live in, every boat is necessarily a compromise between inconsistent objects. In building a boat you must compromise somewhere between speed and stability, weatherliness and the advantages of light draught. And in the case of a yacht's boat freedom of choice in design is limited by some special considerations. She must not be too heavy to carry in the davits; she must not exceed a certain length, say 25 feet; she must not be too broad in the beam to be carried inboard; and her draught of water must be somewhat shallow for the sake of convenience in landing. Subject to these conditions, stability is, I am sure, the object that should principally be aimed at in the construction of a yacht's boat.

The ever-present and the most serious danger of boat-sailing is that of being overpowered by weather: that is to say, of being overtaken by a wind so strong that the boat will not carry any canvas sufficient to work her without instantly capsizing or filling with water. And a very ordinary gale of wind, such as occurs on our coasts once at least in most months of the year, will be enough for this, and will, especially if combined with sea, so overpower any open boat, of a size that can be carried on a yacht, that is exposed to its full strength, that she will be unable to show any canvas to it except just to scud before it.

I am aware that this statement will be felt a little startling, perhaps even by some sailors; but I have tried a good many experiments in sailing boats in rough weather, and I am sure it is true of any boat that the yacht-owner is likely to carry.

Builders of yachts' sailing boats are not, somehow, usually very successful in making boats 'stiff.' They will not make them flat enough in the floor, or, if they do, do not make it the right shape. Their idea, generally, is to build a boat that will beat boats of a similar class in regattas, and sail fast on a fine day in the smooth waters of a harbour; and if you allow them their own way, they will generally provide you with a crank boat, over-masted and over-canvassed, that may sail very fast in a light wind and smooth water, but which will be overpowered at once in a fresh breeze and a choppy sea. And some day, even perhaps after you have done your best to make her more seaworthy by lightening her mast and cutting down her canvas, you may have the mortification of seeing a fishing-boat no larger than your own craft making a good passage and standing up like a stake under her close-reefed sail, whilst you are unable to show a rag to the wind without being at once overpowered.

And remember that you cannot make an open boat stiff by the simple process of loading her with ballast, as even some sailors vainly suppose. Beyond the amount which brings her to her best sailing trim in a good breeze, and which experience of the boat will teach you, additional ballast hardly makes her appreciably stiffer, and does make her very appreciably slower. Make stability, then, your primary object, and impress on your builder that he must not sacrifice it to speed; and that, as it is out of the question to obtain it by means of a lead or iron keel, the weight of such a thing in the case of a large boat being quite prohibitory (not to speak of inconvenience in landing), he must make her flat in the floor and give her plenty of beam.

With the same object in mind, her spread of canvas should be moderate but sufficient, and her masts and spars no heavier than is really necessary. These are generally quite needlessly stout. If the mast is strong enough to capsize the boat without breaking, it is as strong as it need be; anything beyond this merely means additional topweight, decreasing the stability of the boat, and doing no service. A very light mast, if properly stayed by a couple of wire shrouds on each side, will stand an immense strain.

It is a disputable question whether such a boat should be a lifeboat. The air-tight compartments, usually made of copper, certainly add to her weight, and, some say, make her less stiff. On the other hand, it is pleasant to feel that your boat is unsinkable, and that if you knock a hole through her bottom with a rock, or ship an unlucky sea, she will not go down. But if you decide, as I should do, on a lifeboat, be sure that she really is one, and that her air-tight compartments are large enough to float her with ballast and crew on board. A 25-ft. cutter, such as is built by White of Cowes, will carry more than half a ton of ballast and half a dozen people quite comfortably when she is full of water. But I have seen small steam-launches, nominally lifeboats, that would undoubtedly, with their engines and boilers on board, sink like stones if they were filled with water.

Wooden air-tight compartments are lighter than copper tanks, but they are apt to warp and become leaky. Twenty-two years ago, in New Zealand, I had a lifeboat sailing-cutter sent out to me by long sea that I had had built for me in England. As soon as she arrived I took a friend out for a sail on a rough day and filled her with water, just to show him her marvellous properties. The result was ignominious. The water-tight (!) compartments filled, and we drifted helplessly home, thanking the Fates that we had nothing but water ballast on board.

The shape of the stern is another point on which opinions may reasonably differ. There is much to be said in favour of a boat being sharp at both ends. A sharp stern is undoubtedly safer when running through broken water or before a heavy sea, and when a boat 'squats' in running before a strong wind it does not drag dead water behind it, and makes a cleaner wake. But unless increased length can be given to the boat it diminishes stiffness. The square-sterned boat carries her bearings farther aft, and so, if both are of the same length, the square-sterned boat, other things being equal, will be the stiffest of the two. But if you decide for a square stern let the boat have a fine run aft, and let the square surface of the stern be small and well up out of the water.

Any sort of a counter is an abomination, dangerous to a boat in a sea-way.

She should have a good side; that is, a high side above water. It adds to her stability, as well as making her much drier. If her side is rather low, washboards fixed along the top of the gunwale will be found advantageous in rough weather. She should be higher out of water at both ends than amidships, and the line of her rail should describe a graceful curve from bow to stern. A boat that looks quite level from end to end is generally a poor sea-boat, and, if her bottom corresponds with her top, a bad steerer besides.

I think she should certainly have a centreboard. Several of the smartest yachts' cutters use instead a half-moon-shaped keel of galvanised iron, clamped on to the keel of the boat. I cannot see that this contrivance, which makes a boat useless for anything but deep-water sailing, has any advantages of its own over a centreboard, and its disadvantages are serious. It makes it impossible to beach the boat, or to attempt any landing-place when the water may be shallow, and whenever the boat runs aground or hits a rock, as she is sure to do sometimes when fishing or exploring, it is nearly certain to get broken or bent; and whenever it is left behind, a boat of this kind will cease to be very weatherly, and may even miss stays. Moreover, it must be rather an awkward thing to put on and take off when the boat is in the davits.

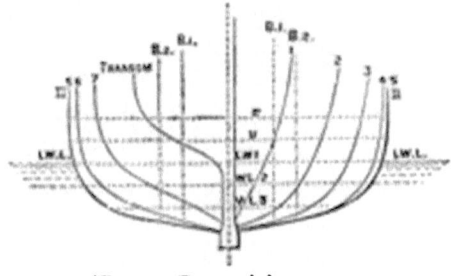

'BLACK PEARL'S' CUTTER,
MIDSHIP SECTION.

A wooden false keel of more graduated shape, deep in the middle and tapering to nothing at the ends, is a better contrivance, but it is open to some of the same objections about landing, in a minor degree.

It is hardly necessary at the present day to combat the prejudice against centreboards. But for many years there was a curious dislike and distrust of them among British boat-sailers and builders. They were excluded altogether from most regattas; and not one in twenty of the boats that would have been vastly improved by them were ever fitted with them. They were regarded, for some mysterious reason, as unseaworthy, unsportsmanlike, and unfair; and when the average boating man found his craft beaten out of sight in going to windward by a centreboard boat, he considered the discovery that she had a centreboard a satisfactory explanation of his defeat, and seldom drew the further conclusion that a centreboard was an excellent thing.

And yet, after nearly twenty-five years' experience of them, I have never been able to discover what the objections to them are. The case of the centreboard is said to get in the way; but unless you want to load your whole boat with very bulky cargo, I am unable to conceive what it can get in the way of. And the merits of a centreboard are many and obvious. It enables you to combine the advantages of deep and shallow draught. You can run your boat up on a beach, and be holding your own to windward against a deep-keeled yacht ten minutes afterwards. It makes the most ordinary boat weatherly, smart, and handy to steer. It gives you timely warning of shallow water, and the only result of its touching the bottom or striking a rock is to send it up into its case. I have never had my centreboard either bent or broken by such contact. But it is well to have it lowered on a chain or wire rather than on an iron shank, with a joint or two near the handle, as in most of White's boats. Because when the centreboard hits the bottom and is forced up into the case, these joints will double up inside the case, and the solid part of the shank be driven through the top of it; which would be unpleasant for anyone who happened to be sitting there.

A centreboard, except in so far as its weight makes ballast, does not make a boat stiffer, as the uninitiated often suppose, but in the case of a broad, shallow boat, rather the reverse, as it prevents her from being blown away to leeward. And in a boat such as is being here considered, it should not be too heavy for one man to haul up. It should be made of a thin sheet of galvanised iron.

As regards her rig, nothing is really so handy and capable as the cutter, or, to speak more accurately, the sloop rig; consisting of mainsail and foresail, as ordinary working canvas. I prefer the sloop rig of a single foresail on a short iron bumpkin, to the end of which the forestay is attached, to the cutter rig of staysail and jib with a regular bowsprit; for a bowsprit is an awkward thing in rounding to and coming alongside a ship, under all sorts of conditions of wind and tide, and a second head-sail gives you more gear to attend to when you are single-handed. And on a boat of this size a single foresail is not too large to be easily handled.

What makes this rig so suitable for the peculiar and varied purposes of a yacht's boat is, that, with mainsheet and peak halliards kept in hand, it gives such absolute control over the pace and direction of the boat at a moment's notice. In whiffing round the rocks after pollack, for instance, in a flawy wind, by lowering and raising the peak, and easing off and hauling in the mainsheet, it is easy to maintain a perfectly level pace of two or three knots. In a squall, or in going alongside a ship or a landing-place, the peak can be dropped and the boat eased or checked at once without becoming unsailable. This constitutes, in my opinion, a very important advantage over the standing lugsail, of which, of course, the peak cannot be lowered. A downhaul should be attached to the end of the gaff, as the peak will not always drop when the wind is pressing the sail against the topping lift.

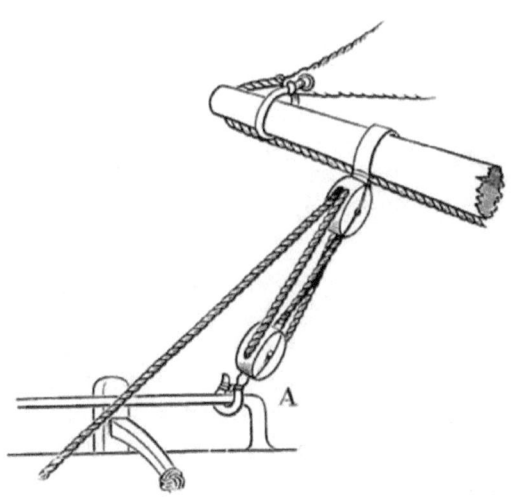

MAINSHEET ON IRON HORSE.

The foresheets should lead aft and be made fast round cleats or pins within reach of the steersman for convenience when sailing single-handed; the mainsheet should travel on an iron horse across the stern; but care should be taken that the shackle, A, that attaches the block to the horse, should be of a size and shape that will not jam when the block hangs down loosely, and perhaps takes a turn, as it may in going about. One squally day this year, the writer, who had always wondered how people could be so foolish as to get drowned through their main-sheets being foul, found himself, after going about, with the lower block of his mainsheet twisted and jammed under the horse, at such an angle that the sheet would not run: while, to make the mischief complete, the tiller was jammed by the block as well, so that he could neither luff nor ease the sheet.

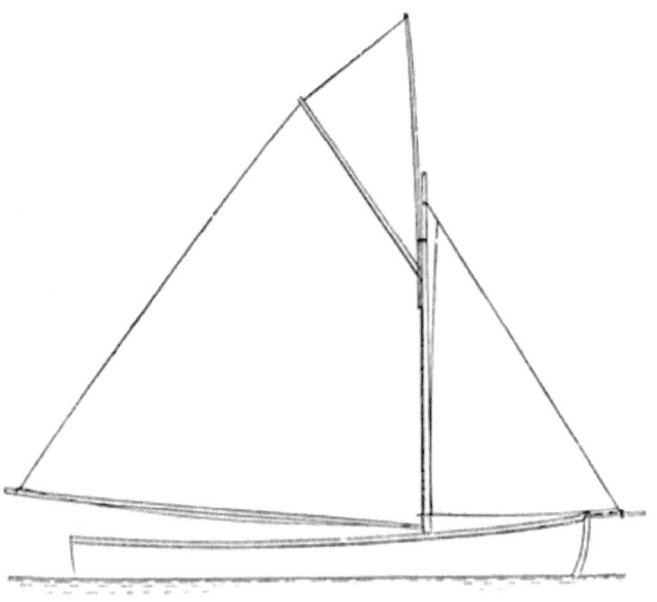

SAIL-PLAN, 'BLACK PEARL'S' CUTTER.

A jackyard topsail that requires no topmast can be set, and a spinnaker will be found very useful for running in light weather. A bowsprit can also be run out and a jib set; but this will probably be found to upset the balance of sail on the centreboard, and make her carry lee-helm, in which case it will be of no use.

If a standing lugsail is preferred, the peak should be cut high, and the long yard should be as light as is consistent with the necessary strength. I can see no advantage over the cutter mainsail, except that the halliards are rather simpler. Old sailors and fishermen will tell you that a boat with a yard is always stiffer than one with a gaff. With a dipping lug, such as fishermen use, or a balance lug, this seems not improbable, as in these rigs a considerable part of the yard and sail is to windward or in front of the mast; but with a standing lugsail, which, if it has a boom, is practically identical in shape with a cutter's mainsail, it is hard to believe that there is much in it—the peak halliards can hardly make much difference.

A balance lug, however excellent for racing or for fine-weather sailing in protected waters, is unsuited for the varied purposes of a yacht's cutter, and the rough experiences to which she will be exposed. For it is not possible either to lower the peak, or to trice up the tack, or to brail up the sail by means of the topping-lift, and in a squall it is not unlikely to jam against the mast and refuse to come down.

Though the yawl may not be quite so handy as the cutter-rig in the matter of instantaneous control of pace and direction—for there is the mizzen as well as the mainsail to think about—it has certain special and important advantages of its own. When it is necessary to shorten sail, to strike the mizzen is equivalent to taking a reef in the mainsail without any of the difficulty and delay involved in that operation; or you can lower the mainsail and reef it at leisure whilst you sail under foresail and mizzen. To lower the mainsail of a cutter in order to reef it involves losing way and falling off to leeward. Moreover, whether the sail be up or down, it is much easier to take reefs down on the main-boom of a yawl, which is well inside the boat, than on that of a cutter, which is right out over the stern. To haul down and secure the earing on the main-boom of a cutter when she is plunging in a sea-way and burying her rail with the force of the wind is a difficult and even dangerous operation, which is not unlikely to end, if you are not careful, in your finding yourself in the sea and your boat careering gaily away without you.

The tiller of a yawl must be shaped or placed so that the mizzen-mast does not get in its way; there are several ways of contriving this. A yoke with lines does not give sufficient power, unless so large as to be inconvenient.

The amount of ballast required will depend somewhat on the shape of the boat, but about 11 cwt. will probably be found to be about the right amount for a 25-ft. boat with three or four men on board under ordinary circumstances. When there is a very strong wind

'ALINE'S' CUTTER (COLONEL GAMBLE).

and fewer hands on board, an extra 2 cwt. or 3 cwt. may be added. But much extra ballast makes a boat slow—much more so, oddly enough, than the same amount of weight in people—without adding very much to her stability.

Blocks of lead about ½ cwt. each make the best ballast. These should be cast so as to fit two long boxes along the floor on each side of the keel in the centre of the boat. But it is well to have some of the ballast in the form of shot-bags weighing about 40 lbs. each, which can be placed further aft and shifted about as required.

Water ballast is unsatisfactory. Its bulk is not the only objection. Its specific gravity is so small that it will not make a boat stiff, and so even a boat that has no water-tight compartments will be safer in a strong wind with lead or iron ballast. A lifeboat that will float ¾ ton of lead or iron is, of course, much more so.

I give here dimensions, drawings, and diagrams of two typical yachts' sailing boats, well suited for knocking about in all sorts of weather, one belonging to the writer, the other to Colonel Gamble of the *Aline*. The former, the *Black Pearl's* cutter, is a 25-ft. lifeboat, with copper air-tanks, built by Messrs. Fay & Co., from a design of T. Soper's, with a centreboard, and sloop-rigged. She has a high side, and a good deal of shear, while her forefoot is somewhat cut away. She is fairly fast, and weatherly, fairly stiff, and a beautiful sea-boat. She carries usually 11 cwt. of ballast, occasionally as much as 14 cwt.

Colonel Gamble's boat is a 22-ft. lifeboat, with wooden air-tight compartments, of the Lamb & White pattern, built by Hansen & Sons. She has no centreboard, but a 9-in. wooden false keel, deepest in the middle, and tapering to nothing at the ends, is screwed on to her keel. She carries a standing lug mainsail, and a foresail. The peak of her lugsail is cut very high, and her mast, yard, and boom are very light and workmanlike. Her side and ends are less high out of the water, and she is in every way a smaller boat than the *Black Pearl's* cutter, and probably less of a boat in a sea-way: but she can sail round the latter in a light wind, and in a strong one is very nearly as fast, and stands up like a stake. The reader will please to notice the flatness of her floor in the drawing of her midship section on the previous page. She has been, I believe, very successful in races against boats of her class, showing that speed and stability are not quite so incompatible as they are sometimes supposed to be. She carries usually about 9 cwt. of ballast in shot-bags, and when full of water will float 4 in. clear of the sea, with that ballast and four men on board.

'BLACK PEARL'S' CUTTER	ft.	in.	'ALINE'S' CUTTER	ft.	in.
Length	25	0	Length	22	0
Beam	7	1	Beam	6	3
Depth amidships from gunwale to outside garboard	3	2¾	Depth inside	2	7
Depth of keel from outside of garboard		5¼	Depth of keel from outside garboard		3½
Draught of water with 11 cwt. of ballast and crew	2	0½	Depth of additional false keel		9
Draught with centreboard down	5	0	Draught of water with 9 cwt. of ballast and crew	1	10
			Ditto with false keel added	2	7
Sail plan					
Length of mast from step to hounds	16	0	*Sail plan*		
Ditto from step to masthead	19	7	Length of mast	14	0
Length of mainboom	20	4	Length of mainboom	16	9
Length of gaff	11	3	Length of yard	19	0

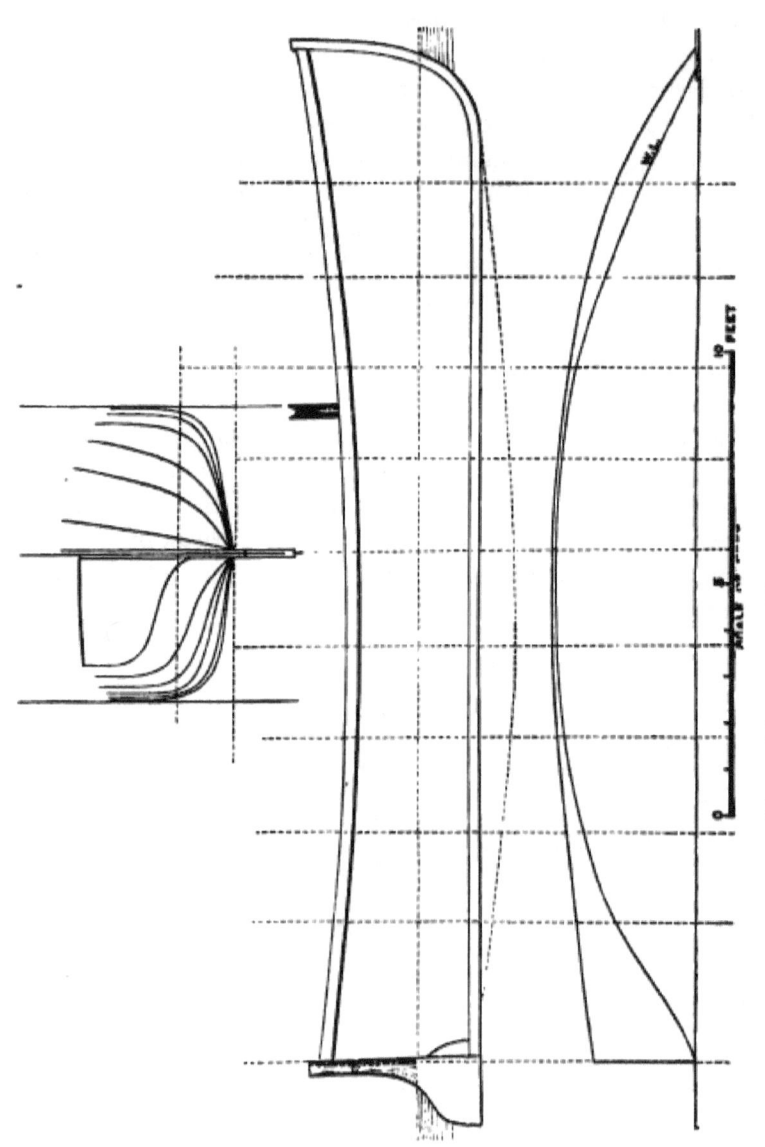

S.S. 'Aline's' Lifeboat (Colonel Gamble, C.B.)

It does not come within the scope of this chapter to give a full and elementary manual of the art of boat-sailing. Descriptions of the thousand and one things belonging to a yacht and the sailing of her, a glossary of nautical terms and their meaning, and a full account of the art of sailing are given in another portion of this work. The leading principles of boat-sailing are the same as those for sailing a larger vessel. The gear of a boat, as far as it goes, is identical, and the knots, bends, and hitches that are most used are common to both. I need not, therefore, describe them, nor waste space by repetition in giving such elementary directions as that a boat should be luffed in a squall, or in explaining what is meant by 'gybing' a boat or 'putting her about.' But there are some things in the art of sailing that have a special application to open boats, so perhaps I may be allowed, even at the cost of an occasional repetition of what has been said elsewhere, to give a few hints and directions, based upon practical experience, as to the handling of a boat, together with some of the simple rules that experience has taught me are the most important to remember, even though some of these may seem to be of a very elementary character.

The yachtsman who is inexperienced, or much out of practice in the management of a boat, had far better take a sailor or a couple of sailors with him. By observing what they do he will learn or remember how to do things properly, and the tiro will pick up in a day or two, from watching an expert, many things that he would take long to learn for himself. Indeed, I think that in dangerous weather it is always as well to have a seaman on board. He will be unnecessary, probably, if nothing happens—that is to say, if nothing carries away or gets jammed; but it is just on such days that things do happen, and it is in such emergencies that the difference between a sailor and an ordinary amateur becomes widest.

A good sailor has some resource for almost everything that can happen, and if one thing will not do he tries something else. Even if the amateur is as quick to know what should be done, he is usually far slower and more clumsy in the doing of it. Suppose, to take a very simple instance, the peak halliards carry away. How many amateurs are there who could make a long splice and re-reeve them with reasonable expedition? In a tumble of a sea, with a lee shore imminent, the mere reeving of them, if no splice is required, will very likely bother him considerably.

Still no one will ever be a passable boat-sailer, or will ever enjoy boat-sailing as it can be enjoyed, until he learns to dispense with pro-

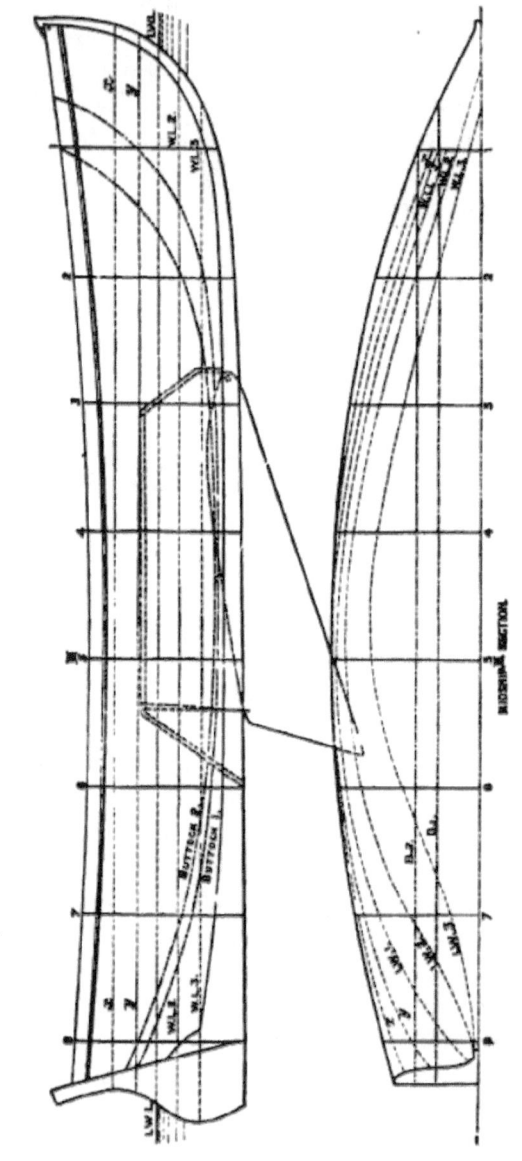

Earl of Pembroke's 'Black Pearl's' cutter.

fessional assistance and to manage his boat single-handed if necessary. So, when he has learnt with his eyes, as far as a man can, how things should be done, other than steering and giving orders, let him go out alone or with an amateur like himself and learn his business. Let him choose a fine day and sail away if possible out of sight of the most powerful glasses on his ship, and then deliberately and of set purpose practise everything essential that is comprised in the art of boat-sailing. He will instantly discover that between knowing how things are done and doing them there is an extraordinary difference, and he will find himself curiously awkward in doing what he has seen his men do a hundred times. He will make acquaintance with the malign tendency of all ropes to get foul of each other, and the strange law that whenever you are trying to put something right on a boat something else always goes wrong.

When he first tries to reef his sails—he will do it at anchor if he is wise—he will find that the foretack is horribly inconvenient to get at, and that the foresail will keep running up the stay and muffling his head, while the main-boom seems to be possessed by a devil and tries to push him overboard whichever side of it he gets. When he gets under way again he finds that he has got the anchor-line foul of the foresheets, and while he is clearing these and re-reeving them through their fairleads, a puff of wind knocks the boat nearly flat and sends him scrambling aft to the tiller and the mainsheet. He will bruise his shins and bark his knuckles all manner of ways—he hardly knows how; he will get hot and blown, and go near to tumbling overboard in the violence of his exertions; he will do things and he will forget to do things that it will make him blush in bed to remember afterwards. But let him not feel too deeply humiliated. For even experienced sailors will make the most monstrous blunders in a boat when they are strange to her, and to boatwork; and he will find that his awkwardness seems to vanish miraculously after a few lessons, and it will not be long before he has the satisfaction of feeling that he can handle his boat as well as any man on the ship.

It is foolish to go far, and especially far to leeward, when there is every appearance of bad weather coming on, and a low glass. You may do it many times with impunity, but some day you are sure to get caught, and the consequences may be serious. Remember that you are always liable to meet with an amount of wind that your boat will not be able to bear under the shortest canvas that you can work her with. Many people do not realise this; and indeed it requires some powers of imagination, when a boat is standing stiffly up under her full canvas in a good breeze, to realise that in a few hours, or even minutes, there may come an amount of wind which will make it impossible to keep her lee-rail out of the water even with close-reefed sails and sheets flying loose. But a few rough and unpleasant experiences will soon convince the young boat-sailer of the fact, and teach him that a boat has no business to be out in a gale of wind, and that when he is caught in one the thing to do, if it is possible, is to gain shelter at once. If he sails much he will come across plenty of bad weather without courting it, and when he does he will probably meet it with more coolness and confidence if he is free from the depressing sensation that the scrape into which he has got himself, and perhaps others as well, is entirely due to his own wanton folly.

It is always best, if possible, to reef down and make everything snug before the squall or storm comes upon you; but you cannot be continually reefing down for every threatening cloud, so this is not always practicable. When the wind has become too strong for the sail you are carrying, you will have to act according to circumstances. It is not always wise to attempt to reef at once. There may not be sea-room enough to lower down the sails to reef them, and to attempt to reef a cutter's mainsail in a squall when she is nearly overpowered by wind is extremely dangerous. For the sheet must be hauled right in, and cannot be eased while the earing is being made fast. It is better under such circumstances to lower your peak altogether, taking up any slack in the topping-lift so as to support the boom. This will ease the boat immensely, and gives you a capital leg-of-mutton sail. Possibly this will be a sufficient reduction, and you may stand on under this canvas until you get shelter, or sea-room to reef in, or there comes a lull in the squall. If it is not, and the boat is still overpowered, haul down the foresail as well and double reef it, and when it is set again you can, if you have then got sea-room, take down the reefs in your mainsail, keeping the peak down all the time.

There are generally three reefs in a cutter's mainsail. If when these are taken down you have still too much canvas, let the throat run down, and lash the jaws of the gaff down to the boom. It is well to have a line of reef points running from the throat of the mainsail to the cringle of the third reef on the after-leach to make this arrangement snug. It is then called a balance reef.

Most boats will stand rather more wind when it is on the beam than they will when they are close hauled. For while they do not feel it quite so hard, it is easier to keep good way on, and you can spill the sails by slacking the sheets as much as you like without fear of losing it. So that in smooth water you will be as safe in a blow with the wind abeam as you are when sailing close to it and luffing up into the puffs. But a beam sea is the most dangerous sea of all, and when it is heavy you must always be ready either to luff up towards it, or to keep right away before it, as may be best. But if you do the former be careful not to have too much way on, or you will run your boat's nose right into the sea. If your course gives you a dangerous beam sea the best plan is to keep your luff until your port is well to leeward, and then up helm and run for it.

In running before a strong wind and a dangerous sea do not attempt to carry much sail. It is a common belief among the inexperienced, founded upon nautical literature absorbed in youth, and even amongst some who ought to know better, that you must carry plenty of sail in order to run away from the sea and avoid being pooped. But, in the first place, you cannot run away from the sea, which travels more than twice as fast as any boat can sail, and a press of canvas which buries the boat's stern as it drags her through the water increases the danger of being pooped. Moreover, it makes her harder to steer, and increases the much greater risks of broaching to or running the boat under water in those desperate rushes on the steep front of the big seas, which are at once the danger and the delight of running before a wind. So far from its being desirable to emulate the pace of the sea, the sooner the wave passes the boat, and the shorter, therefore, these rushes are, the less is the danger.

I learned this once by experience. Many years ago, on the coast of New Zealand, I was caught out at sea by a gale of wind in a 13-ft. sailing dinghy, and had to run home before it in a short, dangerous, rapidly rising sea. The little boat tore before the wind under a reefed mainsail and jib, running her nose and stern alternately level with the water, until it became evident that we should be swamped in a few minutes. I ordered the man who was with me to haul down the sail. The moment he did so the little boat, which was sharp at both ends and was steered with an oar, began to ride the seas like a duck, and we ran home before the gale with ease and safety under a bare stick and a fragment of head-sail.

A boat with a sharp stern, steered with an oar, has a great advantage under such circumstances. For the rudder is sometimes right out of the water and useless; and though the water of a great wave does not really move forward with the wave as it appears to do, the breaking top of it does, and when the rudder is in this water, which is going faster than the boat, it is useless for the moment. It is well to have a place for a crutch in the gunwale far aft, so that an oar can be used to steer with if necessary.

There is generally less wind under the shelter or lee of the land. But this is not always the case, and the most experienced seaman cannot always foretell whether this will be so or not. Sometimes the wind seems to belong to the land, and there may be little or none of it out at sea. Under high land—cliffs or mountains—you may lose the wind altogether; you may find it blowing in occasional baffling puffs of great violence and uncertain direction, or you may find it blowing much harder, not in puffs merely but altogether. It is not an uncommon experience, especially in the Mediterranean, to run down a coast before a fresh breeze, and to find a perfect tornado blowing when you turn a corner and luff up under the land. This is one of nature's paradoxes—one of the undoubted facts that one occasionally meets which seem opposed to all reason and probability. I do not know how far it has ever been scientifically explained.

Some places where there is high land seem to brew their own wind. Loch Scavaig, in Skye, under the Coolin hills, is an instance of this. It may be fine and almost calm outside, but as you sail into its gloomy waters you may find a perfect tempest blowing in or out. It staggers one to think what it must be like in a real gale of wind.

In Carlingford Lough, Ireland, last autumn, when there was but a fine-weather breeze blowing outside, the puffs off the mountain on the south of the lough took the form of a succession of regular waterspouts, any one of which would have twisted the mast out of the boat or capsized her if it had struck her. We kept as far to leeward as we could, and most of them died away before they crossed our track, but they felt very uncanny.

Speaking generally, high land is always dangerous for boat-sailing, as well as trying to the temper. On a day when there is nothing but a fine-weather breeze elsewhere, under high land you are liable to get puffs as violent while they last as a gale of wind. It is as though the hills bottled up and concentrated the wind, so that when it is let loose it comes with double force; and these puffs are specially dangerous to a boat apart from their force: first, because the angle at which they will strike is so uncertain, and secondly, because, coming from above and striking downwards, a boat does not relieve the pressure on her sails by heeling over as she does when the wind blows horizontally along the water. This is the reason why you will probably find that the squalls that go nearest capsizing your boat are not those that you have seen tearing towards you turning the water into smoke as they come, violent as these may be, but those which you have hardly seen a sign of on the water at all, and which strike the sails with a downward blow straight from the mountain side. The Sound of Raasay, outside Portree Harbour, when a westerly wind is blowing over the tremendous cliffs of Skye, is a fine place for the study of these phenomena.

When the wind is blowing up or down a channel with high land on either hand, the fiercest puffs will be near the sides which seem to concentrate the wind, and the safest place will be the middle of the channel. One day, in Loch Scavaig, beating out of that inferno of furious winds against the usual succession of tearing puffs, with double-reefed sails and all passengers down in the bottom of the boat, I stood rather far over one tack under the high mountain on the west side. Just as I was preparing to go about a furious blast struck the boat like a cannon-shot. I thrust the helm down, letting fly the mainsheet. The foresheet fortunately carried away of itself, but for a few seconds a volume of water poured over the rail, and I thought we should go over or fill. A minute later, as we were standing off on the other tack, setting things to rights and pruning our ruffled plumes, my coxswain, a most excellent boat-sailer but a man of a somewhat sardonic humour, re-

THE SQUALL IN LOCH SCAVAIG, SKYE.

marked grimly, 'I should think that would be a lesson to you in future not to stand over too far under high land.' It has been.

Here follow a few of the things which it is well to remember when boat-sailing, whether you are acting as captain or crew, or both in one.

As soon as your sails are set and properly trimmed, coil away the ends of all your halliards, topping-lift, &c., in the bottom of the boat, capsizing the coil after you have made it so that the part of the rope that has to go up first becomes uppermost, and so will not get foul when the halliards are let go.

See that all your blocks are clear. A reef pendant (earing) getting drawn into the mainsheet block, or a bit of bunting or spunyarn into the block of the peak halliards, may easily cause an accident.

See that boathooks, oars, and crutches are all ready for use if required.

Never make fast your sheets in any way that can possibly jam, or that a single pull will not set free. The same is advisable with your halliards also.

Always see that your mainsheet is clear, and that it cannot get foul of anything in running out. The most favoured lady passenger should not be allowed to put her feet on it.

When you have passengers on board in dangerous, squally weather, try to get them to sit down in the bottom of the boat. It adds greatly to stability, besides getting them out of the way. But if there is much water in the boat already, they may require some persuasion.

Always carry an anchor or grapple and a line to attach to it, and see that both are ready for instant use if you are likely to want them. The anchor for a 25-ft. boat should weigh about 30 lbs. If it is heavier it will tax your wind severely to get it up quickly in deep water.

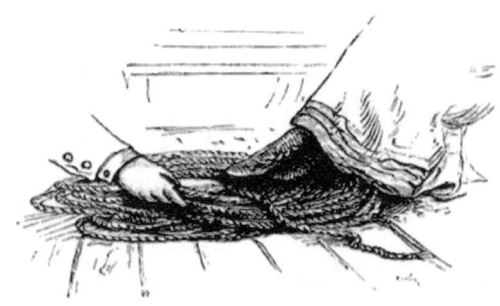

'EXCUSE ME.'

Always carry a knife. A sheath-knife is best: there is no difficulty about opening it when fingers are cold, and it will not shut on them when you are using it.

Always carry a pocket-compass in case of fog.

In what is called a temperate climate always carry oilskins and a sou'wester.

Always carry some spare rope, particularly odds and ends of small rope; you may always want it for something. Your spinnaker gear will probably do at a pinch to replace a broken halliard or sheet.

When you are exploring and have ladies on board, do not forget to take a landing-board.

Always carry some water and biscuits when you may be out many hours.

Always have the centreboard down in coming alongside a ship. The boat will answer her helm better and steer more accurately with the centreboard down, as the wind and sea cannot push her about on the surface.

If it is ever necessary to leave your boat untended, take great care that she can neither damage herself nor get adrift when the tide rises. Nothing will make you feel so intolerably foolish as to come back and find your boat damaged or gone, perhaps still in sight bobbing away without you. The writer was once left stranded on a small island in the Hauraki Gulf, New Zealand, owing to his man having considered a round stone a suitable object to make a boat fast to.

SELF-UNMOORED.

Keep out of the way of steamers and big ships when you can, even when by the rule of the road it is their business to keep out of yours. They will probably expect you to keep clear of them, and, when in narrow waters, are justified in doing so.

NEVER 'MOON.'

Finally, never 'moon,' or think about such things as politics, philosophy, or people, when boat-sailing. Frivolous conversation on subjects unconnected with the boat or the weather should be sternly discouraged in any but the most familiar waters and the finest of weather. Distraction is a real danger in boat-sailing, and is probably the commonest cause of fatal accidents. The attention of the boat-sailer should always be concentrated on his business. He has plenty to attend to and think about. He must always have an eye on his sails, and at the same time must keep watching the wind on the water before it reaches him, and the general appearance of the weather. And in spite of these preoccupations he should be continually noting the features of the coast.

If he is leaving a place to which he is going to return, he should be constantly taking note of the relative bearings of rocks and headlands by which to remember the proper channel when he comes back, not forgetting that the state of the tide will be different, and carefully observing, therefore, if the tide is low, the position of rocks and shoals that may be submerged on his return, or if it is near high water, the bearing of places which his chart tells him will have to be avoided when the tide is out. In short, it is an engrossing occupation, permitting of no distraction, except perhaps fish, and even *then* one man must continue to give his attention almost entirely to the boat. There is a time for all things, and the man who wants to talk or to read his book in the boat has no business there. Shelley used to read, it is true, and he was an ardent boat-sailer. But Shelley's case is a bad one to quote as an example, for his boat-sailing came to an unlucky end, and we shall never know now how much or how little that little volume of poetry had to do with it.

I have said a good deal in these pages of the dangers of boat-sailing. It has been necessary to insist upon them, because the price of safety in boat-sailing is eternal vigilance and a little knowledge. The careless man may drown himself any day, and there is no saying what mess the complete duffer may not get into. But given the habit of carefulness, which soon becomes instinctive and unconscious, together with a little experience, and a moderate amount of prudence as regards weather, and boat-sailing is certainly not a dangerous sport as sports go.

THERE IS NO PLACE LIKE HOME.

CHAPTER 9

Small Yacht Racing on the Solent
By 'Thalassa'

As Lord's is to the cricketer, St. Andrews to the golfer, Newmarket to the lover of the Turf, so is the Solent to the yachtsman—the Solent in its largest sense, not the West Channel only, but the whole of the waters inside the Wight, bounded by fifty miles of shore line, and covering an area of over fifty square sea miles. The West Channel, twelve miles long, is nearly twenty-four square miles; the East Channel, eight miles long, is equal in area; and Southampton Water, six miles long, covers three square miles. Nearly all of it is navigable to yachts, the Brambles being the only midwater shoal which interferes with small vessels of moderate draught.

The water of the Solent is clear as crystal, the air healthy as Switzerland, the scenery nearly as beautiful; here are watering places with mirth and music; cities with docks and shipping; men of war and men of peace; clubs and hotels; piers, slips, jetties, and hards; building and repairing sheds; yacht designers and agents; skippers and 'hands'; sail, flag, and rope makers; yachts' ironmongers and purveyors, &c. &c. &c., which *etceteras* include several snug anchorages and small harbours for those who wish to escape from the general hubbub during the yachting and excursion season. And the whole of this within a two hours' journey of London!

Curiously enough, the advantages of the Solent for yachting have only been fully appreciated during the past few years. It is true that the Royal Yacht Squadron was started early in the century, and the Royal Southern and Royal Victoria Yacht Clubs early in the forties; but yachting on the Solent as we know it now was not dreamt of, and the Thames held for many years the leading position as the centre of this essentially English sport.

Many things have combined to drive yachts from the Thames. Manure, marmalade, cement, gas, and other manufactories now line its banks; the Barking outfall fouls its waters, and an enormous steamer and barge traffic obstructs them. No wonder the yachtsmen deserted the Thames. But this is not all; a new sport has been born—the racing of small yachts, for which the Thames is peculiarly unsuited. Steam yachting has caused this development of small yacht racing. Men who would otherwise have built or purchased large sailing yachts now prefer steam, and, although they may themselves race but little in any craft, their action has destroyed our fleet of large sailing yachts, and with it the market for outclassed racers of any considerable size.

Moreover, the very perfection to which racing has been brought tells in the same direction, because few men can afford to build large racers year by year to replace those which are outclassed. Yacht clubs have increased both in numbers and wealth, and the executives find that racing brings grist to the mill and repays the cost and the trouble. This especially applies to small yacht races, the prizes for which are not a severe tax on a club's exchequer, and can therefore be given more frequently.

Owners were not slow to avail themselves of the sport offered, which on trial proved to possess many advantages over large yacht racing.

In small craft an owner is more his own master, and frequently steers and sails his own boat. Corinthian hands can form all or a large portion of the crew; ladies can take an active part; the sport is less costly and better fun than with large craft; there are more races; fouls and accidents are less dangerous; and people can get home to dinner.

In short, the advantages are so numerous and real that one marvels at any men preferring to act as passengers on board their own yachts in the more ancient sport. Even this adjective belongs really to the boats, as prehistoric men no doubt owned and raced canoes for ages prior to the existence of larger vessels. But we as moderns are concerned with the nineteenth century, during which sailing boats have certainly raced frequently on the Solent. The square stem and stern boat used by the Itchen ferrymen for fishing in Southampton Water and the E. and W. channels is still a favourite type, and during the seventies became almost a class for small yacht racing, inside lead ballast, moulded, being first introduced, then lead keels, until in 1878 heavy lead keels, with fore and aft overhang, became the fashion with racing owners, and the Solent 'Length Classes' were introduced to the yachting world; 21 feet, 25 feet, and 30 feet L.W.L. being the top limits of each class.

A scale of time allowance for length was made by the Y.R.A., and the boats developed into great 'brutes' which were efficient sail-carriers if nothing else, the final outcome being over 70 square feet of canvas to each foot of L.W.L., whereas a modern rater in the small classes is driven almost as effectively with 20 square feet per foot of similar hull length.

There being no limit to sail in the length classes, it was not a difficult matter to outbuild the crack boat of the year every winter. Each succeeding boat had longer overhang, greater beam, draught, and displacement than her predecessor, and consequently won, being a larger boat and carrying more sail. The table of Solent racers prior to 1886, appended to this chapter, gives some details of interest.

A few races were given every year for what was termed the 27-ft. class (*Sorella*, *Whimbrel*, &c.), also for Itchen punts and for fishermen's boats; and, early in the eighties, races under various conditions were provided for small yachts by the Royal Southampton and Royal Portsmouth Corinthian Yacht Clubs, under the energetic direction of their respective Honorary Secretaries, Mr. Wolff and the late Mr. McCheane. These clubs may fairly claim to have started that small yacht racing on the Solent which now employs so many hands in building boats in the winter and sailing them in the summer, and affords so many people a healthy pastime for their leisure hours. The rest of the Solent clubs were not long in following suit, first one then another giving races for small yachts, until in 1891 'The Squadron' so far forgot the distich:

Nothing less than 30 T
Must ever race with our Burgee,

as to permit two 'extra' races for 5- and 2½-raters, the prizes having been subscribed for 'privately' by some sporting members of this distinguished club. The same recurred in 1892 and 1893, but it is impossible to feel overwhelmed with gratitude, as the manner of granting the concession was too like that of an old lady introduced sorely against her will to people and things she deems *infra dig*.

On the other hand, the Royal Victoria, or the 'Red Squadron,' as its friends delight to call it, has since 1890 taken to the sport with becoming enthusiasm, the committee being said to possess more knowledge of the requirements of yacht racing than the Y.R.A. itself. This has produced some strange realities which the racing owner may see for himself at Ryde, in the shape of drums, time-post and semaphores galore, together with a 500-guinea cup and other remarkable 'Gold cups in waiting,' if he step ashore and can make friends with the good-natured secretary. The club gave several special days in 1892 and 1893 for matches in the Solent classes, and the Royal Albert did the same at Southsea, in addition to similar races at their annual regatta—a two days' affair. The Royal London and the Royal Southern Yacht Clubs followed suit. In short, these elderly dames of the Solent are acting in a very proper spirit by adopting and assisting to support the offspring of their younger relatives, requiring them simply to belong to something 'Royal *or* Recognised'—a peculiar distinction somewhat rough on the former word.

One caution to the unwary. Some of the senior clubs are very proud of their ordnance, but racing boats of *modern* construction should give them a clear berth, or the concussion may cause damage. One of the cracks had to proceed to the builder's for repair soon after a race at which that great artillerist the hall porter of the Royal London Yacht Club shook Cowes to its foundations. Certain it is that some racing boats are now built far too light for safety if caught in a gale on the open sea.

Returning to the clubs, the table at the end of the chapter gives some prominent facts at a glance, so it will not be necessary to repeat them.

An aspirant to fame in any of the small classes should belong to the Royal Southampton Yacht Club. It has plenty of members, of vitality, and 'go.' Its house is good and comfortable, with a fair cuisine and attendance, and its position is excellent for the racing sailor-man. The fees are not heavy,[1] and the sport is good.

The beginner will do well to make the acquaintance of the leading members of the committee, for their sound advice and local knowledge may be of service to him; but he may be cautioned not to disturb them after the racing with written memoranda about rounding buoys; the soul of man is not to be worried by such frivolities when absorbed in the worship of crab, tap, or Nap in the cosy cabin of the Committee-boat—and this applies with more or less force to all sailing committees and club secretaries. Some shrug the shoulder and

---

1. This club has raised its fees this year (1894), finding it impossible to exist on the income derived from nearly seven hundred members, whereas formerly it lived joyously on half the amount.

vent an expletive, the more pious sigh deeply and glance to the zenith, while many impose a heavy fine on that enemy of peace and quiet who dares to protest against a breach of the regulations. An exception, however, is said to prove a rule; and the committee of the Castle Yacht Club administers the law with strictness, and perhaps severity. If this policy were general, many of the difficulties connected with yacht racing would disappear, as a large percentage is due to irregularities which sailing committees might easily correct, instead of scanning them with a blind eye at the telescope end.

Real sportsmen like rules to be strictly observed and administered, and the discipline enforced at the Calshot racing has, if possible, increased the popularity of the club which was started in 1887 by some eccentric enthusiasts who considered that small yacht racing required further encouragement. At that date the idea was not so preposterous as it now appears; but whether this and other clubs assisted materially in the production of modern racing, or were themselves the products, is a problem for the Macaulay of sport to solve in the dim future, when he writes on the pursuit of pleasure in the nineteenth century.

The adoption of the present Y.R.A. rating rule in the winter of 1886 practically killed the 'Length' classes; for, although the Solent clubs continued to support them for another year, no more 'lengthers' were built, and, the existing boats gradually dropping out, the racing with 'footers' collapsed.

******

The year 1887 was a turning point in small yacht racing on the Solent, as elsewhere.

There was much diversity of opinion as to the suitability of the new rule for small yachts. Mr. Clayton declared in January that 2½-raters would soon be 29 or 30 feet long. Mr. Dixon Kemp, on the other hand, so late as 1881, when the sixth edition of his book was published, gave 'the lengths of water-line . . . . possible in the classes . . . . as follows':—

60 raters,		60 to 70 feet,		their	1892	developments	being	68 feet	
40	"	50 "	60 "	"		"		59	"
20	"	40 "	50 "	"		"		46	"
10	"	30 "	40 "	"		"		38	"
5	"	20 "	30 "	"		"		34	"
2½	"	16 "	20 "	"		"		28	"
1	"	10 "	12 "	"		"		21	"

This forecast erred in the three smallest classes, where prophetic utterances, if only for six months, are extremely hazardous. The fact gives additional piquancy to small yacht racing.

The Solent clubs most interested in this racing began the year 1887 with a conference on January 28 at Southampton, and another on February 2 at Portsmouth, when it was finally agreed to recommend:—

1. The continuation of length class racing for the season of 1887.

2. The adoption of two new classes of square-sterned boats to race under the new rule, *viz.*—

(a) 2½-raters not exceeding 21 feet L.W.L.

(b) 1-¼ "   "   "   17 "   "

In both classes an overhang limit of 1 foot and a mainsail limit of 55 *per cent.* of the total sail-area.

Special Racing, 1887

Two new boats were built for class (*a*), Miss Cox's *Madcap* and Colonel Bucknill's *Thalassa* (see table). They were well matched, the rig being the same, *viz.* sloop with a small topsail of about 80 square feet. They were capital 'day boats,' with roomy wells, and fairly good performers in a sea-way. At first *Madcap* proved the faster, but towards the end of the season *Thalassa* won most prizes, and captured the class medal of the R.S.Y.C.

Mr. Campbell's *Merrythought* was the only new boat in class (*b*), but she failed to beat *Tootsie* (afterwards named *Minnow*), which belonged to Mr. Payne, and was altered to fit the class. On the whole, the racing in the new classes was somewhat disappointing, owing to the small number of competitors and of races. See the following table, over the page, which also includes the races for the 'Solent Classes' in 1888 and 1892, and shows the great development of the sport during the past five years.

The actual races only are recorded, as clubs deserve but little credit for offering prizes hedged in by such conditions that owners will not compete for them.

Class Racing, 1888.

Early in 1888, delegates from several of the Solent clubs met at the house of the Royal Southampton, to settle the difficult question of the classes of small racing yachts to be encouraged on the Solent, it having become clear that racing under a rating of length alone was played out.

Races in the Solent Classes

Yacht Clubs and Sailing Clubs	1887			1888				1892					
	21'	17'1½	Total	10	5	2½	Total	10	5	2½	1	½	Total
Royal Yacht Squadron	0	0	0	0	0	0	0	1	1	1	0	0	3
Royal London	1	0	1	3	0	3	6	0	1	2	2	2	7
Royal Southern	1	1	2	2	2	2	6	0	2	2	2	2	8
Royal Victoria	0	0	0	0	0	0	0	1	3	9	7	7	27
Royal Albert	0	0	0	2	0	2	4	0	6	6	6	6	24
Royal Southampton	7	6	13	4	2	8	14	4	8	8	8	8	36
Solent Yacht Club	0	0	0	1	0	1	2	0	3	3	1	3	10
Royal Portsmouth Corinthian	1	0	1	7	1	7	15	0	4	9	7	9	29
Castle Yacht Club	(started)			5	0	8	13	1	12	12	9	7	41
Island Sailing Club	—	—	—	—	—	—	—	0	0	9	9	9	27
Minima Sailing Club	—	—	—	—	—	—	—	0	0	2	12	9	23
Bembridge Sailing Club	—	—	—	—	—	—	—	0	0	2	1	13	16
Totals	10	7	17	26	6	34	66	7	40	65	64	75	251

The Y.R.A. recommended that 10-, 5-, and 2½-rating, by the new formula L. × S.A. ÷ 6,000, should be encouraged as the small classes, but the Scotch and Irish clubs favoured 6- and 3-raters as better suiting their 3-tonners, which had been produced under the 1730 rule, and were about 6-rating. After a lively correspondence in the *Field*, in which the editor steered a middle course between the Southern buoys and the Northern shallows, the conference at Southampton decided to adopt the classes recommended by the Y.R.A., and there has been no cause to regret this decision.

10-, 5-, and 2½-raters consequently became known as the 'Solent Classes,' and the limits on S.A. in mainsail and on L.O.A. were quashed, no objection being raised by vested interests.

THE 10-RATERS, 1888.

The 10 class racing this year mainly consisted of a duel between Mr. Clarke's new 10, the *Dis*, and Mr. Arabin's 6½-rater, the *Lollypop*, built for cruising, but a very fast and capable boat (see table opposite).

The lengthers *Verena* and *Frolic*, each about 7-rating, tried their luck on a few occasions, but they were soon proved to be outclassed under the rating rule. *Little Nell*, *Raven*, *Ina*, and *Jenny Wren* also competed. *Dis* finished the season with the excellent figure of merit 52.2, and '*Lollypop*' with 34.6. This figure of merit is found by the formula proposed by Colonel F. J. Smith, R.E., in 1890, *viz.*:

$$M = 100P \div (N + \sqrt{N} + 2)$$

where M is the figure of merit
N is the number of starts
P is the number of first prizes,

all referring to class races only. Colonel Smith subsequently elaborated the formula by allowing points for sails over, and for second prizes when three boats started; but it is practically impossible to get such records with accuracy, and the resulting order of merit is the same whichever figure of merit be adopted.

Hence it is best to employ the simplest formula in which first prizes alone count, as in the one just given, which will be adopted in these pages.

Further details of the 10-rater racing will be found in a tabulated form in of *Land and Water*, Oct. 20, 1888.

THE 5-RATERS, 1888.

Mr. L. M. Ames attempted to start the 5-rating class by building *Fair Geraldine* (see table of dimensions), but the class received but little encouragement from the clubs this year, and there were very few purely class races. The *Flutterby*, 4-rater, designed by her owner, Mr. Fred. Hughes, Mr. Farmer's *Chittywee*, and Mr. Newton-Robinson's *Rose* were the only competitors available.

THE 2½-RATERS, 1888.

Mr. Waller's *Lady Nan*, Mr. Manning's *Ada*, and the late Mr. Sidney Watson's *Chipmunk* were the new boats in this class, the first named being a great success at a moderate cost, the usual oak timbers, bent ash frames, and pine planking being used in her construction. Her lines are given in Mr. Dixon Kemp's *Yacht Architecture*, second edition. *Madcap*, her chief opponent, had been slightly lengthened during the winter, and a counter added; thus improved, she was able to turn the tables on *Thalassa* (see following table).

Racing Records, 1888

1888	Starts	Prizes			Figure of merit
		First	Other	Total	
10-*Rating Class*					
Dis.	29	19	6	25	52
Lollypop	17	8	4	12	34
2½-*Rating Class*					
Lady Nan	31	19	9	28	49
Madcap	24	8	10	18	26
Tottie	6	2	0	2	19
Thalassa	34	3	11	14	7
Fairy	21	2	3	5	7
Minnow	10	1	2	3	6

The feature this year was the birth of the heavy lead fin-keel. Mr. Payne tried it in *Lady Nan*, and Captain Hughes had a similar keel placed on 'Fairy,' thereby improving both her speed and power.

Another excitement was caused by Mr. Simpson very gamely sailing his *Tottie* (4.5 feet beam) round from the Thames, so as to try the Solent 2½-raters. *Tottie* was designed by Mr. G. L. Watson for a special class, 21 feet L.W.L. and 500 S.A. She won easily in this class on the Thames, but only scored on the Solent in light weather, and soon found it expedient to return to her muddy headquarters. *Minnow* also won a few prizes in light weather by means of her time allowance; but

Chipmunk 12 starts, *Ada* 4, *Titu* 2, and *Cormorant* 1 start, failed to score for their figure of merit.

The season's racing was good, and the class evidently established itself in public favour. The Castle Club, then at Hamble, gave a number of races for the class, and several members of the club agreed to build 2½-raters for the coming season.

For the results see the record table for 1888.

CLASS RACING, 1889
THE 10-RATERS, 1889.

The owner of *Lollypop* being encouraged by her performances in 1888, commissioned Mr. Arthur Payne to design a racing 10-rater; whence it came about that the swift and handsome *Decima* was launched from the Belvidere yard in the following spring. She was a few inches shorter than *Dis*, but in every other respect a more powerful boat—more beam, draught, and displacement, also a larger mainsail.

The *Drina* was built at Cowes about the same time, but she was designed simply as a 32-ft. L.W.L. day boat, and her owner, Prince Batthyany Strattmann, only decided to race her when she was already in frame. The lead keel was then dropped 1.8 foot and the sail increased 400, to 1,800 square feet. Unfortunately for *Drina* it was a windy summer.

Mr. Ratsey tuned up his fine square-sterned yacht *Dolly Varden* with a lovely suit of sails. Captain Montagu lengthened *Lil* and converted her into the 9-rater *Nety;* and Mr. Clarke brought out *Dis* from her padlocked abode and did all that he could to make her win—but in this he was disappointed, though when beaten he stuck to the fight as only a true sportsman can.

Towards the end of the season the attention of Clydesiders was drawn to *Decima's* long string of successes, and the sporting owners of the old *Doris* and the new *Yvonne* sailed them round to do battle in the Solent lists.

Yvonne, designed by the famous son of Fife, was narrower and shorter than *Decima*, and had 45 square feet more sail, which placed her in the van in light weather. But *Decima* beat her five times in eight starts, and beat *Doris* eleven times in fourteen starts.

The results for the season are given in the record table over the page.

It was a red-letter year for the 10's on the Solent, nothing like it having occurred either before or since.

Racing Records, 1889

1889	Starts	Prizes			Figure of Merit
		First	Other	Total	
10-Rating Class					
Decima	39	28	6	34	59
Yvonne	32	13	12	25	33
Doris	38	12	7	19	26
Dis.	28	3	9	12	8
5-Rating Class					
Lollypop	10	5	3	8	33
Thief	3	2	0	2	29
Thalassa	12	5	3	8	28
Fair Geraldine	3	1	0	1	15
Cock-a-Whoop	5	1	2	3	10
Blue Bell	9	1	3	4	7
2½-Rating Class					
Humming Bird	38	25	4	29	54
Queen Mab	12	5	2	7	28
Cosette	19	4	6	10	15
G. G.	13	2	3	5	11
Nadador (Lady Nan)	21	2	8	10	7
Madcap	26	2	5	7	6
Thalassa	13	1	3	4	6
Thief	16	1	3	4	5

THE 5-RATERS, 1889.

Energy in one class is often accompanied by stagnation in another, and the 5's were certainly slow enough during 1889 to satisfy the most exacting Puritan.

The clubs did their duty, as fifteen races were given to the class on the Solent. *Lollypop*, cut down to a 5, was the most successful boat. Next came *Thief* (of which boat more *anon*); then *Thalassa, Fair Geraldine, Cock-a-Whoop, Blue Bell, Gleam, Ada, Dorothy*, and *Tar Baby* made up the motley crowd—the four last-named scoring a 'duck' for their figure of merit. *Gleam*, however, caused a little excitement by capsizing in one race, pitching her owner, Mr. Clayton, with several of his friends, into the sweet waters of Southampton, from which they were fortunately rescued with much promptitude by the blue gig carried on board Her Majesty's letter-bag boat, which was steaming past at the time of the accident. The class was nothing more nor less than a harbour of refuge for outclassed boats; and, as the yachts differed in their ratings, the race officers were ever busy calculating their time al-

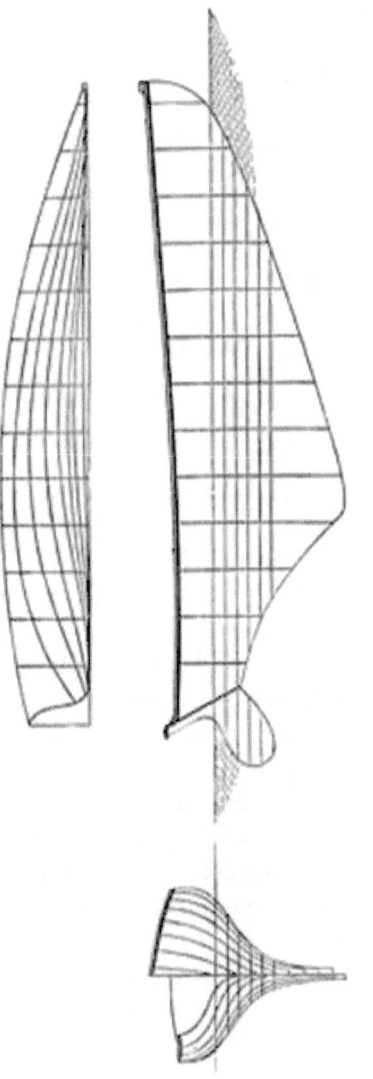

'Cock-a-Whoop', 2½-rater. Designed by A. E. Payne, M.I.N.A., 1889.

lowances, and growling inwardly at 'those confounded decimals.' *Fair Geraldine* was the only boat built for the class, but, curiously enough, when she tried conclusions at the end of the season she found herself 'between the devil and the deep sea,' the 2½-rater *Cock-a-Whoop*, with extra sail to qualify for the class, beating her in light weather on September 14, and the cruiser *Lollypop* beating her in a breeze on the 21st.

The broad results of the racing can be seen in the table of records for 1889.

The 2½-Raters, 1889.

Now began small yacht-racing in earnest, and a determined attempt was made to lower Mr. Payne's colours. Mrs. Schenley, the Earl of Dunraven, and Mr. T. B. C. West all joined the class, all cared but little what it cost to win, all sailed their boats well, all engaged good crews, and all went to Mr. G. L. Watson for the designs. He gave them enlarged 'Totties' (one with a C.B.), excellent boats in their way, but distinctly inferior to the type developing on the Solent under the motto, '*Payne and Pleasure.*'

Such a boat was *Humming Bird*, often called the *Hummer*, nearly 3 feet longer than *Lady Nan*, and about 17 inches longer on W.L. than her Watsonite competitors, but with little O.H. at either end. The fin-keel became more pronounced, the M.S. and scantling were further reduced, and the lug sloop rig was adopted—a combination which made her wonderfully fast on all points of sailing in any but light winds. She was sailed faultlessly by her owner, Captain J. W. Hughes, and made the excellent M. of 54 at the end of the season (see table of records).

Another boat of the year deserves mention—the 26-ft. C.B. sloop built and designed by Stephens of Southampton. She was purchased by Mr. Garrett of plunging boat fame, and named the 'G.G.' She had 10 feet beam, and did best on courses where she could avoid a tide by sailing over the shallows. *Thalassa* was raced in the class during June and July, after which she raised her R. and joined the 5's. She had been lengthened 2 feet aft during the winter, and greatly improved thereby, her speed now being equal to *Madcap* and *Lady Nan* (see record table for 1889.

Heathen Chinee, a yawl of peculiar design, and *Minnow* and *Chipmunk* raced on a few occasions, but failed to win any first prizes.

'Humming Bird,' Payne, 1889.

Solent Sailoresses.

This year was noticeable for the activity of ladies on the Solent. Miss Cox continued to race *Madcap*; her sister, Mrs. Rudston-Read, purchased *Lady Nan*, and raced her under the new name *Nadador*; Mrs. Schenley raced her new 2½ *Thief*; Mrs. Sidney Watson, Miss Harvey (now Mrs. A. Heygate), and the Misses Hughes occasionally steered in the races, and the daughters of *Thalassa* helped to work their father's boat, and sometimes steered her.

Late in the season—in the series of matches, 'ladies up,' between *Cosette* and *Queen Mab*—the earl got two 'daughters of the sea' to help him, and Miss Harvey steered the *Queen* for Mr. West.

It really looked as if ladies were about to take an active part in Solent racing; but next year, although races for ladies were specially provided in the programme of the Castle Club, some owners objected, and this form of sport received a somewhat rude and unexpected check from which it has never quite recovered.

Two sailing clubs were started on the Solent in 1889—the Island Sailing Club at West Cowes, and a branch of the Minima Sailing Club at Hamble. The former club arose during the winter of 1888, and Mr. Barrow, its present hon. secretary, states that it was 'the outcome of much boat-sailing talk in Cowes and in the *Field*..... on the superior charms and advantages of open-boat sailing;' but, 'like many season fashions, open boating soon found its level, and the I.S.C. has had an uphill fight to get open boats together for racing,' . . . . 'The influence of small raters seems to have been too much for the open craft, and though the club has offered very good prizes and a 20-guinea challenge cup, . . . yet the open-boat racing has been so poorly supported that most probably next year' (1893) 'the racing will be entirely confined to small raters, which have given much sport during the past season' (1892). The first 'Commodore, the late General Baring, taking much interest in the club, bought land adjoining the Customs watch, and built thereon the present small but very convenient club house, with its slipway, &c., where it has since passed a ... busy existence, holding in the season its fortnightly races, which have been well supported by 2½-, 1-, and ½-raters.'[2]

The Minima Sailing Club was established in the same year, 1889:

1st. To encourage the building, improvement, and sailing of small boats, and to promote seamanship and sport amongst amateur boat-sailers.

2nd. To arrange cruises and races both on the coast and inland waters.

3rd. To give to members who may wish to visit a coast, river, or lake which is new to them, facilities for obtaining information as to harbourage, boatmen, housing of boats, carriage of boats, and other local matters.

4th. To form branches or out-stations, and to affiliate local clubs as such, or otherwise.

This club has adopted the motto '*Per Mare per Terram,*' very appropriate for an institution which encourages the transport of boats by rail.

Commodore Hallowes is an Admiral, and settles disputes admirably. To him and to Mr. Herbert Ridsdale, the hon. secretary for the Solent, the success of the club in these waters is principally due. Unfortunately for the Solent, Mr. Ridsdale departed for fresh seas and outlets new in 1892.

A little club-house was erected in 1891 on the Hamble river-bank,

---

2. The above was penned at the end of 1892, and applies to that year. In 1893 the programme was enlarged by including races on alternating days for the 5-raters and for handicaps with boats up to 19-rating, not being class racers. A few races were given in 1891 to $2-1/_8$-raters.—.

opposite Warsash village, and the races now start and finish at this point, everything being done by miniature flags, &c., in strict accord with the Y.R.A. rules—altogether a nice little club, well managed, and possessing an excellent general programme which deserves to succeed.

The Castle Club also jumped ahead with a fair breeze in 1889, and a convenient house was built close to Calshot Castle, permission having been obtained from the Admiralty and War Office after much negotiation.

Ladies are encouraged to join the club. A room is set apart for them, and the near relatives of members can join on specially easy terms. This, a somewhat novel experiment, has succeeded admirably, and many ladies now attend the races and take a lively interest in the club. Tea at the club-house has become an afternoon function on race-days. Intoxicating liquors are not sold, but the housekeeper can generally put a square meal before a hungry mariner. The race officers have a tower-room to themselves. The starting gun—a heavy double-barrelled 4-bore—gives as excellent a report in its way as Mr. Parsons, the courteous correspondent for the *Field*—sharp, clear, distinct, and never a hang fire or a doubtful meaning.

We now pass to another year, but adhere to our present subject, because in 1890 the Bembridge Sailing Club first attracted notice by its energy under the diligent direction of its hon. secretary, Mr. Blair Onslow Cochrane, to whom we are indebted for the following characteristic account, which begins by claiming that—

> ....The Bembridge Sailing Club was started in 1886 under the name of the Isle of Wight Corinthian Sailing Club, changed in 1890 to the present name in order to avoid confusion with the Isle of Wight Corinthian Yacht Club (Ryde) since defunct. .... Many men of moderate means, but fond of boat-racing, thought a club whose leading features were:—
>
> 1st. Racing in boats of uniform pattern.
>
> 2nd. Racing in boats of small Y.R.A. rating (2 and under) ... would be a success, and in order to keep down expense and to suit the harbour, draught was limited to 3 feet.
>
> The first feature, which consisted of club boats, sloop-rigged, with rolling jibs and mainsails so as to reef easily, has been very popular; races in this class, both single-handed and otherwise, taking place almost daily. The subscription to these boats being

only 1*l.*, a member is enabled to have a summer's racing and cruising for this small sum, and can, if he be a fair hand in a boat, win good prizes. The boats are as nearly as possible equal, and, lots being drawn for them before racing, the best man wins as a rule. These boats are moored just under the club-house, and amusing incidents frequently occur.

A well-known man from the Emerald Isle, who is a keen and successful yacht-sailer, was the cause of a hearty laugh. Getting into a club boat, he set the mainsail, and, after letting go the moorings, he jumped aft to the helm, but unfortunately for him the hook of the mooring chain caught in the bobstay and held the boat fast. Advice was freely showered upon him from the club-house. 'Haul your port jib sheet aft.' 'Push the boom over.' 'Roll up the jib.' 'Steady your helm.' 'Get your hair cut,' &c., &c., amid roars of laughter; but it was a good ten minutes before he found out what was wrong, the boat sheering wildly all the time!

Races are also held in which each helmsman has to set sail, pick up moorings, &c. &c.

The classes under Y.R.A., 1-raters and ½-raters, also afford great sport, but resulted in the development of a very expensive type of boat, the natural consequence of the ascendency of the 'almighty dollar'; but these boats are exceedingly capable and safe. In 1891 the racing was only stopped one day on account of weather, and that summer was peculiarly stormy.

These small yachts afford an admirable school ... which will do more for the real sport of yacht-racing than anything else. A man who can sail a 1- or a ½-rater will never be out of place in a larger ship, or become a mere passenger, for he won't race a small boat unless he loves the sport.

At Bembridge the club has a slipway and cradle, and members can haul up their boats at any time, either for repairs or drying, at no cost. This is a great boon to a small boat-owner.

There are generally about forty races each season, of from 5 to 10 knot course. The starting is by semaphore, and recalls are effected by blowing a fog-horn to attract attention and then exposing the boat's racing flag painted on zinc ... thus doing away with cards and enabling post entries.

The harbour, capable of much improvement, is in the hands of a ... company. ...

There are two good boat-builders, a good sail-maker, and a ship-chandler.

Tides run very slack, and the railway station, telegraph office, steamboat pier, and first-class hotel are all within fifty yards.

Classes for 2½-raters and deep draught 1-raters have now (1892) been started, and will race outside. . . .

Further details concerning this excellent and flourishing club will be found in a table further on.

Class Racing, 1890

. . . . may be described in the words fives and two-point fives. *Dis* and *Decima* were sold and went away, the 10-R. class collapsed, and the ones and halves were only talked about, not built. The 5-rating class was thoroughly started this year, and a boat which devoured the cakes for two seasons was launched in the 2½-rating class.

Racing Records, 1890

1890	Starts	Prizes			Figure of merit
		First	Other	Total	
5-Rating Class					
Glycera	43	19	12	31	37
Alwida	40	14	16	30	29
Archee	14	4	5	9	20
Valentine	26	5	4	9	15
Quinque	39	2	10	12	4
Fair Geraldine	13	0	1	1	0
2½-Rating Class					
The Babe	27	15	6	21	44
Humming Bird	33	12	3	15	29
Dolphin	26	7	6	13	21
Cock-a-Whoop	33	4	18	22	10
Thalassa	10	1	0	1	6
Mliss	34	2	10	12	5
Troublesome	22	1	5	6	3

Lord Dunraven became Commodore of the Castle Club in the spring. He was already an avowed champion for and a generous supporter of small yacht racing, and during the winter—to be precise, on November 23, 1889—he wrote an epoch-marking letter to the *Field* which produced good fruit. In it he said:—

'May I add a word about the small classes on the Solent? Your remarks in your issue of the 9th inst. were, I think, rather unfair upon the 5's. Roughly speaking, I suppose the cost of a 20 is about three-fifths more than the cost of a 10; a 10 costs nearly two-thirds more than a 5, and a 5 would come to about double the expense of a 2½. The proportional initial expense diminishes according to size; but the converse is the case in respect of working expenses.

The crew of a 2½ can sail a 5, but double the crew of a 5 will be found in a 10, and a 20 will require another couple of hands and a pilot in addition to the crew of a 10.

The 5's and 20's appear to be the cheapest classes. Nothing can be more delightful than a 2½. It is the perfection of racing of its kind; but the absence of any accommodation below is a serious drawback under certain circumstances, especially to persons living at a distance.

In a 5 you can change clothes, boil a kettle, and, on a pinch, sleep.'

THE 5-RATERS, 1890.

Lord Dunraven's boat *Alwida* and Mr. P. Perceval's boat *Glycera* were designed by Payne and built at Southampton; Col. Bucknill's *Quinque* was designed by her owner and built at Hamble in a very substantial manner by Luke & Co.

'QUINQUE,' 5-RATER.
(Lt.-Col. Bucknill, R.E.).

Two new boats were designed by Mr. G. L. Watson—the *Valentine* for Mrs. Schenley, and the *Archee* for Mr. McNish. The elements of all these boats will be found in the table for 5-raters, and detailed drawings of *Valentine* are given in the sixth edition of Dixon Kemp's *Yacht Architecture*. *Archee*, the more capable of the two Watsonites, was built at Wivenhoe. She was beaten on the Solent when she first tried conclusions, but her sail-plan was improved and 5 cwt. of lead transferred from inside to out, after which she made some good matches with *Glycera* and *Alwida*. She scored four firsts for fourteen starts in the Solent, and three more firsts in four ex-Solent races. Her speed probably astonished her designer as much as other people, and this surprise, combined with the success of the 2½-rater C.B. boats on the Clyde in 1891, may account for the best Watsonite in the large classes 1892 belonging to this reviled type. (See Mr. Watson's evidence before the Y.R.A. Committee, 1886.)

But we live to learn. Mr. McNish deserves some credit in this matter, as he thoroughly believed in the centreboard when others (including the designer he employed) were sceptical.

At the end of the season Mr. Payne's boats again headed the list, as will be seen in the table of records. They were built lighter, they drew more water, and they were sailed better than the other boats in the class; $5/_8$-inch mahogany planking was employed, but they leaked freely at the garboards, and their floors had to be strengthened.

Fair Geraldine only scored one third prize in thirteen starts.

THE 2½-RATERS, 1890.

This may be termed *Babe's* year, as a boat of that name built for Mr. W. A. Beauclerk from a design by Mr. Payne won fifteen firsts in twenty-seven starts on the Solent. She was not the longest boat in the class, but had a foot more than *Hummer*. She had fairly good depth and displacement, and in some respects was like her principal rival—especially in the faultless manner in which she was sailed and prepared for every race. Her owner a good helmsman and keen sportsman, her skipper first-rate in every way, she came out of the builder's yard as smooth as a bottle, and after two years' racing everything about her was in the same high-class racing condition.

The *Dolphin*, designed by Mr. Clayton, proved to be fast and capable. In addition, she had the germs of a new type in her—*viz.* the overhanging end to evade the measurement of length, which has since developed such startling proportions. Drawings of this boat are given

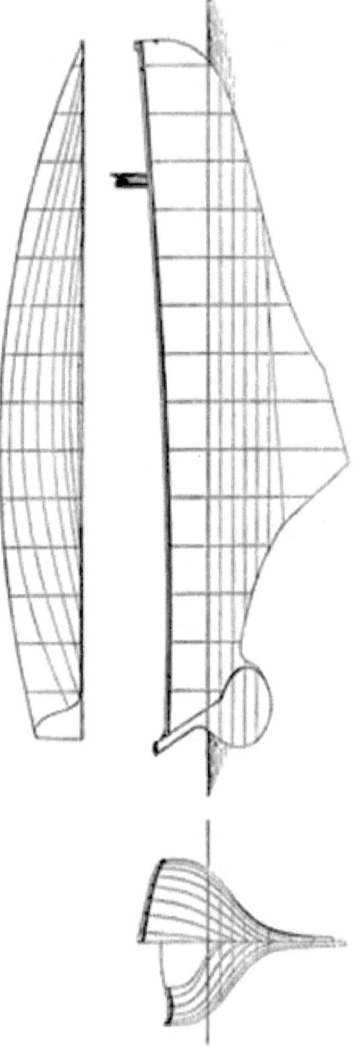

'The Babe,' 2½-rater. Designed by A. E. Payne, 1890.

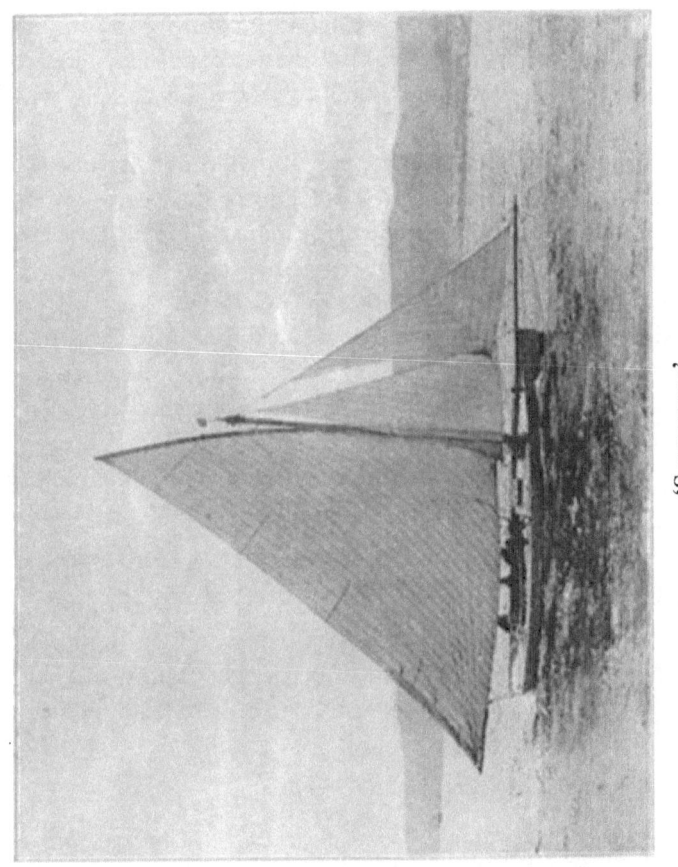

'SAVOURNA'

5-rater. (H. L. Mulholland, Esq.) Designed by A. E. Payne, 1891.

in *Yacht Architecture*. It is difficult to point to any defect in her lines or general design.

Camilla and *Janetta*, 26½ feet, and *Mliss*, 25 feet, were designed by Mr. Payne, *Mliss* only doing well. She belonged to Miss Cox, whose sister, Mrs. Rudston-Read, had the *Troublesome* built at Fay's, from a design by Mr. Soper—a somewhat ugly boat with a counter and flare bow. She was fast in light weather, and won the Challenge Plate given by Mr. George Schenley to the Castle Yacht Club.

Cock-a-Whoop, built in 1889 for Captain Hughes's two sons, from a design by Mr. Payne, was raced, as already stated, in the 5-rater class at first, but in 1890 she was rearranged to fit the 2.5 class, in which she raced.

Two of the narrow boats, *Cosette* and *Thief*, did not fit out for the Solent racing, and the third, *Queen Mab*, did not succeed in winning a single first prize in six starts. The same remark applies to *Camilla* with nineteen starts, to *Janetta* with ten starts, and to *G.G.* with five starts. Four boats, two being new boats by Payne, and one a 'last year's boat' by Watson, failed to score a single point for their figure of merit! These boats are consequently omitted in the table of records, but full particulars of the racing can be found in a table published October 20, in *Land and Water*.

We now pass to 1891, which will be remembered as the ½-raters' year.

Class Racing, 1891

The 10-raters *Dis* and *Decima* raced in a few matches on the Solent; but it was tame work, the old story being constantly retold. In the end, however, *Decima* was found to be over her rating and had to disgorge her prizes. Hence the final results are only misleading, and are not entered in the record table opposite.

The 5-Raters, 1891.

Valentine was replaced by the *Windfall*, and *Glycera*, by the *Savourna*, the two new boats being designed by Mr, Payne and built by the new firm of Summers & Payne, which like a phœnix had risen from the ashes of a disastrous fire at the Belvidere yards of A. R. Payne & Sons and Black & Co. (late Hatcher & Co.).

Mr. Summers, having command of capital, bought up both these firms, took Mr. Arthur Payne into partnership, erected labour-saving machinery, rebuilt the premises in a very substantial manner, and brought a good business capacity to bear upon the whole concern.

In the two new 5-raters the fin-keel, the lug, and the general arrangements on the *Babe* and *Hummer* were carried into the larger class with complete success. Mr. Langrishe joined the class with a new boat, the *Iernia*, built at Gosport and designed by the son of Fife. She differed from Mr. Payne's boats in possessing considerable overhang, in a flare bow, and a long counter. Her hull was somewhat similar to *Valentine*, and she was rigged as a lug sloop like *Savourna*. *Windfall*, however, sported the divided skirt in front of the mast.

Racing Records, 1891

1891	Starts	Prizes			Figure of merit
		First	Other	Total	
5-Rating Class					
Windfall	40	22	12	34	45
Savourna	40	14	20	34	29
Alwida	29	6	8	14	16
Iernia	29	3	4	7	8
2½-Rating Class					
The Babe	45	36	3	39	67
Avadavat	40	12	17	29	25
Fiera	33	7	9	17	17
Janetta	36	1	11	12	2
½-Rating Class					
Spruce	12	6	2	8	35
Tiny	33	14	7	21	34
Narua	25	9	6	15	28
Bairn	29	9	11	20	25
Dee Dee	38	8	19	27	17
Jeanie	50	5	17	22	8

Katherine, a new 5, built, designed, and sailed by Mr. Black (who had retired from business), was a capable boat of 31 L.W.L., with a straight stem and a pretty counter; but she failed to score.

Quinque had been altered during the winter, but was not improved. *Alwida* was not changed until in August the lug was adopted, when the same was done for *Quinque*. Their sailing was improved, but not enough to win.

The racing proved the superiority of Mr. Payne's designs, which now and for the third year headed this class. See table of records, which shows that *Windfall* and *Savourna* competed in no less than

The 'Babe'
2½-rater. Designed by A. E. Payne, 1890.

forty class matches. This was due to the senior yacht clubs like the Squadron, Royal London, Royal Victoria, and Royal Albert giving extra match days for the Solent classes. Coincident with this fashion of giving numerous races there arose in some quarters a desire to do it economically, one club being specially noticeable. For instance, at its annual regatta, 1891, the second prize was not awarded to Lord Dunraven, as only three boats started, although the prize was given to the club by another owner and several rather heavy entrance fees had been collected. In fact, the club cleared 7*l*. 15*s*. by the race. This, and other cases of the kind, may cheer those who tremble at the cost of giving races, and may even point a way whereby less wealthy clubs may 'turn an honest penny.'

THE 2½-RATERS, 1891.

Humming Bird, *Mliss*, *Dolphin*, and *Camilla* did not race, *Hummer* eventually going to Ireland and *Camilla* to the East coast, *Mliss* and *Dolphin* to Plymouth. The new boat *Fiera* was designed for Miss Cox by Mr. Payne, who also turned out the *Avadavat*, 28 feet L.W.L., for Mr. Wilson Hoare. Mr. E. N. Harvey had the *Undine* built at Cowes from a design by Mr. Clayton, and Sir G. Pearce the *Squirrel*, designed by Stone. *Janetta* was raced again.

Not one of them could touch the *Babe*, which seemed to go faster than ever now that her principal antagonist, the *Hummer*, was out of the way.

The record for the season will be found in the table, and *Babe's* figure of merit—67—obtained by thirty-six first prizes in forty-five starts, was a wonderful performance.

THE ½-RATERS, 1891.

Just as the 2½-raters had been the outcome of an agreement among some members of the Castle Club to build and start the class in 1888, so the ½-rating class in 1891 was produced by a similar agreement among certain enthusiastic boat-sailers of the Bembridge Sailing Club. Mr. Payne was consulted, and quite a fleet of these little ships was built in the Belvidere yards during the winter of 1890-91—*viz*. *Narua*, *Eileen*, *Otokesan*, *Dee Dee*, *Idono*, *Ladybird*, *Kittiwake*. These were all capital little boats—miniature yachts, in fact—with rather heavy lead keels of the fin type, and with good displacement—some 11 or 12 cwt.—about three-quarters of it being ballast.

Two more of similar type—*viz. Tiny* and *Dancing Girl*—were built at Hamble from designs by Mr. Herbert Ridsdale, and the *Coquette* was built at Gosport from a design by Mr. C. Nicholson. A boat designed by Fife, the *Jeanie*, had a counter 4.6 feet long. Their L.W.L. usually varied from 15½ to 17 feet. The *Mosquito*, designed by Mr. Soper, was built of cedar; the others were planked with mahogany, and all were good specimens of the modern art of boat-building.

Most of the sail-plans consisted of a large lug and a spitfire jib secured to a roller which could be revolved on the forestay as an axle by means of cords led aft to the well of the boat. Thus the sail could be reefed by rolling it up like a blind. This was the invention of Captain Du Bowlay. It is very convenient, especially for single-handed sailing. By a further contrivance, the roller can be carried on the end of an iron or steel arm pivoted in a goose-neck secured to the front of the mast and worked by guys from the well; in which event the forestay is rigged in front of the roller. Thus the jib can be reefed or unreefed, or set at an angle, and converted into a spinnaker in a few seconds. (See illustration).

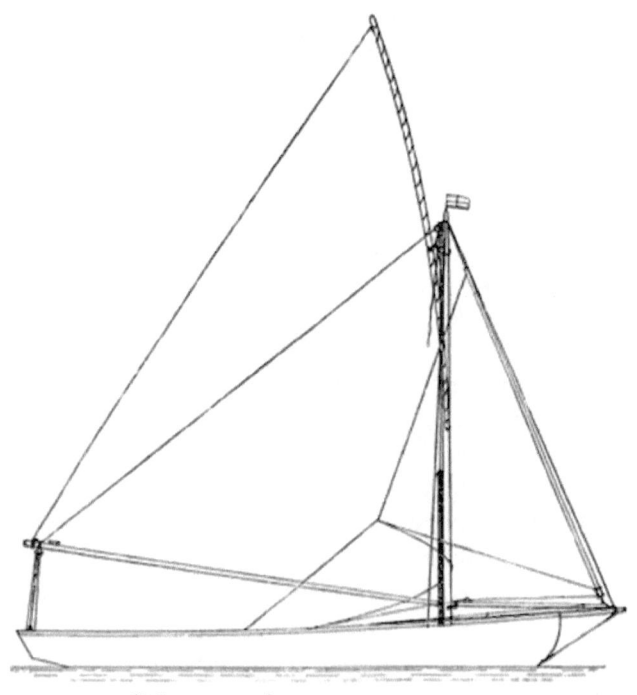

'Mosquito,' with roll foresail.
Designed by Soper, 1892.

These little craft are wonderful sea-boats, and created quite a furore of enthusiastic excitement throughout the season, several ladies taking an active interest in the sport, and some of them steering their own boats in the roughest weather. But they were not destined to have all the fun to themselves. In the middle of the season a spruce young gentleman arrived from the metropolitan waters with a contrivance termed a 'canoe yawl'—a shallow, light, buoyant thing having little or no ballast except the crew, who sat in a canvas-bag arrangement to be emptied as occasion required on rough days. The craft was as easily upset as righted; but the crew combined the acrobat with the water-rat, and showed great skill in keeping the little ship right side up.

The *Torpedo*, another device of the kind, and owned by Mr. Stewart, came from Oxford.

The owners of the Solent half-raters were not too well pleased to see some of the prizes going into the lockers of these canoe yawls, and a fine string of letters appeared in the *Field;* but the excitement moderated when it was found that the raters usually scored honours.

One other type was tried—the C.B. dinghy. *Bairn,* however, was the only example in this class. Many of the clubs limited the crew of half-raters to two hands. This did not suit the *Bairn* type, which requires three or four hands to windward as 'ballast' in the usual Solent weather.

It is impossible to give a summary of the racing in this class, because it is very imperfectly reported in the sporting press, and the club secretaries do not invariably retain correct records even of the starters and winners.

Kittiwake was generally considered the best boat of the year; but several others ran her close. The only boats recorded in the *Yacht-racing Calendar* are *Tiny, Narua, Bairn,* and *Jeanie,* and for these the figures are given in our table of records. *Spruce's* record includes her Solent races only. She won numerous prizes in other waters.

CLASS RACING, 1892

.... began, so to speak, with a conference of club delegates under the hospitable roof of the Royal Southampton Yacht Club, on the last Saturday in February. An amicable meeting agreed to encourage as many open races as possible by withdrawing the restriction that owners and helmsmen should be members of the clubs.[3] It was also decid-

---

[3] The Royal Portsmouth Corinthian Yacht Club, however, still continues, (as at time of first publication), to give races only to those owners who are members of the club; and the Royal Southampton adheres to the condition that the yachts in the small classes shall be steered by members of the club.

ed that the classes 'not exceeding ½-rating,' and 'exceeding ½-rating but not exceeding 1-rating,' should be added to 'the Solent classes,' and be supported by the yacht and sailing clubs on the Solent. Dates for match days were agreed to, and the meeting separated.

The result was satisfactory, as better sport in the small classes was seen on the Solent in 1892 than in any previous year.

Racing Records, 1892

1892	Starts	Prizes			Figure of merit
		First	Other	Total	
5-*Rating Class*					
Dacia	31	23	4	27	59
Cyane	12	6	4	10	34
Windfall	9	4	4	8	29
2½-*Rating Class*					
Gareth	9	5	1	6	36
Faugh-a-Ballagh	49	15	15	30	26
Polynia	25	7	5	12	22
Papoose	41	10	15	25	20
Hoopoo	44	9	17	26	17
Cockatoo	40	7	8	15	14
Molly	41	5	14	19	10
Stork	36	4	5	9	9
Bud	33	2	8	10	5
1-*Rating Class*					
Doushka	23	13	3	16	44
Nansheen	32	15	8	23	38
Pup	23	7	8	15	23
Rogue	45	11	11	22	20
Mahatma	?	12	18	30	?
Barbet	?	1	12	13	?
½-*Rating Class*					
No complete records					

THE 10-RATERS, 1892.

An attempt to revive the 10-R. class was made by Mr. J. Gretton, jun., who built the *Doreen* from a design by Mr. W. Fife, jun. She forms a startling exponent of the modern racer.

Her mainsail, a lug, contains 1,061 square feet of canvas by Y.R.A. measurement, her total S.A. being 1,572, her L.W.L. 38 feet, and her L.O.A. 56.5 feet (see table for 10-raters).

A fine, seaworthy craft, fast in a breeze, but not so good in light winds owing to the absence of a sky-scraper. She has the divided skirt forward, but the forestay is taken through the deck some distance inside the stem-head, this having an O.H. of 8.2 feet. This arrangement was used for a similar reason on the cutter yacht *Margaret*, 265 tons, illustrated in the *Field*, 1853.

'DOREEN,' 20 (J. GRETTON, JUN., ESQ.).
DESIGNED BY FIFE, 1892.

The present owner of *Dis*, Mr. Sparks, came forward very pluckily to battle for some of the class prizes on the Solent and the South Coast, and scored on a few occasions in light weather; in a heeling breeze, however, *Doreen* romped away from him.

Although the 10's form one of the 'Solent classes,' they do not flourish.

If men built to the class they would get plenty of racing, as in 1889, but Lord Dunraven's letter, already quoted, gives ample reasons for the 5- and the 20-raters being preferred.

THE 5-RATERS, 1892.

This may be termed *Dacia's* year, when a young and comparatively unknown designer succeeded in lowering the colours of Mr. Payne where others had so signally failed.

'DACIA'
5-rater (Earl of Dudley).
Designed by C. Nicholson, jun., 1892.

Dacia was built at Gosport for Mr. R. H. Langrishe from a design by Mr. C. Nicholson (jun.). For her dimensions, &c., see table for 5-raters. She carries her sail well, but is probably built too light. In the middle of the racing season she had to lay up for a time and have a new stem fitted, presumably because the bow was straining. She carries a *deep* fin-keel, which draws about 8.5 feet. It is coppered. Her O.H. both fore and aft is extreme, and her sailing length is thereby considerably increased when sailing even at moderate speeds. But her success must also be due to a well-considered design as a whole, because her strongest point is clawing to windward, which she does in a marvellous way, blow high blow low, and her great length cannot assist her much on this point of sailing.

She cost no more than other boats of the same rating, but when the Earl of Dudley took a fancy to her, Mr. Langrishe sold her early in the season for 'four figures,' it is said; and she was worth it, for it is better to have one successful than two unsuccessful racers. Early in September she raced a rubber of matches against the Clyde crack *Natica*, Tor Bay being selected as the 'neutral water.' The stakes were heavy, and she won two out of the three races, being steered to victory by her designer.[4] During the season Lord Dudley generally steered her himself, but her designer steered at Tor Bay.

LORD DUNRAVEN'S 'CYANE,' 1892.

---

4. She subsequently lost the match on a protest, which was referred for settlement to the Council Y.R.A.

The *Cyane*, about the same L.W.L. as the *Dacia*, was built from a design by Mr. Payne for the Earl of Dunraven, who, as commodore of the Castle Club, and one of the first supporters of 5-raters, takes a great interest in the class. *Cyane* started well before *Dacia* and *Windfall* were launched, but afterwards only succeeded in beating *Dacia* once. She was laid up in the middle of the season.

Squall, a sister 5, built for Mr. A. F. S. Crawford, was not so fast, and failed to win pride of place in any race on the Solent.

Windfall, with her new owner, Mr. Gubbins, at the helm, did better against *Dacia* than any other yacht on the Solent, but she left for the Emerald Isle early in the season.

'Windfall,' 5-rater.
Designed by A. E. Payne, 1891.

Savourna was also raced by her owner, the Hon. H. L. Mulholland, M.P., before going to Ireland, but she did not succeed so well as when Mr. Perceval had her, or it may be that *Windfall* went better than in 1891.

Quinque had been lengthened during the winter, and was greatly improved thereby, but she failed to score until in July her keel was lowered, after which she beat *Dacia* twice in light weather, and won twelve prizes before the end of the season.

The full history of *Quinque* during her four years' racing is most instructive to the student on account of her numerous alterations, each of which afforded more trustworthy information on some special point than it is possible to obtain from the examination of new boats, however successful they may be; but the story is too long for these pages.[5]

The records of the Solent racing are entered in the table, wherein it will be found that *Dacia* made the excellent figure of merit 59, in spite of first two prizes lost by minor infractions of the rules, before Lord Dudley raced her.

THE 2½-RATERS, 1892.

This year was full of surprises in the 2½-rating class, as indeed in all the small classes.

These were mainly due to two gentlemen, Mr. Nat Herreshoff of Rhode Island, U.S., and Mr. C. Nicholson (jun.) of Gosport, G.B.

The success of their boats was largely owing to their long overhangs, producing a sailing length greatly in excess of the length measured for their rating.

Mr. Herreshoff also took full advantage of the power given by the bulb-keel to give great stability to a boat of very small displacement. He was therefore content to apply long overhangs to boats of moderate L.W.L. as compared with the English boats in the same class.

Mr. Nicholson, however, placed his long overhangs on boats of long L.W.L., and used fin-keels. Complete success crowned both these types.

Unfortunately the *Gareth* never met *Wenonah*, and the crack 2½ of the year is therefore still a matter of doubt.

Wenonah's elements, so far as known, are added to this list of boats, in order to facilitate comparison. She never raced on the Solent. She is sloop-rigged, with a very short gaff, and a fore-triangle, about the same as *Faugh-a-Ballagh*.

Gareth is 3 feet longer on the L.W.L., but 0.8 foot shorter than *Wenonah* in L.O.A. She is, therefore, a fairer boat than *Wenonah*, a greater percentage of her length being taxed for rating. It is an insult to the intelligence of a designer to suppose that any portion of the hull is useless. Consequently we must assume that all the 37.5 feet of

---

5. For further information and drawings of *Quinque*, see the *Yachtsman* of July 20 and October 5, 1893.

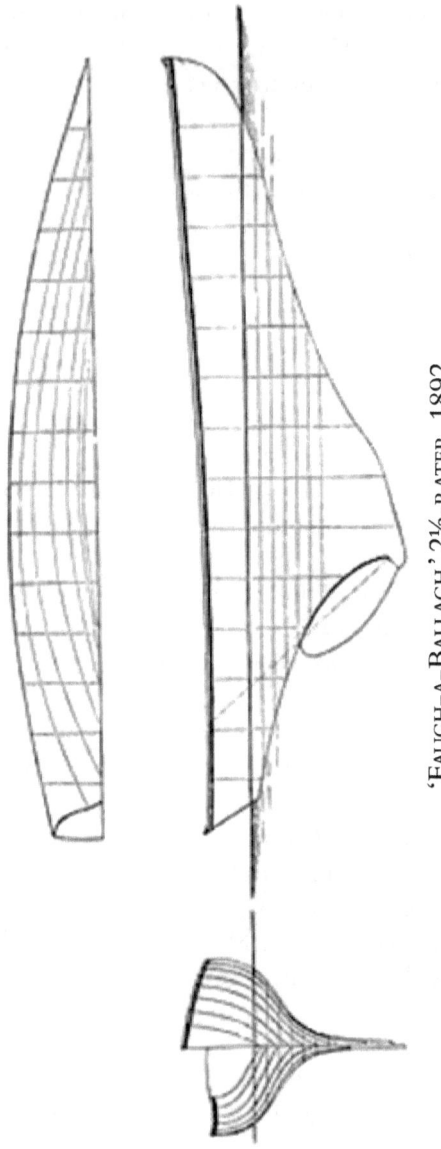

'Faugh-a-Ballagh,' 2½-rater, 1892.

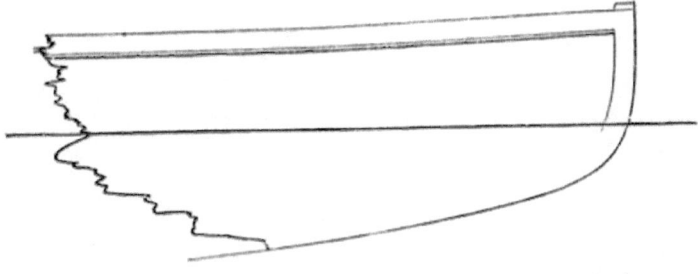

Old Fashion.

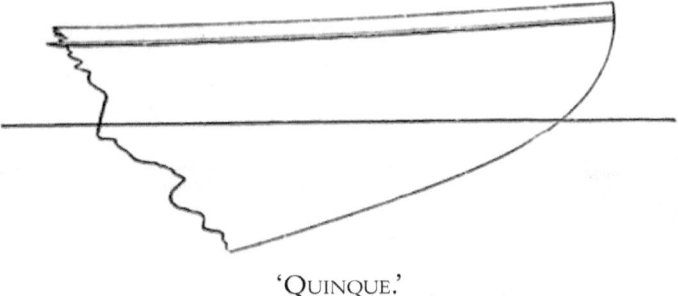

'Quinque.'

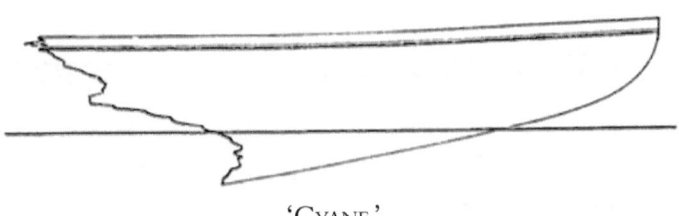

'Cyane.'

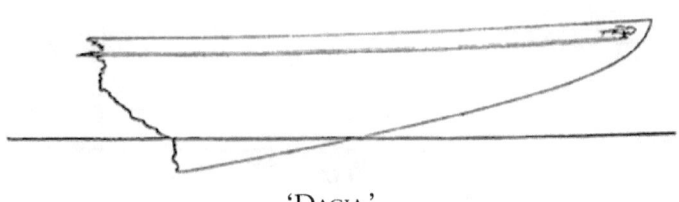

'Dacia.'

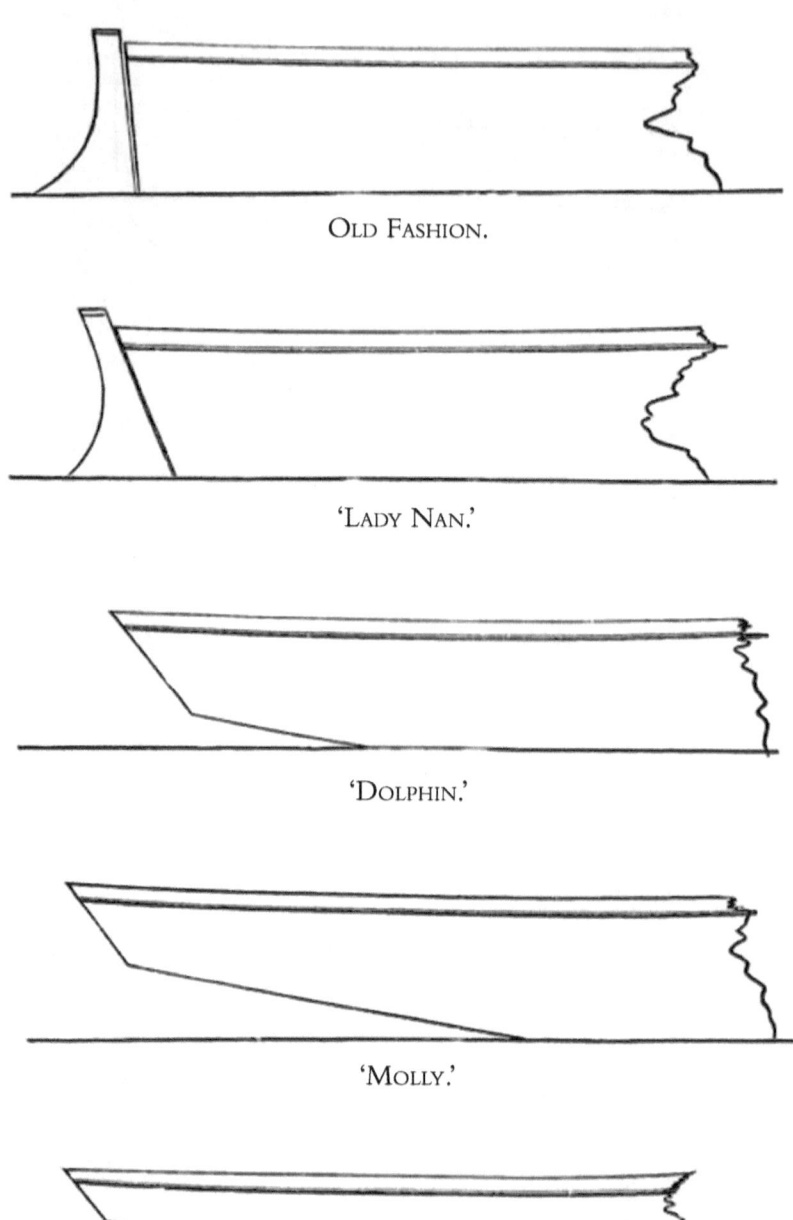

L.O.A. in *Wenonah* is useful, and, as the sailing length was that which the Y.R.A. intended to tax for rating in 1886, the *Wenonah* cannot be regarded as a 'short boat.'

The ability of a designer is legitimately employed in evading a measurement rule as far as possible, as did Mr. Edward Hammond Bentall in designing *Jullanar* in 1875, but the experience that is found at the council table of the Y.R.A. should checkmate such evasions of the spirit in which their rules are framed.

Gareth is not so excessive in type as *Molly* and *Stork* by the same designer, which came out earlier in the season and won a good many prizes before Mr. Payne's boats of the *Cockatoo* type were launched. When this occurred, *Molly's* keel was recast and lowered, after which she was less successful in any weather.

Mr. Payne built a number of 2½-raters for this year's racing; three of them—the *Papoose, Polynia,* and *Cockatoo*—have a canoe-shaped M.S., and fin-keels which taper upwards—not quite bulb-keels, but nearly so. The lead was also shaped like half a dumb-bell in longitudinal elevation. They were beamy boats of small displacement and great stability, and beat the rest of the fleet easily in a heeling breeze until '*Gareth*' appeared. In light weather they were generally beaten by *Hoopoo, Mynah, Faugh-a-Ballagh, Molly,* and *Stork. Faugh-a-Ballagh* perhaps possessed the highest *average* speed of any boat in the class, and seemed to go very much like the *Babe*, which is high praise. At the end of the season her string of flags was the longest, but this is often rather deceptive—especially when better boats are launched late, and when contests are occasionally selected for winning flags rather than the highest class honours.

Hoopoo was well raced; but the owner picked his weather, occasionally refusing to start in a strong wind when he thought he 'hadn't a chance.' No doubt this is correct if the 'Yachtsman's' medal be the object sought for; but few men possess the strength of mind to stand out with their boat at the starting line, crew eager for the fray, and everything all-a-taut-oh.

Mynah, another fast boat, was well sailed by her owner, Lieutenant F. Elwes, of the 68th Light Infantry, whenever he could escape from the duties of camp life, inspections, and summer manoeuvres.

Bud, designed by Mr. Soper for the Earl of Desart, did nothing so long as she stuck to her heavy C.B. made of gun-metal. When it was discarded, and a triangular lead keel fitted, she went better and led the fleet at the finish on two occasions when the weather suited her.

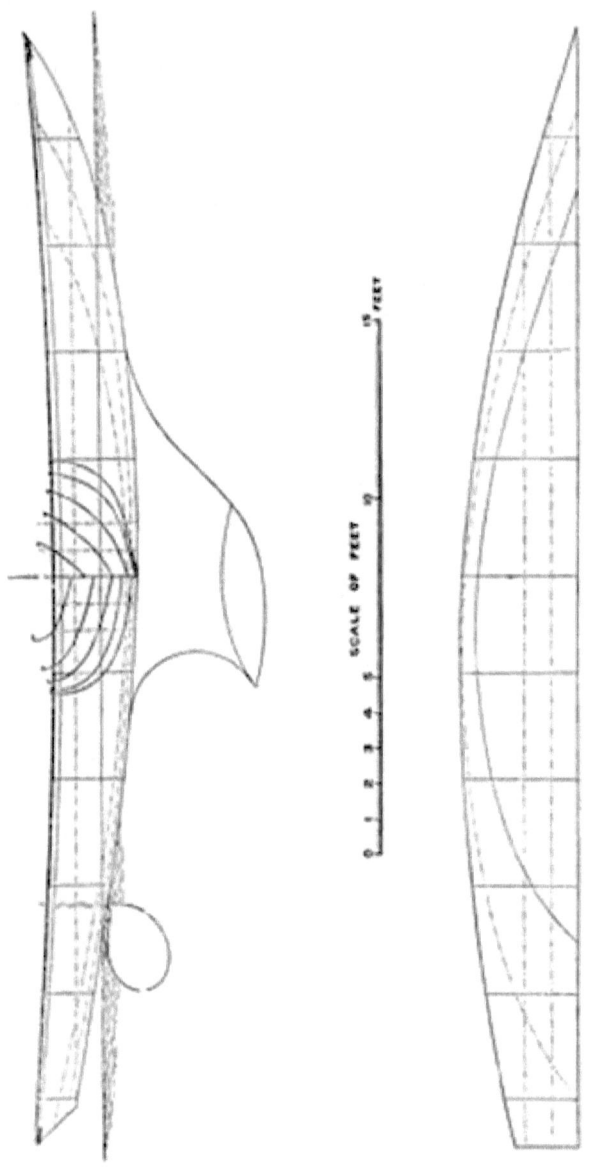

Design for 1-rater by J. M. Soper, 1892.

Calva, a new boat by Mr. Payne, also *Modwen* and *Walrus* by other designers, were failures as prize-winners on the Solent.

There were no less than 66 races for 2½-raters *on the Solent* in 1892, and the records of the best boats are given in the table, *Gareth* leading with a figure of merit, 36.

THE 1-RATERS, 1892.

This class had a half-hearted existence in 1890 and 1891, when Mr. T. Ratsey's *Pup* (see table) won most of the races, easily defeating the yachts' cutters of about the same rating, and generally succeeding in giving the time allowance to the ½-raters in the few mixed races open to her. The club conference, already described, having in 1892 added this class to the 'Solent classes,' a good programme and a full entry resulted.

Pup still competed, and went well in light weather. She is one of the *Bairn* or C.B. dinghy type, with plenty of beam and little ballast, depending upon her crew for much of her stability. A good type, and much less costly than the modern 1-rater, as, for example, the crack *Doushka*, built by Payne for Mr. Perceval. This boat is probably like *Cockatoo* in type. She stands up to her canvas well, and claws to windward in a wonderful way. The harder it blows the better she goes, but she fails in light weather.

Nansheen, another fast boat designed by the son of Fife for Mr. Burrowes, is a good sample of the 'weighted centreboard' type. She was built in Ireland by Doyle, and is a fine specimen of sound work. The C.B. is supported by a wire rope on a drum, worked by worm and wheel so that it is always supported in any position without keying, and can rise if it strike the ground with force.

The *Rogue* was another good boat, designed by Mr. Ridsdale for Mr. R. Vogan. At first she failed in windward work, but a bulb-keel was put upon her which quite cured the defect, and she then won plenty of prizes, her racing with *Nansheen* being close and exciting.

Mahatma, designed by her owner Mr. Flemmich, also went well. She now belongs to the Ladies Fanny and Blanche Stanhope.

The *Argula*, built at Gosport from a design by Mr. C. Nicholson, was a fast boat, but proved to be over rating. She was similar to the 2½-rater *Moll* in general arrangement and appearance.

Barbet was a good boat designed by Mr. Payne for Mr. Wilson Hoare.

All these boats have the fashionable rig, Ratsey's lug, and a small—

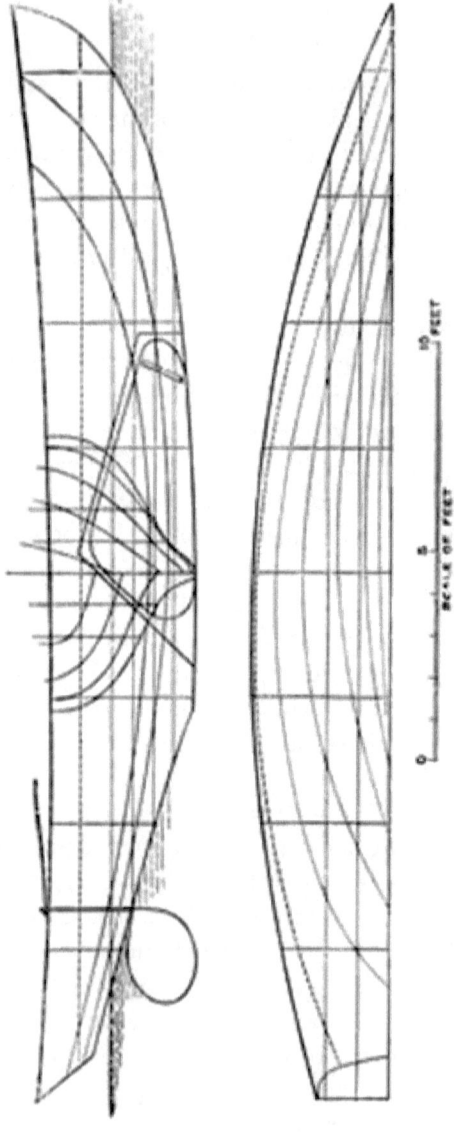

Design for a centreboard 1-rater by J. M. Soper, 1892.

very small—foresail. Dr. Hughes, of East Cowes, however, re-introduced the split lug in his 1-rater *Cariad*, and she went well when this severe handicap is allowed for.

The *Kitten*, built by Mr. Sibbick for the Hon. W. Ruthven, won a few second prizes; but *Oretta* and *Minuet*, built at Cowes for Mr. Lancaster Owen and his son, were not so successful, and the other boats which occasionally started—*viz. Query, Anaconda, Dorothy*, and *Tramp*—failed to score.

Nearly twenty 1-raters competed during the season—pretty good for the first year of a class, and indicative that the class is popular.

A 1-rater is, or ought to be, a good wholesome boat, costing but little more than a ½-rater, either to build or maintain.

Most of the clubs limit the crew to three hands—an excellent rule—to prevent the introduction of a racing canoe with the Malays' system of ballasting.[6]

The racing in the 1-rater class is not fully reported in the sporting press, and the records given in our table have been obtained from the owners.

The ½-Raters, 1892.

This class suffered from the attention bestowed on the 1-raters. *Kittiwake* had been sold to H.R.H. Prince Henry of Prussia, and *Eileen, Jeanie, Bairn, Narua, Spruce*, and *Torpedo* dropped out of the racing from one cause or another. *Coquette, Dancing Girl, Tiny, Dee Dee, Mosquito*, and *Ladybird* continued, however, to race on the Solent, thus forming an 'exhibition of Old Masters' and young mistresses, only one having changed hands during the winter, and Miss Sutton replaced her with the *Pique*, a new boat by Mr. Payne.

The late Mr. Sidney Watson also purchased a new boat from Mr. Payne, and called her the *Lilliput*. She was the last boat he ever sailed in. He much enjoyed racing her, and not infrequently led the little fleet. His sudden death in the prime of life was a great shock to all his numerous friends on the Solent.

English men and women are born lovers of sport, and attached to the tools they employ: the huntsman to his horse and hounds, the shooter to his dogs and guns, the turfman to his thoroughbred, and the sailing man to his yacht. A real devotion may exist for inanimate pieces of wood and metal. Especially is there poetry, and plenty of it,

---

6. This (and other limits of crew for the classes of 5-rating and under) has since been embodied in the Y.R.A. rules.

in a boat—that dancing, playful, wilful thing that only obeys the skilful hand. Ask any old crab-catcher. Yet racing seems to blunt the feeling. Many owners part with their boats and crews at the end of every season, and allow themselves no time really to care for any one of them.

Rather late in the season a new boat appeared designed by Mr. Herreshoff. She belonged to Miss W. Sutton, and was named very appropriately *Wee Winn*. She and her owner certainly did win, in even a more decisive manner than *Wenonah* on the Clyde. There was no mistake about it. The boat showed a clean pair of heels to the rest of the class in every sort of weather. She is a long boat, the true length being concealed in an excessive overhang—15.6 L.W.L., 23.9 L.O.A., M.S. like a canoe, small displacement, bulb-keel 3 cwt., draught under 3 ft. An approximate representation of her lines is given on the opposite page, and the illustration below gives an idea of her appearance when racing.

Towards the end of the season Mr. Soper of Fay's designed and built a fast boat, *The Daisy*, of somewhat similar type; about the same L.O.A., but longer L.W.L., and having more beam, depth, draught, and a heavier bulb-keel than *Wee Winn*. They only met twice, and *Daisy* was beaten; but she got away from the rest easily enough, and these two boats are certainly the fastest ½-raters on the Solent at the present time.[7]

Miss Sutton's 'Wee Winn,' ½ rater.
Designed by Herreshoft, 1892.

---

[7]. The *Daisy* was exhibited at the Royal Aquarium in 1893, and sold to some gentleman in the Antipodes; so that her keel, instead of her stern, is now pointing at the Solent ½-raters.

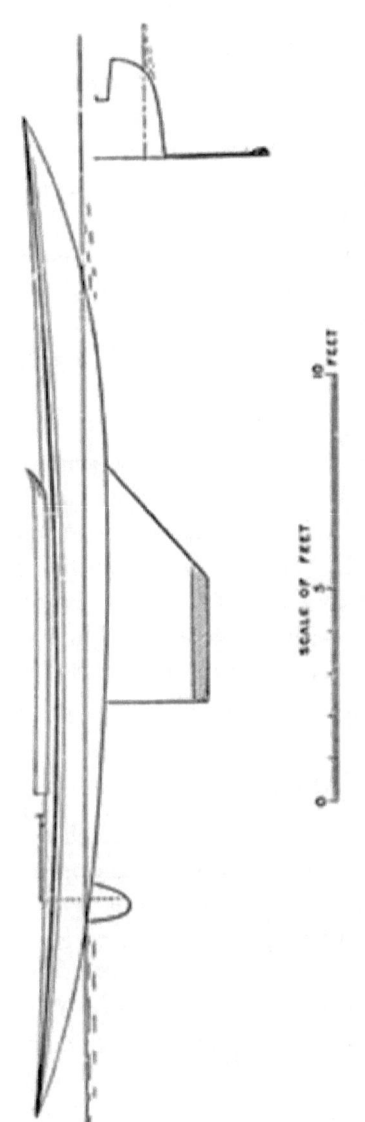

'Wee Winn,' ½-rater. Designed by Herreshoff for Miss Sutton, 1892.

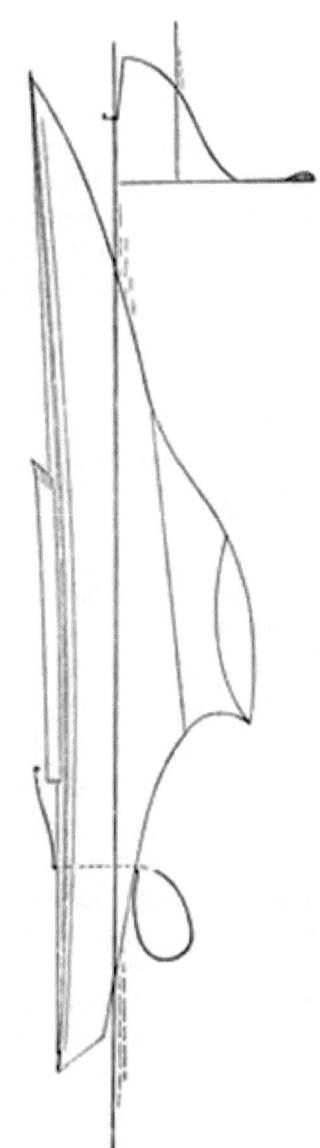

'Daisy.' Designed by J. M. Soper, 1892.

Class Racing, 1893

The racing on the Solent (apart from the large classes) during the season of 1893 will be principally remembered by the advent of the 20-rater class. It was not adopted at the Conference of Clubs held at the Club House of the R.P.C.Y.C, in February as one of the Solent Classes, which remained at ½-raters, 1-raters, 2½-raters, 5-raters, and 10-raters; but the 10-rater class being practically defunct on the Solent during this year, the clubs were enabled to offer a capital programme to the 20-raters, for which class the Earl of Dunraven built the *Deirdre* (L. 46.2, S. 2,590) from a design by Mr. G. L. Watson, the Earl of Dudley built the *Vigorna* (L. 46.7, S. 2,569) at Gosport from a design by Mr. C. Nicholson (jun.), and Mr. F. C. Hill built the *Dragon* III. (L. 45.3, S. 2,593) from a design by Mr. Fife (jun.); Mr. E. Jessop also purchased Mr. Hill's *Dragon* II. (L. 45.7, S. 2,624), and raced her on the Solent for the first half of the season under the new name of *Molly*.

The *Maladetta* (L.46, S. 2,608), designed by her owner, Mr. J. E. McGildowny, also competed in a few races in August, but without much success. The most extreme boat, Lord Dudley's, proved a complete failure as a racing machine. In type she was similar to the *Pilgrim*, built in America for the cup competition. *Deirdre* was also a highly developed machine, but she was beaten by *Dragon III.*, the more moderate design. However, both she and *Dragon III.* generally found no difficulty in defeating *Molly*, and on several occasions during the season *Deirdre* was able to win the principal prize, as will be seen in the table opposite.

The 5-Raters, 1893.

Red Lancer's record of 11 first prizes in 13 starts is exceedingly good. The start for the Squadron race on Aug. 3 is not counted against her, as the first prize should have been awarded to her. She always won easily in light weather, and it required half a gale for *Dacia* to get in front of her.

Before *Red Lancer's* arrival, at the end of July, *Dacia* scored by far the best of the Solent trio, the other two boats (*Quinque* and *Fleur-de-Lis*) being a good match *inter se*.

Valentine was sailed capitally, and made a good fight for a place in light weather; but she never won first honours, and was as clearly outclassed as she was in 1890 when she competed against *Alwida*, *Glycera*, *Quinque*, and *Archee*.

Racing Records for 1893

1893	Starts	Prizes		Total	Figure of merit
		First	Other		
20-Rating Class					
Dragon III.	29	19	8	27	52
Deirdré	29	9	10	19	25
Molly (Dragon II.)	19	1	5	6	4
5-Rating Class					
Red Lancer	13	11	1	12	59
Dacia	27	12	10	22	35
Fleur-de-Lis (Squall)	41	11	9	20	22
Quinque	37	9	11	20	20
Valentine	12	0	2	2	0
2½-Rating Class					
Meueen	49	26	14	40	44·8
Gareth	53	25	17	42	40·1
Elf	34	6	5	11	14·3
Manx Cat (Polynia)	46	3	16	19	5·4
Papoose	48	3	16	19	5·1
Kismet	34	2	6	8	4·8
Faugh-a-Ballagh	10	1	6	7	4·5
Gavotte	26	1	2	3	3·0
1-Rating Class					
Morwena	36	20	8	28	45·4
Sacharissa	49	21	14	35	36·2
Scud	20	6	7	13	22·6
Tipcat	33	8	13	21	19·6
Tartar	34	6	12	18	14·3
Wolfhound	32	5	5	10	12·0
Whisper	4	1	1	2	12·5
Doushka	12	2	5	7	11·4
Hark Holla	5	1	1	2	10·7
Whoo Whoop	18	2	3	5	8·2
Kitten	10	1	2	3	6·5
Roulette	11	1	2	3	6·1
Javelin	33	1	5	6	2·5
Fantasy	36	1	11	12	2·3
½-Rating Class					
Wee Winn	11	8	3	11	49·1
Coquette	52	25	14	39	40·8
Koodoo	7	4	2	6	34·5
Ragamuffin	12	5	4	9	28·6
Pique	14	3	8	11	15·2
Mosquito	51	9	18	27	14·97
Queen Bee	3	1	1	2	14·92
Ladybird	37	6	7	13	13·3
Humming-top	20	3	5	8	11·3
Spruce	18	2	3	5	8·2
Lady Grizel	21	2	6	8	7·2
Idono	18	1	6	7	4·1

THE 2½-RATERS, 1893.

The racing in this class soon became principally interesting in the duel for first honours between the Gosport boat *Gareth*, owned by Mr. Henderson, and frequently sailed by Mr. Collingwood Hughes, and the Herreshoff boat *Meueen*, owned and sailed by Mr. Hardie Jackson, who did so well with *Faugh-a-Ballagh* in 1892. *Meueen* was fully 'up to date' except her rig, which was sloop with a gaff-mainsail. This, however, she soon discarded for the more fashionable rig in the small classes, and she always made a fine race with *Gareth*, except in the hardest weather. Even in strong winds and heavy seas she did well after her lead was increased. She has great overhang, like *Wenonah* and *Wee Winn*; but there is nothing excessive in beam or in shallowness of body. Her elements are not at present obtainable, except L.W.L. 24.82 feet, and sail-area 596 square feet. *Gareth* raced this year on a length for rating of 29.15, and a sail-area of 533 square feet, which together produced a rating of 2.58, and she had to allow time for the excess of rating over 2.5, in accordance with Rule 3, Y.R.A., as revised in 1893.

The *Elf*, a new boat built at Gosport for Mr. Dudley Ward from a design by Mr. C. Nicholson (jun.), was rather too advanced in type. She did fairly well at first, but fell off as the other boats were gradually tuned up to their maxima of efficiency. Her figure of merit was 14.3, *Gareth's* being 40.1, and *Meueen* heading the class with 44.8. *Kismet*, another new boat, built and designed by Payne for Miss Cox, proved to be a disappointment, as the record table indicates.

Mr. Gurtside Tipping, R.N., purchased *Polynia* during the winter of 1892, and raced her in '93 under the new name *Manx Cat*. She did very well until her keel and attached rudder were removed and replaced by a fin with bulb and a 'disconnected' rudder. This made her very hard on the helm, and she rarely scored afterwards.

Mr. Paul Ralli stuck to his good boat *Papoose*, and tried to invade the 5-rater class with her; but this was frustrated mainly by the clubs promptly adopting conditions to stop this form of inter-class racing.

The *Faugh-a-Ballagh* started in 16 races and scored one first prize; as did '*Gavotte*,' which started 26 times on the Solent. *Undine* started twice, *Fiera* and *Cassowary* seven times, but no prizes came to the lockers of these three boats.

It is questionable whether this class will retain its popularity. The 2½-rater is decidedly an expensive boat; the first cost and maintenance being nearly as much as a 5-rater, and the comfort very much less. Moreover, it is severely pressed by the class below of 1-rating, which is becoming very popular, and deservedly so. A 1-rater can be built complete for 100 to 150 guineas, whereas some of the new 2½-raters cost nearly 400*l*.; and a 5-rater can be built for 500*l*., although it is stated that some of them cost 600*l*.

THE 1-RATERS, 1893.

It has been very difficult to draw up a record of the class racing in the two smaller classes, because many of the sailing clubs and some of the yacht clubs do not send full reports of their numerous matches to the press. The winners only are mentioned in some reports, but it is necessary to know the number of starts for each boat if her figure of merit is to be calculated. The figures given in the table of winners in the Y. R. Calendar are not trustworthy; first, because the owners often make mistakes in sending in their returns; and, secondly, because some of the results are taken from mixed races, not class races, and some from races outside the Solent.

The record table is compiled from the reports of the regattas given in the Y. R. Calendar, and in the *Yachtsman*. Two of the Portsmouth match days were omitted, and the winners only were mentioned on one of the Royal Albert days, one of the Victoria days, and on the Squadron day.

There may, therefore, be a small decimal error in the figure of merit of a few of the boats, but the order of merit may be regarded to be correct as it stands in the table.

The best 1-rater was the Yankee boat *Morwena* with the high M. of 45.4. She is similar to the other Herreshoff boats in the small classes, and has been well sailed.

Sacharissa came next with the excellent M. of 36.2. She was sailed faultlessly by Mr. P. Perceval (jun.), and was the best boat turned out by Payne in 1893.

Scud came third with an M. of 22.6. She is one of the wide and shallow type, answering well to her name when going over rather than through the water.

Tipcat went well; also *Tartar* and *Wolfhound*. *Whisper* was not seen often enough to judge of her merits accurately, but the old 1892 crack *Doushka* went as well as ever when Mr. Perceval brought her out at the end of the season.

Fantasy, a novelty built at Hamble for Mr. Randal Vogan from his own design, went far better than anyone expected. She has a ram bow, long counter, and fin-bulb keel, with narrow beam and sides that tumble home above the water-line. She often scored second honours.

Mahatma, Viva, Cariad, Rogue, Vlekendor, Leading Article did not race often on the Solent, and did not score any first prizes.

Roulette, Dona, and *Rogue* did most of their racing on the Thames, which has been tabulated by Mr. Winser, and published in the *Field* of November 11, 1893.

THE ½-RATERS, 1893.

The smallest class suffered from the extreme popularity of the 1-rater class, and it often occurred that only two or three ½-raters started in a race. *Wee Winn* again proved herself to be the champion boat in the class, but she only competed about a dozen times. She made the fine M. of 49.1. *Coquette,* which was raced hard all the season, also did remarkably well, and made a fine figure of merit, 40.8. *Koodoo* and *Ragamuffin,* which came out late, also did well. *Sagamore, Nautilus, Tiny, Vega, Khistie, Coral,* and *Haha* raced occasionally, but failed to score first honours.

******

When this chapter was begun the writer feared that designers would refuse to give any information about successful boats, but the tables have been filled in by many of them in a most liberal manner; and the author begs to tender them his thanks, and he hopes those of his readers, for so doing. The elements thus recorded are hull-dimensions, but the sail-dimensions are often equally interesting and instructive. These are given on the certificates and are public property; but they become more valuable for comparison when collected in a tabular form. The table has therefore been made.

At present the lugsail, invented by Mr. Tom Ratsey of Cowes, reigns supreme in the small classes, *Doreen* leading the list with a mainsail about 1,000 sq. ft. in area. Nevertheless, we find *Wee Winn* beating the other ½-raters with a cutter mainsail; but all our experience points to the belief that she would go still better with a lug. The table deserves careful study, and it will be seen that the proportion of head-sail to total S.A. has steadily decreased, until in some boats it has almost reached the vanishing point, and *Coquette* came out with all her sail in the lug. This tendency is bad, and will be still further encouraged if the actual area of head-sail be measured as proposed by the Council of the Y.R.A.[8]

---

[8] The resolution to measure the actual area of head-sails in yachts of 10-rating and under, as proposed by the Council, was lost at the general meeting of the Association held December 6, 1892.

******

Here ends the summary of the Solent racing under the Y.R.A. rule of rating. The type of boat which was produced up to the end of 1891 is excellent, being dry, seaworthy, fast, and easily driven with small sails; but it is easy to see that the most recent developments are not equally satisfactory. In the words of the *Field*, October 29, 1892:—

> It seems that all which is good has been got out of the present rating rule, and there is nothing more to be derived from it but an increase of speed, with a possible decrease of weight, internal space, and sail-spread.

This sums up the much-debated rule question in a single sentence.

What the next period will bring depends greatly, perhaps entirely, upon some small mathematical sign in the form for the rule of rating. For instance, the American rules use a sign indicating addition where we use one indicating multiplication, the consequence being that the former is a more adjustable rule than ours—more easily controlled by coefficients. But it is not necessary to enter into these matters now, as they are specially treated in Chapter 7. The racing man on the Solent or the Clyde cares more for the sport than the science involved in questions of displacement, length, and what not; and we may rest assured that whatever the Council of the Y.R.A. do, or leave undone, the sport will proceed in the same enthusiastic manner.

There cannot be the smallest doubt that an immense advantage to yachting would be gained if England, France, and America raced under the same rule of rating and a similar classification; and if an international conference were invited to meet in London the thing would be done without much difficulty.

The table of clubs shown later in the chapter shows that 2,761*l*. in cash and 933*l*. in cups, plate, &c. were won on the Solent in 1892, or a total of 3,723*l*. This does not include the prizes won at the Town Regattas—Cowes, Southampton, Lymington, Yarmouth, Totland Bay, Ryde, and Portsmouth. Good prizes are offered to the raters at several of these regattas, probably increasing the above total to nearly 4,000*l*.[9]

Some of these town regattas are managed in a most remarkable manner, the fireworks at night being perhaps the most important matter for consideration in the eyes of the committee.

---

9. These amounts were all larger in 1893.

Table of Rig,

	Name of Yacht	Rig	Date	Rating	L.W.L.	Sail Total	Sail Main
10-raters	Yvonne	Cutter	1889	9·80	34·10	1,726	813
	Doreen	Lugger	July 15, 1892	9·96	38·05	1,572	1,061
5-raters	Alwida	Cutter	May 15, 1890	4·95	29·66	1,002	684
	Glycera	Cutter	May 15, 1890	4·93	30·97	957	657
	Archee	Cutter	Aug. 21, 1890	4·96	30·43	980	675
	Quinque	Cutter	May 29, 1890	4·99	31·56	951	645
	Windfall	Lug. cut.	May 19, 1891	4·57	32·89	909	659
	Savourna	Lug. slp.	June 2, 1891	4·94	33·40	888	669
	Iernia	Lug. slp.	June 5, 1891	4·99	31·48	953	774
	Cyane	Lug. slp.	June 3, 1892	4·95	33·75	880	668
	Quinque	Lug. slp.	July 21, 1892	4·96	33·15	898	677
	Dacia	Lug. slp.	June 15, 1892	5·00	33·83	888	700
2½-raters	Thalassa	Sloop	1887	2·46	20·94	706	422
	Thalassa	Sloop	May 17, 1889	2·49	22·95	652	452
	Humming Bird	Lug. slp.	July 12, 1889	2·44	25·90	567	432
	Mliss	Sloop	May 15, 1890	2·50	24·97	603	448
	Cock-a-Whoop	Lug. slp.	June 18, 1890	2·50	25·00	600	438
	Babe	Lug. slp.	1890 and 1891	2·48	26·76	557	429
	Fiera	Lug. slp. {	June 12, 1891	2·49	28·00	536	} 425
			June 18, 1892	2·45	27·36	539	
	Avadavat	Lug. slp.	June 10, 1891	2·49	28·00	536	425
	Janetta	Lug. slp.	Aug. 14, 1891	2·48	26·45	563	430
	Molly	Lug. slp.	1892	2·49	28·26	531	439
	Stork	Lug. slp.	1892	2·50	28·52	527	442
	Faugh-a-Ballagh	Lug. slp.	May 30, 1892	2·48	27·48	543	433
	Cockatoo	Lug. slp.	June 28, 1892	2·41	27·24	533	436
	Papoose	Lug. slp.	June 11, 1892	2·50	27·65	543	446
	Polynia	Lug. slp.	July 1892	2·47	28·15	528	431
	Gareth	Lug. slp.	July 30, 1892	2·48	28·02	533	442
	Wenonah	Sloop	Aug. 3, 1892	2·40	25·05	577	449
1-raters	Pup	Lug. slp. {	July 1890	0·99	18·21	328	} 272
			July 1892	0·99	17·37	344	
	Rogue	Lug. slp.	Aug. 18, 1892	0·99	20·91	285	238
	Barbet	Lug. slp.	Aug. 23, 1892	0·97	20·27	288	249
	Doushka	Lug. slp.	June 30, 1892	0·98	21·07	281	245
	Nansheen	Lug. slp.	May 28, 1892	0·99	20·24	297	251
	Mahatma	Lug. slp.	April 27, 1892	0·99	20·61	289	242
½-raters	Coquette	Lug. slp.	May 14, 1891	0·50	15·58	192	192
	Dee Dee	Lug. slp.	July 14, 1891	0·50	17·17	177	149
	Jeanie	Lug. slp.	June 18, 1891	0·50	16·25	187	162
	Spruce	Yawl	Aug. 27, 1891	0·41	16·20	154	123
	Eileen	Lug. slp.	May 13, 1891	0·49	15·90	185	144
	Narua	Lug. slp.	May 19, 1891	0·49	15·97	183	143
	Dancing Girl	Lug. slp. {	1891	0·50	15·99	189	167
			July 13, 1892				
	Daisy	Lug. slp.	Aug. 26, 1892	0·50	17·10	176	152
	Wee Winn	Sloop	July 23, 1892	0·46	15·61	178	141

266

Dimensions, &c.

Areas		Spars			Lines					
Head	Top	Boom	Gaff	Yard	Luff	A	B	C	D	I	J
658	254	34·00	21·6	—	22·85	44·3	19·2	40·2	19·3	46·2	28·5
511	—	38·38	—	33·38	18·75	57·8	24·3	42·4	16·9	34·4	29·7
318	—	29·7	19·5	—	22·1	41·1	17·3	36·0	18·3	28·8	22·1
300	—	29·3	19·3	—	21·5	40·7	16·7	35·8	17·7	28·0	21·4
305	—	30·5	19·5	—	21·4	40·5	17·25	36·0	18·1	29·0	21·0
306	—	28·8	19·0	—	?	40·0	16·7	35·3	17·6	25·9	23·6
250	—	30·4	—	27·0	17·7	47·0	19·1	33·8	12·4	25·0	20·0
219	—	31·65	—	28·6	12·0	47·0	20·5	34·0	11·0	26·5	16·53
179	—	35·75	—	29·3	12·0	48·0	22·6	37·5	11·5	26·05	13·75
212	—	30·5	—	28·0	13·25	46·0	19·5	33·0	12·2	29·2	14·5
221	—	30·95	—	29·6	12·75	46·3	21·0	33·5	11·4	27·45	16·1
188	—	31·87	—	31·0	13·0	49·4	20·2	33·0	12·2	28·13	13·33
208	76	22·58	15·82	—	?	31·5	?	27·8	14·5	25·41	16·33
200	—	22·6	14·8	—	?	34·8	12·5	29·8	15·7	24·9	16·1
135	—	23·46	—	23·2	11·5	39·0	15·2	26·5	10·2	23·54	12·0
155	—	24·5	16·0	—	17·7	32·5	14·2	29·5	14·7	22·2	14·0
162	—	24·1	—	23·0	?	36·2	16·8	26·8	10·0	24·1	13·4
127	—	23·6	—	22·9	11·6	36·5	15·6	25·4	10·5	21·7	11·7
111 114	—	23·8	—	23·0	11·3	38·0	15·5	26·2	10·0	20·5	10·8 11·1
111	—	23·8	—	23·0	11·3	38·0	15·5	26·2	10·0	20·5	10·8
133	—	23·8	—	23·0	11·6	38·0	15·5	28·8	10·5	22·6	11·8
92	—	25·3	—	24·5	9·5	38·0	17·0	26·7	8·7	17·1	10·7
85	—	25·3	—	24·5	9·1	38·4	17·0	27·0	8·5	15·7	10·8
110	—	23·8	—	23·7	11·3	38·5	15·3	25·8	10·3	20·0	11·0
97	—	23·3	—	24·0	12·3	40·3	14·5	25·6	?	20·1	9·7
97	—	23·6	—	24·0	12·5	40·5	14·8	26·2	11·2	20·1	9·7
97	—	23·6	—	24·6	10·75	39·4	15·4	25·4	10·0	18·5	10·5
91	—	24·9	—	24·5	10·6	40·3	15·4	26·2	10·0	10·7	9·7
128	—	27·4	14·9	—	?	?	?	?	?	19·6	13·1
72	—	20·0	—	18·4	7·8	29·5	13·2	21·2	7·3	15·2	9·4
47	—	18·5	—	18·3	7·00	28·0	12·5	19·4	6·5	13·5	7·0
39	—	19·0	—	18·9	6·25	29·0	12·9	20·0	6·2	10·2	7·6
36	—	?	—	19·0	5·75	28·8	13·2	20·0	5·5	10·0	7·2
46	—	19·5	—	17·0	8·00	28·0	12·4	20·5	7·5	12·8	7·2
47	—	18·4	—	17·7	6·5	27·0	13·1	20·0	5·9	14·7	6·5
—	—	16·8	—	14·9	7·6	25·2	10·3	17·8	7·0	—	—
28	—	14·8	—	14·9	4·6	21·5	10·8	15·8	4·2	11·00	5·1
25	—	?	—	12·7	6·1	22·9	9·7	17·0	5·6	12·3	4·1
—	—	?	12·9	—	4·75	17·0	10·4	13·8	4·4	—	—
(mizzen | 30·5)	5·95	7·0	—	2·83	8·5	5·2	6·5	2·6	mizzen	—
41	—	14·5	—	14·9	4·8	20·3	11·0	15·0	4·3	12·6	6·5
40	—	14·6	—	14·8	4·8	20·0	11·0	15·0	4·3	12·6	6·4
22	—	16·4	—	15·0	4·8	23·4	11·0	17·1	4·5	11·1	4·0
24	—	15·6	—	14·1	5·3	22·2	10·0	16·0	5·1	9·0	?
37	—	15·1	9·16	—	8·6	18·8	8·2	16·6	7·7	10·9	6·7

A year or two back, the raters at Cowes were started in a line with the committee vessel, with no outside limit! On the day of the race it was a lee shore; consequently Lord Dunraven, Mr. Perceval, and one or two others who were wider awake than the rest, started in the dim distance, well to windward, and romped down full and bye to the first mark.

At Lymington the 5-raters are started from a line at the rivermouth from a little boat, by a little man, with a little gun and a big flag, and the finish is right up the river, in a narrow place thronged with small boats, with probably a four-oared race in progress. After an accident has taken place and a few people are drowned, this may be altered.

At Totland Bay in 1892 there was a handicap for which two very unequal boats had entered. The sailing committee could not agree about the handicap; some bright genius therefore proposed that the difference of time between the boats at the end of the first round should be multiplied by 3 for the handicap on the three rounds, and it is said that this was actually done! And so on. These regattas are very good fun, if only because the unexpected usually occurs.

The men who have made the Solent racing what it is must now be mentioned:—

Mr. Wolff, the Hon. Sec. of the R.S.Y.C., and the late Mr. McCheane, Hon. Sec. of the R.P.C.Y.C., have already been alluded to. Colonel Bucknill, Hon. Sec. of the Castle Yacht Club; Mr. Blair Onslow Cochrane, Hon. Sec. of the Bembridge Sailing Club; Mr. Barrow, Hon. Sec. of the Island Sailing Club; Mr. Herbert Ridsdale, Hon. Sec. of the Hamble Branch of the Minima Sailing Club, have in like manner worked hard and very successfully in the cause. So also have many of the flag officers in the various clubs, and especially should be mentioned Mr. Frederick Cox, who for years has been a persevering patron of the sport—both in the Solent length classes and afterwards in the present Solent classes (Y.R.A. rating). Mr. Cox's sons and daughters have raced a number of yachts: *Lil, Verena, Madcap, Merrythought, Kitten, Ethel, Mliss, Troublesome, Fiera, Mosquito*, all under the protecting wing of the head centre, typified by the steamer *Zinaida*. Mr. Cox is Commodore of the Royal Southampton, Rear Commodore (or is it Rear Admiral now?) of the Royal London, and Rear Commodore of the Castle Yacht Clubs. He is also a member of the Council Y.R.A.

Captain Hughes and his family of sons and daughters have followed the sport for a long time in the same enthusiastic way, and have raced

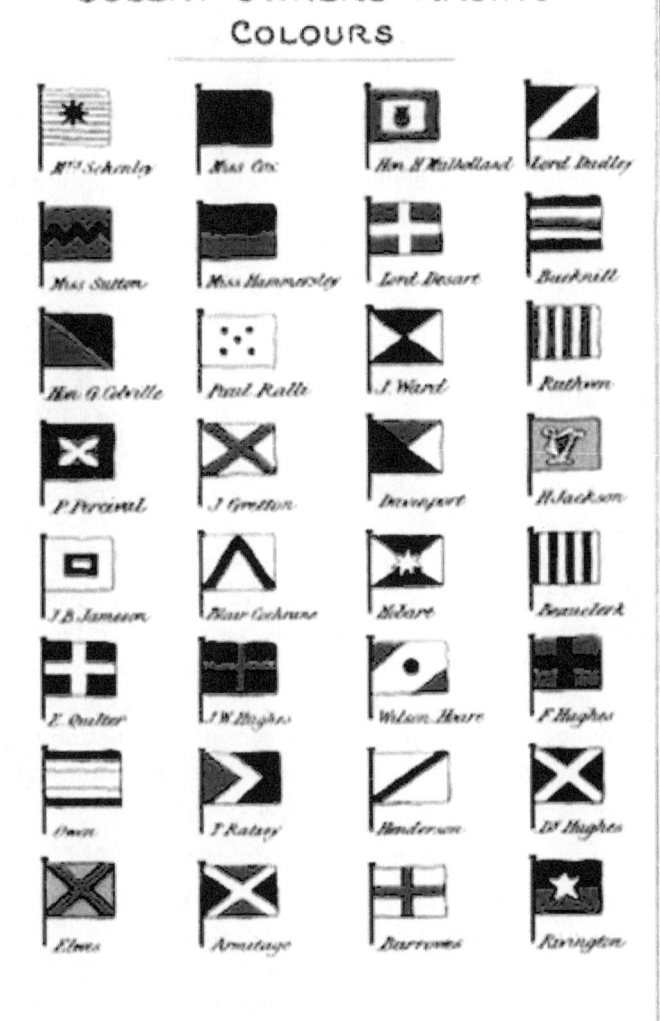

SOLENT OWNERS' RACING COLOURS.

the following boats: *Lil, Fairy, Jenny Wren, Madcap, Flutterby, Humming Bird, Cock-a-Whoop,* and *Cockatoo.* Captain Hughes was most active in starting the Castle Yacht Club, and for a short time was the Hon. Sec.

In addition to the above, the chief patrons and promoters of the sport during the past few years have been the Marquis of Exeter, the Marquis of Ailsa, the Earl of Dunraven, the Earl of Desart, the Earl of Dudley, the late Mr. Sidney Watson, Colonel the Hon. H. G. L. Crichton, Captain the Hon. J. M. Yorke, Colonel F. Dugmore, Captain J. R. F. Fullerton, R.N., Admiral the Hon. Victor Montagu, R.N., Mr. W. H. Forster, Mr. R. S. Hankinson, Mr. P. Perceval, jun., Mr. George Schenley, the Hon. G. Colville, Captain Cecil Drummond, Captain Du Boulay, Captain Davenport, Mr. Wilson Hoare, R.N., Mr. Granville Keele, Admiral Hallowes, R.N., Mr. Paul Ralli, Mr. W. A. Beauclerk, Mr. A. D. Clarke, Mr. H. R. Langrishe, Captain C. E. Haynes, R.E., Lieut.-Colonel Moreton, Mr. F. L. Popham, Mr. E. F. Quilter, Mr. W. S. Nicholson, Mr. J. P. Ranwell, Mr. L. M. Ames, Captain R. Alexander, Mr. G. F. Flemmich, Mr. H. L. Hewitt, Mr. A. Manning, Mr. R. Vogan, and a number more, whose names would fill a page.

The ladies who have taken an active part in the racing should also be mentioned, as their presence has done much to make the sport popular and fashionable.

Prominent among them are Ladies Fanny and Blanche Stanhope, Mrs. Sidney Watson, Mrs. Schenley and her sisters the Misses Hughes, Mrs. Rudston-Read and her sister Miss Cox, Mrs. H. Duff-Gordon and her sister Miss Hammersley, Mrs. Arthur Heygate, Mrs. Blair Onslow Cochrane, the Misses Sutton, and Colonel Bucknill's daughters.

Oilskins and sou'-westers are really very becoming, and if this fact were generally known, the ranks of the ladies might gain recruits, and this word leads to the next division of our subject:—

Hints to the Novice

If a beginner wish to learn the art of small-yacht racing he cannot do better than start with a second-hand 1-rater, costing say from 50*l.* to 80*l.* Such a boat if new would cost from 100*l.* to 150*l.*

The next step is to hire a good lad (sixteen or seventeen years old) for the crew, wages from 16 *s.* to 20*s.* a week, and some racing money, say 5*s.* for a first, and 2*s.* 6*d.* for a second or third prize. No prize, no racing money. The lad will ask for a suit of clothes, and if he seem likely to suit, the suit may be given on the distinct understanding that, should he leave the job voluntarily or on account of misbehaviour, the clothes will be kept by the owner. The clothes are part of the equipment of the yacht, and belong to the owner, who should see that they are worn on board, and not kept entirely for shore service. Nothing looks worse than a ramshackle, untidy fellow on a smart little yacht. Racing boats and crews should be as smart at the starting line as guns and gunners on parade.

The young owner must then settle how much racing he can manage, and on what days it will be most convenient. '*Thalassa's*' *Almanac*, published by King & Co., High Street, Southampton, may be consulted with advantage, as an attempt is made therein to give the whole of the club programmes for the season, so far as they are known by the secretaries at the beginning of the year.

It will be found that Saturdays are practically secured by the Royal Southampton and the Royal Portsmouth Clubs; Mondays by the Royal London and the Castle Clubs; Wednesdays by the Royal Albert Yacht Club and the Island Sailing Club; Thursdays are chosen by the Royal Victoria Yacht Club, and Fridays by the Solent Yacht Club and the Minima Sailing Club.

Examine the *Almanac* again, note which of the clubs give 'open' races and which 'club' races; and then it will be easy to settle which clubs are most convenient, and to take the necessary steps for being entered as a candidate.

The next point to settle is the best headquarters for the little ship, and this depends on so many personal considerations that advice is impossible. Remember, however, that a 1-rater requires a sheltered anchorage, and that moorings keep mud off the decks, and save time and bother. The best anchorages for *small* boats are: (1) the Itchen River, at or above the Floating Bridge; (2) the Hamble River, at or above the Salterns; (3) Calshot, up the Creek; (4) Portsmouth Harbour, especially up Haslar Creek; (5) Bembridge Harbour; (6) Wooton Creek; (7) Cowes, above the ferry; (8) Beaulieu River, inside the coastguard station; (9) Newtown River; (10) Yarmouth, the harbour; (11) Lymington River; (12) Keyhaven.

Do *not* anchor for the night, or moor so small a boat as a 1-rater off the pier at Southampton, off Hythe, at Calshot (except up the creek), in Cowes Harbour (except up the river), off Ryde, off Southsea, in Yarmouth Roads, or in Totland Bay. If you do so, you will wake some stormy morning to find her more or less damaged, and possibly wrecked. The boy will have very strong opinions concerning the best place for moorings. Don't listen to him. Fix on the place that suits yourself and your friends best.

Next decide where you will go for the everlasting scrub, paint up, and frequent repairs. If on the Itchen, there are Fay & Co., Summers & Payne, and Field close to the Floating Bridge to choose from. If on the Medina, either White, Ratsey, or Sibbick. If on the Hamble, there are Luke & Co. If in Portsmouth Harbour, Camper & Nicholson at Gosport, or Reid on the Portsmouth basin. If sails give out, repairs can be quickly done at reasonable charges by Beaton of Bugle Street, Southampton; but new sails for racing should be obtained from Ratsey at Cowes or Lapthorn at Gosport.

The next step to take is very interesting. Collect your lady friends, and ask each of them to design a racing flag; paint each design full size, and examine them simultaneously from a distance, say one cable at least, as a flag should be easily distinguished at this distance in any weather. Two colours are generally sufficient. Black, or some dark colour, with white or yellow; also red, with white or yellow. If three colours be used, separate the red from the dark colours by white or yellow. Employ strong contrasts. Remember that a simple design shows best and costs least. Also that a flag with horizontal seams flies better than any other, except one with no seams at all. However small the boat, the racing flag should never be less than 10 inches wide by 8½ inches high. The winning flags may be smaller, say 6 or 7 inches square, for a ½- or a 1-rater. The following dimensions may be regarded as 'suitable sizes' (see Rule 11, Y.R.A.) for the racing flags in the 'Solent classes':—

	height	width
1/2-raters and 1-raters	8 inches	by 10 inches
2-1/2-raters	10 "	" 12 "
5-raters	12 "	" 14 "
10-raters	14 "	" 17 "

Having settled on the size and pattern of flag, proceed to Mr. Wolff, High Street, Southampton, and order two or three, and (say) a dozen of the smaller size to hoist as winning flags. Make a solemn vow to win a dozen flags in the season, and if you fail the first year, stick to your colours and try again.

The boat must now be prepared for the racing; all ropes and gear carefully examined, her top sides and bottom carefully rubbed down, painted, and varnished, until everything is as fit as a fiddle, and the bottom smooth as a bottle.

Next buy a copy of the Y.R.A. Rules, Dixon Kemp's book on *Yacht and Boat Sailing*, and King's *Channel Pilot*. Study each carefully, especially Chapter 8 of Kemp's book. More than half the difficulties and troubles connected with the sport are due to ignorance of the rules.[10] In every other sport such ignorance is regarded with the contempt it deserves, but in yacht and boat racing the rules are somewhat complex and difficult—all the more reason for learning them carefully.

Every racing owner should enter his yacht strictly in accordance with Rule 5, Y.R.A., and it saves trouble if an owner has a card with the declaration at entry, his personal address, and the yacht's racing flag printed upon it.

Care should be taken to post this 'entry' so that the club secretary receives it in proper time. Do not rely on the 48 hours' clause, but examine the club programme, as the entries are not unfrequently closed earlier.

The day before the race give the most distinct instructions to crew as to the time and place of meeting on the morrow, and keep the appointment punctually.

Provide yourself with a chronograph, and it may help you to win prizes by means of good starts.

Get to the starting line half an hour before your start if you can, and get a card of the races if one has not already reached you through the post. Read it carefully, and, should anything appear to be doubtful, have it cleared up by the race officer, or by the club secretary.

If other races start before you, do not get in the way of the starting boats.

Note when the ten minutes preparatory flag for your own race is hoisted; you will then be the better prepared to start your chronograph at the first gun. See Rule 17.

After first gun, stand off and on *near* the starting line. Remember that you are now 'under the rules.' Have Rule 18 by heart, and understand each clause of it. During the last half-minute before the second or starting gun, manoeuvre for the place you wish to secure, be there at the flash of gun, and if possible just to windward, or just ahead of your most dangerous antagonist. If you think you are over the line at gunfire, keep a sharp look out for your recall numeral (Rule 12), and directly it is displayed return, and cross the line; but keep clear of other competitors in doing so.

After the start do not go in for a luffing match or allow yourself to

---

10. See chapter on the Racing Rules and Rules of Rating.

be luffed by a yacht you do not fear. Stick to the boat you fear most. Remember Rule 19 in rounding the marks. If the weather be light, keep your weather eye open for every cat's-paw, and do not lose an inch during the whole race by careless steering. Be careful when you come to the run to put spinnaker up on the best side; and, if you run by the lee, shift it over at once without parleying with the boy. After the finish, if you win, sign the declaration (Rule 10, Y.R.A.) and send it ashore as soon as possible. If you have any cause for protest against another yacht, or should any protest be lodged against your own yacht, go ashore at once and see the matter through.

After the race it has been customary for the second yacht to cheer the winner—like shaking hands after a boxing match—but this old custom is now dying out. Never permit your crew to bandy remarks with the hands on other yachts, either during a race or after it. If your boat wins, lower the racing flag, and hoist the club burgee with your winning flag one fathom below it. If she do not win, sail home with the racing flag still flying, this being the label of your boat's *raison d'être*. Never accept a prize unless you feel that every rule and regulation has been properly followed; see that your opponents follow them too; cut those men who do not race honourably, and show them up if you can.

Keep a log, and enter upon it everything of interest concerning the boat and the racing. Every little change of gear should be carefully noted; the position of crew when the boat goes best, and every detail which may help to point the way to any improvement, either in the boat herself or in the type which she represents. Such a log enables you to draw up an accurate record at the end of the season, and is valuable in later years as a reminder of past pleasures and adventures.

At the end of the first or second season you may decide to have a larger boat and crew. If so, consider carefully whether you will not skip the 2½ rating class and start a 5-rater.

Two paid hands are required with a 2½, and a 5 can be managed with the same crew if Corinthian help be obtainable. The maintenance of a 2½ is not much smaller than that of a 5, and the latter is a little ship in which you can sleep with comfort and cook a meal. A modern 5 is 11 tons Thames measurement, and can go anywhere when properly built, like the *Windfall*, *Quinque*, and *Savourna*.

As Lord Dunraven truly said, 'the 5's and the 20's are the cheapest classes'; and to these I would add the 1's. The ½-, 2½-, and 10-raters are the dearest classes. Many men may, like yourself, be wishing to go a

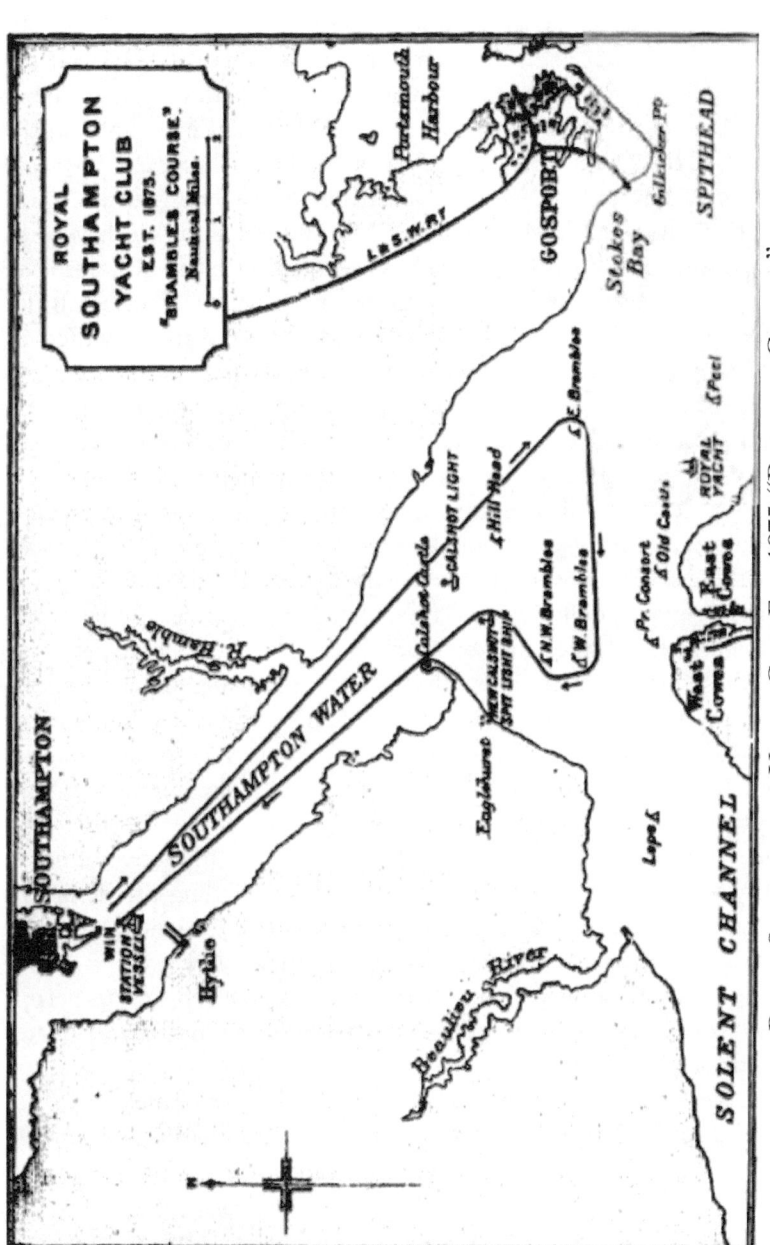

Royal Southampton Yacht Club Est. 1875. "Brambles Course."

class higher, and you may therefore pick up a good boat at a low price towards the end of the racing season. If not, you must build; and the great question then arises, who to go to?

The most successful designers on the Solent in the 2½ and the 5-rater classes are Mr. Arthur Payne and Mr. Charles Nicholson; but Mr. G. L. Watson and Mr. Willie Fife were equally invincible on the Clyde, until the appearance in 1892 of Mr. Herreshoff's 2½ *Wenonah*. Mr. C. P. Clayton and Mr. A. Richardson are also designers of great ability, while Mr. G. M. Soper and Mr. Herbert Ridsdale have produced some fast boats for the orders they have received. Whomsoever you select, have your boat built under his very eye. If a Scotch designer, build in Scotland; if a Solent designer, build there. Moreover, look after the boat yourself when she is building, and learn the tricks of the trade—if you can. Insist upon having your boat fitted out at least a fortnight before the first race, as a new boat often requires no end of doctoring before her best trim is discovered.

Her new sails also require to be carefully stretched, in suitable weather; and finally she should be officially measured before she races. For these several reasons it is necessary to specify date of completion in the contract, and to have a clause whereby the builder can be heavily fined week by week for non-fulfilment—such fines being deducted from the final payment. There should also be a clause empowering the owner to complete the work in the builder's yard himself in the event of the builder, from any cause whatever, being unable to carry out the contract. An arbitration clause in the event of a disagreement is very desirable. Insure the yacht against fire to the full amount of the work done as it proceeds. A 5-rater, complete with sails, properly 'found' in every way, should not cost more than 500*l*., including the designer's fee, and a modern 2½ rater should not cost more than 300*l*. They cost less than 260*l*. in 1887-8 and 1888-9. The difference is due to higher pay per hour for labour, the Societies now refusing to permit piecework, also to more expensive materials, higher finish, and greater length of hull.

As for the crew, the owner of a 5 may consider himself fortunate if he can secure the services of a good man as skipper for 30*s*. a week, clothes (about 5*l*. worth), 20*s*. racing money for a first prize, and 10*s*. for a second or a third prize.

It is a mistake to give racing money for losing. At present it is only done by a few wealthy and thoughtless owners, who will soon ruin the sport unless the majority combine to put a stop to their extravagance.

Losing money is legitimate enough in the large racers, where the yachts make long passages by night and day in all weathers from regatta to regatta. By such crews the losing money is earned, but the crews of small Solent racers, who sleep comfortably at home in their beds, and often have little or nothing to do between the races, should not get it.

It costs from 100*l.* to 150*l.* to maintain and race a 5- or a 2½ rater for the twenty weeks of the season, from which may be deducted the value of the prizes won, less entrance fees and racing money. This sum covers a crew of two paid hands, and the owner of a 5 must enlist two or three Corinthians to help at each race. Unfortunately, there is a lamentable deficiency of these mariners on the Solent.

DETAILS OF YACHT CLUBS AND SAILING CLUBS ON THE SOLENT

	Royal Yacht Squadron	Royal London Yacht Club	Royal Southern Yacht Club	Royal Victoria Yacht Club	Royal Albert Yacht Club	Royal Southampton Yacht Club	Solent Yacht Club	Royal Portsmouth Corinthian Yacht Club	Castle Yacht Club	Bembridge Sailing Club	Island Sailing Club	Minima Sailing Club	Totals
Established	1812	1838 1882	1843	1844	1864	1875	1878	1880	1887	1886	1889	1889	
Head-quarters	Cowes	Cowes	Sthmptn	Ryde	Sthsea	Sthmptn	Yrmth	Prtsmth	Calshot	Bmbrdg	Cowes	Hamble	
Entrance fee	£100	...	2 g.	5 g.	4 g.	2 g.	1 g.	2 g.	£3	2 g.	1 g.	½ g.	
Ann. subscription	£11	{4 g. / 6 g.}	{3 g. / 4 g.}	6 g.	4 g.	{1½ g. / 2 g.}	1 g.	2 g.	£3	1 g.	1 g.	½ g.	
1892													
No. of members	224	650	300	300	300	711	90	500	100	150	140	250	2,761
Prizes, cash, won	£409	£128	£207	£400	£227	£435	£40	£434	£204	£85	£105	£87	£933
Cups, value	£110	...	£75	£235	£207	Medals	£20	£10	£148	£85	£25	£18	
Races 60-R. &c. sailed	4	1	1	3	1	1	...	1	...	...	...	...	12
,, 40-R.	1	1	2	4	1	4	...	1	2	...	...	...	14
,, 20-R.	...	...	1	...	...	2	...	...	1	...	...	...	5
,, 10-R.	1	...	...	1	...	...	...	...	1	...	...	1	7
,, 5-R.	1	...	2	3	6	8	3	4	12	2	...	...	40
,, 2½-R.	1	2	2	9	6	8	3	9	12	1	9	2	65
,, 1-R.	...	2	2	7	6	8	1	7	9	13	9	12	64
,, ½-R.	...	2	2	7	6	8	3	9	7	...	9	9	75
Yachts' cutters	...	...	...	...	...	...	...	1	2	...	...	...	5
Handicaps sailed	2	1	2	2	2	4	1	2	2	...	...	1	19
Other races	...	...	...	...	...	...	...	...	...	22	4	6	32
Total races	10	10	16	35	28	47	11	34	47	38	31	39	338
Race days	4	3	2	10	6	11	3	11	12	33	9	12	116

SOME SOLENT RACERS, PRIOR TO 1886

Rig	Yacht	Owner and Designer	R.	S.A.	L.W.L.	O.H. Fwrd.	O.H. Aft	L.O.A.	B.	D.	Drght.	Displ. tons	Ballast tons	When built
					21-FOOTERS									
S.	Fairy	Capt. J. W. Hughes Stockham	2·5	717	20·8	?	?	?	8·5	3·4	?	?	?	1881
C.	Bird-o' Freedom	Mr. H. L. Popham Feltham	?	?	21	?	?	?	6·3	5·0	?	?	?	1883
S.	Tootsie (Minnow)	M. A. E. Payne	1·25	?	16·5	·25	·16	?	6·6	4·5	4·0	2·25	1·5	1885
C.	Minima	Mr. St. J. Arabin Payne	4·65	1,333	20·8	?	?	33·0	8·4	6·6	6·7	6·0	4·0	1886
C.	Volador	Lt.A.H.Oliver,R.N. Clayton	?	1,300	21	4·5	8	33·5	8·5	6·6	6·5	6·6	3·2	1886
C.	Scylla	Mr. L. Egremont Luke	?	?	21	?	?	?	8·9	5·3	?	?	?	1886
					25-FOOTERS									
C.	Frolic	Mr. E. Bridges Webb Hatcher	7·26	1,741	25	?	?	?	9·0	?	?	?	?	1882
C.	Lil	Mr. F. Cox Clayton	7·26	1,742	25	4·6	6·3	35·9	9·1	6·8	6·7	8·6	5·3	1884
C.	Verena	Mr. R. H. Cox Clayton	7·96	1,910	25	5·5	8·4	38·9	9·8	?	7·2	9·4	5·3	1886
					30-FOOTERS									
C.	Bonina	Mr. A. O. Baylay Dixon Kemp	9·74	1,830	30	?	?	41	9·7	7·4	7·3	13·1	7·5	1882
C.	Keepsake	Mr. H. W. Forster Clayton	8·66	1,730	30	4·4	6·3	40·7	9·7	?	7·0	13·7	7·8	1882
C.	Eclipse	Mr. A. Manning Clayton	9·4	2,090	30	5·2	8·0	43·2	10·1	7·5	7·7	13·5	8·0	1884
C.	Curtsey	Mr. H. W. Forster Clayton	10·8	2,180	30	6·0	8·3	44·3	10·5	8·0	7·8	13·8	7·6	1885

10-RATERS, 1882-92

Rig	Yacht	Owner and designer	R.	S.A.	L.W.L.	O.H. Fwrd.	O.H. A ft	L.O.A.	B.	D.	Drght.	Displ. tons	Ballast tons	When built
C.	Dolly Varden	Mr. T. W. Ratsey J. S. White	9·99	1,663	36·09	0·5	0·4	37	11·3	4·6	6·10	13	6·5	1872
C.	Frolic	Mr. Bridges Webb Hatcher	7·21	1,704	25·41	?	?	?	9·0	?	?	?	?	1882
C.	Doris	Messrs. R. & B. Allan Watson	9·48	1,681	33·86	?	?	?	5·6	6·6	?	?	?	1885
C.	Jenny Wren	Mr. R. E. Froude Owner	9·59	1,705	33·79	?	?	?	5·5	6·8	?	?	?	1885
C.	Verena	Mr. R. H. Cox Clayton	7·10	1,716	24·85	5·6	8·4	38·9	9·8	7·2	7·2	9·4	5·3	1886
C.	Wanderer	Mr. J. Lee Barber Brighton	9·00	1,580	34·15	?	?	?	9·0	5·0	?	?	?	1886
C.	Lollipop	Mr. Arabin Payne	6·49	1,325	29·3	0·2	8·0	37·5	9·2	7·3	?	10·7	?	1888
C.	Dis	Mr. A. D. Clarke Soper	9·94	1,658	36·0	6·0	9·1	51·1	9·1	7·1	7·7	14·8	8	1888
C.	Decima	Mr. Arabin Payne	9·98	1,679	36·0	1·0	9·4	46·4	11·0	7·5	8·5	14·3	?	1889
C.	Yvonne	Mr. P. Donaldson Fife	9·80	1,726	34·10	5·5	8·5	48·1	8·9	6·6	8·1	12·9	7·75	1889
C.	Drina	Prince B. Strattmann Dixon Kemp	9·95	1,801	33·17	0·48	7·80	41·45	9·8	6·7	8·4	15·0	7·2	1889
C.	Nety (Lil)	Admiral the Hon. Victor Montagu, R.N. Clayton	8·82	1,764	30·0	4·5	6·2	40·7	9·5	6·8	6·8	8·6	?	1884 1889
L.C.	Doreen	Mr. J. Gretton Fife	9·96	1,572	38·05	8·2	10·3	56·5	11·2	7·5	8·5	14	8	1892

½-RATERS, 1888-92

Rig	Yacht	Owner and Designer	R.	S.A.	L.W.L.	O.H. Fwrd.	O.H. Aft	L.O.A.	B.	D.	Drght	Displ. tons	Ballast tons	When built
C.	Chittywee	Mr. H. Farmer / Ash	4·8	1,213	28·2	?	?	?	4·8	?	?	?	?	1882
C.	Fair Geraldine	Mr. L. M. Ames / Clayton	4·98	1,000	30·0	4·5	7·5	42·0	7·5	5·5	5·3	8·0	4·6	1888
C.	Flutterby	Mr. F. Hughes / Owner	3·98	938	25·5	?	?	?	8·1	4·5	?	?	?	1888
C.	Lollipop	Mr. Perceval / Payne	4·98	1,000	29·5	0·21	8·08	37·79	9·2	7·3	7·0	?	?	1888
C.	Alwida	Earl of Dunraven / Payne	4·97	1,003	29·75	1·31	1·79	32·85	8·4	6·0	7·2	8·2	?	1890
S.	Glycera	Mr. Perceval / Payne	4·98	967	31·16	1·04	1·41	33·61	8·6	5·6	7·0	8·3	?	1890
C.	Quinque	Col. Bucknill / Owner	4·99	948	31·61	1·34	?	?	9·0	6·1	6·6	8·6	5·3	1890
L.S.	Ditto	Ditto	4·98	997	30·02	1·34	1·9	33·26	9·0	6·1	7·0	8·7	5·0	1891
L.S.	Ditto	Ditto	4·96	898	33·15	1·45	2·5	37·1	9·0	6·1	7·5	8·7	4·7	1892
C.	Archee (C.B.)	Mr. J. McNish / Watson	4·96	980	30·43	6·67	7·9	45·0	9·3	4·4	{5·1 / 18·0}	8·8	4·5	1890
C.	Valentine	Mrs. Schenley / Watson	4·95	997	29·83	6·17	8·0	44·0	7·2	6·3	7·4	8·2	?	1890
L.C.	Windfall	Mrs. Schenley / Payne	4·97	909	32·89	1·11	1·3	35·3	8·66	6·0	7·0	?	?	1891
I.S.	Savourna	Mr. Perceval / Payne	4·94	888	33·4	1·18	1·22	35·80	8·75	6·0	7·2	?	?	1891
C.	Katherine	Mr. W. A. Black / Owner	4·99	969	30·94	?	?	?	7·5	?	6·5	?	5·4	1891
L.S.	Iernia	Mr. H. R. Langrishe / Fife	4·99	953	31·48	6·0	8·42	45·9	8·0	6·0	7·2	8·7	5·4	1891
L.S.	Cyane	Earl of Dunraven / Payne	4·95	880	33·75	3·1	1·5	38·35	8·4	5·5	7·75	?	?	1892
L.S.	Dacia	Mr. H. R. Langrishe / Nicholson	5·00	888	33·83	5·14	9·17	48·14	8·3	?	8·6	?	?	1892

2½-RATERS, 1887-92

Rig	Yacht	Owner and Designer	R.	S.A.	L.W.L.	O.H. Fwrd.	O.H. Aft	L.O.A.	B.	D.	Drght.	Displ. tons	Ballast tons	When built
L.	Heathen Chinee	Mr. W. A. Beauclerk. Mackenzie	2·34	571	24·70	?	?	?	6·0	3·2	?	?	?	1879
C.	Bird-o'-Freedom	Mr. H. S. Popham Feltham	2·5	625	21·00 24·00	?	?	?	6·3 6·3	5·0 6·0	?	?	altd. altd.	1883 1886
S.	Fairy	Captain J. W. Hughes Pickett	2·5	723	20·77	?	?	?	8·4	3·3	?	?	?	1881 1887
S.	Thalassa	Col. Bucknill. Payne	2·49	714	20·94	?	?	?	7·4	4·9	5·8	?	?	1887
S.	Madcap	Miss Cox Clayton	2·49 2·49	714 694	21·0 21·62	? 0·2	? 6·3	? 27·5	7·3 7·3	4·0 4·0	5·4	4·1	2·7	1887 1888
S.	Ada	Mr. A. Manning Owner	2·5	612	24·48	3·5	4·35	32·33	7·0	5·0	5·0	?	?	1888
C.	Chipmunk	Mr. Sidney C. Watson Luke	2·48	749	19·87	4	8	32	7·7	4·5	6	3·2	2·5	1888
S.	Lady Nan	Mr. W. Waller Payne	2·5	653	22·97	0·5	1·25	24·65	8·3	4·7	5·7	4·1	?	1888
C.	Trixy	Mr. G. Sibbick Ratsey	2·4	600	20·0	3·95	6·25	30·0	8·0	5·0	5·2	4·0	2·5	1888
S.	Tottie	Mr. Simpson Watson	1·75	500	21·00	4·2	4·6	29·8	4·5	4·3	?	?	?	1888
L.	Queen Mab	Mrs. J. B. C. West Watson	2·49	619	24·21	5·0	6·2	35·4	5·1	4·7	6·0	4·3	?	1889
L.	Thief	Mrs. G. A. Schenley Watson	2·45	606	24·34	4·9	6·2	35·4	5·1	4·7	6·0	4·3	?	1889

	Name	Owner									Year
L.	Cosette, C.B.	Earl of Dunraven Watson	2·48	609	24·46	4·8	6·0	35·3	5·7	4·0	4·5	4·5	?	1889
L.	G.G.	Capt. G. W. Garrett Stevens	2·48	574	25·94	2·9	2·0	30·8	10·0	4·0	{2· / 7·}	3·5	2·1	1889
L.	Humming Bird	Capt. J. W. Hughes Payne	2·44	567	25·90	0·75	0·72	27·35	7·41	4·2	6·0	?	?	1889
L.	Cock-a-Whoop	Lt. F. & Mr. A. C. Hughes Payne	2·50	600	25·00	1·25	0·91	27·16	8·6	4·5	5·75	?	?	1889
L.	Babe	Mr. W. A. Beauclerk Payne	2·46	553	26·76	0·75	0·91	28·76	6·7	4·25	6·0	?	?	1890
C.	Camilla	Mr. G. Keele Payne	2·47	563	26·45	0·91	1·16	28·52	7·2	4·0	4·8	?	?	1890
L.	Janetta	Mr. Newton Robinson Payne	2·49	566	26·51	0·92	1·10	28·53	7·5	4·3	5·8	?	?	1890
L.	Mliss	M.s. R. Read & Miss Cox Payne	2·50	603	24·97	1·0	1·25	27·22	7·0	4·5	5·8	?	?	1890
L.	Dolphin	Mr. A. C. Kennedy Clayton	2·48	581	25·08	2·7	2·6	30·4	7·5	4·5	5·8	3·6	?	1890
L.	Troublesome	Mrs. Rudston Read Soper	2·47	566	26·3	4·8	6·2	37·3	7·3	5·8	5·8	5·7	3	1890
L.	Avadavat	Mr. Wilson Hoare Payne	2·49	536	28·00	0·75	1·23	29·98	6·5	4·5	6·4	?	?	1891
L.	Flera	Miss Cox Payne	2·49 / 2·44	535 / 536	28·00 / 27·36	? / 2·7	? / 1·23	? / 31·29	6·5	4·5	6·4	?	altd.	1891 / 1892
L.	Squirrel	Sir W. G. Pearce Stone	2·50	578	25·95	?	?	?	6·5	?	?	?	?	1891
L.	Undine	Mr. E. N. Harvey Clayton	2·49	577	25·99	2·5	3·2	30·7	7·2	4·5	6·0	3·8	2·3	1891
L.	Calva	Mr. F. R. Jameson Payne	2·50	565	26·55	4·0	1·29	31·84	7·25	4·0	6·0	?	?	1892

2½-RATERS, 1887-92—continued

Rig	Yacht	Owner and Designer	R.	S.A.	L.W.L.	O.H. Fwrd.	O.H. Aft	L.O.A.	B.	D.	Drght	Displ. tons	Ballast tons	When built
L.	Cockatoo	Lt. F. and Mr. A. C. Hughes / Payne	2·47	545	27·24	3·66	1·24	32·14	8·0	5·0	6·0	?	?	1892
L.	Hoopoe	Capt. Britten, R.N., & the Hon. G. Colville / Payne	2·49	539	27·83	2·5	1·20	31·53	6·8	5·0	6·0	?	?	1892
L.	Papoose	Mr. Paul Ralli / Payne	2·50	543	27·65	3·5	1·25	32·4	7·0	4·5	6·0	?	?	1892
L.	Poÿnir	Mr. W. S. Armitage / Payne	2·47	528	28·15	3·7	1·22	33·1	7·2	4·5	6·0	?	?	1892
L.	Faugh-a-Ballagh	Mr. A. Hardie Jackson / Payne	2·48	542	27·48	2·25	1·16	30·9	7·0	4·25	6·5	?	?	1892
L.	Mynah	Lieut. F. Elwes / Payne	2·50	544	27·65	2·25	1·3	31·2	7·0	4·25	6·5	?	?	1892
L.	Molly	Mr. Jessop / Nicholson	2·41	531	28·26	3·98	5·99	38·23	6·6	?	6·5	3·7	2·3	1892
L.	Stork, C.B.	Capt. S. Y. H. Davenport / Nicholson	2·43	527	28·52	3·66	6·08	38·26	7·0	?	3·7 {?}	3·6	2·2	1892
L.	Gareth	Mr. Henderson / Nicholson	2·48	533	28·02	3·78	4·9	36·7	?	?	?	?	?	1892
L.	Bud	Earl of Desart / Soper	2·47	534	28·0	1·8	2·7	32·5	7·3	?	6·4	4·3	2·4	1892
L.	Modwen	Mr. C. MacIver / Livingstone	2·50	564	26·69	2·59	5·99	35·27	7·33	3·8	3·2	3·6	2·1	1892
S.	Wenonah	Mr. H. Allan / Herreshoff	2·40	577	25·05	?	?	37·5	7·5	3·0	6·1	?	?	1892

½-RATERS, 1891-92

Rig	Yacht	Owner and Designer	R.	S.A.	L.W.L.	O.H. Fwrd.	O.H. Aft	L.O.A.	B.	D.	Drght.	Displ. cwt.	Ballast cwt.	When built
L.S.	Pup (C.B.)	Mr. T. W. Ratsey. Clayton.	0·99	343	17·37	1·46	2·32	21·15	6·6	2·9	{1·9 / 5·0}	22	7·5	1890
—	Unit	Mr. G. F. Flemmich. Owner	0·94	308	18·40	?	?	?	5·4	4·0	?	?	?	1890
—	Cobweb	Mr. B. O. Cochrane ? Designer	0·75	?	?	?	?	?	5·8	4·5	?	?	?	1890
Split L.	Cariad	Dr. P. W. Hughes Sibbick	1·00	285	21·00	?	?	26·6	6·6	2·6	?	?	?	1892
L.S.	Barbet	Mr. Wilson Hoare Payne	0·97	288	20·27	3·05	1·00	24·32	5·95	2·5	4·0	?	?	1892
L.S.	Argula	Mr. H. R. Langrishe and E. K. B. Tighe Nicholson	over rating			?	?	?	5·9	?	2·6	34	15	1892
L.S.	Nansheef (C.B.)	Mr. T. C. Burrowes Fife	0·99	297	20·24	4·18	3·38	27·80	6·6	2·3	2·5	30	17	1892
L.S.	Rogue (Bulb Keel)	Mr. K. Vogan, Ridsdale	0·99	285	20·91	5·06	2·51	28·48	5·75	2·2	4·5	21	13	1892
L.S.	Doushka	Mr. P. Perceval Payne	0·98	281	21·07	3·1	1·7	25·87	6·0	2·5	4·5	?	?	1892
—	Mahatma	Mr. G. F. Flemmich. Owner	0·99	289	20·61	2·67	1·36	24·64	5·3	2·7	?	?	?	1892

½-RATERS, 1890-92

Rig	Yacht	Owner and Designer	R.	S.A.	L.W.L.	O.H. Fwrd.	O.H. Aft	L.O.A.	B.	D	Drght.	Displ. cwt.	Ballast cwt.	When built
L.S.	Tiny	Mr. Vogan, Ridsdale	0·50	193	15·52	1·25	0·4	17·17	5·0	2·45	3·0	18	14	1890
L.S.	Bairn	Mr. E. F. Quilter, Clayton	0·49	185	16·10	1·65	1·0	18·75	6·1	1·3	1·3	14	4	1891
L.S.	Coquette	Mr. E. Jessop, Nicholson	0·49	191	15·58	1·53	1·97	19·08	4·5	3·0	3·0	15	9	1891
L.S.	Eileen	Miss Sutton, Payne	0·48	185	15·90	0·82	0·61	17·33	4·8	2·7	3·0	?	?	1891
L.S.	Jeanie	Mr. Cochrane, Fife	0·48	182	15·94	0·88	4·51	21·33	5·2	3·0	2·9	22	12	1891
L.S.	Narua	Mr. Perceval, Payne	0·48	183	15·97	0·81	0·58	17·36	5·0	2·8	3·0	?	?	1891
L.S.	Dancing Girl	Mr. Hewitt, Ridsdale	0·50	189	15·99	1·03	0·7	17·72	4·8	2·4	3·0	16	12	1891
L.S.	Kittiwake	Lt. L. C. Elwes, Payne	0·50	178	17·16	1·25	0·5	18·91	5·0	2·7	3·0	?	?	1891
L.S.	Dee Dee	Mr. Paul Ralli, Payne	0·50	177	17·17	0·25	0·71	19·13	4·41	2·7	3·0	?	?	1891
L.S.	Mosquito	Mr. Rudston Read, Soper	0·49	179	16·6	0·9	2·1	19·6	4·9	?	2·9	20	6	1891
L.S.	Ladybird	Miss Hammersley, Payne	0·49	176	17·04	1·00	0·4	18·65	5·0	2·5	2·9	?	?	1891
L.Ywl.	Spruce	Mr. Brand, T. L. Smith	0·41	154	16·20	0·15	1·75	18·1	5·0	1·5	0·5	?	nil	1891
Ywl.	Torpedo	Mr. Stewart, ?	0·5	170	17·30	?	?	?	?	?	?	?	?	1891
L.S.	Daisy	Mr. Soper, Soper	0·5	176	17·10	4·23	2·65	23·98	5·8	?	3·3	15	7	1892
S.	Wee Winn	Miss W. Sutton, Herreshoff	0·46	178	15·61	3·78	4·53	23·92	4·8	1·3	2·9	8	3	1892
L.S.	Lilliput	The late Mr. S. Watson, Payne	0·5	180	16·5	3·0	0·5	20·0	4·9	2·0	3·0	?	?	1892
L.S.	Pique	Miss Sutton, Payne	0·5	176	17·0	3·12	0·66	20·78	5·0	2·0	2·9	?	?	1892

CHAPTER 10

Fitting Out a Fifty-Tonner to Go Foreign
By E. F. Knight

There is no reason why ocean cruising should be confined to those who are fortunate enough to possess big steam yachts, or schooners of considerable tonnage. A good 50-tonner, or even a smaller craft, is probably as safe under any circumstances as the larger vessel; she can go where the latter cannot, and in many ways gives her owner better sport.

When a man really fond of the sea—and he must be so to undertake the task—sets to work to fit out a 50-tonner for a lengthy voyage, to the South Atlantic for example, his method must necessarily be somewhat different from that of the owner of the large yacht. He has to rely a good deal on his own wits, for much of the work of preparation is quite out of the line of his shipwright and of the ordinary nautical tradesmen with whom he has to deal. He is not likely to employ one of the regular ocean-going skippers, who would of course know exactly what was required, and the yachtsman making ready for his first expedition of this nature is sure to do some things wrong; but he will gradually pick up many wrinkles to help him on another occasion.

Such a voyage must to a great extent be an amateur business, by which I mean one to be undertaken only by a pleasure sailor of experience, accompanied by friends of like tastes; for I can imagine nothing so remote from an amusement as for a novice to sail away on a vessel of this size with a purely professional skipper and crew on whom he has to implicitly rely. He is completely at the mercy of his servants; hands who are well enough when carrying their employer about in home waters and on short foreign cruises are apt, unless they are exceptional men indeed, to take advantage of his ignorance and helplessness in many ways when the vessel is thousands of miles from home and on coasts where—and they are thoroughly well aware of this—he cannot discharge them, since it would be impossible satisfactorily to replace them. To travel in such a fashion would be productive of so much annoyance and anxiety as to sicken one forever of the sea. With a larger vessel it is of course a different matter; a first-class skipper is engaged, the crew is carefully picked, all is properly ordered, and a discipline not altogether feasible on the small craft is maintained; and yet I have heard it whispered that discord and trouble are not always absent even from the big vessel on a lengthened cruise.

There is no man I would rather have at sea with me than the honest British yachting tar of the right sort; but it is difficult to get him to ship for a long voyage on a small craft, and as a rule one has to put up with an inferior article. The owner of our roaming 50-tonner therefore, if he wish to enjoy any comfort and have an easy mind, must know sufficient to be entirely independent of his crew; and if he is not his own skipper—which he ought to be—he should at any rate be entered on the ship's papers as captain, and every man on board should sign articles under him. Should the skipper choose to leave the vessel, the owner must be capable of taking his place. The men must be made to understand that their employer can do without them; that, in case of their attempting any nonsense, he is quite prepared to put all hands on shore and ship a crew of any sort of foreigners in any port if necessary; if he cannot do this, he had far better stay on shore, or only cruise in home waters. But when once the owner has attained this absolute independence, he will find there is no more fascinating pursuit than that of navigating his little vessel across the seas from country to country, to whatsoever corner of the world he may fancy to betake himself.

It is important that our cruiser should be so rigged and fitted out generally as to be capable of being handled by as small a crew as possible. Every trick of tackle, purchase, and what not that can economise labour should be taken advantage of, and it is astonishing how few men can then work a vessel. One does not do everything in recognised yachting fashion when making ocean runs; there is comparatively little work to do, and the large crew that is required on the Channel cruise is not necessary on the long voyage. For several good reasons the owner should keep his crew as small as is compatible with the safety of the vessel. Crowding is thus avoided, a matter of moment when one is sailing the tropical seas; for there the confinement of several men on a small yacht is unhealthy for them, despite all arrangements that may be made for their comfort. When the mouths are few, it will be easier to carry a sufficiency of supplies, and the question of water, more especially, will not be so difficult to deal with; it will moreover be a much less troublesome business to get one's complement of men made up in a foreign port in the event of desertion or dismissal.

It must be remembered that the owner is very likely to have a few disturbances and to get rid of some of his men in the course of such a cruise. It would be strange if it were otherwise. It is a monotonous life for the hands cooped up in the small vessel. If they have no other reason for becoming discontented, they will do so merely because they have too much to eat and too little to do; there will be dissensions; each man will reveal what bad qualities he may possess; there may be that fearful thing a sea lawyer on board, but he should not be permitted to stay long. This period of trouble, however, will probably be only of short duration—else such a cruise would be a purgatory; the worthless are weeded out, others are shipped; and it is a man's own fault if he has not soon gathered around him a compact if miscellaneous crew, willing, cheery, ready to go anywhere he may choose to take them.

It is my opinion that there should not be a single yacht sailor on board the foreign-cruising 50-tonner. It is difficult, as I have said, to get the right ones, and it will be bad for the owner if he fall in with the wrong ones—men who have been spoilt by foolish employers, for instance; a numerous class, I fear. We all know them. Smart-looking fellows enough maybe, but shirkers of honest work, they prefer to ship on show yachts belonging to owners who like to exhibit themselves and their vessels in the fashionable yachting ports each season, but who are not sailors in any sense of the word, and have no real love of the sport, following it only for the swagger of the thing. Men who have served such owners would prove a great nuisance on an ocean cruise, and would not be likely to go far. I have heard such hands grumbling on a friend's yacht because they were to pass one night at sea instead of in some port where they happened to have friends. They look to frequent tips from the 'governor's' visitors, and to other less legitimate perquisites; these they cannot get in mid-Atlantic, so it is not the place for them.

Hands from fishing-boats, sailing barges, and small coasters are the best men for the foreign cruiser of small tonnage. Among these one is not likely to come across spoilt and pampered mariners, and they are accustomed to roughing it, and to the shifts of short-handed craft. But were I undertaking a lengthened tropical voyage, I think I should ship my English crew simply for the run over to my first West Indian or South American port, and there engage a negro crew. These blacks are excellent fore-and-aft sailors, easy to manage, and always happy and ready for any amount of hard work if kindly but firmly treated; while they are, of course, far better fitted than white men to withstand the debilitating influence of sultry climates, an influence which, as everyone knows, has caused the ruin of many a good British sailor, driving hitherto sober men to injure their health by excess whenever they get shore leave.

And now for our vessel, of what sort should she be? She must, of course, be of fair beam. We are beginning to believe in beam again, and are returning to the wisdom of our ancestors, recognising the fact that beam is not incompatible with speed, whilst it is indispensable for comfort both on deck and below on an ocean cruise. I remember, when we sailed away in the *Falcon* to South America twelve years ago, yachting men shook their heads at our beam; I was assured that I should never get more than six knots an hour out of such a tubby craft, more especially as she was snugly sparred and could fly so little canvas. She had a length of 42 feet to a beam of 13 feet. As it turned out, we often got nine knots out of her, and made one voyage of 2,000 nautical miles in ten days, the current, it must be said, being favourable to us on this occasion. But the proportionate beaminess of the *Falcon* is not necessary for the bigger craft, and the beam of our 50-tonner should be about a quarter of her length.

When choosing my vessel I should prefer, for other reasons than economy, to buy an old one that had been well cared for to building or purchasing a new one. Tropical climates soon develop defects in wood, and though it may be impossible to detect any flaws or signs of early decay in a new vessel, the timber of which she is constructed may have been put in sappy, and she may be ready to break out into dry rot on the slightest provocation. Tough old human beings who have weathered the ailments of youth are not likely to fall into consumption, and so it is with the ship. If she has knocked about for years and shown no symptoms of decay, then she has proved herself to have been put together of the right stuff, and she will remain sound in her good old age.

If one came across some old teak vessel, such as my *Alerte* was, a quarter of a century old, constructed by a good builder in the strong, honest fashion of those days, not put together in a hurry, but leisurely; with not a plank in her that was not well seasoned and selected, and that had not been lying in the builder's loft for a year before it was used, and with timbers and deadwood stouter than are employed now, and if, after careful examination, she proved from stem to stern, from deck to keel, as sound as when she was put on the stocks, even in those treacherous and usually ill-ventilated corners inside the counter, then that vessel is the one to be possessed of by the man who would go foreign; for she can be more safely trusted than many a brand-new craft, scamped, pleasing to the eye, but of unsound constitution, like some fair pulmonary with the germs of disease latent in her bones. The *Alerte* was a vessel of this good old sort—I say was, for after I had left her, this yawl, which properly cared for would have completed her century of cruising, was lost by a piece of wicked negligence off the West Indian island of Trinidad, and is now lying at the bottom in one hundred fathoms of water.

A yawl is the favourite rig for the cruising 50-tonner; personally, I should prefer a ketch, the easiest vessel afloat to handle. A 50-ton ketch requires a very small crew indeed; a couple of men on deck can tackle any job that turns up. But a yawl is nearly as handy as the ketch. Two of us used to knock about for days at a time on the *Alerte* in the South Atlantic, and she was a 56-ton yawl, with somewhat heavy spars. We never had any difficulty with her; but when we were short-handed, we used to employ 'un-yachty' methods. We could only hoist our mainsail by using our mast-winch, which we also employed for hauling out the reefing tackle when shortening sail. There are many little dodges that soon occur to a sailor, and I have no doubt that if one man who knew what he was about were left alone in mid ocean on such a vessel, he would have little difficulty in taking her into port.

There should, of course, be a good supply of sails on board, not omitting a stout storm trysail and a handy spinnaker. The latter should have a boom short enough to pass under the forestay when topped up, so that it has not to be unshipped for a gybe. Such a spinnaker will be more effective than a big one on an ocean cruise. It can be carried when the wind is strong and the sea high—an important matter; for how often one has seen a fore-and-after, that has been rolling gun-wales under when running under mainsail and head-sail alone, skim along steadily with dry decks as soon as the little spinnaker is put on her to balance the other canvas? When we left England with the *Alerte*, we had with us her racing spinnaker only. We soon discovered we had made a mistake. Short-handed as we were, we often refrained from using it when it would have been of service; for the unshipping of its mighty boom was a heavy bit of work. Then we had a small boom made, and used the balloon-foresail as the working spinnaker. One man could handle this, and it was seldom allowed to lie idle when the breeze was aft.

It is better thus to provide oneself with a sail that can serve both as balloon-foresail and spinnaker, according to how the wind may be, than to encumber oneself with a large square-sail, such as yachts were wont to carry, and such as one still sees on revenue cutters.[1] But there is a square-sail of another sort that should be found in the sail-locker of every little foreign cruiser; this is the small stout storm square-sail, a sail which would be seldom used, it is true, but which, on certain occasions, would prove of inestimable advantage.

With the *Falcon* we once ran on before a favourable gale till the gale became a hurricane—a River Plate *pampero*—and then the sea was dangerously high, so that we were unable to do what should have been done hours before; that is, bring her up into the wind and heave to. Not daring to attempt this now, we had to make the best of the position, and run on under trysail and storm jib. The steering was a most difficult and anxious matter; there was considerable danger of broaching to, and our lives depended upon the watchful skill of the helmsman. The trysail had no boom, and was ever violently gybing, while so low was the body of the sail that it lost the wind when we were in the trough of those great seas.

Now that was the very time when we needed the little storm square-sail. Under that snug bit of canvas the vessel would have steered with far greater ease and safety; there would have been no risk of a gybe; the tendency to broach to would have been much lessened, and a topsail of this sort, moreover, is, like a jib, a lifting sail, and helps to keep a vessel afloat. Hoisted well up, as it should be, right under the forestay, it is high enough to catch the wind between the seas.

If the owner does not carry a storm square-sail, he should have a boom to his trysail.

When the yachtsman, having purchased his 50-tonner, begins to fit her out for the ocean cruise, he is certain to discover that he will have

---

1. The *Navahoe*, before returning to America, ordered a square-sail from Tilley, of Southampton.

to make considerable alterations in the arrangement of her ballast. The vessel that hitherto has been cruising in home waters only is sure to have a great deal more ballast in her than is necessary or advisable for his purpose. In the first place, when on a long voyage, he is not going to crack on as if he were racing for a cup. He will most probably have reduced his vessel's spars before starting, and has no ambition, when he is on the ocean for weeks at a stretch, to carry the huge spread of canvas under which his craft was wont to stagger in the Solent.

The ocean rover, who loves blue water for its own sake, is a quiet plodding sort of person, in no extreme hurry to reach his port. He wishes to be as comfortable and free from anxiety as possible, and, like the master of an East Indiaman of the olden time, is more likely than not to make things snug each sunset and take in his kites—the big topsail for example—as he does not approve of the watch below having to be summoned on deck at each squall.

So our foreign cruiser, snugly sparred and moderately canvassed, need not be nearly so stiff as when she used to fly up and down the Channel, straining and quivering as if acutely jealous lest any other craft should outstrip her; and she can now be relieved of a considerable portion of her ballast. It is of such importance that the 50-tonner should be light and buoyant, so that she may leap over the Atlantic storm waves and not plunge into their curling crests, that I think the less ballast one can do with the better. I lay stress on this, because I know that the usual wiseacres and others, who frequent the shipwright's yard to proffer all manner of advice to the yachtsman while he is preparing for his voyage, will shake their heads if he speaks of lightening his craft to the extent I should advocate, and warn him that a perilous crankiness will be the result. There is, of course, a limit to this lightening process which must not be overstepped; but that limit—at any rate so far as my practice is concerned—does not, as a rule, find favour in the eyes of the forementioned advisers.

If the vessel be ballasted with lead when she comes into one's possession, the weight can be reduced to the exact amount that is required by selling a sufficient quantity of the lead and substituting the same bulk of iron, the specific gravity of one metal to the other being roughly as 11 to 7. A spare chain, spare anchors, and any iron implements not liable to be damaged by damp, can with advantage be employed as ballast in this way, but must, of course, be stowed so that they can be got at without difficulty. Whilst adjusting the ballast it is necessary to remember that, unlike the coasting yacht, the ocean cruiser will have to be laden with a considerable quantity of water and other stores—probably some six tons weight of these.

The question of what boats should be carried on the ocean-going 50-tonner is one to be considered carefully. The ordinary yacht's gig, that does very well to land passengers in Channel ports, is not adapted for our purpose; she would be cumbersome, occupying too much room on deck, and, most probably, would not be a sufficiently good sea-boat. A shorter dinghy of lifeboat shape, with plenty of sheer and a pointed stern, will be found much more serviceable, especially if one has to effect a landing on small oceanic islands or at other exposed spots where access is rendered difficult by heavy surf. The boat should be beamy and rather shallow; for if she is too deep she is likely, while lying on deck, to get very much in the way of the main boom, which will have to be topped up to an awkward height to clear her; or, worse still, she may even make it impossible for the main boom to be swung sufficiently forward when the vessel is running before the wind—a terrible nuisance on which it is unnecessary to dilate. I believe one of the principal reasons why the revenue cutters carry their large square-sails is that they could not otherwise get any speed out of them before a fair wind, to such an extent do their boats cramp the boom and prevent the easing off of the mainsheet.

In my opinion one cannot do better than carry a medium-sized Berthon collapsible in addition to one's big dinghy. A Berthon occupies very little room, and is so easily dropped into the water and hoisted on board again that she is sure to be used on many occasions when one would not take the trouble to put the heavier boat out. I was once shipmate with a delightful Berthon which had an iron centreboard and a balance lugsail. We gave her plenty of work in every port, creek, or river we entered; for she sailed admirably, and was one of the handiest little craft possible. She contributed a great deal to our enjoyment of the cruise.

A few remarks on that most important subject, the commissariat, may not be amiss. When fitting an ocean-going 50-tonner for the first time, one asks oneself with considerable misgiving how it will be possible to find room for all the necessary stores. I remember coming down to the *Falcon* one morning, when we were getting her ready for her South Atlantic voyage, to find the quay, alongside which she lay, covered with barrels, sacks, cases, &c., the provisions for five men for nine months, which I had ordered from London. I stood aghast before this mighty mass, the bulk of which appeared to exceed by far the capacity of my vessel's hold; but it is wonderful what an amount of stowage room there is in the lockers and corners of a beamy vessel; however much is put into her, there seems to be place for more. I was much relieved in my mind to get my tons of stores snugly stowed out of sight, and all below the water-line too, so serving as good ballast. On the *Alerte* we found no difficulty in carrying nearly a year's supply of provisions for thirteen hands.

As for water, extra tanks will have to be fitted up in all convenient places. On the *Alerte* we had a gallon tank under the saloon table, while the cabin fireplace was removed and a large tank was built into the space thus gained. We carried 600 gallons in all, which ought to suffice for the longest run one is likely to make, allowing for calms in the doldrums and unforeseen delays. All the drinking water should be in tanks below. To carry any weight of water in casks on deck is a mistake for various reasons; but of course it is well to have some breakers on deck to hold any rain-water that may be caught on the voyage.

It is my firm opinion that one should carry plenty of good salt meat when bound on a long cruise, and rely as little as possible on tinned provisions. The temperature is very high on small vessels in the tropics, and this does undoubtedly in time set up some sort of chemical change in tinned meat—a change which, though it may not be perceptible to the senses, can be productive of much ill health. The salt meat should be of the right sort too. It is not advisable to go, as I myself once did, to even the best of butchers in a seaport town and have fresh meat salted down. This is excellent at first, but it will not keep long on the small vessel. It is far better to procure the older, much-travelled, well-tested salt meat, less tasty though it be. The good firms of purveyors empty the cask, examine each piece of beef, and repickle it, before sending it on board; such beef will keep through the longest voyage and in any climate.

It is certain that no sort of food will remain sweet and wholesome so long on a small as on a big craft. It is amongst other things essential to have the supply of biscuit divided into a number of hermetically sealed tins. The best made bread locker will not prevent maggots, weevils, and other loathsome insects from swarming among the biscuit as soon as the 50-tonner reaches the tropics, and the better the quality of the biscuit the more rapid and complete will be the spoiling of it. It must not be forgotten that tinned ship's bread can only be procured in England, so a sufficient supply must be laid in before one sails.

This brings me to another point. It is not only advisable to take from England all the biscuit wanted, but also, if possible, all the tinned meats and suchlike stores. If more be needed in the course of the voyage, it should be sent out from England and transshipped. In the ports of the West Indies, of the Indian Ocean, or indeed on any tropical coast, though one may come across honest ship-chandlers—I have frequently been lucky enough to do so myself—it will be found that, even with them, prices are apt to be exorbitant; while their goods are often of inferior quality, or, when of good brands, old and damaged. With the dishonest ship-chandlers, who are not rare, one is likely to have still worse experiences. Were I again to fit out a yacht for a lengthy cruise, I should take everything of this sort with me, or make arrangements with a good English firm to send me out relays of supplies to certain places at which it was my intention to call. I should only rely on the ports for fresh meat, vegetables, fruit and suchlike perishable commodities.

Neither should one go to the ship-chandler of the foreign harbour for rope, blocks, canvas, or boatswain's necessaries of any description. Provision should be carefully made against running short of these; plenty and to spare should be taken from home.

On an English 50-ton yacht it is usual to carry on all the cooking in the forecastle; but when the vessel is on tropical seas it is very uncomfortable for the hands forward to have a fire burning for the greater part of the day in their close quarters. On the *Alerte* the fire was only lit once a day in order to cook the dinner, a large spirit stove being employed or the preparation of breakfast and tea, to boil water, and so forth. A good spirit stove is indispensable on our 50-tonner. On the *Falcon* we used even to cook our dinner with one. Spirits-of-wine is among the few things that can always be got of satisfactory quality and at moderate cost in every foreign port. I have never found difficulty in procuring this in any part of the world, and as a rule considerably cheaper than methylated spirits in England.

I have always preferred a spirit to a paraffin stove. I have never come across a sea cook yet who could deal satisfactorily with the latter. The lampblack is apt to make a terrible mess of the pots and pans and everything else, including the sea cook. I know that, if the lamp is properly trimmed and the stove is carefully looked after, this should not happen. But somehow or other it generally does happen; consequently paraffin is not suitable fuel for the sea-going stove, and the cleanly alcohol, though a little more expensive, is far better for the purpose.

On plenty of smart West Indian and other foreign sloops and schooners of about the size of our 50-tonners, it is customary to do all the cooking on deck; and I do not see why this method should not be adopted on our small ocean-going yacht when she is at sea in fine weather or lying at anchor. A tiny temporary galley or fireplace—very 'un-yachty,' it must be confessed—might be fitted up on deck forward, and if the cook be a West Indian negro of the right sort, he will probably be found as clever as an Indian '*bobbachee*' on the march at turning out a capital meal without the aid of cumbersome stove or oven—and that, too, without making any mess whatever, so that the skipper need feel no anxiety for his spotless deck and sails.

THE DROGUE, OFF THE KULLEN HEAD.

CHAPTER 11

Baltic Cruising
By E. F. Knight

A few English sailing yachts visit the Baltic every year, but that wind-swept sea can scarcely be termed one of the favourite cruising grounds of our pleasure fleet. This is not altogether strange; for the voyage is a long and rough one round the Skaw into the squally Cattegat; chilly gales and choppy seas in many summers form the rule rather than the exception among the Danish Islands, and the principal seaports of the inland sea are singularly dull and uninteresting.

Nevertheless—and the reader will soon understand that what I am about to say is in no wise inconsistent with my opening sentence—I am confident that the yachtsman who undertakes a summer's cruise on the Baltic in a *small* vessel will afterwards remember it as one of his very pleasantest experiences. This is a sea which is often coldly repelling to the cursory traveller, but it is strangely fascinating to him who takes the trouble to explore it, and the charm of it increases with further knowledge.

How interesting, to begin with, is the voyage out! For, with the small vessel I am speaking of, the yachtsman does not double the stormy Skaw, but sails in and out along all the winding coasts that were the cradle of our race, the lands of the Frisians, Saxons, Jutes, Angles, and Danes. Having waited for a slant in one of our Eastern ports—Harwich, for example—he crosses the North Sea to a Dutch harbour, follows the shores of the Zuider Zee, picks his way up the narrow channels that divide the sandy Frisian Islands from the mainland, enters the River Eider, and passes up the ship canal to Kiel.

And that port once reached, what possibilities of glorious cruising are before him! He has now left behind the discoloured waves of the North Sea, and his keel is cleaving water so limpid that every stone and weed is visible fathoms beneath. He can sail up narrow sounds between park-like glades and forests of pines and magnificent oaks and beeches; or up long winding fiords which take him beyond the coast belt of forest and pasture, and past the undulating corn lands, into the very heart of the Cimbrian peninsula, where the desolate moorlands of the Ahl, grand in their northern savagery, spread far on either side of the sinuous creek. There is the long Slie, a succession of lakes and narrows that leads to old Schleswig; there are the deep inlets of Flensborg, Apenrade, Veile, and many-islanded Liim; Ise Fiord, perhaps the fairest of all, with its promontories of noble forest; the lovely sounds of Svendborg and the Little Belt; and a score of other straits and lochs that make this in many respects the finest cruising ground in Europe.

I do not know where else, when the sun shines out between the rain squalls, the sea appears so blue, the grass and the foliage seem so green and luxuriant, as in this land of Denmark. It is pleasant to sail, as one often does, suddenly out of the choppy windy open Baltic into the shelter of these narrows, where the great trees dip their branches into the smooth water, where one comes upon scene after scene of tender and restful beauty, and where the traveller knows, too, that whenever he may choose to land, at some trim village or opposite some snug old farmhouse, he is sure of a welcome from the kindly people. Then, if the yachtsman wishes for more open water, he can sail out of the *fiord* mouth and steer for one of the many delightful little islands that stud the Baltic. Remote many of them are, set in the middle of that treacherous sea, inhabited by a few primitive fishermen. The advent of a stranger is rare in the extreme. I spent two summers in these waters, and found that no British yacht had ever come before to most of the fiords and islets I explored.

For it happens that nearly all the charms I speak of are lost to him who sails these waters in a big vessel. It is a coasting voyage in a small craft I am advocating here. Of the fiords that penetrate the Cimbrian peninsula and the larger islands, only a few are available for a yacht of deep draught, and in order to visit some of the most beautiful of the inland waters one's vessel should not draw more than two feet. Again, though harbours that will admit coasters of even light tonnage are far apart on much of the iron-bound coast of the Baltic, there are to be found everywhere, at short intervals, little artificial havens that have been built for the accommodation of the craft of the herring fishermen; while the only shelter afforded by many of the islets consists of similar havens, frequented solely by the fishing and ferry boats. At the entrance of most of these miniature harbours there is a depth of about four feet of water at high tide.

Now bad weather springs up frequently and with wonderful suddenness in the Baltic, and a dangerous sea soon rises on those shallow waters. It is therefore of great advantage to have a boat of so light a draught as to be able to run for refuge into any of these little havens. Such a craft has nearly always a snug port not far under her lee while coasting here; whereas a larger craft can find no harbour for many leagues, and has to make the best she can of it on the open sea. The shallow boat is the safest for such a cruise, besides being the only one with which the most interesting inlets and islets can be visited. She must be small, but at the same time she must be as good a sea-boat as is possible for her size; for she is not likely to escape bad weather altogether on the Baltic.

DANSKE FISHING-BOAT AND ANCHOR.

To some it may appear foolhardy to go so far on a small yacht like the one I am speaking of; but as a matter of fact it will be found that it is nearly always the cautious sailor and not the reckless one who succeeds in sailing his little vessel to distant shores. The imprudent and thoughtless man soon encounters such experiences, soon gets into such scrapes, on attempting a foreign cruise as will keep him for the future in the home waters he happens to know something about.

A voyage from England to the uttermost ends of the Baltic does not necessitate any really long runs for a yacht of small draught, and it is seldom that one need remain out at sea at night. It is well that it is so; for these are surely the most wind-vexed waters of Europe; violent north-westers rise in the most unexpected manner, and the stillest of summer mornings will as likely as not be succeeded by a howling wintry afternoon. It behoves the skipper of the small yacht to watch his weather very carefully in this treacherous region. Whenever a run of some distance is before him, from isle to isle, or along some portion of the coast where the havens of refuge are rare, he must patiently wait for a slant, and the advice of the aneroid in the cabin must be implicitly followed.

It is this last precaution that makes what otherwise would certainly be a dangerous cruise for a small craft an amusement less risky than are the majority of sports. It ought to be unnecessary to repeat such trite admonition as this; but in my experience it is the skipper of the small vessel who pays the least attention to his glass; and in all cases that have come under my notice when small yachts that have started to cross the North Sea or the Channel, or to make some other run of a dozen hours or so, have come to grief in any way in consequence of having encountered weather dangerously heavy for them, it is for the one reason that the skipper, possibly an excellent sailor in other respects, has neglected his aneroid. One may indeed make occasional runs in this blind fashion, trusting to the appearance of the sky alone, and yet no harm come of it; but on the sort of Baltic cruise I am describing there will, of course, be a number of such short runs; short, but quite long enough to make disaster a probability sooner or later if proper precautions be not taken, and it may be found that the pitcher has gone to the well once too often.

The life of the man who undertakes long coasting voyages in small craft depends more on his knowledge of the use of the barometer, and on his close observation of it, than it does on his good seamanship. A man I know had his dinghy carried away, and nearly lost his little yacht and his life, on a run from Ryde to Havre. The longshore wiseacres shook their heads when they heard of it, and spoke of the foolhardiness of sailing across Channel in so tiny a vessel. In this I maintain the wiseacres were wrong; the foolhardiness lay in the skipper's blinking at the heavens to windward and lee, and putting absolute faith in their deceptive appearance, while he entirely omitted to see what the glass was doing before he tripped his anchor. It is possible to practically insure for oneself fine weather, or at any rate the absence of dangerously bad weather, for a run of say a day and night, provided one have the patience to wait for it.

I cannot recall an instance of having experienced really bad weather when my reading of the barometer had told me that it would be fine; but I have seen the weather-wisdom of many an old sea-dog at fault. In the Baltic the fishermen fail signally to read the signs of their own skies, as the following incident will show. I had sailed into a fish-

ROSKILDE FROM THE FIORD.

ing-haven on Zeeland called Gillelie. I found a *fête* in progress which had detained the fishermen who would otherwise have sailed on that day to the distant island of Anholt for the autumn herring fishery. 'But we will all be off tomorrow,' said one to me. 'I do not think any of you will sail tomorrow or the day after; it will be blowing a gale of wind from the north-west,' I remarked, for my glass had been falling in most ominous fashion for some days.

But my friends thought they knew better. 'You are a stranger here,' said they; 'we fishing-folk know the signs of the sky in our country. The wind is south-west, and it will remain fine. The barometer is not to be trusted in the Baltic.' Well, at midnight the wind had shifted to north-west, and was howling through the bending pines; by dawn the gale had burst upon us, for two days it blew a very hurricane, and there was much loss of life and shipping on the Cattegat. Had it not been for the *fête* the fishermen would have put to sea, and few would ever have been seen again. I converted the fishermen of Gillelie to a belief in the barometer, and I believe that they forthwith applied to the Danish Government for one of those glasses which it supplies to seaports for the public use.

Having given my reasons for recommending a small vessel of light draught for Baltic cruising, I will now explain what I consider that vessel should be like. I am about to preach rank heresy, but I should certainly act up to my preaching were I ever again to make preparations for a similar voyage.

The craft that last carried me about those seas was an old teak P. & O. lifeboat, 29 feet in length, which had been decked, rigged as a ketch, provided with six inches of false keel, and so converted into a yacht of three tons register. A boat something like this one appears to me to be the best adapted for the purpose in question—a boat with pointed stern and considerable sheer, such as my lifeboat was, and such, too, as are the herring fishing boats of the Cattegat. Her beam should be about one-quarter of her length, her draught should not exceed 2 ft. 6 in., and she should have less ballast by a good deal than is generally put into a boat of her tonnage; for she must be comfortable when in rough water, be light and lively, and leap over the steep seas of the Baltic instead of driving herself through them.

My old lifeboat was the best sea-boat of her size I have ever come across. Once I was caught with her in a north-wester in the Gulf of Heligoland, and had to run to Cuxhaven before a really heavy sea. That little boat acquitted herself in a way that astonished us; presenting as she did a sharp stern to the steep following seas, she showed no tendency to broach to, but steered with beautiful ease, rising like a duck to every roller. Why more of our little cruisers are not constructed with these lifeboat sterns I could never understand. Anyone who has run before a high breaking sea in both styles of craft will appreciate the enormous difference between the behaviour of the long-countered vessel and the one with the pointed stern. The latter is undoubtedly the boat for comfort and safety in a sea-way.

In such a boat as I am describing one could sail, single-handed, if one was so minded, to Finland or to the furthest depths of the Gulf of Bothnia, and run less risk than one would in most vessels four times her size.

We have now got a good sea-boat almost as safe as a lifeboat—but the next question is, how will she sail? A double-ended craft like the one I am speaking of will run or reach as well as anything of her size; but, being of such light draught, though she will turn to windward well enough, maybe, in smooth water, she will be a very slow boat,

A Danske craft.

making scarcely any headway, but considerable leeway, when she encounters the tumbling waters of the Zuider Zee or Baltic on a breezy day. This, of course, must be remedied by some means; for we cannot always have fair winds and smooth waters. And now I am coming to my greatest heresy—I would not make a hole in the bottom of my boat and pass the orthodox centreboard through it; but I should sling on either side of her the heterodox leeboard.

In this country we are not accustomed to see leeboards on pleasure craft, and they are considered to be ugly. In Holland, where they also know something about small yachts, elegant polished oak brass-bound leeboards are invariably attached to the brightly polished little oaken vessel. One soon comes to consider a leeboard as an ornament. The appearance of a long double-ended boat is distinctly improved by these wing-like appendages. Finding that my lifeboat was so unsatisfactory on a wind, I got a Dutch shipwright at Harlingen to fit two shapely oaken leeboards upon her, which suited her well, for she herself was of polished teak. I remember that when her leeboards were once temporarily removed we felt quite ashamed of her, so lank and naked did she appear in our eyes. But the leeboards were still more useful than they were beautiful. When I put out with them into the choppy Zuider Zee I was astounded at the success of my plan. The vessel turned to windward as she had never done before, and I soon came to the conclusion that I had almost arrived at the ideal of a shallow-water cruiser.

Leeboards have many undoubted advantages over centreboards. To make a long hole through the bottom of a boat cannot but weaken her. The trunk of a centreboard is ever in the way in a small cabin. In rough water a centreboard must strain a boat more than a leeboard does. On a little vessel like the one in question the leeboards are not cumbersome, but can be readily unshipped and stowed on deck or below when there is a leading wind, or when one is hove-to in bad weather, or rolling about at anchor. And, most important of all, if the boat runs ashore, the leeboards will come gently up, whereas a centre-plate may become jammed, and so bend or break. A leeboard never refuses to be hauled up or dropped down.

In many of the shallow Baltic fiords one is apt to run ashore pretty frequently, and sometimes on rough ground that would subject a boat to severe strain unless the centreboard were pulled up very smartly. Again, some portions of these fiords in summer present the appearance of green fields, so thickly are they overgrown with weeds whose branches float on the surface of the brackish water. It is impossible to bring a centreboard boat into this tangle. The weeds gather round the plate, choke the trunk, and cannot be cleared in many cases until the boat has been hauled up on dry land. But leeboards can be lifted and cleared in a moment, and the boat provided with them can sail over meadows of aquatic growth that would effectually bar the approach of the orthodox yacht. To reach the inland *brednings* or 'broads' of the Baltic, far larger and as fair as those of Norfolk, one must often pass through these weedy passages, and this is not one of the least of my reasons for advocating the leeboard.

A GOOD CRAFT FOR THE BALTIC.

I should like to see leeboards more employed in this country. I remember as a small boy coming into possession of my first boat, some old ship's dinghy. I put sails in her, but, to my disgust, not a bit would she turn to windward. I tried to fix a false keel on her, but my appliances were few, and I was unsuccessful. Now, had I known of the simple expedient of the leeboard, limited as was my carpentering skill, I should have had no trouble in making my boat tack. The pleasure of sailing was thus denied to me for several years afterwards, and all through my ignorance of the leeboard. There must be plenty of boys at the present time in similar plight, in parts of the Far West for instance, where, as I discovered the other day, the very name of leeboard is unknown. In an hour or so anyone can convert almost anything that will float into something that will sail by means of leeboards; and this is a fact well worth knowing when one finds oneself in some wild corner of the earth and wishes to extemporise a sailing-craft.

I have done something of the sort on more than one occasion. Once I was living by the shores of a lake in Florida. I started at short notice for a fortnight's cruise inside the keys that line the coast of the Gulf of Mexico above Tampa. Nothing else being procurable, I borrowed one of the canoes of the country, a flat-bottomed punt with no more lines than a horse-trough. I manufactured a sail, and one leeboard which I could throw over from one side to the other according to the tack I was on; and away I went with rod and gun down the shallow passes, up winding bayous and across broad lakes; a delightful little cruise; and my strange craft, to the astonishment of the crackers, sailed like a witch. It was the very coast for a leeboard; for the channels between the keys and the mainland are often very shallow—so shallow, indeed, that when the tempestuous north wind blew and the rising waves poured into my vessel, so that she would soon have filled and settled to the bottom, I was sometimes enabled to lighten her, and so save her, by stepping overboard; and then I would walk ahead of her, painter in hand, and tow her against wind and sea until the weather moderated—a manoeuvre that can be recommended under such circumstances.

To return to our little Baltic cruiser—I have only given the broad features of what I consider to be the most fitting craft. As for the details of rig, cabin arrangements, and so forth, each man knows best what he requires. But were I having such a boat made ready for myself, she should be built of oak. Her sides and leeboard should not be painted, but be varnished and kept brightly polished after the Dutch fashion—

TOWING HEAD TO WIND.

boiled oil and rosin is the mixture for the purpose. She should have a small well. There should be the usual hatch on the cabin-roof to slide back and facilitate entrance to the cabin; but, instead of the usual cabin-doors, I should have a water-tight bulkhead between the well and cabin, with only a small square opening at the top, which could be closed with a sliding shutter when necessary. The cabin would then be kept snug and dry.

It is, of course, the right thing for the skipper of a small vessel to run for a port when bad weather is coming on; but this cannot always be done, and it is by far the wiser policy to remain on the open sea and make the best of it than to rush blindly before the gale towards a harbour whose dangers and difficulties are unknown to one. I remember once being with some men who, because the sea was rather ugly, were very anxious to run into a most dangerous river mouth, to the almost certain perdition of our vessel. This was the suggestion of panic, but they called it prudence. Some small vessels, even though they be rather shallow, like the one I am speaking of, can claw off a lee shore in pretty heavy weather.

Unless one have the misfortune to be embayed, there is generally one tack on which the boat can keep off the land—despite the leeway—well snugged down, with as little head-sail as possible on her, and forging slowly ahead all the time. But on such occasions there must be a good man at the tiller. Mr. ———, the most skilful sailor of small craft we have ever had, who used to knock about single-handed in all sorts of weather, and who, it will be remembered, at last died alone of heart-disease on his vessel in mid-channel—a fitting death for such a man—made it a rule to beat to sea instead of running for a port on the appearance of bad weather. He proved what can be done with a tiny yacht properly handled. But then he was a consummate seaman—so much so, indeed, that those who knew him affirm that no other man than he could have performed some of his exploits.

A little vessel may be blown away from the land, or have plenty of sea-room to leeward when the storm attacks her. Then it is not so difficult to know and to do the right thing. If the craft be such as I am imagining her to be, she should be able to ride out almost any weather with drogue out, and possibly a bit of trysail or mizzen set, sheeted well amidships. Every small yacht should be provided with one of these drogues or sea-anchors when a long cruise is to be undertaken. I have never seen one employed; but I was in the habit of carrying one, which consisted of an iron ring some 3 feet broad, to which was bent a stout canvas bag with a pointed end. A bridle was attached to the ring by which it could be made fast to a 20-fathom grass-rope. A very good drogue, which serves as a breakwater as well, can be extemporised with a spar. If one side of a small strong jib be bent on the spar, and a weight be attached to the lower corner of the jib, this ought to form a very efficient drag.

To sum up—for cruising on the charming inland waters of the Baltic, and for getting about from one part of that sea to another, the most fitting craft is, I believe, such a one as I have sketched out, sharp-sterned, with ample freeboard, with good sheer, of shallow draught, lightly ballasted, and provided with leeboards. With a boat constructed on these lines, a man who neglects not his aneroid should be able to make a very delightful voyage along the coasts of our Viking ancestors, and very much further from home, too, if he wishes it; while she would also be found a capital craft for sailing about the mouth of the Thames, the Norfolk Broads, and Dutch waters. But at Cowes they might stare at her with the eye of prejudice.

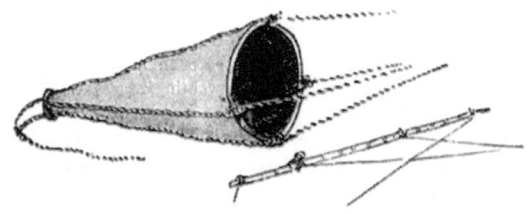

CHAPTER 12

Five-Tonners and Five-Raters in the North
By G. L. Blake

A few years ago a great sportsman, whose privilege it had been to take an active part in nearly every form of sport known to the British Isles, was asked which of them all he thought should be placed at the head of the list as being most conducive to make its follower manly, and at the same time least open to the criticism of those who are always inclined to find fault with their neighbours' methods of employing their spare time. There was some little hesitation before he gave an answer, but at length he expressed an opinion that yachting excelled all others. To enumerate a few of his reasons will not be out of place here.

The first and foremost was the utter absence of any possibility of cruelty, as calls could only be made on inanimate materials and the yachtsmen themselves. Then it was quite out of the question for a man to be a thorough yachtsman without courage and endurance being brought into play. Quickness of action, or the ability to think and act at the same time, was also a necessity in yachting, as it was in most other sports; but it was an absolute one here, because the elements were an unknown force, and sudden contingencies, not to be equalled in intensity or severity by any possible emergency ashore, had frequently to be faced. This quality—quickness of resource—was, of all others, the characteristic of the sailor.

Two more points were added, which certainly tend to place yachting, and yacht racing especially, in the fore rank of sports. The first was that yacht racing and cruising are carried on by those who enter upon them, not in any way as a business, but solely for the love of the sea.

The prizes, such as they are, when bestowed in money are so small in comparison with the outlay and cost in building and sailing a racing crack, that in most of the recognised classes they only go a very little way towards lessening the general expenditure, whilst as for betting on the races, such a thing was rare in the extreme.

The last argument was that 'unfair sailing' was a thing almost, if not quite, unknown, and if there was an argument in favour of extra money for yachts' crews on racing days, it was that it helped to encourage all hands to do their utmost to make their vessels, let the look-out be ever so bad, come in and win.

To one desirous not only of enjoying the sport, but also of really understanding every detail connected with it, from splicing, knotting, sail-making, varnishing, painting, cleaning brasswork, setting, taking in, reefing or shifting sail, to steering a clean full-and-bye against a head-sea, or learning to make himself comfortable on the smallest possible fit-out, an old yachtsman's advice is, the smaller the boat chosen to begin with the better; and after a quarter of a century's experience of small yachts in all weathers, seas, and climates, he believes the vessel of about 30 feet in length, with a moderate beam and draught of water, is the smallest capable of keeping the sea with any degree of comfort and safety.

There are no more suitable yachts of the size referred to than those built under the old Thames Rule of Measurement, or the late Rule of the Yacht Racing Association, to sail in the class for yachts of 5 tons and under. A restriction might be added to the exclusion of such yachts as were the extreme outcome of the rule; but as only three were built—one designed by Mr. G. L. Watson and the late Mr. Payton's two vessels, both of which were lost—there is no need for the limitation; and on looking back into the eighties it will be found that the 3-ton class in the South and the 3½-ton class in the North altogether monopolised the true plank-on-edge model entirely for themselves. Though the extreme types under the old rule were long, narrow, and deep, they were fine weatherly little sea-boats to the practised hand, but as a school for the tiro, except in racing, too heavily sparred and too narrow.

The main point in favour of the 5-ton yacht built under the old rule—for the 5-rater of today is almost as large as the former 10-tonner, and requires quite as many, if not more, hands to work her on a racing day with her present lugsail rig—is that she is easily worked with one good hand, can be raced with three, or easily with four; and those whose early practical yachting experience was gained as small yacht sailors and yacht-owners will agree in this, that their happiest hours were spent in the boat that required fewest paid hands, or when their ship was of such a size that they were able to put to sea single-handed, or perhaps in company with a friend who could make himself useful.

There are many who will say that a 10-ton or even a 20-ton yacht is too small to stand out to sea in; but when a yacht is of such a size that she requires more hands than one to work her there will be little or nothing learned, whereas, if the yacht is just a little too much for one man to handle, the owner is bound to do his portion of work each day, and what he does not know will soon be taught him by his man, so that he may enjoy his fair share of rest and not have to be called up in the middle of his watch below. Besides, if the cost is a consideration, a 5-ton yacht can be built for just half the price of a 10-tonner, and the keeping it up is very much smaller in proportion.

It is not quite twenty years since the racing yachts of 5 tons were formed into a class, and prizes awarded them. The Clyde yachtsmen were the first to appreciate the value and capabilities of the little ships for affording good all-round sport, and the small expenditure entailed at that date in building them was a consideration in their favour. It has been a favourite class ever since.

In Dublin Bay small yacht racing is far from a novelty, but it is only within the last few years that boats have been built to the class adopted in the seventies, *viz.*, for 'yachts of 6 tons and under,' time allowance having previously been used to bring the small fry together. At that time Liverpool had two pet classes, the 20-ton and 10-ton, and such small yachts as were located on the Sloyne entered in the latter class.

It was about the middle of the summer of 1873 that the writer's attention was first drawn to small racing yachts under 7 tons, and the way in which they could face almost all weathers. It had been, as it is at the present day, the custom to decry and run down racing yachts as unfit to be made into cruisers. 'The scantlings were light,' 'the framework was weak,' 'the plank, especially at the garboards and towards the run under the counter, may have been dubbed down to almost the thickness of brown paper.'

This latter process was often resorted to some twenty-five years ago, so that ballast in the form of lead sheeting might be padded on to the keel and garboards. More than one large yacht at that period had been so treated that she was supposed to have not much more than half-an-inch planking at her two lowest strakes. 'I would not buy an old racing yacht if I were you.' Such were the comments and never-ceasing advice dinned into the ear; 'besides, they are fearfully wet in a sea-way, and most uncomfortable,' and, therefore, at that time the writer's vessel was a strong, able, high free-boarded schooner of 11 tons. In that year there could not have been a dozen yachts, taking our coasts round, which were being raced as 5-tonners, but there were classes made up of yachts of 7 tons and under, which took in some stray 3- and 4-tonners, and here and there a casual 5- or 6-tonner.

One of the best of these 6-ton yachts (and this is including all the Scotch and South-country boats) was a little vessel built in 1871 for Mr. W. A. Tomlinson, by Mr. Dickenson, of Birkenhead, the well-known builder and designer of the principal pioneer Liverpool 10-tonners. Unfortunately her dimensions cannot be correctly stated, but she was about 32 feet between stem and sternpost on deck, some 6 ft. 6 in. in beam, and had a draught of 5 feet or a little more—that is, she was as nearly as possible the size of the 5-tonner of a five or six years' later date.

The occasion on which the *Wyvern* came under the writer's special notice was one long to be remembered on account of the anxiety created among the little yacht's admirers at Kingstown, owing to the severity of the gale that blew after she had left that port for Liverpool. There had been a regatta in Dublin Bay, where, as is usual, all the small boats of the St. George's Channel had collected to do battle. The *Wyvern* had come over from the Mersey, and having won, her owner (at that time Mr. Colin Napier, of Liverpool) had left her in the hands of his two men, that he might hurry back to his business by steamer. The men were ordered to make the best of their way to Birkenhead, as the yacht had been entered for a local regatta the same week.

They started early on a Wednesday, but unfortunately ran aground on the rocks at the end of the eastern breakwater on which the light-house is built. For the greater part of the day the boat was standing high and dry some feet above the low-water mark, but she sustained no damage, was floated off at the return of the tide, and left at once for her destination. The hour of her departure was about three or four o'clock in the afternoon. Three yachts left the harbour in company with her, bound for the same port, all three being at least 25-tonners.

As the barometer had been falling ever since the morning, and there was every indication of bad weather, the skipper in charge of the *Wyvern* was repeatedly advised to postpone his start till the following day, or till a change in the weather should take place; but it was to no purpose, since he was very anxious to reach the Mersey as soon as possible.

Towards 6 p.m. the north-westerly breeze, which had been blowing since noon, increased considerably, so much so, that first one and then the other of the larger yachts gave up and turned tail before it might become too late, the last to say goodbye being the largest of the three. This yacht, a well-known hard-weather vessel of over 40 tons measurement, after trying to signal a last advice to the little *Wyvern* to return, put her helm down (though she was well past the Kish Lightship), and made herself snug for the dusting she was in for on the journey back to Kingstown.

On shore, at both club-houses, the greatest alarm was being felt not only for the *Wyvern's* safety, but also for the welfare of her three larger sisters, and the anxiety on the *Wyvern's* account increased still more when her three companions put in their appearance again at their moorings. During the evening and through the night the wind increased to a whole gale, and the meteorological report next morning proved anything but pleasant reading, whilst among the old salts and those best acquainted with the capabilities of small yachts little hope was felt of ever seeing the *Wyvern* again.

On the evening of the next day the writer left Kingstown for Liverpool in his yacht, and fell in with the Mersey 10-tonners making the best of their way down river. The nearest yacht hailed informed him that the *Wyvern* had arrived all safe, and had made a very fast passage across to the Sloyne. A few days after, meeting the skipper, a full account of the trip was given, and there was no limit to the eulogies he had to bestow on the yacht. During the night the sea had increased the further they sailed from under the lee of the land, but for all that the only time any seas were shipped was when off Holyhead. Twice only had they to free the yacht of water, and on those occasions very little had gone into the cabin.

The *Wyvern* was not a yacht of large displacement; she inclined, indeed, rather the other way. Those who have seen the *Naiad* or *Pastime* hauled up out of water (two of Dickenson's old crack 10-tonners which now frequent the South Coast ports) will have a better idea than any words can give of the *Wyvern's* style of model and midship section. Built for length on deck, there was no necessity for shortening up the water-line, and her sternpost had no very great rake. Her buttock lines were as easy and fair as could be, giving her a slightly

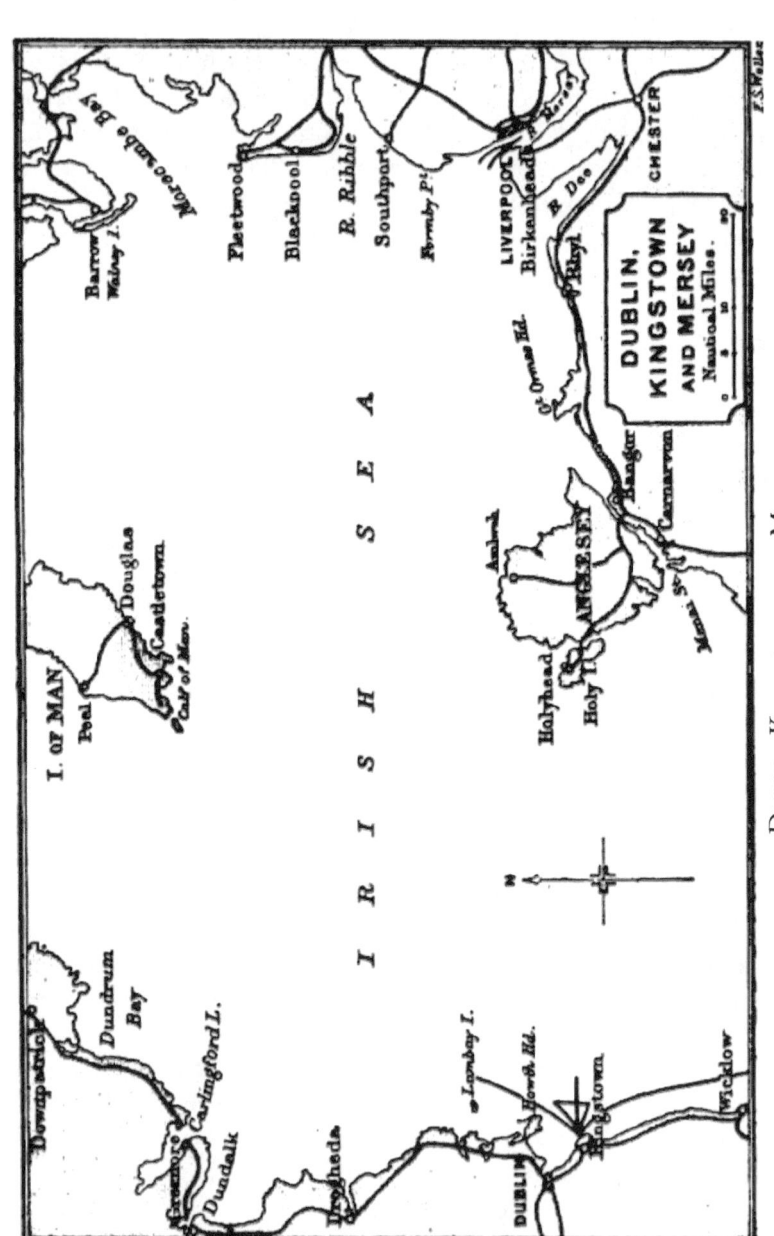

DUBLIN, KINGSTOWN AND MERSEY

hollowed entrance with a nice clean run aft. Her extreme draught was not much over 5 feet, and her keel ran almost straight from the heel of the sternpost to the foot of the stem—that is, with very little if any rocker (or rounding) to it. Dickenson had a very admirable method of finishing off the after end of his yachts, and their counters were all light, and neatly put on. The *Wyvern's* counter was particularly so. She was flush-decked save a large cockpit, which opened into the cabin, and which was surrounded by a 5-inch combing.

This was the only weak or vulnerable part about her; for if a really heavy lump of water had filled it, there was nothing to prevent the cabin being swamped. Her fittings below were of the simplest description, though very comfortable. The sofas on each side of the saloon formed lockers and berths, and beyond these a pantry and a fitting for a lavatory, which was forward on the starboard side, with the usual two square lockers at the after ends of the sofas, were all the furniture of any consequence she contained. She had wood floors, iron not having come into fashion at that time, and carried the greater part of her ballast inside to the tune of 3 tons of lead and 10 cwt. of iron. Her outside ballast consisted of a 14-cwt. lead keel, which was considered in those days a very heavy keel for so small a yacht. She was one of the first small yachts of 6 tons or under that was fitted with a flush deck and ordinary skylight, and in every way she looked the picture of smartness.

When she was first built her principal antagonists about her own size were the *Adèle*, a small 5-ton yacht also by Dickenson, the *Pet*, 5 tons, built at Douglas, Isle of Man, in 1871, and a very fast 3-tonner, the *Barracouta*, built by Bishop in 1860, for Mr. J. M. Hannay. She was altered in 1874 into a yawl in order to race in the 5-ton class, which was at that time just beginning to be popular.

Among the most celebrated of the early 5-tonners were three yachts, the *Pearl, Torment,* and *Arrow*. Of the three, the *Pearl* and *Torment* were the best known, and are still held in loving memory by many a yachting enthusiast. The *Torment*, owned by that well-known yachtsman the late Secretary to the Royal Irish Yacht Club, was raced from the day of her birth, some time about the year 1850, and was always a leader of the van. Her racing career lasted not much less than twenty years, and it was only the lead keels and the deep bodies given to the later yachts that brought it to a close. It is when looking back on such good old warriors as the *Torment* and the *Mosquito*, among the larger racers, that lovers of the sport whose incomes are limited must agree that the old days were good indeed.

It was not necessary then to be the fortunate possessor of a new vessel each season to enable the lover of yacht racing to win prizes and keep well in with the flyers of the year. When an old boat appeared to be not quite up to the mark, or lacking in the requisite turn of speed, little was done to make her beat some new comer beyond a few alterations, which as a rule took the form of doctoring up one or other of her ends, or, perhaps, lengthening her out amidships. The most remarkable example of how a yacht's racing life could be made to outlive many competitors and leave her a winner to the last, by effecting alteration after alteration on her hull, was that of the old *Arrow*, which belonged to Mr. Tankerville Chamberlayne. Alas! the days when an alteration was quite sufficient to keep a yacht successful have long since passed away, and from the present outlook seem as if they will never again return.

The *Pearl*, like the *Torment*, was a hard nut to crack for all the new aspirants to fame which were built to beat her, and she kept her position as the fastest of the *Mosquito* fleet for an untold number of years. She hailed from Fairlie, that birthplace of hundreds of fast, powerful winners, so dear to the hearts of all Scotch yachtsmen, and so well known in almost, every corner of the globe. She was owned and built by Mr. Fife early in the sixties, and after ending her racing career in the Clyde has found her way over to France, where she is as much appreciated as she was in the height of her day in Scotch waters, and has kept up her reputation of being a difficult boat to beat. Her dimensions were: length, 25 feet; beam, 7 feet; and draught, 4 feet. There were many yachts built to beat her, among them being the 5-tonners *Hilda* and *Viola*, designed, owned, and built by Mr. Inglis.

This well-known yachtsman also launched a very pretty schooner of 8 tons called the *Cordelia*, now, unhappily, lying at the bottom of the sea. She, like his other two ventures, was designed to race in the 5-ton class, and also to put the wee *Pearl's* nose out of joint. They were all three big boats, fully decked, and veritable ships when compared with the *Pearl*. They drew a foot or two more water, had big midship sections, and were in every way larger and more powerful yachts. Their success, however, was only partial, and it was a question whether, after all, the old boat did not in the long run hold her own.

The *Arrow's* reputation was only of short duration in comparison with the *Torment* and *Pearl*, but she was a remarkably small boat, and very like them in the main features of her design. She was got out originally to play a part very different from that in which she proved herself so successful, having been built and launched for a fishing-boat to trawl in the Thames; but her speed, like that of the Liverpool 10-tonner *Wonderful*, showed up so conspicuously when sailing in company with other fast boats that she was forthwith bought, turned into a yacht, and made to fly a racing burgee. As may be supposed, both the *Torment* and *Arrow*, as well as the *Pearl*, were only half-decked boats with waterways round them.

In the year 1873, Mr. Stowe, of Shoreham, built the *Diamond* to the design of her owner, Mr. W. Baden-Powell. She won some few races under his flag, but the chief reason of her name appearing in these pages is that she was, if the writer is not very much mistaken, the first of all the yachts of 5 tons and under in the south of England to go from port to port and race, her owner and his friends living on board. The *Diamond* was a decided advance on the boats of her tonnage stationed between the Thames and Southampton; yet she looked small indeed when moored alongside the yachts of a year or two later date. Her length was 26 feet, with a beam of 7 feet, and an extreme draught of 4 ft. 6 in. She ran her fore and aft lines right fair to her taffrail, and had a long counter, part of which was submerged when she was down to her load-water-line. With such a small draught of water her height under the deck was necessarily low; she had however a high fixed coach roof, which helped her out of that difficulty to a certain extent. The cabin was roomy and made up four berths, but her weak point, like that of the *Wyvern*, was her immense cockpit, which was almost as capacious as her cabin.

In 1874 the late Mr. Charles Weguelin illustrated in a prophetical manner what were to be the dimensions and proportion of length to beam of the yacht of the future. The *Alouette* was a 5-tonner, 33 ft. 7 in. in length from stem to sternpost on deck, 5 ft. 9 in. in beam, and with an extreme draught of 6 feet. She was built from Mr. Weguelin's design by Robertson, of Ipswich, but was not a great beauty to look at out of the water. Her body was long and full, and her displacement naturally large, though nothing like that given to vessels constructed on similar dimensions during the ensuing decade. Her chief antagonists were yachts of quite an opposite design, beamy, and of no great draught, besides being of a greater tonnage, such as the *Virago*, 6 tons, *Rayonette*, 8 tons, and *Zephyr*, 9 tons. Against these the *Alouette* was very successful, but her course was run as a successful racer when the season of 1876 ushered in one of the late Mr. Dan Hatcher's most triumphant achievements.

Mr. Weguelin was so satisfied with what his 5-tonner had done that he set to work, and in 1875 placed the design of a 40-tonner in the late Mr. Ratsey's hands, who launched from his yard the *Christine*, the counterpart of the *Alouette*, only twice her size; that is, by doubling all the dimensions of the 5-tonner, the *Christine*, a 40-tonner, was the result. The *Christine*, however, did not fulfil the expectations of her designer, and though her length approached as nearly as possible to that of the 60-tonners of her date, still she could do nothing with them.

Before saying farewell to the *Alouette*, it is as well to remember that, notwithstanding her small amount of beam, she was a grand sea-boat. On one occasion she sailed from Southampton to Algiers and made a very good passage, considering that she had to face some very heavy weather on her journey. It has become the custom to run down the seaworthiness of the yachts built under the old rule, but the number of examples that could be produced, if time and space permitted, of what the old 5-tonner would go through, and that at her ease and without any fuss, would more than astonish many who now, in the faith they bestow on the boat with three beams to her length, forget the comfort and safety in which they were carried about by the old boats of five to six beams to their length. The *Alouette* was wrecked at Algiers in 1890. She broke adrift from her moorings during a gale of wind, and was smashed up into matchwood. Nothing was saved from her.

The season of 1876 was one especially to be remembered among those interested in the now established 5-ton class, as it witnessed the advent of three grand additions to the greatly increased fleet sailing in that class. Each yacht was from the well-thought-out drawing of a master-hand, and each was the representative of the three several schools of yacht-design, the *Freda* being the work of the late Mr. Dan Hatcher of Belvidere, Northam, near Southampton; the *Camellia* the offspring of Mr. William Fife, jun., of Fairlie, on the Clyde; while the *Vril* was built from the design of Mr. G. L. Watson, of Glasgow.

The *Vril* holds the right of precedence in that she was not only designed, but built and sailed, by her three owners, Messrs. G. L. Watson, John Lawrence and J. B. Hilliard, who, assisted by two carpenters, put her together in the Messrs. Henderson's yard at Partick, Glasgow. She was a fine, round-bodied little vessel, with a large sectional area and great sail-carrying powers. She had less waste surface for friction and skin resistance in proportion to her size than many a yacht of a much smaller tonnage. In several ways she might be said to have been a novelty, as she was the first yacht that was fitted with a heavy lead keel consisting of the whole of her ballast. Her counter was short and tucked up with a knuckle on the quarter. She had no bulkheads, and her fittings were only such as were absolutely necessary; still very little goes a long way towards making a small yacht comfortable, and her head-room under her deck made her 'tween decks look like a palace. She was about the last yacht that was supplied with the fore and aft studding-sail (or stu'n's'l, as it is called) known as the 'ringtail'; but it was seldom, if ever, called into use. For small yachts such wind scrapers are more trouble than they are worth, to say nothing of the room the extra spars take up. The *Vril's* record was remarkably good, and though the three friends, assisted by an amateur or two, were her only crew during her first season—for her owners would not have a paid hand on board—she won a full quantum of first prizes, and with the clever boats she had for rivals praise must be meted out not only to the little yacht herself, but to those who sailed her for the smart manner in which she was handled.

The *Camellia* and *Vril* were, with the exception of their draught, almost identical in their dimensions, the *Vril* being 28 ft. 3 in. long and the *Camellia* 28 feet. Their respective beams were the same, 6 ft. 6 in., and they drew, the *Vril* 6 feet and *Camellia* about 5 feet of water. The *Vril* at the end of her third season was sold and turned into a fast cruiser. Her fittings, as they are now, are very elaborate and are well illustrated and explained in the seventh edition of that handy and serviceable book, *A Manual of Yacht- and Boat-Sailing*. She has been laid up for some time at Mr. Robertson's yard at Sandbank in the Holy Loch, where her proximity to many new yachts makes the signs of the sere and yellow-leaf stage of her existence, which is creeping upon her, very apparent. But there is life in the old boat yet, and her owner has in the *Vril* a fine, able, comfortable little cruiser.

It is now some six year, (as at time of first publication), since the writer had the pleasure of seeing the *Camellia*. She had just been sold to a gentleman to go to Stranraer, where she is at the present time. She was hauled up on Fairlie beach in charge of the late Mr. Boag, and was awaiting a suitable tide for being launched. The *Camellia*, though of like dimensions to the *Vril*, was altogether different in form, and to those acquainted with the Fairlie type was as pretty an example of what the Messrs. Fife were in the habit of turning out at that period as it was possible to select. She and her sister ship the *Clio* were both built from the same drawing, and were the first boats in which Mr.

William Fife, jun., whose name is now a household word among men interested in yachting matters, played the conspicuous part of designer. The *Camellia* was a smaller-bodied boat altogether, more compact than either the *Vril* or *Freda*, with a powerful entrance and fine run, and ribbands as fair as they could be. Messrs. Craig and Lawson, for whom she was built, possessed in her a little sea-boat capable of being driven in all weathers, and the harder it blew the more she seemed to like it. With less bilge and somewhat higher floor than *Vril*, she was fitted, like her predecessor the *Pearl*, with simply a half-deck and waterways, and was strengthened by a strong beam running across her to which the pump was attached. Of course in smooth water it was a great advantage being able to work the yacht from below, but in anything like very heavy weather she carried hatches for covering in the open space.

Both the *Vril* and *Freda* were fitted with topmasts, but giving the *Camellia* the same fitting was only an afterthought, for when she was launched, like the *Clio*, she was supplied with a polemast. Three or four years after her appearance she was decked in and provided with a very neat coach roof, or booby hatch, but her head-room below in her cabin could not have been more than 4 feet. She makes a very good cruiser now, and from the grand work put into her, as into all yachts which hail from the great Fairlie yard, her sides looked when last seen

'FREDA.'

as fresh and as smooth as on the day when she first saw the water.

The *Freda* is (for she is still hale, strong, and fit to show her tail to many a vessel of her size on cruising terms) a fine able boat, some 30 ft. 4 in. on the L.W.L., with a beam of 6 ft. 1-¼ in. and draught of water 6 ft. 6 in. She is, like all the Belvidere yachts of those days, a boat of large displacement with a grand midship section, with Hatcher's well-known entrance, and a rather lighter quarter than usual. Her sternpost has very little rake in it; in fact, excessive rake of sternpost was a rarity during the seventies, and her keel was only slightly rockered. Most of her ballast, about 2 tons 14 cwt., was carried inside, and the lead on her keel was under 2 tons. She was built for Mr. Freake, her planking being altogether of mahogany. All the wood, dead woods, ribs, and planking were got out in Mr. Hatcher's yard and then taken to Mr. Freake's estate, where she was put together and finished off.

As a model yacht she is a perfect picture both above and below water, as well as on deck and in the cabin. With a flush deck and a small water-tight cockpit, after the fashion of the 10-tonners, and a neat skylight, the *Freda* looks all over fit to go, and equal to all emergencies. She has proved herself quite as much at home when cutting her way through a head sea as when smooth water and dry decks have been the rule. She was the home of her racing crew, and Mr. Beavor Webb, who sailed her during her racing career, and afterwards bought her from Mr. Freake, could spin many a yarn of the little boat's great weatherly capabilities.

No three yachts were more unlike each other, and after all the *Freda* had done down South, and the *Vril* and *Camellia's* successes in the Clyde, so much attention was attracted to them that at last a series of matches was arranged to take place between them off Holyhead the following season of 1877. The place was well chosen, as in bringing the several matches off on the coast of Holyhead Island there was no chance of favouritism, since the locality was strange to all concerned, and the yachts had to prove their worth in a sea quite different from that to which any of them had been accustomed. It is not too much to say that, owing to the distance that had to be covered before the three yachts could reach Holyhead, and the fame of their doings in the yacht-racing world, no more interesting racing has since taken place, either in America or in our own home waters, than the matches that were sailed off by these little opponents.

The arrangement was that *Freda* should sail *Camellia* and *Vril* separately, and the yacht that pulled off two out of each three races was to be declared the winner. The weather for some days prior to and during the race week was anything but inviting, and the manner in which the yachts worked their way to their port showed at once what kind of stuff they were. The *Vril* was unfortunate, for owing to some gross carelessness the men who brought the yacht round from the Clyde allowed her mainsail to get damaged to such an extent that during the trials it could scarcely be made to stand. The stakes were for 100*l*. a side. The first match between *Freda* and *Vril* took place on May 14, 1877. The courses on each occasion were arranged by Messrs. G. L. Watson and Dixon Kemp. On the first day the course lay from the New Harbour across a line between the 20-ton yacht *Challenge* and a buoy, round the end of the breakwater westward, rounding a flag-boat outside the inner end of the breakwater, thence eastward three miles round the Bolivar buoy; thence to a mark-boat off the old pier, twice round, finishing between the *Challenge* and the starting buoy, 14 miles.

There could not have been a finer trial than these three matches afforded. The wind on the 14th was light from E.S.E., shifting to the eastward, accompanied by rain, whilst on the second day it veered round between S.W. and N.W., and brought up with it the usual sea that most yachtsmen frequenting St. George's Channel know so well and hate so cordially. Space will not permit a full account of the races to be given here, but should details be required, they will be found most faithfully recorded in an article in *Hunt's Magazine* for the year 1877, which has greatly assisted the writer in refreshing his memory, or in the *Field* newspaper that was published on the Saturday following the races.

The first match was the *Vril's*. She was the first over the line, and though the *Freda* very soon after passed her to leeward, she soon regained her original position, and gradually so increased her lead that at the end of the first round she was 1 min. 30 secs. ahead of her rival. The two little flyers had donned for the occasion all plain lower sail with working topsails aloft. On the run out for the breakwater the second time spinnakers were set, when the *Vril* was unfortunate enough to carry away the goose-neck of her spinnaker boom. This was followed by the boom slipping into the water and at once snapping in two. Her crew smartly cleared the wreck, the outer end of the boom was lashed to the weather rigging, and the spinnaker set once more. Those familiar with such matters will readily understand how well things must have been done on board the Scotch yacht, when it is said that 50 seconds were all that the *Freda* made out of the mishap. Before reaching the Bolivar buoy, the *Vril* had more than made up her lost ground; and though on the journey home the *Freda* gained a little, she was decidedly beaten, as she came in nearly 6 minutes astern of the *Vril*, the times being—*Vril*, 3 hrs. 40 mins. 40 secs., and *Freda*, 3 hrs. 46 mins. 10 secs.

'CHALLENGE,' 20 TONS, 1876.

The second match on the following day was sailed in about as dirty weather as it was possible for the concentrated energy of the elements to provide, and the result was that *Freda* turned the tables on *Vril* and beat her by about the same amount of time. The start was made at 10.20 a.m., and this time the *Freda* got away first. Both yachts were reefed down, the *Freda* showing a single-reefed mainsail and foresail with the third jib, while the *Vril* carried a whole foresail with a double-reefed mainsail and second jib. The *Vril* also started with her topmast housed. Outside the breakwater the little boats had to face a bad wind-against-tide sea, and quite a third part of the trip was made under water. For the run to the Bolivar buoy the *Freda* set her spinnaker with a Paddy's reef in it, which gave her a tremendous lead, because, though her extra length told, still the *Vril* had no spinnaker boom on board, having left it ashore, and could therefore only boom out her balloon foresail.

On the thrash to windward, however, the *Vril* gained twelve seconds on her antagonist, so that the first round finished *Freda*, 1 hr. 49 mins. 2 secs.; *Vril*, 1 hr. 54 mins. For the second round, the *Vril* sent her topmast on end and set a topsail, but her mainsail had been so badly treated before the races began that it was found impossible to make it stand properly, and the remarkable thing is that the little yacht worked as well as she did under the trying circumstances. The *Freda* kept to the sail she started with. The sea smoothed down considerably during the second round, which made the sailing somewhat easier. With the exception of a slight miscalculation in distance on the part of the *Vril*, and a consequent extra board on the beat up for the harbour buoy, nothing of any importance took place, and the two yachts came in, *Freda* first at 2 hrs. 44 mins. 40 secs., followed by *Vril*, 5 mins. 15 secs. after her.

The interest occasioned by the third day's sailing was extraordinary. All over the country an eagerness was displayed for news of the match almost equal to that seen on a Derby day. The wind was at about the same force, and blowing from the same quarter as on the previous day, with the addition of a harder feel in it. Both yachts, therefore, set the same amount of sail and had their topmasts housed. At the time of the start, which was made at 11 a.m., the sea was breaking over the lighthouse, and made the journey look anything but inviting.

Both yachts, keeping a sharp look out on each other, were too keen on crossing the line, and had to return and make a fresh start, which they did side by side. There were not 10 seconds between them when they jibbed round the first mark, the *Vril* leading, and the difference was further shortened by 5 seconds at the Bolivar buoy, this run having been made under boomed-out balloon foresails. The time between the yachts might have been lessened still more had not the *Freda* been obliged to busy herself about her boom, which came adrift. From the Bolivar buoy home the little vessels danced it merrily to the tune of 'Blow, breezes blow.'

The *Freda*, before she made a fresh start, had placed herself 30 seconds ahead of her rival, but going out again, the *Vril*, owing to the *Freda's* not being able to make use of her balloon foresail, passed her before they had rounded the first mark-boat, only to be repassed on the running-reach to the Bolivar. The *Freda's* best point of sailing brought her to the Bolivar 1 min. 30 secs. ahead, and though for the last time the *Vril* showed her superior power in beating to windward, the *Freda* had made up her mind to walk off with the dollars, and win she did by a few seconds over the minute. Considering the sea that was running, and the amount of broken water that was throwing itself about, this last race is one to be long remembered and handed down in the annals of small-yacht racing; and now and hereafter, when racing and cruising men feel a tendency arising in them to croak and speak ill of the little yachts that were built under the old rule of measurement, let them call to mind their mighty deeds, their racing and their voyages under circumstances and in weather that would frighten many a 50-tonner into harbour and to her moorings.

The fourth day ushered in a new competitor, and the *Freda* had to cross the line with the *Camellia*, which she did five minutes after the second gun. The wind and weather had changed during the night, an unfortunate circumstance for the *Camellia*, a hard-weather boat. The wind was unsettled, hung about between N. and N.E., and was at times very shy. The *Freda* at first, not being able to hold the wind that the *Camellia* did, lost ground considerably in the beat up to the Bolivar buoy, and the latter had reached on her so cleverly that the *Freda* was fully a minute astern on rounding for the run into the harbour. The *Freda* here had the pull over the Fairlie clipper, for she was provided with two spinnakers, while the *Camellia* had but one, and as a shift had to be made (since they had left the Bolivar with spinnakers set on the bowsprit end) before setting off for the second round, the *Camellia* was left in the lurch, her one spinnaker having to be taken in and boomed out.

Standing out again, the *Camellia* tried her best to pass the *Freda* to windward, but to no purpose, as the *Freda* was always ready for her each time the attempt was made, and at the Bolivar the *Freda* was first round by 30 seconds. Coming into the harbour, the *Freda*, again at her best, kept increasing her lead, and finally won by 1 min. 40 secs. Hunt's correspondent writes: 'This was a closely sailed race, in which the English boat owed much of, if not all, her success to smart handling.'

The fifth day's race was sailed under something like the *Vril* and *Freda* weather. The wind had hardened up and freshened during the early morning, and kept increasing as the day went on. Both yachts started with housed topmasts, single-reefed mainsails, and No. 2 jibs, the *Freda* running up and booming out her balloon foresail as she crossed the line. During the first round the *Freda* showed herself the better boat when on a reach as well as in beating to windward in the teeth of the heavy, solid sea which was running. She, however, was only 1 min. 30 secs. ahead at the mark-boat.

On the second round the boats were literally more under water than above; they were simply smothered in their efforts to windward, and had the *Camellia* not been so persistently squeezed in order to make her look up closer to the wind than her rival, she might have gained more than she did. As it was, what she gained on one point she lost on the other, and allowed the *Freda* to come in a winner by 1 min. 45 secs.

On the sixth and last day the umpires were obliged to alter the course owing to the heavy sea running outside the breakwater. There had been no lull during the night, and with the northerly gale blowing it was thought too dangerous a matter to allow the small yachts to face the hazards of a lee shore. The mark-boat outside was therefore brought within the breakwater, the other was left in its place off the Old Harbour, and the course made nine miles, or three times round the two marks, which lay now in more or less smooth water. The start was made at 11.50 a.m. under double-reefed mainsails and small jibs, *Freda* having sent her topmast on deck. The *Camellia* got away 45 seconds ahead of the *Freda* owing to the latter not having heard the gun, and increased her lead till she came to the mark-boat.

Her lead, however, did not last long, for in the beat to the next mark she missed stays and allowed the *Freda* so to gain upon her that by the time the mark was rounded the *Freda* had put herself 1 min. 5 secs. ahead. The yachts had quite as much as they could do, the next time they had to haul their wind, to stagger under their small canvas, as the wind blew harder than ever and with more real venom in it. The *Freda* finished the nine miles in 1 hr. 30 mins.—quick work taking everything into consideration—but the *Camellia*, having again missed stays, up helm and made for her anchorage. This last match exhibited the powers of the two yachts in a different way, perhaps, and under conditions other than any met with in the previous races. If the third and fifth matches showed what fine sea-boats these small 5-tonners were, and how capable, handy, and powerful, when driven in a big, broken, heavy sea, the sixth day's racing proved that they could stand up to their canvas and bear pressing when many a much larger yacht would have had to be close-reefed.

No apology need be offered for introducing these six matches into this work, because not only do they form a good precedent in the manner in which all the arrangements and the choice of fighting ground were made, but it is impossible in any other way to discover how one stay-at-home small yacht compares with another at a distance, unless they are brought right away from their respective localities and allowed to fight it out in open water unfamiliar to both. Before bidding *adieu* to the above three little beauties, it may not be amiss to add that the *Freda* was sailed on all six occasions by Mr. Beavor Webb with a professional crew, the *Camellia* was in the hands of Tom Dudley, of Southampton fame, and the *Vril* piloted by one of her owners, Mr. Hilliard.

Each year now introduces new aspirants to the Blue Ribbon fame of the well-established 5-ton class, and though few methods, if any, had been resorted to up to this time for the purpose of cheating the tonnage rule, which then took the length on deck between stem and sternpost as its measure, instead of the length along the L.W.L., still the year 1878 saw a notable tonnage-cheater launched from the Cheshire side of the Mersey in the formidable 5-tonner *Lorelei*, designed by Mr. Wynne Eyton, her owner, and built by Messrs. Buckley & Sherlock.

The *Lorelei* was a yacht worked out purely and simply on the wave-line theory, as defined by Mr. Colin Archer, of Christiania, and her counter was partly submerged, not only to enable the lines of her after body to be carried out fair, but at the same time, without adding to her tonnage, to give her a foot and a half more length on the L.W.L., since she was 31 ft. 6 in., whether the measurement was taken on deck or along the L.W.L. Her beam was 6 feet, and she drew 5 ft. 6 in. Like the *Vril*, her ballast, 4 tons in all, was on her keel, and her sail area 770 square feet, or 30 square feet less than that of the *Freda*. The displacement of both these yachts was almost identically the same; yet the *Freda* would have had a very hard struggle to keep within sight of the *Lorelei* on an ordinary 5-ton yacht course.

Frequently the *Lorelei* very nearly beat her 10-tonner competitors on even terms, and was always fit and ready to save her time. In the smaller class, such as she would race in at Kingstown or Liverpool, there was not one boat that she could not beat. Mr. Richardson designed for the Messrs. Anderson, who used to own Hatcher's old crack the *Queen*, 15-tonner, a 5-tonner called the *Urchin*. She was intended to beat the *Lorelei*, but she never could do anything when sailing against her. The *Lorelei* carried rather a deep bilge, and her keel was well rockered. After Mr. Wynne Eyton parted with her, she went up to the Clyde, where she has done little or no racing, but has proved herself a first-class little cruiser. Her fittings below, when she was in the height of her racing career, were very good and rather unique.

She had no bulkhead, but was entirely open fore and aft. She was flush-decked, and her main cabin was partly divided off by a double set of rails made of 3-inch planks, which formed an open, but double, partition to hold all her kites and other sails. This open sail locker or pen stretched right across from side to side, and was about 2 feet deep. It formed a good roomy receptacle for the sails, kept the weight amidships, and sails well aired. Something of the same kind of fitting has been applied to one or two 10-tonners, the open gratings in their case being carried right up to the deck on the starboard side, leaving the door and pantry in its usual place. The upper half of the grating facing the main cabin was on hinges, and could be removed altogether to allow of sails being taken out or replaced quickly, as, for instance, on a racing day.

As regards tonnage cheaters, the chief method employed for walking through the 'length on deck' rule was that of bending up the sternpost. The first yacht built with a knuckle in her sternpost came from Messrs. Buckley & Sherlock's yard at Tranmere, on the Mersey, and belonged to the Sloyne. She was a 10-tonner, and with the others, which followed after her, very soon brought the authorities' attention to the rule, which was promptly altered to the L.W.L. measurement. Those who wish to know more about the *Lorelei* will find a very good description of her, with drawings, as they will also of the '*Freda*,' in the third edition of Mr. Dixon Kemp's work on *Yacht and Boat Sailing*.

In 1879 and 1880 two yachts were turned out which perhaps did more fighting as first-class 5-ton racers, and lasted throughout a greater number of seasons at the top of the tree, than any others had done since the days of the *Torment* and *Pearl*. The *Cyprus* and *Nora*, the one designed and built by Mr. William Fife, jun., the other parented on Mr. George Watson, were as distinct types in their way as were the *Vril* and the *Camellia* three years before. They were, besides, equally interesting, if not more so, since in them the practised eye could see how wonderfully the Fife and Watson designs had respectively developed and improved.

The *Nora*, built in 1880 for those keen racing yachtsmen of the Clyde, the Messrs. Allan, with 32 ft. 4 in. length on deck, 6 ft. 2 in. beam, and a rather deeper draught, was a veritable ship in comparison with her predecessor. More cut away forward and with greater rake of sternpost, big body and large sail-area, long counter and straight stem, nothing could touch her in light winds. The only antagonist that gave her any trouble was the *Cyprus*, built the previous year.

This yacht, designed to sail under either measurement, length on deck, or L.W.L., was exactly 30 feet when measured along the one, and 29.5 when measured along the other. Her beam was 6 ft. 4 in., draught 5 ft 4 in., with a displacement barely equal to that of the 3-tonners, which between the years 1880 and 1884 gave so much sport and became so popular. She was one of the smartest of the small fry Fairlie had ever turned out. Certainly few would gainsay the fact that the *Cyprus* was by far the prettiest of her class at that date afloat, and at the same time looked a racer all over. Out of the water she was a perfect study to the lover of gentle curves and fine lines, and as sweet a model as any connoisseur would wish to feast his eye on.

Without a straight line up or down, diagonal or horizontal, to be found about her, to all appearance, looking at her from a beam view, she presented a longer and finer entrance than had up to that time been given to any of the Fairlie small yachts. Such an increase had been meted out to her that at first sight it was difficult to free the mind of the impression that she must be a regular diver. An end-on view, however, soon dispelled all misgivings on that score, for her vertical sections showed a round floaty bow of extraordinary power. With a low freeboard of 1 ft. 9 in. at the waist, and a grand midship section, there was no wall-sidedness about the *Cyprus*, whilst her run was fine and clean, and her buttock lines beautifully easy. Perhaps the prettiest features about the little yacht were her shear and the sit of her counter. This latter was light and long, and had a spring upwards towards the taffrail, rather after the fashion of a duck desirous of keeping her tail dry, though the yacht was a little more moderate as regards the height necessary for so carrying her appendage.

The *Cyprus* was kept in the family during her career in the Clyde, and was very successful during those seasons that her racing flag was seen at her topmast head, being always piloted by that prince of helmsmen, her designer and owner. In the winter of 1884 this yacht became the property of the writer, when she began a most successful career of a more all-round character than she had up to that time undergone, and it is principally from the practical experience derived from racing and cruising in her that he has been enabled to form his ideas and recommend the 5-ton yacht of ordinary dimensions as the best size and class of vessel for an inexperienced yachtsman to ship himself aboard as owner, captain, and hand.

When the *Cyprus* came into his possession her fittings below were practically *nil*. Like the *Vril* in her early days, she had only such contrivances as were absolutely essential for one living on board during a time bounded by hours rather than weeks or months. He was therefore obliged to make a few alterations below, such as turning her sofas into lockers, having iron bed-frames fitted in the cabin on hooks so as to be easily removable, and a box made to stand in between the after-provision sideboards and under the ladder to hold a bucket, washing basin, and lavatory conveniences. On deck the fittings were almost perfect. The jib, throat, and peak halliards led below through brass fairleads let into the deck a few inches on either side of the mast.

The forestay, instead of coming down through the stem-head along the deck, and being purchased up to the bits, was led through the stem close under the deck and set up by tackles to the mast. In place of the regular tackles to the bowsprit shrouds, two sets of selvagee strops were used, the one short and the other long. The long strops were doubled round the forearm of the belaying rail on each side, abreast of the rigging, and the standing part of the bowsprit shroud shackled on and set up with galvanised rigging screws. The short strop was employed whenever the bowsprit was reefed in. It was found strong and neat, and much better altogether than the old plan of tackles, which formed the original fitting.

The *Cyprus* was not entirely flush-decked—that is, she had a low very neat-looking 'booby hatch,' which fitted on a combing some three inches high. The combing ran from about two feet abaft the mast to within a couple of feet of the rudder-head. The after part enclosed a small water-tight lead-lined cockpit, then a foot of deck, ahead of which came the hatch, containing the after sliding hatch into the cabin and a low skylight. The width between the combings was 2 ft. 4 in. A transparent compass and binnacle fitted into the deck space ahead of the cockpit, and this was lighted by a lamp below in the cabin. This arrangement was excellent, as it prevented any of the troubles which so often arise in small yachts from the lights being washed out.

At sea the boat was stowed below in the cabin, and as the hatch was very simple and easy to adjust, it was always taken off for the boat to be lowered down into its place. Another point in favour of this hatch was that on fine sunny days it could be removed and the yacht kept well-aired and sweet. A narrow strip of india-rubber, doubled, was nailed round, close up to the combing, and this proved a thoroughly effective method for keeping the hatch tight and preventing any water from coming into the cabin.

The *Cyprus* was a particularly handy boat. As the writer had to take her round to Plymouth from Scotland, he invited an old friend, and with the help of a boy of seventeen years of age out of one of the Plymouth trawlers, left the Clyde for Kingstown, the port of call, after enjoying a few days' cruising about by way of letting everything shake into its place. It was a Tuesday morning when the start was made from Lamlash, in Arran, and the *Camellia*, which was on her way to Stranraer, left about half an hour before. The wind was N.W. and came down off the hills in strong squalls; but the water was smooth, and under all plain sail the little vessel simply flew along.

After leaving Ailsa Craig astern, the sea began to show signs of getting up, and about 5 p.m., before reaching Corsewall Point, it had begun to take such liberties, and make such encroachments on deck whenever a big curler chose to break over aft, sometimes to the depth of three inches to four inches, that it was thought advisable to heave her to and shorten sail. About 6 p.m. the helm was put down and the foresail hauled to windward, whilst a reef was taken in the mainsail, No. 3 jib set, and our ship made snug.

It was a treat to see how well the yacht lay to, and it is impossible to describe the feeling of confidence it inspired, for not a drop of water was shipped, and she rode like a duck the whole time, coming up and falling off as each sea passed under her. From the time the foresheet was let draw to the time she dropped anchor in Kingstown Harbour all went well, the only incident being the writer's coming on deck at 6 a.m. to find that the boy, who was on watch, had mistaken the Morne Mountains to the north of Dundalk Bay for the south of Ireland, on the strength of which he had given up steering by compass, and was taking a course into Dundalk, which would have soon led to a disastrous end. The compass, though a spirit one, was rather sluggish, and his idea of safety was steering by the land.

Wednesday night was spent at Kingstown, and with the first of the ebb the *Cyprus* was again on her way with gaff-topsail set over all. Light flukey airs from the southward and westward helped the yacht along during the greater part of the forenoon, but these were eaten up by the sun as the day wore on, and gradually died out altogether, leaving us to drift along till the tide began to make, when, being in easy soundings on the edge of the Arklow Bank, the anchor was let go, and the yacht brought up to await the beginning of the ebb or the wooing of a breeze.

The next morning—Friday—there was no wind of any kind; but the tides run strong on the east coast of Ireland, and a whole ebb meant many miles to the good. The time during this drifting was well employed in having a thorough clean down, in opening up the cabin, airing the bedding, and improving the stowage of the general cargo shipped on board, consisting of sails, luggage, provisions, and numerous other necessary items. In the afternoon the yacht was again brought to an anchor, and remained so till Saturday, about 4 a.m., when a breeze springing up from the southward, her head was pointed towards the Welsh coast. Travelling was very slow, for the wind was very light, and not at all true. Two short boards were made on reaching the other side, and about 8 a.m. on Sunday the yacht was laying up on the port tack for the Smalls. The wind had now some westing in it, but not sufficient to let a course be laid for the Longships; and as long rollers were coming in from the south-west, it was settled to go well away to windward in order to make Land's End in one tack and obtain a clear offing.

The Smalls was left behind about 3 p.m., and at 5 p.m. the whole face of the sky was beginning to look so threatening, and the clouds to drive past at such a rate from the southward, while the quiet rollers had already begun to break up and require such extra attention, that at 6 p.m. the *Cyprus* was hove to, and made ready for a dirty night. The mainsail was taken off her and trysail set, the topmast housed and bowsprit reefed in, the second jib shifted for a spitfire, and the foresail double-reefed. Two hours later, the wind having sprung up into something near akin to a gale, and the yacht dancing with a light heart and by no means wet deck away out to sea, everyone on board was glad that she was under snug canvas and that time had been taken by the forelock. She could not have been more comfortable or cosy had she been a sea-going rocking-chair.

On going about, the first land sighted was Cape Cornwall, but the wind, having had its say, again went down, till the yacht was left with just sufficient to keep her going, but not enough to make her steady, or prevent her knocking about in the choppy sea that remained. About noon, however, a breeze sprang up, and the Seven Stones Lightship was passed close to about 3 o'clock on Tuesday morning. Towards 8 a.m. the wind had veered round to the N.W., coming off the land in strong puffs; sail was made once more, and with fairly smooth water all the way the yacht lay herself down to her work, and finally brought to off the Hoe at 10 p.m. the same night.

The lesson learnt during this cruise was a useful one—*viz.* that if sail is attended to in time, a 5-ton yacht is fit to face almost any weather, provided she has sea-room. During the whole trip round the crew were never without hot water when they required it, so easy was the yacht's motion to those below, even during the most disagreeable part of the journey; and no water went below even when it lay thick on deck, as, for instance, off Stranraer, and once or twice before sail was taken off her when near the Smalls.

The *Cyprus* was raced, whenever an opportunity presented itself, in the then A, B, and C classes, and in every case the racing was against yachts larger than herself. Any amount of Channel groping had to be undertaken, both from one English port to another, as well as between the French coast and England, ocean racing being quite as much in her line as the *Meteor's*. Her best performances took place in strong breezes, and it was a sight worth seeing to watch the wonderful manner in which she could drive through a head-sea. At Bembridge Regatta the *Cyprus* sailed the course round the Nab on a day when the 30-ft. class of yachts (15-tonners in reality) begged to have their course, which was identically the same, altered.

No matter on what point of sailing she was engaged (and she is only given in these pages as a very fair type of the 5-tonner built to sail under the old Y.R.A. Rule), blow high or blow low, a lady might have handled her tiller without experiencing any of that muscular arm exercise so common in boats built under the length and sail-area rule, or even the slightest inconvenience. The *Cyprus* was sent out to Toronto on board an Allan Liner from London, and became an ornament to Lake Ontario, where she is at the present time.

Between the years 1880 and 1886 four 5-tonners were built from the designs of one of the most rising young naval architects the Clyde has ever produced—Mr. Payton. The first of this team was the *Trident*, which, though not by any means a successful racer, was a fine able boat and moderately fast. She is mentioned here on account of her having made a long ocean voyage to the South of France. She was altogether bigger and a much heavier boat than the *Nora* or *Cyprus*, but could be worked just as easily. Five Frenchmen, however, were employed to take her South. Her behaviour under a very trying state of the weather, while crossing the Bay of Biscay, was highly spoken of, and the men who went in her declared their faith in her to such an extent as to be quite willing to take her out to the Cape.

The *Olga* was Mr. Payton's next attempt at a flyer. She was 32 feet long, with a beam of 5.73 feet, and had a great draught of water. She was a very large-bodied boat, was built on the most advanced scientific principles, and, what is more to the point, was a complete success; but she was a most unfortunate yacht. With a very wide keel her midships section was anything but shapely, and ran down almost in a straight line from her bilge, which was very low and square, to the bottom of the lead. At the Royal Irish Yacht Club Regatta, Mr. Power's steam yacht ran into her and sank her in Kingstown Harbour, but she was brought up and floated again, Mr. Power having bought her as she lay under water. The *Olga* after this mishap won her full share of races, and ended her first season flying 18 winning flags, of which 15 were firsts. Mr. G. B. Thompson bought her during the winter, and the following season won four first prizes with her; but before the season was half over she was again unlucky, and on June 22 was once more run into and sent to the bottom, whilst in the Mersey. She was fished out, and put up for auction, but who bought her or what became of her is not generally known.

The third yacht of 5 tons was the *Luath*. She, however, was not such a phenomenon as the *Olga*, and after the *Olga's* short but brilliant existence, what was expected of her did not come off. She was, as may be supposed, very much like the *Olga* in looks and of about the same dimensions, though of rather larger displacement. The last of the four was the *Oona*. Her melancholy end is still fresh in the memory of many a small-yacht sailor. She was built in 1886 at Wivenhoe, in Messrs. Harvey & Co.'s yard, for Mr. Plunket, of Belfast, and was an extreme example of what could be designed under the old Y.R.A. Rule. Her length was 33 ft. 10 in. on the L.W.L., her beam 5 ft. 6 in., and draught 8 feet, but her chief characteristic was her marvellous body, which displaced 12 tons, both displacement and sail-area of 2,000 square feet and more being greater than many racing 10-tonners, and the latter over 1,300 square feet more than *Freda* or *Nora's* sail-spread. What she might have done as a prize-winner it is impossible to say, for she never reached her station. Coming from the eastward, she put into Southampton to effect some small repairs, and after remaining there a few days, on May 4, with her owner Mr. Payton, her designer, and a crew of three men on board, left for Belfast. It appeared that shortly after passing Dublin Bay—for she did not put into Kingstown, as might have been expected—her owner must have intended to make the best of his way up Channel, but, unhappily, terrible weather set in about the night of the 12th, and the general opinion was that, from some weakness in or lack of roping, the trysail was burst up, and that becoming unmanageable, or through her crew having been swept overboard, the yacht was driven on to the sands off Malahide and so became a wreck. Her hull was washed up without its lead keel and its fastenings or the iron floors; in fact, the whole of her keel and lower garboards had gone.

Mr. Payton's name will always be associated more especially with the 3-tonner *Currytush*. She was a more brilliant success than even the *Olga*; but the old 3-tonners do not come within the scope of this paper.

The last of the race of 5-tonners, if the *Oona* be left out, is the *Doris*, one of Mr. Watson's greatest successes in small-yacht design. She was built in 1885 for the Messrs. Allan, who had owned and sailed the little *Nora* so pluckily and so well. Her length is 33.6 feet on the load-water-line, beam 5.6 feet, and draught about 7 feet, or a little more. The *Doris*, like the *Oona*, is an extreme representative of the old rule. Her displacement is very large, but there is far more shape and comeliness about her body plan than was to be found in any of Mr. Payton's designs. She has proved herself a clever boat in all weathers, and in light winds particularly so. Her chief rival, had she not been lost, would have been the *Oona*, for there was no other 5-tonner afloat capable of tackling her, and her principal racing was against boats of a larger tonnage. She could always save her time on the crack 10-tonners of her day, such as the *Uleerin*, *Queen Mab*, and *Malissa*, and the only matches of any interest that she was mixed up in were three that came off between her and Mr. Froude's 5-tonner *Jenny Wren*.

This yacht, designed by her owner, and built at Messrs. Simpson & Dennison's yard at Dartmouth, was made double-skinned for the sake of lightness. She, like the *Doris*, was a large, big-bodied boat, but her form did not give that idea of power with which a look at the *Doris* at once inspired the observer. Both the *Doris* and *Jenny Wren* are cut away forward, and carry the curve of the keel up to the water-line, finishing at the deck-line in a fiddle-head. The *Jenny Wren* had shown herself remarkably fast in light winds and smooth water, and on certain days could leave the length classes to follow her up. Bad weather, however, was her weak point, and even in strong breezes and smooth water she did not always appear to be sailing at her best. At Plymouth, then, when the *Doris* and *Jenny Wren* met, everything depended on certain conditions what kind of a fight the latter would make. As the *Doris* beat her, there is every reason to believe that it was either blowing hard or that the wind was shy and there was a certain amount of roll outside the breakwater.

Since the measurement rule was altered, the *Doris* has been im-

Good Start of Small Raters in the Clyde.

proved by being spread out and given more beam. She still races, but cannot do much against the 10-raters, the class to which she now belongs, and has lately been sold to spend the rest of her days as a cruiser. Should she race in the future, it will be in the many Clyde handicap cruising races. With such bodies and draught there was no lack of head-room in the cabins of the latter day 'plank on edge' 'lead mines,' but the want of beam made the accommodation not exactly as grateful as it might have been had there been a little more elbow-room. The alteration in the *Doris* has given her the requisite amount of beam, and she ought to make a very comfortable fast and able boat for cruising purposes.

The Y.R.A. Rule and Its 5-Raters

In the year 1886 the Yacht Racing Association brought in a new rule for yacht measurement, or, more properly speaking, for rating yachts to be used in racing. There is no other reason why a rule for rating should be required at all, as under the old rule, or any true capacity measurement, a naval architect or yacht designer would be sure to produce a good, serviceable vessel for cruising purposes, and according as the owner's requirements might be speed, accommodation, or light draught, so the several dimensions and design would be arranged to suit.

With regard to this rule of rating by 'length and sail-area,' and the boats which are the result of it, there appear to be many and diverse opinions; and prior to noticing any particular yacht built under it, it will be as well to look at all its points before declaring for or against it. Experience declares them to be good sea-boats, in that they rarely ship solid water, and they are very fast when sailing on a wind. Their spoon and fiddle-headed bows would help to throw the water off, while their mast being stepped almost in the eyes of the yacht, would make them eat up into the wind, because it permits of most of the driving power being concentrated in one big sail.

Their sailmaker's bill is a small item, on account of the tendency to keep the sail-area down. For instance, the *Archee*, Mr. Lepper's 5-rater, of Belfast, with a length of 30.4 feet, a beam of 9.2 feet, and a draught of nearly 5 ft. 6 in., a length on deck of 39.5 feet, the tonnage of which, by the last rule, would have been a little over 6½ tons, has a sail-area of 979 square feet against the 1,680 square feet of the *Doris* 5-tonner.

They are bigger boats than the old 5-tonners, but then they have so much more beam. The *Cyprus* was the same length as two-thirds of the 5-raters that have been built, but she had only 6 ft. 4 in. beam against the raters' 8 feet to 9 feet. They have very little gear with the lugsail rig, and the decks are always clear.

They can lay to, but it is on the same principle as that of a Una boat, and they would not remain on one tack all the time but for the little jib they carry, while they forge ahead at a great speed, and cannot be stopped unless a man is left at the helm to look after it.

If properly trimmed the rater can be steered by the lightest hand when beating to windward and close hauled, and she is remarkably quick in stays.

Experience, however, shows that, though the rater rarely ships a sea, still, when she does put her nose in the water, it becomes a general question on board her whether she will ever bring it out again. This is not altogether enjoyable, and such sensations were never experienced in boats built under the old rule. The one large lugsail, too, and little jib form a most unhandy rig.

Experience has also proved that, with regard to the two factors, sail-area and length, the tendency is to make the body of as small displacement as possible, taking the length into account, so that with the small area of canvas employed there may be very little weight to propel. Thus, though the early raters were big-bodied and roomy boats, with good head-room below, the boats built lately are inferior in those qualities, and those which will be put on the stocks in the future will be merely big canoes with bulb-keels.

Experience prefers for Channel seas a boat that can be driven through the water when necessity compels without any sense of danger, and that, if allowed to do so, will ride over the waves when no object is to be gained by making a short cut through. A yacht of four beams to her length or more will do this far more comfortably and with less commotion and fuss than one of three beams or less to her length.

Experience furthermore says that, though the lugsail requires very little gear, and can be hoisted with a certain amount of ease, yet if sail has to be shortened, or the lugsail to be taken in hurriedly, it requires more than three men to do it smartly; at no time is the job an easy one, but if any sea is running, or the weather squally, three men have as much as they can do to handle it. This is never the case with the gaff-mainsail. In a 5-tonner a man and a boy could have shortened sail easily, and though the sail-area was great, one man and the owner could always sail her from port to port.

Money may be saved through a small sailmaker's bill, but it must go out in wages to the crew and extra hands.

It is a good point to have very little gear about, but the *Wenonah* and *Wee Winn* both prove that a gaff-mainsail is quite as suitable as the lug and a better all-round sail.

Experientia docet that the rater, though she can lay to, cannot be hove to and have her way stopped. And the risk with her is, that in a sudden rush, caused by her aftersail filling, she may bury herself by jumping right into a head-sea—a most dangerous performance when the weather is so bad and the seas so high that travelling can only be carried on at peril.

Again, experience tells a tale that raters are not all so very tender on the helm even when sailing on their best point, and are what would be called in horsey phraseology very hard-mouthed; and that whilst off the wind they are like star-gazers, all over the place, and ready to rush anywhere and everywhere rather than straight ahead or where the helmsmen want them to go. Some of the small yachts built latterly under the old rule had a similar inclination, but it was generally at a time when they were being very heavily pressed, carrying too much sail, or when badly trimmed.

Of the two kinds of overhang forward, the spoon-shaped bow, which Mr. G. L. Watson has given his new boats, is the best, because it adds flotation as well as length on the L.W.L. when the yacht is sailing down to her bearings, and fairs all her longitudinal curves. The fiddle-headed bow may be thought by some to look prettier, but it is not so effective, unless it helps by its flam, or flare out (which some new yachts with this kind of bow do not have), to keep the decks clear of water. The overhang bow means an extra top weight, which has to be provided for and counteracted when the calculation is being made for the ballasting; but, on the other hand, it gives enlarged deck-room. It also saves having a long outboard spar in the shape of a bowsprit, and so does away with any need of reefing. This is really only a small matter after all, since even with a rough sea there is never very much difficulty in reefing in the bowsprit providing it is properly fitted.

Years ago in American waters there was scarcely a sloop built that had not an Aberdeen stem or fiddle-headed bow, but for some years they were discarded, and it is only lately they have been brought into fashion again. No American would give up anything that he had pinned his faith to unless he saw some real advantage to be gained by so doing. It is quite easy to understand why Americans should come back to the old stem now, for their waters like it, and it helps to cheat the rating for length.

The main design so common in the rating classes is perfect when regarded from two points of view only. The long, very gentle curve that runs up from the heel of the sternpost to the stem-head, and the excessive rake of the sternpost itself, allow of no more outside deadwood than is absolutely necessary to keep the yacht together, hang the rudder, and fix the lead keel on, so that whatever surface there may be to cause friction is doing its duty—that is, is caused by the skin or planking. The form thus given has its drawbacks; this experience has shown us and they are far more prominent and, therefore, serious when met with in the smaller raters than when seen in a 40- or 100-rater.

The second point is the quickness with which yachts of this new design 'stay' and 'get away.' This is a more practical benefit to large yachts than to small ones; for vessels like the *Doris* or the old *Solent*, 30-ft. and 25-ft. classes, could all stay and move off quite quickly enough, although they might not have manifested a desire to spin round twice when not stopped on their wild career, which is a marked peculiarity with the modern mosquitos. In the large classes a few years ago it was a common thing to make use of the time occupied in going about to take in or shake out a reef when circumstances demanded it; at the present day the skipper or sailing-master has to keep his wits about him, otherwise he may find his beauty turning round and looking him in the face; for the large rater can whip round like a top.

Now, in regard to the courses round Great Britain, two-thirds are what may be called reaching courses—that is, there is more running and reaching to be done than there is beating to windward—and though the distance to be sailed over in tacks may be only a third of the whole course, still the tacks that have to be taken will make the distance almost as long as two-thirds of the whole course itself; hence comes the advantage of having a yacht that will travel the distance quickly on a wind. Nevertheless it seems foolish to place the eggs all in one basket, and as it is an absolutely useless accomplishment for a yacht to be able to go round two or three times to the once putting down of the helm, the question may be asked whether she would not be equally quick and a better racing, to say nothing of a cruising, yacht if she were not quite so much cut away forward, or, better still, if her sternpost were not quite so much raked; and could not this be done without materially affecting the speed?

If the idea is to give the yacht a great hold of the water by a deep draught, then it is easy to understand that the present fin-shaped keel is necessary; but Mr. Herreshoff has given practical proof that such a shaped keel or such excessive draught is by no means necessary to make a boat weatherly or a successful prize-winner. With a straighter sternpost a certain length of horizontal keel might be required to keep the centre of lateral resistance in the best place, but that again would only be following Mr. Herreshoff at a near distance, and would make the boats run and reach better and under a steadier helm, whilst a very imperceptible difference would be found in their rate of travelling to windward.

The two Herreshoff boats that have been sent over to England have certainly shown their tails to our smartest raters in the two rating classes, *viz.* the 2½ and ½. Both the *Wenonah* and *Wee Winn* are fitted with bulb-keels, which run their length horizontally to their L.W.L., and they are good on all points of sailing as well as remarkably quick in stays. These two boats are rigged with regular gaff-mainsails too, so that notwithstanding the craze for lugsails, they are not essential to make a boat sail past the winning marks first. To the cruising yachtsman who lives on board his little vessel, with such an alteration or improvement as the one referred to above there would be the comfort and satisfaction, when hauled alongside the pier of a tidal harbour, of knowing, after the yacht had begun to take the ground, that he had not to sit up all night watching her, or waiting till her bow started to lift before he could turn in to his bunk, because his yacht would take the ground on a more even keel. It is no child's play looking after a fin-keeled yacht taking the ground, and the very greatest of care and most subtle precautions have to be used to avoid a fall over on the side.

In designing a small yacht there are matters that have to be considered which scarcely affect larger vessels except when comparing them, again, with larger vessels still. One of these points almost makes it worthwhile looking back at the reasons why certain types of small yachts have become so prominent and so much sought after and believed in. The great American designer, Mr. Herreshoff, and our own clever yacht architects here, are taking the canoe of the savage as their model; and as this is the case, it may be interesting to see how, starting from the canoe, all yachts have taken their form (no matter how deep or beamy they may have been), and perhaps, too, by so doing, it will

'WENONAH'
2½-rater (Mr. H. Allen). Designed by Nat. Herreshoff, 1893.

be easier to discern and arrive at the kind of form best suited to meet special requirements, apart from the trammels of the rules, measurements, or ratings such as are or have been laid down for yachtsmen and yacht-owners by the Royal Thames, the Yacht Racing Association, the American and French yacht clubs, or other societies and authorities.

The canoe of the South Seas or the *kyak* of the Greenlander could not have been better chosen, had they been worked out on the most scientific principles, for the work they have to do. The shape is that best adapted for speed, lightness (which means light displacement), and, under certain conditions, for sea-going qualities. Those conditions are, of course, smooth water or big ocean rollers, which seldom if ever break, and a propulsion easy, strong, and yet not exaggerated, longitudinal and not transverse in its tendency (as in propulsion by sail). Now if this model be taken, which invariably possesses a U-shaped section, there will be no great difficulty in understanding the whys and wherefores of the several transformations it has undergone.

If it is desired that a small boat should keep the sea, the nearer she approaches to the canoe form, as far as is compatible with the limited requirements, the better able will she be to cope with the difficulties which she ought, under the circumstances, to be ready to encounter. Hence it is that those men who make great ocean voyages, as, for instance, across the Atlantic, in boats about 15 feet or thereabouts, always have their boats built as round and floaty in form as it is possible to design them, taking into account that they must be decked, have sufficient depth of hold to allow of stowage for provision and water, which act as the greater part of the ballast, with the addition of just sufficient room for lying down at full length under deck covering: 2 ft. 6 in. to 3 feet is the outside depth under the deck of any of these diminutive ocean cruisers.

The entrance given to such boats is always full and buoyant, though not bluff. Rarely do they have a vertical stem, but one rather rounded up, with a slight overhang. The after-body is generally whale-shaped, with the sternpost at a somewhat less angle than the stem. Both stem and stern-posts have this inclination given them, not with the idea of making them quick in stays, but rather for the purpose of meeting and throwing off head or following seas, and adding buoyancy to both ends. The main principle in these boats is to obtain buoyancy and speed, while great sail-carrying power for driving at abnormal speeds does not so much as receive a thought. This is why it so seldom occurs that any of these little vessels fail in reaching their destination.

They go over the seas and not through them, owing to lack of weight and want of power. Their worst experiences during their long, uninteresting, and perilous voyages generally begin on nearing our shores and the chops of the Channel, where the seas begin to assume a broken, short, uneven, or at the best a deep ridge and furrow, shape. These boats may be considered the first remove from the early canoe form.

The general requirements, however, in a yacht are speed, accommodation, sail-carrying power, and weight. This latter property means, in other words, the ability to drive through a sea which, from its wall-sidedness, makes it an impracticable barrier to get over. When a vessel has not the weight or power to meet such a sea, as a rule, it spells disaster, or, to say the least, very disagreeable consequences; whereas if she can climb a part of the way up and then send her nose through the top, all is sure to end well.

Accommodation is very near akin to weight, for it is impossible to have a roomy boat without weight being concerned in it as a factor of some consequence. Accommodation in a yacht of 30 feet length and 6 feet to 7 feet beam means that there should be a height between the cabin floor and the deck beams of 4 ft. 6 in. to 5 ft. 6 in. at least, and this will demand a big-bodied boat of rather large displacement, otherwise the deepening in the water of the original U shape. Such a boat will require a large sail-spread to propel her. Supposing, however, that such height between decks is not required—that is to say, the boat is to be only partially decked with a large open cockpit—in that case the designer can, if he chooses, give the boat very much less displacement, which, in its turn, will require less driving power. The tendency, as it has been shown, of the Length and Sail-Area Rule is to provide just such a small displacement yacht, and accordingly a large yacht will someday be launched without any accommodation whatever.

Sail-carrying power is almost entirely a matter of displacement, for it is only a large-bodied boat that will have buoyancy sufficient to carry a great weight of ballast, and the deeper that ballast is placed, the more leverage will there be to counter-balance the sail, and hence the greater may be the sail-spread. Under the new system of deep plates, with the whole of the ballast bolted on at the bottom of the plate in the shape of a cigar or Whitehead torpedo, it is impossible to say how much area of sail could not be given to a boat of a certain length, beam, and depth of hull, and the only questionable difficulty that would come in the way would be the weight of the mast and spars necessary to carry the sail.

For instance, take the three principal methods of stowing ballast, inboard, outboard, as in the ordinary keel, and the plate with a bulb. The dimensions of the boat to be supplied with sails are, length 30 feet, beam 7 feet, draught to bottom of wooden keel 4 feet. If the ballast is stowed inboard (lead ballast is presumed in all the cases), and the displacement permits, the sail-area may be 800 square feet. If the ballast is taken out and moulded in a keel, the sail-area may be increased to close upon 900 square feet. Should the lead be taken out and a plate some 2 feet or 3 feet deep be fitted, with the lead in the form of a bulb fixed at the bottom, the weight of the spars and the sails would be the only obstacle to the great increase of canvas that might be spread.

Suppose, again, another hull be employed for experiments, having the length the same, but the beam increased to make up for the smaller depth of body below L.W.L. of 3 feet, the new hull may have the same displacement, and therefore the power to support the same weight of ballast as the last example. If this hull were supplied with a plate 4 feet or 5 feet deep, with the same bulb of lead, she would carry a still greater amount of sail; but with such a shallow boat there would be no accommodation.

Speed, that element in design which everybody cries after, whether they be practical scientific yachting men (and there is one thing Great Britain can boast of in her yacht designers, professional or amateur, and that is, they are all, without exception, first-rate helmsmen and seamen), or only graduating in the first principles of yacht-racing, is dependent on many conditions. In the first place, it forbids the presence of all superfluous deadwood, so that the outside surface presented to the water may be all of a useful description (that is, by being part of the planking or skin, or only as much deadwood as is necessary for the strength of the vessel), and the friction caused thereby may be reduced to a minimum. With a hull of large displacement there must naturally be very much greater surface friction than in one of smaller body, and therefore the question will arise—Will not the smaller yacht be the faster of the two? This involves still deeper sifting, because sometimes the smaller yacht will beat the one built on the same length and beam, though she may be very much larger.

Before we can choose which of the two kinds of boat will be the better to have for a successful racer, a second great condition has to be looked into and satisfactorily settled. This is nothing less than what kind of waters the yacht will have to race or cruise in. The question of the element water is one very frequently forgotten and lost sight of by those buying yachts, especially second-hand ones; and the purchaser, who perhaps buys a most successful small vessel in the South, is astonished to find that when he has tried her against the local Scotch cracks, her performances prove of a very poor description in comparison, and disappointment is the consequence. Water may be in the eyes of some all the same, wherever it may be, and so it is round our coasts in its smooth state; but when it is set in motion there are scarcely two of our great yachting stations alike, while the seas in our three Channels all vary in form.

At the mouth of the English Channel the seas, as soon as the 'chops' are left astern, become regular, are long and deep, and more or less easy for a small yacht to negotiate; that is, she has room to work in and out of them, and at the same time avoid receiving a comber aboard as passenger. As she sails farther up and the channel narrows, the seas become more of the deep ridge and furrow order, steep, narrow, and difficult to sail over, whilst each sea will contain its full weight of water. On nearing Calais the seas have less water in them, but are very short and steep; the consequence is they are more inclined to break. In the North Sea the sea disturbance takes another and larger form, and sailing North becomes still larger, and, of course, wider and deeper, till the Northern Ocean is opened out. St. George's Channel is very much like the English Channel, except that between Port Patrick in Scotland and the Irish coast the waves are more regular than between Calais and Dover, where currents and banks tend to make dangerous cross seas.

So it is found that off Plymouth and Falmouth and outside Dartmouth there is often an ocean swell running, especially after there has been a south-westerly gale. The Solent, again, is different from the Clyde in its sea disturbance, and when acted upon by a south-easterly gale the seas off Spithead, owing to the shallowness of its water, have not nearly so much weight of water in them as those of the Scotch estuary when worked up by a northerly or southerly breeze. The Liverpool and London rivers are very much alike, though perhaps of the two the Liverpool has the greater sea disturbance, owing to the strength of its tides, which at some seasons are very rapid.

To large yachts of 40 tons and over the difference in character of the seas just spoken of is not a matter of great importance. What a large yacht may treat as a mere ripple to a 5-tonner may be a 'nasty sea'; and as these pages are dealing with the smaller craft of about 30 feet length, the sea disturbance must be regarded as it affects them. On rivers and inland waters the waves, as a rule, have not much weight in them, and there is no reason why the small yacht should not be able to go through the waves she is unable to rise over. Yachts of large displacement are more likely to do that at better speed than a small vessel of the same beam and length, because they have more weight.

Where ocean rollers are concerned, or a heavy swell, while there is wind both types may be equal; but when the wind is shy and light, then the yacht of large displacement will walk past her small rival. It would be noticed that the heavy displacement vessel would forge ahead apparently moved by no other force than the 'send' of her weight as she lazily pitches to the movement of each succeeding wave. The courses for small yachts where such conditions are met with are Plymouth, Dartmouth, and Queenstown, and some parts of the Clyde and St. George's Channel to a very much lessened degree. Then, if a thought be cast across the Atlantic and a look be taken at the characteristics of the waters of Long Island Sound, that favourite haunt of all American racing and cruising yachtsmen, as on our own inland waters, the seas that much disturb the small fry are, it will be observed, scarcely noticeable to the large schooners and cutters of which so much is heard.

The principal form in America laid down for all yachts used to be a long flat floor with very small displacement, great beam with a centreboard—the immense beam giving great initial stability. Large as well as small yachts were built to this design, and much used to be heard about their remarkable speed. A few years ago, however, two or three small yachts, amongst them the little *Delvin* 5-tonner, built by Mr. W. Fife, jun., were sent over, all of fairly large displacement. These, without exception, put the extinguisher on all the American small yachts, by beating them time after time. The reason of it was that the English-built yachts could drive through what broken water or sea disturbance they met with, while the 'skim-dishes' could do little against it. Since those days the Americans have very materially altered their model, and both large and small yachts have been given more power; *vide* the examples brought out to compete with our yachts for the 'America Cup,' and those to which the *Minerva* has so lately shown her tail.

Where, therefore, great speed is required, and there is no limitation to sail-carrying power, a large displacement vessel is the best type to choose. Some small-yacht racing men do not like to be always remaining in their home waters, but prefer to go round to the regattas at other ports, and try their luck against the small yachts that gather at these meetings. They live on board, and sail their yachts round the coast. To such the large bodied boat is a regular frigate. The head-room is good, no lack of space is wanted for a comfortable lie down, and the owner and two friends, with racing sails and all other yacht paraphernalia, can stow away in the main cabin as cosily as can be.

During the last six years yacht designers have been spending their time in perfecting a vessel to be rated by length and sail-area alone. Boats of large displacement and moderate length, with good sail-spread, limited so that the boats might be rated under their several classes, gradually, but surely, gave place to boats of greater length, smaller bodies, and a smaller sail-spread. It does not appear, from the opinions of many who have published their views, that there is at the present time any particular desire to have good accommodation in racing yachts.

The owners of the greater number of the 5-raters do not live in them, and the owners of the 40-raters have been so accustomed to great head-room in their vessels, that now, when, instead of having 7 feet to 8 feet, they still find they can walk about in the cabins, no complaints are heard; but with the lessons that Mr. Herreshoff has been teaching, there is every reason to believe that we may live to see a 40-rater launched with about 3 to 4 feet depth of body under water, and then perhaps there may come a reaction, and a return may be made to a moderately large displacement. Up to the present time the 5-raters have been kept fairly large, and owing to their beam, as far as internal accommodation is concerned, have room enough and to spare; but the raters of 1893 were not nearly of such large displacement as the boats of two years before, and they are wonderful to look at outside.

The fin-keel requires great depth if it is to be of any real use, and it is in this particular point that small yachts suffer. If a 5-rater is to sail in all waters, and go the round of the coast regattas, then her draught should be limited; of course, if the sole intention of the owner is that his yacht is never to race in any other locality than his own home waters, then, if the home waters be the Clyde, or Windermere, or Kingstown, there is no reason why depth should not be unlimited. On the other hand, should the yacht be intended for a sea-going vessel, then a heavy draught of water is not altogether desirable.

There are times when a 5-tonner or rater may be overtaken by bad weather while making a passage, and when a comfortable harbour under the lee would be a most acceptable refuge to make for. There are

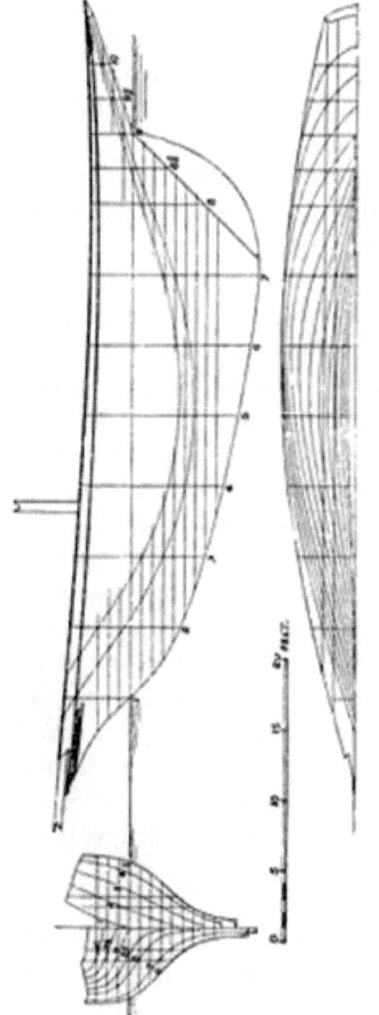

'Minerva,' 23 tons. Designed by W. Fife, 1888.

scores of snug little places round the coast where a small craft could lie peacefully enough, provided her draught of water allowed her to make use of any one of them. The average depth of water at these bays or harbours is about 6 feet at low-water spring tides. Hence no yacht or rater of 30 feet or under should have a draught of more than 6 feet. The writer remembers only too well an occasion when, after leaving Campbeltown, in Cantyre, for a northern port in Ireland, a north-westerly gale sprang up, bringing with it rain and a sea fog. The distance across from the Mull is not more than a few miles, but when his yacht made the land it was blowing so hard he had to run for the nearest shelter.

Alas! when he sighted the little tidal harbour he was steering for, it was low water, and his yacht, which drew 7 feet 6 in., could not enter. He had to lie at two anchors outside in the Roads with some half-a-dozen coasters, expecting, with every shift of the wind, that the anchorage might become one on a lee shore. The *Humming Bird*, in 1891, left the Solent for Queenstown. She is a 2½-rater. After leaving Land's End the weather, which had been more or less fine, changed, and the sea getting up, it was decided to take her into St. Ives Harbour. She unfortunately drew more than 6 feet; the consequence was, though only 25 feet on the water-line, she was compelled to take her chance and drop anchor in the bay outside, because there was only 6 feet of water in the harbour.

None know the value of a moderate draught of water better than those who have cruised or raced afar from home, and groped their way into all kinds of out-of-the-way bays and harbours in small craft. The yachtsman who builds for racing only, possesses the means, and is ready to launch a new yacht to his name every other year, should (if he be a sensible man and proposes to himself to sell the yachts he has no further use for) think of the requirements of the market and his ability to sell. Soon the yacht mart will be flooded with a number of cast-off 5-and 2½-raters, all with a draught of water which would limit their sale to only a few places.

There are many living at the present moment who will remember the time when even the large yachts of 100 to 200 tons were never given more than 12 feet draught. This was done to enable them to enter tidal harbours, the greater number of which only have a depth of 15 feet at high-water neeps. But there is another argument in favour of not having too great a draught of water, and that is, it is not an element of speed, beyond helping the sail power; and the existence of yachts like the old *Fiery Cross*, which only drew 8 feet and was a most successful winner, and of the Herreshoff boats, which do not draw so much as the English-built raters and are the cracks of the day, points the lesson that it is well to put a limit where a limit may be altogether an advantage.

Great care is necessary in apportioning out beam, no matter whether the yacht is to be of large or small displacement; great beam in the case of a yacht of small displacement is only suitable for waters such as Long Island Sound, or long rolling seas, and is useless in heavy broken water like that met with in our channels; because it is a difficult matter, without weight, to drive through the seas. When great beam is given to a yacht of large displacement, she may be able to fight her way through the water, but it will not be at the greatest speed for the given length, since it was proved by the old Solent 30-ft. and 25-ft. classes that when beating through a head sea a yacht of the same length, but of small beam, such as the *Currytush* and the late Lord Francis Cecil's little 3-tonner *Chittywee*, were able to travel faster through the water whenever it was a hard thrash to windward.

The general opinion of those competent to judge is, that 3½ to 4½ beams to the length on L.W.L. is about the most advantageous proportion, some going even so far as to assert that three beams may be given; but, in dealing with small yachts, 5-raters and 5-tonners, as this chapter does, the writer believes that four beams to length is a good proportion to meet all kinds of weather with; and if 30 feet be the length 7 ft. 6 in. the beam, and 5 ft. 6 in. the draught, such proportions will be found to give quite sufficient scope to any designer in order that a remarkably fast weatherly little ship may be the result of his calculations. The height between the decks with a large displacement would give 4 ft. 6 in. to 5 feet head-room. Nothing has been said about the sail-area, which should not be taxed.

The element sail-area appears to be the stumbling-block in the present rating rule. It is limited, and the consequence is the cart is put before the horse, and the hull is built to the sail-spread. Thus the hull is being minimised to carry the small area allotted to certain lengths.

There have been so many raters built since the present rule came in that it would take too much space to mention them all with their several points, but there is this fact to notice, which backs up what has been said before, that South-country designed boats seem to do well in their own waters, while those brought out in the Clyde fare best there. When Clyde 5-raters have gone South, they have performed badly—though the *Red Lancer* in 1893 proved the exception to the rule—and the Solent raters that have found their way up North have made but a poor show. Mr. Arthur Payne is the king of draughtsmen on the Solent, and his yachts, with those designed by Mr. Clayton, also a prince among naval architects, have all had their turn at winning prizes when they have been properly sailed.

Mr. Payne's designs mostly favour a fair amount of displacement, and *Alwida*, built by him for Lord Dunraven in 1890, is a very fine example of the kind of craft he can produce. The workmanship is fit to compare with the very neatest cabinet work. The following year the beam was increased by some inches, the length underwent a drawing out, and at the same time the body was tucked up to decrease the displacement. The next movement, if it is possible to judge by the 2½-raters, will be to follow in the steps of Mr. Herreshoff—who speaks for himself in other chapters. The *Cyane*, another of Mr. Payne's 5-raters and an improvement on the *Alwida*, has few fittings below, but there is great height between decks, and if she were changed into a cruiser, she has enough room to make her everything that can be desired, without greatly decreasing her speed.

To describe all the 5-raters sent out to do battle by those Northern champions, Messrs. Fife and G. L. Watson, would be equally out of place here. Their boats are too well known all over the world both for speed and beauty of design, and if there is a point peculiar to either of them that marks their vessels and makes their meetings interesting and exciting, it is that while Mr. Watson's are extra smart in topsail breezes, Messrs. Fife's yachts are specially good in strong winds.

In mentioning these well-known names, it would be impossible to forget a name which will always be linked with the year 1892—*viz.* Mr. J. H. Nicholson, jun., of the firm of Messrs. Nicholson & Sons, Gosport, the successful designer of the 5-rater *Dacia* and the 2½-rater *Gareth*. His boats are unique, and though they partake of the canoe form, still it is the shape adopted by Mr. Nicholson for his keel, and the design itself, which brought his name so prominently forward during the season of 1892 as one of the most successful designers in England. The 5-rater *Dacia*, which he designed and built in 1892 for Mr. H. R. Langrishe, and which now belongs to Lord Dudley, proved herself far superior in all weathers to the yachts of her rating in the South.

Most of the raters were designed with a square stern above water, whatever their shape might have been below; but the *Dacia* is counter-

'RED LANCER'
11 tons T.M., 5-rater (Capt. Sharman–Crawford). Designed by Fife of Fairlie, 1892.

sterned, and carries her ribbands fair from stem to taffrail, as far as can be judged from a long-distance view when she was hauled up. Whatever her length may be on the L.W.L., it must with a large crew aboard be so considerably increased as to almost make her another boat. At all events, she is a fine specimen of the advanced type of rater, and is good in all weathers.

The *Natica* and *Red Lancer*, 5-raters by Mr. Watson and Mr. Fife, jun., must not be passed over unmentioned. Both these yachts belong to Belfast, which is at present, (as at time of first publication), the home of 5-rater racing. In the Clyde, where 5-tonners and 5-raters were once the fashionable classes, there is now not a single representative. The *Red Lancer* is a fin-keel shaped vessel with great angle of sternpost, from the heel of which to the stem-head the line is run in a very easy curve. She has a very long counter, more than a third of which is submerged; but she is very pretty as a design, and though not of large displacement, is very roomy both on deck and below. She was originally fitted with a centreboard, but as it was not considered of any material benefit to her, this was taken out and the hole in the keel filled up with lead. The *Natica* has a spoon bow, and is one of Mr. Watson's prettiest models as far as the modern racer can be termed pretty. She has been very successful in the North, and as great curiosity was felt regarding her capabilities when compared with the South-country boats, she sailed round, and met the *Dacia* at Torquay Regatta,

'NATICA.' DESIGNED BY G. L. WATSON, 1892.

where the best of three matches were won by *Dacia*.

It would have been better, perhaps, had the matches taken place off Holyhead—*vide* the case of the *Vril*, *Camellia*, and *Freda*; however, there is no reason to disparage them as not giving a true indication of the respective merits of both yachts. So many races come off, both on the Solent and on the Clyde, in numerical comparison with what took place a few years ago, that the owners of small yachts rarely care now to go far away from home on the chance of obtaining sport when it lies comfortably to hand; but it is a thing to be encouraged, and when yachts have proved themselves champions in any particular waters, a trysting place should be chosen for the little winners to meet and try conclusions. This would also make yachtsmen anxious to possess not merely a racing machine, but a boat capable of going from port to port with a certain amount of comfort to her crew.

Practical Hints

Buying

In choosing a yacht there is, as with most other occupations, a right and a wrong way of going about it. First of all, the size has to be determined upon; but this can soon be done by referring to the length of the purse out of which the funds for keeping the yacht in commission are to be supplied. Yachts are very much like houses, and it is quite possible to buy a yacht or a house for such an insignificantly small outlay that to all unconcerned in the bargain it will appear a ridiculously cheap purchase. But this might not really be the case, because, though the original outlay may have been small, if a large number of servants or hands are required to keep either the one or the other up, it would be dear at any price should money not be forthcoming to meet the annual expenditure.

It is, therefore, necessary, before making a purchase, to look ahead at the probable annual cost. At a rough estimate it may be laid down that each extra hand required (this does not refer to those necessary on racing days) will cost at least 25*l*. per season. A skipper may for his wages, clothes, &c., make a hole in any sum from 30*l*. to 100*l*. *per annum*. In a 5-tonner, or a yacht of 30 feet and under, provided she has a gaff-mainsail and not a lugsail, one hand will be quite crew sufficient, with the owner, to take her about. The writer worked a 10-tonner with one hand for two seasons without finding her too heavy, but the addition of a boy made all the difference in the comfort.

The cost of sails, gear, and the many small items of equipment which have to be renewed from time to time, cannot or should not be treated as if such casual expenses could only come about in some dim vista of futurity; for where in the case of sails 60*l.* might see the fortunate owner of a racing 5 in possession of a brand-new suit, the man with a 20 would find that sum barely sufficient to supply his yacht with a new mainsail and topsail.

In making a purchase, it is as well if it be possible to find out what kind of a yachtsman the owner of the yacht for sale is—that is, if he is a man who has made yachts and yachting his sole hobby, and has therefore been in the habit of keeping his vessels in the best condition. It makes all the difference whether you purchase from such a man, or from one who, having extracted all the good out of his yacht's gear and sails, has placed her in the market rather than go to the expense of giving her a new fit-out. In the case of a 5-tonner the difference in price between the purchase money of vessels owned by the two men might be from 50*l.* to 80*l.* or 100*l.*; but then in the case of the one there will only be one expense, *viz.*—that of the purchase money, whereas with the other it might be difficult to say how much might be required as outlay before the yacht could be made ready for sea.

The Clyde and Southampton are the best and most likely places to find yachts for sale which have been well kept up and cared for. Buying from a thorough yachtsman who is known to spare no expense on his yacht will mean an absence of all bitterness and wrath, whereas in making the purchase from the skinflint, until a small fortune has been paid away the new owner will find that he has no satisfaction.

In buying a small yacht, in fact any yacht, unless the purchaser has met with a vessel that combines all his requirements, it is always the wisest plan for him to spend as little as possible the first season on his new purchase—of course it is taken for granted that her sails and gear are in thoroughly good order—in altering any of her fittings to suit his own private fads; for if he changes his mind about his yacht's points, or sees a vessel he may like better, he should remember that he must not expect to get his money back again when wanting to sell. By the end of the first season, he will most likely have found out whether he will keep the yacht, and therefore whether she really suits him, when he can do what he likes to her. It must be borne in mind, too, that the inside fittings of a yacht's cabin form the most expensive part of her hull; and alterations below always mean a goodly expenditure.

Avoid all yachts which are either coated outside or filled in at the garboards inside with cement, as water will leak in between the cement and skin, and rot must ensue.

Fitting out.

In fitting out, two very important points have to be thought of—*viz.*, if the yacht is not coppered, what is the best paint to coat her with, and what is the best method of treating the decks? With regard to the first question, there are two paints which the writer has never yet seen used in the yachting world, except on his own boat, and which can be highly recommended. One is the black priming varnish used on iron ships, and especially in the navy. He gave this, some years ago on the Clyde, four months' good trial. It was used on a boat kept out for winter work which lay in a little harbour well-known for its fouling propensities. At the end of the four months there was absolutely no growth or sign of weed of any kind. Where it is to be obtained he is unable to say, as the coat of paint that was put on his boat was given him by a naval officer.

The other paint is called after the inventor, 'Harvey's Patent.' The writer's experience of this is as follows:—A friend sent him a tin to try, and to give his opinion upon. Accordingly his boat, which had been lying up Portsmouth Harbour some six months at her moorings, was brought down to Priddy's Hard and hauled up. She had, though coated with a very well-known patent, from 7 to 10 feet of weed floating astern of her at the time, which had to be removed. After being thoroughly cleaned, left to dry for a few days, and having her paint burnt off, a coat of priming was given, followed by two coats of the Harvey. The boat was then launched and towed back to her moorings, where she was left for over 20 months. At the end of that time she was hauled up, prior to being put into commission; and there was no sign of grass or weed; slime, with an almost imperceptible shell-fish growth, being all that was visible on her bottom. The boat was seen by a good many naval and other men during the time she was at her moorings, and they remarked on the quality of the paint.

One great point about the Harvey must be mentioned, and that is, it dries very quickly when put on. It is a good thing to warm it before using, as it is apt to get hard and soak up the oil; but it soon softens, and after being properly mixed works well.

Before touching the decks, the spars and blocks will always require to have the old varnish of the past season scraped off them, and will have then to be re-varnished. In scraping the spars care should be taken that the knife, scraper, or glass be drawn with, and not against, the grain of the wood. The scraping will always be achieved with greater facility if the spar or block in hand is slightly damped, and the scraper or knife-blade employed has its edge turned over a little. This latter is done by drawing the side of the edge along the back of a knife or steel tool. After scraping, the whole spar should be rubbed down with sand-paper, prior to its receiving a coat of varnish. The brushes employed should be either well-used ones, or, if new, ought to be well soaked in water prior to use, as this will prevent the bristles falling out during the process of varnishing.

Nothing is so provoking as to have to be continually picking out bristles from the varnish; of course, what holds good about varnishing holds good in the matter of painting. When using copal varnish, it is as well to pour out only as much as may be wanted for the time being into an old tin or jar, because it very soon hardens on exposure to the air, and then becomes useless. For the same reason the varnish bottle or can should never be left uncorked. Two coats of varnish thinly laid on ought to suffice at the beginning of the season, and a third coat may be given as the season progresses.

With regard to the decks. Everything depends on the state of the decks themselves and how they are laid. If they are made of wide planking, which is rarely, if ever, the case when the workmanship is that of a yacht-builder, they should be painted; if, however, the decks are laid with narrow planking fined off with the deck curves at the bow and stern, then, notwithstanding the beauty of white decks, it is better to varnish them. Varnishing keeps them hard, and saves many a heart pang when the little yacht is visited by a friend with nails in his boots or a lady in small heels. If the decks be worn at all, a coat of varnish is a capital thing. After trying decks varnished and unvarnished, experience confesses that the joys of beholding a white, spotless deck in a small yacht are more than outweighed by the sorrow and annoyance of seeing deep nail-marks imprinted on it.

As decks, when cared for, are always varnished when a yacht is laid up for the winter, this varnish has necessarily to be removed prior to a start on a season's yachting. The best method by which this can be carried out is as follows:—Black ashes, *Sooji Mooji,* or one of the many preparations of caustic potash, should be procured from a ship-chandler, and mixed in an iron bucket with warm water in the proportion of one-third black ashes to two-thirds water, according to the strength required. As soon as the sun has set the mixture must be poured over the deck, which must be left well covered with it till an hour before sunrise. The mixture, which will have dried during the night, must now be treated with hot water and well rubbed into the varnish, and fresh buckets of water must be kept applied till every particle of the mixture with the varnish has been cleared off and out of the deck planking. If the mixture is applied or allowed to remain on the deck while the sun is up, it will be certain to eat into and burn it.

There are two or three ways of laying decks. One is to have the planks nailed down to the beams, the nails countersunk, and the holes filled up with wood plugs to hide the nail-heads. This is generally done by men who have not had much to do with yacht-building. The common method employed is to drive the nails diagonally through the edge of the plank into the beam. Nails let in horizontally and driven into the next plank, two or three cotton threads having been placed between, keep the two planks in position. Each plank is similarly treated, and when all the planks have been fitted and jammed together, marine glue is poured into the seams. As soon as the glue has set and hardened the decks are planed, and finished off.

The third method is not so pretty perhaps, but is believed from practical experience to be the best. The planks are mortised together, varnished, and then brought tight up. The whole deck is often built and made ready to fit before it is put into position, so that when it is laid on the beams, all that is required is to nail it down into its place. The writer has had experience with the second kind of deck mentioned here in nearly all of his yachts, and of the third method of laying decks in the *Cyprus*. She was about five years old when he bought her, and that is a good age for a racing 5-tonner's decks to last sound and without a leaky spot to be found anywhere. Her decks were certainly kept varnished, for the simple reason stated above, that visitors might be always welcome, no matter what description of foot-gear had been supplied to them by their bootmakers.

It is not an uncommon practice to have a yacht recoppered, though her copper may be in good condition and even new. When such a proposition is made, which is not infrequently done by skippers wishing to play into the yacht-builder's hands, and thinking more of their own pockets than their master's interests, the yachtsman must remember that every time his yacht is coppered her skin is made more porous, and she herself heavier in the water, since the planking will naturally sodden with greater rapidity.

If the incipient yachtsman has bought the hull and spars of a yacht that is only partially built or finished off, a few more hints must be added, which will give him food for reflection, and may prove of service.

When a yacht likely to suit has been heard of, nothing being known of the owner, the next thing should be to try to discover whether she is sound or possesses any weak places. The purchaser should overhaul her outside just below the channels, and examine if the yacht has been frequently caulked between the seams of the planking, or if there are any signs of weeps of any kind about that part or elsewhere. The weeps will be shown most likely by a rusty discolouration. If the yacht is coppered, wrinkles must be looked for under the channels, runners, and about the bilge. They will show if the yacht has been strained at all. A knife should next be taken, and the point driven into the planking about the water-line, where it joins the sternpost and stem, and then along the two lower garboard strakes, especially if cement has been used to fill in between the keel and planking, to discover if there is any sign of dry rot, sap rot, &c.

Inside, under the cabin floor, the timbers, deadwoods, and the garboard strakes if the yacht be coppered, should be tested in the same way. If the yacht has iron floors, these should be carefully examined for galvanic action or decay. The heads of the bolts which go through the lead keel should be scraped to see whether they are made of iron, metal composition, or copper. If they are iron or steel, most likely they will require to be renewed, because galvanic action is very soon set up between the lead and steel. Outside, copper shows wear and tear more quickly near the stem and sternpost and along the water-line. In the cabin itself the deck ceiling should be examined for weeps and leaks, especially about the bits forward and near the mast, also wherever a bolt-head is visible.

On deck, a look round the covering board will discover whether it has been often recaulked, by the seam being extra wide. The heat of a stove below is frequently the cause of the deck forward leaking. The deck seams should not be wider there than at any other part. All the spars should be examined, and if there are no transverse cracks, longitudinal ones may be held of no consequence. The weak parts of the mast are generally to be found between the yoke and cap, where the eyes of the rigging rest. Rot is often found there, and strains are met with up the masthead. The boom shows its weakness at the outer end by small cracks, and the bowsprit by the gammon iron and stem-head. If the above rough survey proves all correct, attention must be given next to the rigging, sails, and gear. Wear in the wire rigging is shown by its being rusty, the strands stretched, or by the broken threads of a strand appearing here and there.

If the jib, throat, peak halliards, and mainsheet are new, or have seen the work of one season only, they will not require much overhauling. With the other running rigging the strands should be untwisted, just enough to see whether the heart of the rope is fresh and not rotten. The blocks ought to be of a light colour without cracks in them, and iron strapped inside. The sails will not show either mildew marks or discolouration if they are in good condition. The chain and anchors to be in good order should not be rusty, but clean and well galvanised. They should be looked at to discover whether they have ever been regalvanised. This will be noticed by the links presenting a rough, uneven surface, where there was rust or decay before the repetition of the process of galvanising.

Sometimes at fitting-out time an owner finds that he has to provide his yacht with a new anchor. It may help him, therefore, in his choice if the writer gives his experience in the matter of ground tackle or mud-hooks. There are a number of patents in the market, the most patronised of which are Trotman's, Martin's, Smith's, and Thomas & Nicholson's. All these have many good points, with a weak one here and there to keep the competition in anchor designing open to improvement.

Trotman's anchor has movable arms and stock, stows away well, and is a fine holding anchor when once it bites; but it is often very slow at catching hold, and this is dangerous when the anchorage happens to be close and crowded, as, for instance, is frequently the case at Kingstown, Cowes, &c., during regatta time. If the anchor does not catch at once on such occasions the yacht may drift some distance before she is brought up, and with little room this operation is performed, more often than not, by collision with some vessel astern.

The Martin anchor and the Smith both work on a different principle from any of the others, in that their arms move together so as to allow both flukes to act at the same time. Of the two the Smith, which has no stock, is preferable for yacht work. The Martin has a stock which is fixed on the same plane with the arms. Both anchors catch quickly and hold well as long as the bottom is not rocky or very uneven, when they are apt to get tilted over and lose any hold they may have at first obtained. Their worst failing is that of coming home under the following conditions. If the yacht yaws about, owing to strong tides, winds, or boisterous weather, the flukes of the anchor are prone, when working in their holes, to make them so large that they gradually meet each other and finally become one big hole; the anchor then invariably trips, comes home, and the yacht drags. On the other hand, the Smith and Martin anchors stow away better than any others, and when on deck lie flat and compact. The Smith anchor makes a capital kedge. Its holding power is so great that it is not necessary to carry one of anything like the weight that would be required were any other patent anchor employed.

The great point in favour of Smith's over that of Martin's anchor is that, should it foul a mooring or warp, it can be easily tripped. The tripping is done by letting the bight of a bowline slip down the chain and anchor till it reaches the arms, and then hauling on it.

The best of the patents, however, is an anchor that was brought out some years ago by Messrs. Thomas & Nicholson, of Southampton and Gosport. It can be stowed away in a very small space, since the arms are removable. It is a quick catcher, and is, at the same time, very powerful and trustworthy.

The arms stand out at the most effective angle for insuring strength of grip, while the shank is long, and, though light and neat-looking— it is flat-sided—has sufficient weight and substance in it to stand any ordinary crucial test. The flukes from their shape appear somewhat longer in proportion to their width than the usual patterns; but this arises from the sides being slightly bent back, with the object of making the fluke more penetrating, which it certainly is.

The old fisherman's anchor with a movable stock is, after all, as good an anchor as any yachtsman need want. It is not a patent, and is accordingly very much less expensive. Should necessity ever compel the making of a small anchor, then the two great points which it must possess are, length of shank (because greater will be the leverage), and the placing of the arms so that they do not make a less angle with the stock than, say, 53°. After a long practical experience with almost every kind of anchor, the writer believes that two good, old-pattern fisherman's anchors, with movable stocks (the movable stock was a Mr. Rogers' patent), are all that any yacht need require or her mud-hooks; but if it is thought fit to have patent anchors, then either a couple of Thomas & Nicholson's anchors, or one of these and a Smith, ought to form the yacht's complement.

All being satisfactory, if the yacht is a 5-rater the first thing to be done will be to have the lugsail altered into a gaff-mainsail for handiness sake. This will be only a small expense, since the great peak of the lugsail will allow of its head being squared. Very little if anything need be taken off the head of a high-peaked lugsail when the gaff employed is hinged on to the jaws, as such a gaff can be peaked with far greater ease and to a much greater extent than when fitted in the ordinary. The writer has employed the following method for fitting up the interior accommodation of a 5-ton yacht, and he can highly recommend it as most convenient, and at the same time handy to clear out either on a racing day or when about to lay the yacht up:—All woodwork, such as lockers or fore-and-aft boards (used for turning the sofas into lockers), should be fixed in their places by hooks, or at any rate by screws.

Nothing should be a fixture except the two sofa-seats in the main cabin, the one forward of the mast, and the two sideboards fitted aft at each end of the sofas. If the yacht has to race, these sideboards should be made self-contained, and to shape, so that they may fit into their places and be kept there by hooks or catches. There should be only a curtain forward between the forecastle and main cabin, and instead of a regular solid bulkhead aft, gratings should take its place, with one wide grating as a door. This will keep the store room aft ventilated. If there is sufficient length to permit of transverse gratings about 20 inches apart and 2 feet high by the mast, as before explained when describing the *Lorelei*, by all means let these form one of the fittings to hold the sail bags. In the locker astern of the after bulkhead gratings, the skin should be protected by battens 2½ to 3 inches wide and from 1 to 2 inches apart. This will keep whatever is stowed there dry from any little weep or leakage that may occur in the planking.

There should be no ceiling either in the main or fore cabin, and if battens are thought necessary to prevent damp getting to the beds when left folded up in the bed-frames, then three, or at the outside four, some 4 or 5 inches apart, should be screwed up just in the position where the shoulders of a sitter would be likely to rest against them. Four or five may be fitted up on each side of the forecastle. The upper batten should be higher up than the top one in the main cabin, as it may be useful for screwing hooks into. The writer, however, prefers in the main cabin, instead of any battens, clean pieces of duck, or, what is better still, Willesden cloth (waterproof), made to hang loosely from hooks, reaching down to the sofas, and cut to the shape of the after sideboards, holes being sewn in to allow the iron hooks which carry the bed-frames to come through. This fitting always lightens up the cabin, and is easily taken down and scrubbed.

For beds, the iron frames supplied to all yachts' forecastles for the men, with canvas bottoms to them, are far the best and most comfortable. They take up less room than a hammock, and stow away nicely against the cabin's side when not in use. With these frames the writer has used quilted mattresses, the heads of which have ticking covers large enough to hold a pillow, and the whole is sewn on to strong American or waterproof cloth, which forms a covering when the bed and its blankets are rolled up and have to be stowed away.

In the forecastle, a movable pantry may be screwed up against the battens on the port side (the bed will be on the starboard side). This should be an open case with three shelves and two drawers underneath. The upper shelf must be divided off to take the three sizes—dinner, soup, and small plates. Between the plates, outside the divisions, there can be uprights on which to thread double egg-cups. On the lower shelf there should be holes cut to carry tumblers, and between the tumblers slots for wineglasses. The bottom shelf is for cups and saucers. One of the drawers ought to be lined with green baize to hold silver plate and knives. If the sideboards aft are fixtures, a tin case made to the shape of the yacht's side, to rest on the part of the sideboard on which the lid hinges, and reaching up to the deck, is a capital fitting to have.

The inside should be arranged in partitions to hold tea, coffee, sugar, biscuit, and other square canisters, also Dutch square spirit bottles. The door may be double, or if single, should open from the bottom and trice up to a hook overhead, so that it may not in any way hinder the opening of the sideboard lid at the same time. Two or three movable shelves placed right in the eyes of the yacht forward make useful stowage room for a man to keep his clothes, as there they stand less chance of getting wet. Between the sideboards aft a removable box ought to be fixed with screws, of sufficient depth to hold an iron bucket, washing basin, and all the conveniences of a lavatory. This will be directly under the cabin hatch, and from 8 to 10 inches abaft it. The lid should leave a few inches space clear to receive it when opened back.

Curtains made of duck or Willesden cloth, to hang down loose over the sideboards at each side to the depth of 6 inches, and hung from hooks in the deck above, will be found useful for keeping all stray splashes, that may fall inboard, from going on the sideboard lids, and thence among the dry goods and provisions stowed away in them. At the back of the lavatory box will be the after-grating and locker, and standing out from the grating, about 10 inches to a foot square, and 15 to 18 inches deep from the deck, there should be a cupboard, painted white inside, or, better still, lined with copper silver-plated to reflect the light, and a transparent spirit compass should then be fitted to hang through the deck above it. The brass rim for carrying the gimbles and binnacle lid outside must be screwed down to the deck on doubled india-rubber to prevent leakage. The cupboard door must have ventilating holes in it at the top and bottom, and a square hole to hold the lamp should be cut in the door between the upper and lower ventilators.

On the opposite side from that on which the tin case is fixed, and coming out from the grating the same distance as the compass box, two bookshelves can be fitted, which will prove most useful. On deck, the fittings and leads that are mentioned in the description of the *Cyprus* cannot be improved upon, except that rigging screws are neater, and give less trouble than dead-eyes and lanyards, which have to be continually set up. Lanyards, however, give more life to a mast, though it may appear almost imperceptible, and by so doing ought to render it less liable to be carried away. The sliding lid of the companion hatch should padlock on to a transverse partition between the combings, and it is a good plan to have this partition on hinges, so that at night, when the hatch-cover is drawn over, the partition may lie on the deck and so leave an aperture for ventilation.

The windows of the skylight will be all the better for being fixtures and should not open; if ventilation be required, the whole skylight can be taken off; this will prevent the leakage so common with hinged windows. A mainsheet horse and traveller with two quarter leading blocks are better than a double block shackled on to an eyebolt amidships, because a more direct up and down strain can be obtained when the boom is well in.

In any yacht of 25 feet in length or under, the wisest plan to adopt with regard to a forehatch is to do away with it and only have a large screw deadlight; if a small deadlight be preferred, then it ought to be placed about 12 to 18 inches ahead of the bits, and a copper cowl, to screw into the deadlight frame, should form part of the fittings, for use when the yacht is laid up, in order to let air into and so ventilate the cabin. It is certainly a great advantage to have the spinnaker ready in the forecastle for sending up through a hatch, but as this is the only good reason why a hatch should be thought requisite in a small yacht, and since it is a fruitful source of leakage and danger, especially when, as is sometimes the case, the lid has not been fastened down and a sea sweeps it off the deck, it is better to abolish the fitting altogether.

A small rail ahead of the mast, bolted through the deck and stayed to the mast below (in order to take off all weight from the deck and beams), and a rail abreast of the lee and weather rigging, should form all that is required for belaying halliards, purchases, tacks, &c. In most of the 5- and 2½-raters the halliard for the lugsail is led below the deck, and the purchase is worked by taking turns round a small mast-winch in the cabin. It is a great advantage to have a clear deck free from ropes, and it would be a saving of labour to have all a cutter's purchases led below to a winch.

For a small yacht it is as well to have the jib, throat, and peak halliards of four-strand Manilla rope, but wire topsail halliards are a very decided improvement on hemp or Manilla. Wire has little or no stretch in it, and a topsail halliard is the last rope a seaman cares to disturb after it has once been belayed, it may be to lower and take in the sail. All purchases ought to be made of European hemp-rope, with the exception of that attached to the copper rod bobstay. All headsheets should lead aft and belay on cleats bolted on to the combing of the cockpit. It is becoming the custom to have all the bowsprit fittings fixtures. A steel or copper rod from the stem to the cranze iron at the bowsprit end serves as a bobstay, which, with the shrouds, are screwed up with rigging screws.

No such thing as reefing, or bringing the useless outside weight of the spar inboard, is thought of by many racing men now-a-days. Fiddle-headed and spoon bows have introduced this fashion, but 14 to 16 feet of a 5½-inch spar is no trifle to have bobbing into seas, and making the boat uneasy, when half the length, or less, would be quite sufficient to carry all the jib that can be set. No bowsprit belonging to a straight-stemmed cutter should be a fixture, and the best and neatest fitting for the bobstay is a rod with a steel wire purchase at the end. The shrouds should be in two lengths of wire shackled together, as in topmast backstays, and, leading through the bulwark, should screw up to bolts in the deck especially formed to take a horizontal strain. Selvagee strops can be used for setting up the intermediate lengths.

If the eyes of the rigging are covered with leather which has not been painted, then the bight of each eye ought to be left standing in a shallow dish of oil. The leather will thus soak itself, and the oiling will preserve it from perishing.

In sending up rigging it must always be remembered that the lengths of the port and starboard rigging are arranged so as to allow of the starboard fore rigging being placed into position first, then that to port, the starboard backstay rigging going up next, followed by that to port, after which the eye of the forestay will go over the masthead and will rest on the throat halliard eyebolt in the masthead.

All block-hooks should be moused. A mousing is made by taking two or three turns of spunyarn round the neck and lip of the hook followed by a cross turn or two to finish off. This prevents the hook from becoming disengaged.

In some yachts double topmasts and double forestays are used. The former are only fitted where the yacht carries two sizes of jib-topsail, one for reaching and the other for beating to windward. Whilst one is up, the other can be hooked on, so that no time need be lost in setting. A medium-sized sail, however, capable of being used for reaching or beating, is all that is really required. The shifting of two jib-topsails entails the presence for some time of one man at least forward on the bowsprit end, and the less the men are forward of the mast the better, if it is desired to get the best work out of a small yacht, and the yacht herself is in proper trim. There is more to be said, however, in favour of double forestays, since they allow of a foresail being sent up whilst another is already set and drawing, and the work is done inboard, while the difference between a working and a balloon foresail is far greater than in that of two jib-topsails.

The writer has never used double forestays, but he believes so thoroughly in the foresail, as a sail, that he has always carried three—a working, reaching, and a balloon. He has the luff of each foresail fitted with loops at regular intervals, after the manner of gaiter lacings, otherwise called 'lacing on the bight.' These are made either of light wire or small roping. The upper loop reaches down to the next below it, so that the loop below may be passed through, and so on, till the tack is reached. When setting a foresail the upper loop is passed over the forestay before the lower one is threaded through it, and so on with all the loops in turn.

The tack has a single part, which, after it has been passed through the lowest loop, is made fast to the tack-downhaul. When shifting foresails, the sail is lowered, tack let go, and the lacing comes away by itself; then the new sail can be hooked on to the halliards and laced to the forestay as quickly as it can be hauled up. When the sea is smooth there may be no necessity for unlacing the working foresail should the shift have to be made from that sail, especially if it has soon to be called into use again. The above method will be found far superior to that of hanks, which are always getting out of order and not infrequently refuse to do their duty altogether.

In mentioning the shifting of sails, there is one point to which nothing like sufficient attention is paid, and that is to the lead of sheets. Many a good jib has been destroyed and pulled out of shape through a bad lead, and more than one race has been lost through the bad lead of a reaching or balloon foresail sheet. When jibs or foresails are changed, the greatest care should be taken to see that the leads told off for their sheets are really fair—that is, that the pull on the sheet does not favour the foot more than the leach of the sail, or *vice versâ*. In the case of a balloon-foresail its sheet leads outside the lee rigging and belays somewhere aft. The man attending the sheet should take it as far aft as a direct strain will permit, and not belay it to the first cleat that comes to hand; otherwise the sail will simply prove a windbag taking the yacht to leeward rather than ahead.

There is a fitting which must not be passed over that is now almost universally adopted on large yachts, but is equally important on small ones—that is, an iron horse at the main-boom end for the mainsail outhaul to travel on. It was originally invented by that most skilful helmsman Mr. W. Adams, of Greenock, to obviate a difficulty so common in square stern boats with booms stretching to n length over the transom. He fitted the boom of his little racing boat with a horse, which came from the boom end to within easy reach for unhooking the clew of the sail, and so saved the trouble of having to use a dinghy for the purpose. The idea was soon taken up by Clyde yachtsmen, for it was found so much easier to get the mainsail out on the boom than with the traveller working on the boom itself.

Whilst on a subject connected with mainsails, the writer can recommend for the gaff and head of the mainsail, instead of the ordinary long rope lacing commonly in use, separate stops or seizings to each eyelet-hole. The seizing can be done in half the time it takes to properly lace the head of the sail to the spar; it looks quite as well and does its work better. For fastening the luff of the mainsail to the masthoops, instead of seizings he has used hanks, and has found them very handy and neat. The hanks used are riveted on to the mast-hoops. He has now had them in constant use for over twelve years, and has never had occasion to find any fault whatever with them. In one yacht he kept two mainsails in use for cruising and racing, and thus preserved the racing mainsail in good condition for a considerably longer period than would otherwise have been the case, and with the fittings just named the shift of sails was a small matter.

Topsails, perhaps, are the sails which require renewing more frequently than any other, as they get out of shape so quickly if very much is demanded from them. For a small yacht, if she carries a topmast, three topsails are a sufficient outfit. They should be a jibheader, a gaff, and a balloon or jackyarder. One yard ought to serve for both the gaff and jackyard topsail, and these sails should be made the same length on the head. This will save having to carry about a deckload of timber.

Outfit

It is frequently a question of great moment, what kind and what amount of outfit it is necessary to take away on a summer's cruise, and the writer finds it a great convenience to keep a list of everything that goes to form not only his sea kit, but stores and necessaries as well. Such a list prevents one from forgetting small necessaries.

A small air-tight 'uniform tin case' and a painted seaman's bag are the best equipment for carrying clothes. The lists are as follows:—

First List: the Kit

A dress suit and shoes	Gloves
A shore-going suit	Ink, blotting paper, paper and
3 linen shirts	envelopes
6 collars	Mr. Lloyd's Euxesis
White ties	

As may be seen, the tin box only contains the shore-going outfit. The Euxesis mentioned is for those who shave, as with it there is no need of hot water to perform the operation.

4 flannel shirts	4 bath towels and ½ doz. others
2 pairs of flannel pygamas	Sponge bag
½ doz. pairs of socks, 2 pairs of which should be thick	Dressing case
	1 suit of thick pilot cloth
2 pairs of thick warm stockings	1 old pair of thick blue trousers
1 pair of warm slippers	1 large thick square comforter
2 pairs of common blue india-rubber solid shoes	1 common serge suit
	1 pair of mittens
1 pair of brown leather shoes	1 pair of tanned leather boots
2 blue guernseys, hand knit	

For comfort in a small yacht it is impossible to do with less. Of course it may be thought foolish taking the tin case stocked as it is, but experience has taught that even in the wildest and most out-of-the-way spots occasions arise when all pleasure is spoiled by not having the evening change of kit at hand.

Matches	3-lb. tin of marmalade
½ doz. boxes of floats for oil lamp	Pepper
	Mustard
½ doz. boxes of night-lights	Jar of salt
6 lbs. of candles 8 to the lb. and	1 doz. tins of sardines
2 bedroom candlesticks	3 tins of herring à la sardines
1 doz. tins of unsweetened tinned milk	2 lb. captain's biscuits
	1 doz. packages of jelly powder
1 lb. of tea	6 doz. tinned soups
½ doz. coffee and milk in tins	Soap, 1 bar of common brown
½ doz. tins of chocolate and milk	Soap, 1 bar of scented
	Wicks for stoves
Plate powder	Plate, clothes, and boot brushes
Varnish for yellow leather shoes	2 chamois leathers. Cheese, butter, bread, ½ loaf per diem per man
Corkscrew	
Sardine-box opener	
Marlinespike	4 thick common cups and saucers
Pricker	½ doz. tumblers
Mop and twiddlers	½ doz. wineglasses
Hatchet	3 sodawater tumblers
Heavy hammer	½ doz. enamel plates
Small hammer	½ doz. enamel soup plates
Screw-driver	2 enamel slop basins
Gimlet	2 enamel flat dishes
Bradawl	1 enamel double vegetable dish
Pincers	1 deep dish for stews, &c.
Brass screws	
Copper nails	3 tablespoons
Brass hooks	3 table forks
1 tin of black paint	3 table knives
1 tin of Harvey's Anti-fouling Paint	½ doz. small forks
	½ doz. dessert spoons
1 tin of Copal varnish	½ doz. teaspoons
Spare shackles, clip hooks, hooks and thimbles	½ doz. small knives
	Fish knife and fork
1 4-lb. lead and line	2 kitchen knives and forks
1 can of methylated spirits	2 kitchen table- and 2 tea-spoons
1 can of mineral oil	
1 can of colza oil	Binocular glasses
Lamp showing red, white, or green, as required	Parallel rulers
	Compasses
Riding light	Isle of Man almanac
Binnacle and light	Charts: Irish Sea, West Scotland, English Channel, &c.
1 small-sized patent log	
20 fathoms of Kaia grass warp	Books of sailing directions
	Channel pilot

1 tail 4-in. block
2 spare blocks with hooks or thimbles
1 canvas bucket, medium size
1 iron bucket
2 brass holders for oil glass lamp, and to hold tumbler if required for flowers

Flags: Club Burgee, Pilot Jack, and Ensign. The Pilot Jack is useful in case a pilot be required, and the Ensign to hoist upside down in case of distress, or in the rigging as a protest when racing
Fishing tackle

Third List: Yacht Necessaries

Medic Brandy
Friar's balsam
Lint

Bottle of Condy's fluid
Carlsbad salts

Such lists as are given above should be kept in a small book labelled *Fitting-out Necessaries*, because they save much time at that season, and all alterations in them that experience dictates should be noted before or at the period of laying the yacht up.

Racing.

The yacht, let it be supposed, is fitted out. She has a racing outfit, and was the crack boat of the past season. There is a smart young fellow engaged to look after her, and the only thing that remains to be settled now is the question—Shall I give myself up to racing or shall I cruise this year? If it is to be racing, here are two or three words of advice well worth noting. The first is, never pinch the yacht when sailing on a wind. Always keep a clean full and bye—*i.e.* the yacht must be headed, as near as she will go, to the point whence the wind is blowing, but the sails must be kept well full. Then the yacht will travel. Do not, because some other yachts seem to be lying closer to the wind, try to make the little vessel head in the same direction, if she will not do so without her sails shaking.

Many races are lost through this form of bad sailing. The next point to be noted is, 'mind your jibsheet.' No sheet requires such tender handling. The foresheet can be left to a tiro. All he has to do when on a wind is to take and harden in all he can, and belay. The mainsheet can also be hauled in pretty close; but when that is all done, the sailing-master must not think that he can go any closer to the wind by treating his jibsheet after the same simple fashion; for if he does he will find himself very much at fault, as it will take all the life out of the yacht, and the jib will make her bury her head in the seas. He will only stop his ship.

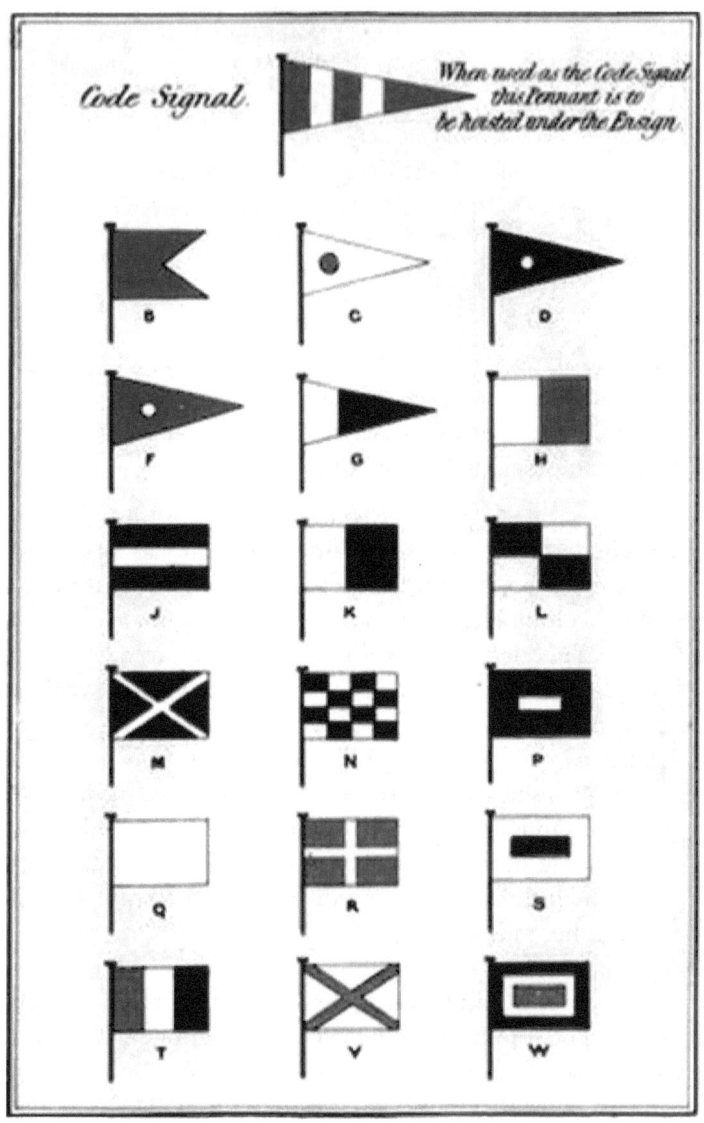

COMMERCIAL CODE OF SIGNALS.
When used as the code signal this pennant is to be hoisted under the ensign

The best plan to adopt is to get the sheet in before the yacht's head is pointed as close as it will go to the wind, and then check out inch by inch till the luff of the sail near the tack has a slight inclination to lift. At first, it is somewhat astonishing to see how much jibsheet a vessel will stand when close hauled. Pinning in the sheet tends to stop the boat, whilst, on the other hand, giving her as much as she can stand will make her fairly jump ahead. The helmsman who knows his duties ought to keep an eye open for this, and watch, in the excitement of going about or hauling round a buoy, that the poor jibsheet is not pinned in or unfairly treated.

Another piece of advice is about that other jib and yachtsman's friend, called the spinnaker. Of the two jibs, this latter suffers most at the hands of the racing sailing-master. When he sees his antagonist carrying his spinnaker with the boom right forward on the bow, only too frequently does he leave his up with the boom in the same position, too fearful lest, should he take his in, or shift it to the bowsprit end, the other yacht may steal an advantage over him. The writer has seen more than one race lost through this hanging on to the boomed-out spinnaker too long. It is a safe and wise plan to take the sail in as soon as the wind obliges the boom to be pointed forward at an angle very much under a right angle to the beam.

Some years ago this was brought before the writer's notice in a clear, unmistakable way. He happened to be on the Breakwater at Plymouth on a Regatta day, when the yachts were making the harbour. They were running with the wind right aft and their booms squared off. As each yacht neared the Breakwater, the wind came round gradually on the beam, and one by one the spinnaker-booms were allowed to go right over the bow to an acute angle with the bowsprit. The spinnakers were certainly all kept full, but as each yacht's after-guy was checked, she gradually ceased to travel and almost stopped dead. Her spinnaker bellied against the topmast stay and forestay, and formed at once a backsail, if anything. Those on board a yacht do not notice the faults of the moment so quickly as those looking on, and only when the race is over does the sailing-master regret that he has not acted differently.

Frequently since then has the writer, having taken note of what he saw, managed to make up a considerable amount of time by having the courage to take in his spinnaker as soon as it refused to stand without the boom going well forward. If the balloon-foresail jib and jib-topsails sheets are ready belayed, so that the sails may take the weight of the wind as soon as the spinnaker is taken in, there will be no fear whatever of the yacht losing ground, but rather she will spring into life, and most likely leave her antagonists behind. The method adopted by American yachtsmen for setting the spinnaker has many points in its favour.

Instead of bringing the tack close in to the mast, the sail is taken outside the forestay and the tack downhaul belayed on the opposite side to which the sail is set. By setting the sail in this way the back draught from it goes into the jib-topsail and balloon-jib, so keeping them full and drawing. The spinnaker boom can also be allowed to range further forward on the bow than under our system. In hoisting the spinnaker it will be found a great saving of labour to send it up in stops ready for breaking out when the pull at the outhaul is taken. It can be stopped up before the race begins.

When running before the wind, it is no uncommon sight to see all hands sent aft, and as many as possible on the counter. Now there is a vast amount of 'follow my leader' in this practice. Because one crack yacht does well under this trim, therefore others are supposed to steer and sail better with the weight aft too, so that when witnessing a number of yachts sailing before the wind with spinnaker set, frequently yacht after yacht may be seen struggling along with her taffrail about level with the water, and the whole counter being sucked back by the wave raised in the yacht's run. Some yachts are bad to steer when running; this is, to say the least of it, a fault or gross peculiarity in their design, for there is no use in the helm unless it is answered, and to help to keep boats steady all available weight is fleeted aft. These must, therefore, bear the penalty and lose ground on this particular point of sailing; but there are others with fine runs, which require no weight aft, and placing weight there causes the counter to go into the water and lie flat on it.

These would steer equally well with the weight forward of the helmsman, and instead of being kept back by the drag put upon them, would leave their heavy-quartered rivals away in the rear. 'Keep the counter as much as possible out of water' is a maxim to be laid to heart by all, on all points of sailing. Of course, in yachts designed to have part of the counter immersed, the maxim applies only to that part above water. A fine run is a most valuable form for a vessel large or small, especially when sailing on any point with the wind abaft the beam; and the man who is wise will do his best to keep it fine, in order that the water may be left clean and without so much as a ripple.

Before naming good cruising grounds and touching on cruising, just a word must be said about dinghies. A dinghy is a big piece of furniture for a small yacht, and at times becomes almost a white elephant, especially if the yacht has to make passages or go foreign. The writer has no hesitation in recommending the Berthon dinghy as the most useful, compact, and stow-awayable of any at present in use. After having had practical experience of nearly all sizes of Mr. Berthon's boats, from the 40-ft. launch supplied to the navy down to the small 7-ft. dinghy, the size found to be most useful is the boat of 8 feet in length.

A boat of 7 feet which he has, and which has been in use for fifteen years in all parts of the world, is a most clever little contrivance. She has carried on many occasions two big men with a portmanteau and other baggage, and when sitting on the bottom boards is hard to capsize—in fact, she has never turned turtle as yet. She is very easy to pull and light to carry, but is a little too small to ask a lady to take passage in. The odd foot, however, makes a great difference. A 9-ft. boat was the lifeboat complement of the *Cyprus*, and this is the largest size of any real value to a small yacht, as the larger boats take too long to open out, and when in the water, unless well filled up and almost brought down to the gunwale, are too light to pull against a head wind. The 9-ft. boat is sometimes difficult to move when it is blowing very hard from the quarter to which it is desired to go, but this occurs seldom, and she is opened out so easily that there may be a question whether a 9-ft. boat might not be, after all, the best to have. The boats will stand any amount of sea, and they travel under sail or oar propulsion, when not too much pressed, very dry and easily.

Should the canvas happen to get cut, the best stitch with which to sew up the wound is that known as the 'Cobbler's.' An awl is required to make the holes for the stitches and a couple of ends similar to those used by a cobbler. This stitch is not so likely to tear the canvas, and brings it closer together than the sailmaker's stitch called 'herring-boning,' which is no use at all for making a water-tight mend. The outer skin may want a coat of paint once a year, and if so, the paint should be mixed up with boiled oil; then, when it is put on, the canvas will remain flexible and will not harden up and crack. Mr. Berthon supplies a special paint for his boats, but it is not always procurable, and any paint mixed with boiled oil will serve the purpose.

Cruising.

Fitted out with an old 5-tonner, or a yacht about the size already recommended, the whole world lies before the cruising yachtsman. She can easily be shipped on board a steamer, and can, for the sum of 50*l*. to 70*l*. or less, be launched off New York, whence there is nothing to hinder a most enjoyable cruise on the lakes (which can be reached by canal) or in the vicinity of Long Island, and along the coast. Racing can be done in the American waters should it so please the voyageur, and a hearty welcome will be met with wherever he goes. There is great scope for cruising and racing in Australia and New Zealand (as set forth at length in another chapter); but the expenses of shipping and taking out the yacht will not be much less than 100*l*.

Sydney Harbour and Port Phillip are both great yachting centres, while the coast of New Zealand is a complete network of bays, inland seas, and natural harbours. The Mediterranean is a much puffed-up yachtsman's cruising ground, but during the best time of year, which is winter, it is as nasty and treacherous an expanse of water as it is possible to meet with in any part of the world. In the summer the great drawback there is lack of wind during the daytime, and calms prevail most days of the week. Among the islands of the Grecian Archipelago, however, and off the coast of Asia Minor, a breeze is always certain to spring up after sunset. There is no difficulty in reaching the Mediterranean, as a yacht drawing 5 to 6 feet can go through France by canal without any trouble, or else she can sail round. Five-tonners, it must be remembered, are serviceable for an ocean cruise should it be necessary, as has already been shown in two cases.

There are cruising grounds on the West Coast of Scotland which may well make yachtsmen in England envious, and some lovely harbours and rivers along the South Coast of England, which would delight the heart of many a Clyde yachtsman, whilst Ireland, on her West and South coasts, has very beautiful and well-sheltered bays. To a yachtsman who lives in the South, and to whom time is an object, the best plan to adopt, if a Scotch cruise be on the cards, is either to put the yacht on a truck and send her up to Gourock, or ship a second hand for the trip and let the men sail her round.

Of the two ways, the latter is much to be preferred, since it will cost less money, and the yacht will not be so likely to get knocked about. If time permitted, the owner might meet the yacht at Kingstown, near Dublin. This is always a good starting point, as he can make for Campbeltown, in Cantyre, stay a night there, and go on to Gourock Bay, near Greenock, which he should make his base of operations, and where he should pick up a mooring if possible rather than drop his own anchor.

If St. George's Channel is to be the cruising ground, then Kingstown, Belfast (Bangor Bay), or the Sloyne (Liverpool) are the best ports to start from. Between Belfast and Kingstown the yachtsman will find Loch Strangford (although it has strong tides), Ardglass, and Carlingford Lough, with little Howth, all places worth peeping into; and a run over to the Isle of Man will well repay any time taken up in a visit. The best ports in the island are Ramsey and Douglas, and of the two Ramsey is to be preferred, because the yacht can always lie at anchor, and it is well sheltered from all winds with any westing in them; but Douglas ought not to be left out on that account, and the yacht, when there, should be sailed up the harbour, where she will have to take the ground. It is a first-rate place to clean a yacht's copper, as there is something in the mud which is very conducive to brightening up the metal. Peel can be seen by crossing the island. Castletown, also, is a very quaint old town, and coaches run regularly between it and Douglas. Anyone visiting the Isle of Man ought to read Sir Walter Scott's novel *Peveril of the Peak*, for the main portion of the story lies at Peel and Castletown.

If interest is taken in iron and smelting works, from Douglas to Barrow is about 70 miles; but as the roughest sea in the Channel is met with on a line between Mougold Head (between Douglas and Ramsey) and Liverpool, where the north and south currents meet, perhaps it will be as well, unless the weather be favourable, to keep clear of that part of the English coast.

Kingstown itself is the finest artificial harbour in the world, and to anyone anchoring there for the first time there will be found plenty to occupy at least a week. The clubs are most hospitably inclined, and Dublin being so near makes it a very pleasant spot to frequent.

For the South of Ireland, Queenstown must be the centre from which to work. There are good fishing and lovely bays all round the coast westward, and nothing can equal Bantry Bay, with Glengariff, which are practically land-locked.

The Shannon and West are in no way inferior to the South coast, and there are many nooks and anchorages, too numerous to mention here, where a yacht such as the one described can very comfortably lie, fearless of ocean billows. Now and then seals are to be met with on the West coast, and care should be taken to avoid rowing into any of the numerous caves, which abound round that coast, and are frequented by them, when the tide is on the rise and at three-quarters flood; more than one shooting party has been caught in a trap through the egress having been blocked up.

The North coast is a wild one; but there, again, Port Rush and Londonderry are very safe, and Port Rush is an especially snug little harbour. Care should be taken to work Rathlin Island Sound with the tide, whichever way it is wished to sail, as the tide rush there is very strong. Between Rathlin and Belfast are bays, each of which has its small tidal harbour, and, if the weather is threatening, the distances between them are so short that opportunities can be snatched for going from one to the other. Larne itself is a fine harbour.

Coming from the North to the South of England, a yacht of 30 ft. and 5 ft. 6 in. draught can be taken by train and launched with the greatest ease in Southampton Dock, and Southampton being so near London makes it the rendezvous of many cruising yachts. A good cruise from there is to run across to Havre (Rouen is easily reached by train from Havre, and well worth a visit), thence to Cherbourg, thence through the Alderney Race, between Cape La Hogue and the back of Sark, to Guernsey.

At Guernsey the yacht's copper should be cleaned, if necessary. It is the best harbour in the English Channel for scrubbing the bottom, as there is good mud and a capital supply of running water close and handy at low water. From Guernsey, weather permitting, with the aid of a fisherman or pilot, the yacht can be taken across to Sark one day and to Herm another. Sark is one of the loveliest and most picturesque islands on our coasts. Any trip to Jersey ought to be made by steamer, as it is an abominable harbour for a yacht, the rise and fall of the tide being over 40 feet.

The next sea run may be to Falmouth, thence to Fowey, Polperro (this port had better not be entered except by dinghy, but it is a very quaint little fishing village and not much frequented except by trawlers), Looe (this is an open anchorage), and Plymouth. All these places have beautiful rivers, with the exception of Polperro, and the Fal and Tamar are both navigable at high water some considerable distance up.

Leaving Plymouth, the yacht might very well touch at the mouth of the Yalme, and the dinghy be rowed up the river. Salcomb and Dartmouth should not be left out, and both have rivers, the heads of which should be seen. Dartmouth is a well-known yachting station, and its club is very prettily situated, so that the members have a full view of the anchorage. The tide there is strong, and two anchors will prove better than one.

Torbay comes next in order, working back to Southampton, with Brixham and Torquay; both so often described that it would be wasting space to add anything to what has already been said.

The only gauntlets to be run are West Bay, which can be very troublesome at times, and the Race off Portland Bill, which can generally be avoided by hugging the shore of the Bill. Weymouth, again, requires no words of encomium. It is as well to anchor off Portland or go right up Weymouth Harbour, where the yacht will have to take the ground.

From Weymouth to Swanage is an afternoon's sail, but it is scarcely worthwhile going into the bay, unless the weather is boisterous from the west or south-west, when the yacht will find a very good berth free from the turmoil of the elements. There is a race off St. Alban's Head, which can always be avoided by keeping well out a couple of miles. When Swanage has been left behind, the course should be steered for the Needles. Once inside the Solent, Yarmouth in the Isle of Wight, and Lymington on the Hampshire coast, Cowes, Ryde, Bembridge, and Portsmouth all open up ports and land, not only different in scenery from any that is visible in the North, but spots and localities interesting on account of the history attached to them.

The Dutch coast with its canals, Norway with its *fiords*, and Sweden with its canal running from Christiania to Stockholm, all merit a description did these pages permit, and are well worth the time taken up in a summer cruise; but whichever way the yacht's head may be turned, or whatever seas may be chosen to be cruised over, the following few hints may prove serviceable.

In cruising along an unknown coast, it is always well to keep a good look out for buoys or boats at anchor inshore. It may be a great help in cheating tides. For instance if the yacht is struggling against a strong tide, an inshore eddy may be discovered from the way the boats are lying, and so, by making use of it, a long journey may be shortened and time saved.

Barges and coasters, especially small ones, should be watched. They, in ninety-nine cases out of a hundred, know the tides, currents, and eddies thoroughly, and the best course to be steered from one point to another. If a short cut can be taken, the coaster is sure to know it, and he can be followed through narrow channels with the greatest safety. A coaster rarely draws less than 6 feet when full up with cargo, or a barge less than 4 to 5 feet.

When sailing along the bight of a bay, with the wind off the shore and close-hauled, because in the bight itself the wind may come off a point or so free, the yacht's sheets should not therefore be checked, but she should be still kept a clean full and bye; for, as the further point of the bay is reached, the wind will be sure to head and come off the land, and instead of being able to round the head close in shore, most likely the yacht will have to be kept away, and much valuable time and distance lost.

When passing high land, with the wind off the shore, care should be exercised should a gully, valley, or ravine open out, for fear a sudden squall may take the yacht aback, and a topsail and topmast be sent flying. The wind is very much influenced by the lay of the land, not only in the matter of the direction in which it blows, but also the power of its gusts.

Regard should always be paid, on entering land-locked waters from the open sea, to the force of the wind. Many open-sea sailors, from being accustomed to a fair amount of wave disturbance whenever the wind has any strength in it, are misled when sailing in enclosed lochs by the smoothness of the water, and so, misjudging the force of the wind, are apt to carry on longer than is desirable, to the danger of spars.

When cruising in the vicinity of yachts racing, the yacht should be kept well out of the way to leeward; and if by chance she happens to find herself to windward of an approaching racing yacht, her head should be turned in whatever direction will seem the best for not taking the wind out of the racer's sails.

When coming to in unknown or any other roads or anchorage, the prevailing wind should not be forgotten, and the spot chosen for letting go the killick should be one from which a speedy retreat can be made should necessity compel. An outside berth in a close-crowded anchorage is therefore always the safest, though, perhaps, not always the most agreeable. The writer hopes that these few wrinkles may prove as serviceable to the readers of these pages as they have been from time to time to himself.

It must be remembered that, when the yachtsman is caught out in a breeze of wind and is obliged to take in a couple of reefs in the mainsail, house his topmast, and shift his jibs, it does not necessarily mean the presence of 'great guns.' It takes very little wind to raise a sea in the channels round our coasts, and to make the small yachtsman sniff a hurricane. In order, therefore, to become accurate about the force of the wind or sea, the writer recommends the *Meteorological Notes*, supplied (at 5*s. per annum*) by Mr. Scott from the Meteorological Office, London, as being most useful for the purpose, and most interesting for reference. His principle is to have the papers sent to his home address, where they remain till the yacht's return to lay up. Then the log or note-book is brought out, notes of the dates on which he relieved his bark and had been more severely knocked about than usual are referred back to, and a very fair idea as to the true local weather is obtained. A knowledge of wind and weather is soon acquired thus.

IN THE CHANNEL.

CHAPTER 13

Yacht Insurance
By G. L. Blake

A book on yachting would not be complete without a few words relating to yacht insurance. There are hundreds of owners who never think of taking out a Marine policy on their boats, simply because they do not know how easy it is; twenty-five years ago indeed only a few insured because it was not generally understood that Lloyd's Agents were willing to underwrite their names against all yachting risks. All yachts should be insured, and therefore the writer will endeavour to explain some of the special clauses contained under a yachting policy.

The ordinary form for a Marine policy, printed and supplied by Government prior to August 1887, is in the main only suitable for merchant shipping; hence clauses have to be added to make that form of service in the case of yachts. Thus the time and dates between which the policy is to hold good must be stated, after which should come what may be called the—

No. 1 Yachting Clause, taking in the following conditions under which Lloyd's hold themselves liable. It runs thus:—

> In port and at sea, in docks and graving docks, and on ways, gridirons, and pontoons, and/or on the mud, and/or hard, at all times, in all places, and on all occasions, services and trades whatsoever and wheresoever, under steam or sail, with leave to sail with or without pilots, to tow and assist vessels or craft in all situations, and to be towed, and to go trial trips. Including all risks and accidents arising from navigation by steam or otherwise. To include the risk of launching.

No. 2 Yachting Clause should allow the yacht to 'touch and stay at any ports or places whatsoever and wheresoever, and for any and all purposes.'

The No. 3 Yachting Clause makes the liability cover the hulls, spars, sails, materials, fittings, boats (including launch, steam or otherwise, if any), &c.

The No. 4 Yachting Clause is a promise to return a certain sum for every fifteen consecutive days cancelled, and for every fifteen consecutive days laid up dismantling, overhauling, repairing, altering, or fitting out.

No. 5 the Collision Clause.

No. 6 the Twenty-pound Clause.

No. 7 the Prevention Clause, No. 1.

No. 8 the Prevention Clause, No. 2.

With regard to the main clauses of the original government form, it will be specially noticed that not one makes it necessary for the owner or skipper, or whoever may be in charge of the yacht, to be the holder of a Board of Trade Certificate. Then, after enumerating all the perils from which a vessel may run the risk of total loss, the form finishes up by stating that where only partial damage takes place, the underwriters are ready to pay an average for the repair of such damage at the rate of 3 *per cent*. That is to say, supposing a 10-tonner is insured at 900*l.* and she splits her mainsail and carries away her mast, which in its fall smashes up the boat, the policy will cover up to 27*l.* of the average value only, and the difference between that and the true value will become a loss to the insurer. This is known as the Average Clause.

To enable the insurer to claim on a partial loss to the full amount of that loss the Twenty-pound Clause is added, and for this in all policies over the value of 700*l.* a small extra premium has to be paid. This clause is decidedly in favour of the man who insures a large yacht, but is of little use to the owner of a small craft. In the first place, it leaves the underwriters liable only for losses above the value of 20*l.* and nothing under. It must be remembered that the general casualties on board a cruising yacht, *when cruising only*, are the carrying away of a bowsprit or topmast, the splitting of a topsail or spinnaker jib, and the whole lot would have to come to grief in a 10-tonner, for instance, before the owner would find his bill for damages sufficiently large to present to the underwriters for payment. With a 60-ton yacht it would be otherwise, as a topmast and topsail would alone run into 20*l.*; so it follows that the larger the yacht the more advantageous will be the addition of the Twenty-pound Clause, since the less will be the difficulty to make out a claim for a sum above that amount.

In a small 5-ton yacht for which the policy need not exceed 500*l.*, the addition of this clause naturally lies in favour of the underwriters, for it is next to impossible for the yacht to receive such damage as will necessitate the outlay of 20*l.* to put her all to rights again. That is, such a catastrophe as must happen to oblige such an expenditure does not occur to one small yacht in a thousand, unless it brings with it at the same time very nearly, if not altogether, total loss. Some agents, however, are willing to lower the twenty and make the clause ten pounds, but of course this risk will mean again a slight extra payment. It is better for the small yacht-owner to pay for a ten-pound clause than have an extra clause which will be of no practical use to him.

The No. 1 Yachting Clause contains some very useful matter. A few years ago, for example, a 20-tonner left by the tide high and dry on the mud at one of our West of England ports, with a leg at each side to support her (her copper required cleaning), fell over and was considerably damaged. On the owner, who had insured his yacht at the beginning of the season, claiming for the damage she had sustained, the claim was disallowed, and after the powers that be had been invoked, the case was given against the owner, the accident not having taken place on the high seas. The form under which the 20-tonner was insured could not have contained the No. 1 Yachting Clause, otherwise the claim would have been in favour of the owner. All contingencies of that kind are met under this clause.

The No. 2 Yachting Clause allows the yacht to voyage to any part of the world and over any seas.

The No. 3 and No. 4 Clauses explain themselves.

The Collision Clause is a very necessary addition to all Marine policies. In case of a collision with another vessel, although the yacht may be in fault, the underwriters are liable under the clause to pay up to three-fourths of the value of the policy towards the repairs of the damaged vessel or the general repairs. The writer has a policy before him for 1,000*l.* with the Collision Clause inserted. Let it be supposed that the yacht for which this policy was taken out has run into another vessel, which has received damage to the amount of 800*l.*, then the underwriters are responsible up to the amount of 750*l.*

Collisions with piers or the removal of obstructions do not come under this clause, and if thought worth insuring against, have to be freed by what has been termed in this notice No. 7, or the Prevention Clause No. 1. This clause enables the insurer to claim for the fourth quarter over and above the three quarters for which the underwriters are liable under the Collision Clause. It will enable him to hand over the business and cost of raising and removing from a fairway, for example, any vessel that he may have sunk through collision with his yacht, or repair any piers that may have been damaged through contact with the boat. Few, however, have this clause inserted in their policies, as so small a risk can safely be borne by an owner.

No. 8, or the Prevention Clause No. 2, only concerns yachtsmen who race their vessels. Its correct title is 'The Racing Clause.' This wipes out those few words from the policy that free the underwriters from all liability in the Twenty-pound Clause, and makes them responsible for total or other loss, should such take place, while the yacht is in the act of racing; for no simple policy or ordinary form provides against '*racing risks.*'

The above remarks refer to policies of insurance on yachts of all sizes; the following will be interesting to the owners of small craft, as giving the average premiums that should be paid under the several conditions named.

For a 250*l.* policy covering five months, two guineas *per cent.* This policy should include the Twenty-pound and Collision Clauses.

The Protection Clause to cover five months should be added for the payment of 5 *per cent.* extra.

The Racing Protection Clause covering a similar length of time should be inserted at the rate of 10 *per cent.* extra.

A laying-up policy freeing the owner of all risks during the winter months should cost 6*s.* 8*d.* or about that sum, for a policy worth 350*l.* This policy will cover risks from fire, falling over, and all such accidents as may take place whilst a yacht is hauled up in a yard or elsewhere.

A laying-up policy to cover the winter months ought to be obtained at the rate of 2*s.* 6*d.* to 5*s.* for a like policy of 350*l.* This policy will cover all risks that may be incurred by a yacht laid up, dismantled, and left at her moorings, such as from fire, dragging ashore, being run into, &c.

Of course insurances differ as to the amount of premium to be paid according to the age of the yacht, her size, and the amount of the policy. Thus for a 100*l.* policy on an old worn-out 5-tonner, to cover summer sailing risks, as much as 5 per cent. has been paid, while for a 150*l.* policy for an old but well-kept-up yacht of a similar tonnage, 50*s.* has been the premium covering the five summer months.

In conclusion, it may be as well to mention that on no account is it a wise plan for the yacht-owner to insure his vessel for a less amount than her full value, including gear, furniture, such valuables as he keeps on board, stores, &c. There are times when, a yacht having suffered partial disablement, the underwriters may propose a composition, owing to there having been no fixed expense incurred in carrying out the repairs. Should a certain sum be agreed upon, and the owner happen to have only insured for a portion of the yacht's true value, whatever ratio that portion bears to the actual value, as laid down by him to the agents, will be deducted from the sum given as compensation. For instance, a friend of the writer insured his small yacht for 200*l*., her true value as given in by him at the time to Lloyd's agent being 250*l*.

During the season, owing to a heavy gale of wind, she dragged her anchor, and, no one being on board, was picked up out at sea by a fishing-boat and towed back a derelict. The owner agreed to accept 25*l*. in compensation for the expenses incurred; but he was astonished when the amount handed over to him only proved to be 20*l*. On going into the matter, he was told that he had undertaken a fifth part of the risk on the yacht himself, in that he had insured for 200*l*., the yacht's real worth being 250*l*., and therefore he would have to bear a fifth part of the expense; and since he had agreed that 25*l*. was sufficient compensation, so the underwriters could only be liable to the amount of 20*l*. The case was brought into court and judgment given in favour of the underwriters. The yachting clauses described above are inserted on the usual Marine policy form, and the yacht insurer cannot do better than have the clauses as given in this chapter inserted in any policy form he may accept.

Attempts have been made from time to time to launch a Mutual Yacht Insurance Company, by which yachtsmen would be able to undertake their own risks by mutual co-operation and without reference to Lloyd's; but there are points, where a system of mutual insurance may benefit householders, who may be said to be localised, which would create difficulties almost sufficient to prevent any general Mutual Yacht Insurance from covering its expenses. The changes that occur in yacht-ownership are very many and frequent, and it must be often the case, that when a yacht-owner ceases to be such, any interest he may have had in a Mutual Insurance Company would have to cease too. Such changes rarely take place among the members of a Mutual House Insurance Company, and it thrives accordingly; but the constant shift of ownership, which may be seen annually by anyone who will take the trouble to study the *Yacht List*, would surely prove a serious drawback to a Mutual Yacht Insurance Company.

In localities like the Clyde, however, where a yacht is almost as great a necessity as the possession of a stone frigate (house ashore), there seems no reason why Mutual Insurance among the local yacht-owners should not do well and prove a most successful undertaking; but then great judgment would have to be exercised as to the kind of risks such a company should incur, and many would have to be excluded, which Lloyd's agents up to the present time have been very willing to accept, such as the insurance of all yachts whose crews do not live on board while in commission, and the like. If the above remarks prove of use as well as interesting to yacht-owners, it must in justice be said that the writer is much indebted for the kindly help given him by his friend Mr. York, the secretary of the Royal Clyde Yacht Club, when compiling the information given.

ALSO FROM LEONAUR
AVAILABLE IN SOFTCOVER OR HARDCOVER WITH DUST JACKET

BOOTS AND SADDLES by *Elizabeth B. Custer*—The experiences of General Custer's Wife on the Western Plains.

FANNIE BEERS' CIVIL WAR by *Fannie A. Beers*—A Confederate Lady's Experiences of Nursing During the Campaigns & Battles of the American Civil War.

LADY SALE'S AFGHANISTAN by *Florentia Sale*—An Indomitable Victorian Lady's Account of the Retreat from Kabul During the First Afghan War.

THE TWO WARS OF MRS DUBERLY by *Frances Isabella Duberly*—An Intrepid Victorian Lady's Experience of the Crimea and Indian Mutiny.

LADIES OF WATERLOO by *Charlotte A. Eaton, Magdalene de Lancey & Juana Smith*—The Experiences of Three Women During the Campaign of 1815: Waterloo Days by Charlotte A. Eaton, A Week at Waterloo by Magdalene de Lancey & Juana's Story by Juana Smith.

DESPATCH RIDER by *W. H. L. Watson*—The Experiences of a British Army Motorcycle Despatch Rider During the Opening Battles of the Great War in Europe.

TWO YEARS BEFORE THE MAST by *Richard Henry Dana. Jr.*—The account of one young man's experiences serving on board a sailing brig—the Penelope—bound for California, between the years 1834-36.

A SAILOR OF KING GEORGE by *Frederick Hoffman*—From Midshipman to Captain—Recollections of War at Sea in the Napoleonic Age 1793-1815.

LORDS OF THE SEA by *A. T. Mahan*—Great Captains of the Royal Navy During the Age of Sail.

COGGESHALL'S VOYAGES: VOLUME 1 by *George Coggeshall*—The Recollections of an American Schooner Captain.

COGGESHALL'S VOYAGES: VOLUME 2 by *George Coggeshall*—The Recollections of an American Schooner Captain.

TWILIGHT OF EMPIRE by *Sir Thomas Ussher & Sir George Cockburn*—Two accounts of Napoleon's Journeys in Exile to Elba and St. Helena: Narrative of Events by Sir Thomas Ussher & Napoleon's Last Voyage: Extract of a diary by Sir George Cockburn.

KIEL AND JUTLAND by *Georg Von Hase*—The Famous Naval Battle of the First World War from the German Perspective.

AVAILABLE ONLINE AT **www.leonaur.com**
AND FROM ALL GOOD BOOK STORES

ALSO FROM LEONAUR
AVAILABLE IN SOFTCOVER OR HARDCOVER WITH DUST JACKET

FARAWAY CAMPAIGN *by F. James*—Experiences of an Indian Army Cavalry Officer in Persia & Russia During the Great War.

REVOLT IN THE DESERT *by T. E. Lawrence*—An account of the experiences of one remarkable British officer's war from his own perspective.

MACHINE-GUN SQUADRON *by A. M. G.*—The 20th Machine Gunners from British Yeomanry Regiments in the Middle East Campaign of the First World War.

A GUNNER'S CRUSADE *by Antony Bluett*—The Campaign in the Desert, Palestine & Syria as Experienced by the Honourable Artillery Company During the Great War.

DESPATCH RIDER *by W. H. L. Watson*—The Experiences of a British Army Motorcycle Despatch Rider During the Opening Battles of the Great War in Europe.

TIGERS ALONG THE TIGRIS *by E. J. Thompson*—The Leicestershire Regiment in Mesopotamia During the First World War.

HEARTS & DRAGONS *by Charles R. M. F. Crutwell*—The 4th Royal Berkshire Regiment in France and Italy During the Great War, 1914-1918.

INFANTRY BRIGADE: 1914 *by John Ward*—The Diary of a Commander of the 15th Infantry Brigade, 5th Division, British Army, During the Retreat from Mons.

DOING OUR 'BIT' *by Ian Hay*—Two Classic Accounts of the Men of Kitchener's 'New Army' During the Great War including *The First 100,000 & All In It.*

AN EYE IN THE STORM *by Arthur Ruhl*—An American War Correspondent's Experiences of the First World War from the Western Front to Gallipoli-and Beyond.

STAND & FALL *by Joe Cassells*—With the Middlesex Regiment Against the Bolsheviks 1918-19.

RIFLEMAN MACGILL'S WAR *by Patrick MacGill*—A Soldier of the London Irish During the Great War in Europe including *The Amateur Army, The Red Horizon & The Great Push.*

WITH THE GUNS *by C. A. Rose & Hugh Dalton*—Two First Hand Accounts of British Gunners at War in Europe During World War 1- Three Years in France with the Guns and With the British Guns in Italy.

THE BUSH WAR DOCTOR *by Robert V. Dolbey*—The Experiences of a British Army Doctor During the East African Campaign of the First World War.

AVAILABLE ONLINE AT **www.leonaur.com**
AND FROM ALL GOOD BOOK STORES

ALSO FROM LEONAUR
AVAILABLE IN SOFTCOVER OR HARDCOVER WITH DUST JACKET

ESCAPE FROM THE FRENCH by Edward Boys—A Young Royal Navy Midshipman's Adventures During the Napoleonic War.

THE VOYAGE OF H.M.S. PANDORA by Edward Edwards R. N. & George Hamilton, edited by Basil Thomson—In Pursuit of the Mutineers of the Bounty in the South Seas—1790-1791.

MEDUSA by J. B. Henry Savigny and Alexander Correard and Charlotte-Adélaïde Dard —Narrative of a Voyage to Senegal in 1816 & The Sufferings of the Picard Family After the Shipwreck of the Medusa.

THE SEA WAR OF 1812 VOLUME 1 by A. T. Mahan—A History of the Maritime Conflict.

THE SEA WAR OF 1812 VOLUME 2 by A. T. Mahan—A History of the Maritime Conflict.

WETHERELL OF H. M. S. HUSSAR by John Wetherell—The Recollections of an Ordinary Seaman of the Royal Navy During the Napoleonic Wars.

THE NAVAL BRIGADE IN NATAL by C. R. N. Burne—With the Guns of H. M. S. Terrible & H. M. S. Tartar during the Boer War 1899-1900.

THE VOYAGE OF H. M. S. BOUNTY by William Bligh—The True Story of an 18th Century Voyage of Exploration and Mutiny.

SHIPWRECK! by William Gilly—The Royal Navy's Disasters at Sea 1793-1849.

KING'S CUTTERS AND SMUGGLERS: 1700-1855 by E. Keble Chatterton—A unique period of maritime history-from the beginning of the eighteenth to the middle of the nineteenth century when British seamen risked all to smuggle valuable goods from wool to tea and spirits from and to the Continent.

CONFEDERATE BLOCKADE RUNNER by John Wilkinson—The Personal Recollections of an Officer of the Confederate Navy.

NAVAL BATTLES OF THE NAPOLEONIC WARS by W. H. Fitchett—Cape St. Vincent, the Nile, Cadiz, Copenhagen, Trafalgar & Others.

PRISONERS OF THE RED DESERT by R. S. Gwatkin-Williams—The Adventures of the Crew of the Tara During the First World War.

U-BOAT WAR 1914-1918 by James B. Connolly/Karl von Schenk—Two Contrasting Accounts from Both Sides of the Conflict at Sea D uring the Great War.

AVAILABLE ONLINE AT **www.leonaur.com**
AND FROM ALL GOOD BOOK STORES

www.ingramcontent.com/pod-product-compliance
Lightning Source LLC
Chambersburg PA
CBHW021958160426
43197CB00007B/172